THE WELFARE STATE AS PIGGY BANK

The Welfare State as Piggy Bank

Information, Risk, Uncertainty, and the Role of the State

NICHOLAS BARR

OXFORD
UNIVERSITY PRESS

OXFORD

UNIVERSITY PRESS

Great Clarendon Street, Oxford OX2 6DP

Oxford University Press is a department of the University of Oxford.
It furthers the University's objective of excellence in research, scholarship,
and education by publishing worldwide in

Oxford New York

Athens Auckland Bangkok Bogotá Buenos Aires Cape Town
Chennai Dar es Salaam Delhi Florence Hong Kong Istanbul Karachi
Kolkata Kuala Lumpur Madrid Melbourne Mexico City Mumbai Nairobi
Paris São Paulo Shanghai Singapore Taipei Tokyo Toronto Warsaw

and associated companies in Berlin Ibadan

Oxford is a registered trade mark of Oxford University Press
in the UK and in certain other countries

Published in the United States
by Oxford University Press Inc., New York

© Nicholas Barr 2001

The moral rights of the author have been asserted

Database right Oxford University Press (maker)

First published 2001

British Library Cataloguing in Publication Data

Data available

Library of Congress Cataloging in Publication Data

Data available

ISBN 0–19–924659–9

1 3 5 7 9 10 8 6 4 2

Typeset by Hope Services (Abingdon) Ltd.
Printed in Great Britain
on acid-free paper by
T.J. International,
Padstow, Cornwall

For Gill

For Gill

Preface

This book is about economics and its application to the welfare state. Its core message is that—contrary to widely held views—the welfare state exists for reasons additional to and separate from poverty relief, reasons that arise out of pervasive problems of imperfect information, risk, and uncertainty. Flowing from that analysis, the book argues, secondly, that the welfare state is here to stay, since twenty-first-century developments do nothing to undermine those reasons—if anything the reverse. To argue that the welfare state is robust does not, however, mean that it is static. A third set of arguments concerns the ways it can and will adapt to economic and social change, including discussion of the direction of change and also specific (and in some cases novel) solutions.

The book grows out of a series of papers whose intellectual roots lie in my earlier work on the microeconomic foundations of the welfare state, notably the first (1987) edition of *The Economics of the Welfare State*. Presented as an integrated whole—the purpose here—they tell a more powerful story than each individually. This book contrasts with my earlier volume, first, in its exclusive focus on the efficiency argument for the welfare state, an underdeveloped area that this book strengthens. Its analytical reach is thus narrower but deeper. Secondly, the analysis is international: it applies to the advanced industrial countries, includes discussion of post-communist countries, and reaches out towards middle-income developing countries. Finally, the story is forward looking, with some chapters explicitly about twenty-first-century issues.

Topics that are new, or that go further than previous discussion, include: forces leading to convergence of private and social insurance; genetic screening and its impact on insurance; approaches to financing long-term care; a new slant on options for pension reform, including pension design in the face of fluid family structures, and where workers are occupationally and internationally mobile; designing loans to finance investment in human capital, including options that incorporate an element of social insurance; and new ways of involving private finance in tertiary education, including new forms of domestic and international financial instruments.

In the academic world, the book will be of interest, first, to economists, as applying the economics of information systematically to the welfare state, and to colleagues in departments of social policy because of its subject matter. The book should be of interest also in related areas such as political economy, as an explanation of the durability of certain types of institution despite apparently adverse economic and political pressures, and to colleagues studying post-communist transition or economic development. The book is also acutely relevant to policy-makers in the OECD, and in post-communist and middle-income developing countries, including Treasury officials bent on fiscal sustainability, policy-makers in departments of Social Security, of Health, and of Education, who have to assess how to reshape institutions in the face of twenty-first-century pressures such as demographic change, global economic competition, and technological advance, and officials in international organizations such as the International Monetary Fund, the World Bank, and the United Nations. Readers with selective interests or short of time should read Chapters 1 and 2, after which any of the remaining chapters can be read as free-standing.

My intellectual debts are many and great, though none of the kind people mentioned below should be held responsible for remaining errors. The idea of the book emerged from conversations with Howard Glennerster and Julian Le Grand, both of whom read and commented on the whole. Conversations and writing with them over more than twenty years has been a wonderful education. I am grateful also to two anonymous reviewers, and to Hilary Walford for her customary sparkling copy-editing. Chapter 2 (the underpinning economic theory) draws on chapters 4 and 5 of *The Economics of the Welfare State* (Barr 1998a). Chapter 3 (unemployment insurance) is based on a long-ago discussion paper on which I received helpful comments from John Hills, Julian Le Grand, Richard Jackman, and David Piachaud. Chapter 4, based on my graduate lectures on health finance, benefited from helpful comments from Alain Enthoven. The discussion of genetic screening in Chapter 5 draws on my evidence to the Parliamentary Select Committee on Science and Technology prompted by Dr Jeremy Bray, at the time the Chair of the Committee. Tanya Burchardt commented helpfully on the section on long-term care, which draws on my evidence to the Royal Commission on Long-Term Care.

The section on pensions draws on my times at the World Bank—periods of splendidly robust fights, alarums, and debates—and on a period of quiet reflection as Visiting Scholar at the International Monetary Fund in spring 2000. I am grateful to the IMF for permission to draw on the resulting IMF Working Paper 00/139, on which Chapter 7 is based. I have benefited from discussions with many colleagues at the World Bank over the past ten years, latterly including Robert Holzmann, David Lindeman, Michal Rutkowski, Alan Thompson, and Dimitri Vittas. I am also grateful to colleagues in the Fiscal Affairs Department at the IMF, including Ke-Young Chu, Peter Heller, Richard Hemming, George Kopits, and Vito Tanzi, and to participants in two seminars at the IMF in April 2000. Others who have commented on the material in the pensions chapters include Phil Agulnik, Gary Burtless, Peter Diamond, Pierre Pestieau, Stanford Ross, and Lawrence Thompson. The section on pensions in the context of labour mobility benefited from comments from participants at a seminar at HM Treasury in 1997.

The section on education draws on writing in the context of UK policy debate from the late 1980s onwards, deepened by involvement in policy development in Australia and New Zealand and, latterly, in some of the advanced post-communist countries. I owe a huge debt to Iain Crawford, my companion-in-arms in the UK debate, and to joint work with Jane Falkingham. I am also grateful to Tony Atkinson and Nick Stern, as successive Chairs of the Suntory–Toyota International Centre for Economics and Related Disciplines, for encouragement and financial support for my early research, to the Nuffield Foundation for financial support, to Mark Blaug for tutorials over the years on the underlying theory, to Mervyn King for pointing towards the link to social insurance, to Bruce Chapman for many illuminating conversations, and to Colin Ward for sharing his wisdom about implementation and, most particularly, about private finance.

The discussion of post-communist countries draws on two periods at the World Bank, one in operations, the other as one of the authors of the World Bank's 1996 *World Development Report: From Plan to Market*. My particular debts are to Ralph Harbison, to Alan Gelb, and to the late and greatly lamented Michael Bruno.

My wife, Gill, listened patiently to my doubts and enthusiasms, argued ferociously when she thought I was wrong, diagnosed with unerring accuracy writing that did not work, and put up (more or less) cheerfully with truncated weekends. My final and enormous thanks are to her.

Nicholas Barr

November 2000

Contents

List of Tables   xviii

List of Figures   xix

1. Introduction   1

Part 1. Economic Theory

2. The Market and Information   11

Part 2. Insurance

Introduction to Part 2   31

3. The Mirage of Private Unemployment Insurance   33

4. Problems with Medical Insurance   50

5. Twenty-First-Century Insurance Issues   72

Part 3. Pensions

Introduction to Part 3   87

6. The Economics of Pensions   89

7. Misleading Guides to Pension Design   96

8. Pension Design: The Options   125

9. Twenty-First-Century Pensions Issues   144

Part 4. Education

Introduction to Part 4   159

10. Core Issues in the Economics of Education   161

11. Information Problems   171

12. Designing Student Loans   179

13. Financing Higher Education: The Options   191

14. Twenty-First-Century Education Issues   223

Contents

Part 5. The Welfare State in a Changing World

Introduction to Part 5   239

15. The Welfare State in Post-Communist Countries   241

16. The Welfare State in a Changing World   263

References   273
Index   287

Detailed Contents

List of Tables   xviii

List of Figures   xix

1. Introduction   1
    1. Core Arguments   1
    2. The Welfare State and its Objectives   4
    3. Organization of the Book   5

Part 1. Economic Theory

2. The Market and Information   11
    1. The Welfare State with Perfect Information   11
    2. Imperfect Information in the Goods Market   13
        2.1. *Types of intervention*   13
        2.2. *Information and other problems*   14
    3. Imperfect Information in Insurance Markets   18
        3.1. *Actuarial insurance with perfect information*   18
        3.2. *Information problems*   19
        3.3. *Social insurance as a response to information failure* 23
    4. Implications   24
        4.1. *Market success*   24
        4.2. *Market failure and government failure*   26
        4.3. *State intervention: When, why, and how*   28

Part 2. Insurance

Introduction to Part 2   31

3. The Mirage of Private Unemployment Insurance   33
    1. Objectives   34
    2. Information Problems   35
        2.1. *The simple model*   35
        2.2. *The technical conditions*   35
        2.3. *Moral hazard*   37
        2.4. *The inapplicability of private-sector examples*   40

3. Operational Problems   42
    3.1. *Compulsion*   42
    3.2. *Protecting individuals*   43
    3.3. *Calculating the relevant probabilities*   45
4. Conclusions   46
    4.1. *Theoretical arguments*   46
    4.2. *Policy implications*   47
    4.3. *The bottom line*   48

4. Problems with Medical Insurance   50
    1. Objectives   50
    2. Information Problems   52
        2.1. *Health care*   52
        2.2. *Medical insurance*   54
    3. Funding Health Care: The Options   62
        3.1. *Private funding plus private production*   62
        3.2. *Public funding plus public production*   66
        3.3. *Public funding plus private production*   67
    4. Conclusions   70

5. Twenty-First-Century Insurance Issues   72
    1. Genetic Screening   72
        1.1. *Problems*   72
        1.2. *Approaches to a solution*   75
        1.3. *Preferred options*   78
    2. Long-Term-Care Insurance   79
        2.1. *Information problems*   80
        2.2. *Preferred options*   83

                Part 3. **Pensions**

Introduction to Part 3   87

6. The Economics of Pensions   89
    1. Objectives   89
    2. The Centrality of Output   89
    3. Uncertainty and Risk   91
        3.1. *Uncertainty and risk facing pension schemes*   91
        3.2. *Risks facing individual pensioners*   92
    4. Information Problems   93

7. Misleading Guides to Pension Design   96
    1. Macroeconomic Mythology   96
        1.1. *Myth 1: Funding resolves adverse demographics* 96

1.2. *Myth 2: The only way to pre-fund is through pension accumulations*   100

1.3. *Myth 3: There is a direct link between funding and growth*   101

1.4. *Myth 4: Funding reduces public pension spending*   104

1.5. *Myth 5: Paying off debt is always good policy*   105

2. Myths about Pension Design   110

    2.1. *Myth 6: Funded schemes have better labour-market incentive effects*   110

    2.2. *Myth 7: Funded pensions diversify risk*   112

    2.3. *Myth 8: Increased choice is welfare improving*   116

    2.4. *Myth 9: Funding does better if real returns exceed real wage growth*   118

3. The Role of Government   122

    3.1. *Myth 10: Private pensions get government out of the pensions business*   122

8. Pension Design: The Options   125

1. Lessons from Economic Theory   125

2. Essential Elements in Pension Reform   126

    2.1. *Public-sector prerequisites*   126

    2.2. *Private-sector prerequisites*   129

3. Policy Choices   132

    3.1. *Building blocks*   132

    3.2. *Fitting the pieces together*   135

4. Conclusions   141

9. Twenty-First-Century Pensions Issues   144

1. Population Ageing: Are Pensions Affordable?   144

2. Portable Pensions: The Welfare State as Snail Shell   148

    2.1. *The issue*   148

    2.2. *Defined-contribution schemes*   149

    2.3. *Defined-benefit schemes*   152

    2.4. *State pensions*   155

    2.5. *Conclusion*   156

Part 4. **Education**

Introduction to Part 4   159

10. Core Issues in the Economics of Education   161

1. Objectives: What do we Mean by a 'Good' Education?   161

2. Measuring the Benefits of Education   164

    2.1. *Measuring output and inputs*   164

    2.2. *Establishing causality: The screening hypothesis*   166

3. What is the Efficient Level of Education Spending?   167

    3.1. *Quantitative analysis*   167

    3.2. *Qualitative arguments*   168

11. Information Problems   171
    1. Information Problems in the Market for Education   171
        1.1. *School education: The case against the market*   171
        1.2. *Tertiary education: The case for the market*   173
        1.3. *Implications for policy*   174
    2. Information Problems, Risk and Uncertainty in Capital Markets   175
        2.1. *Risk and uncertainty facing borrowers*   175
        2.2. *Risk and uncertainty facing lenders*   176

12. Designing Student Loans   179
    1. Why Student Loans?   180
    2. Organizing Repayments: Mortgage-Type Schemes   181
        2.1. *Efficiency and equity problems*   182
        2.2. *Administrative problems*   183
    3. Organizing Repayments: Income-Contingent Schemes   184
        3.1. *Addressing capital market imperfections*   184
        3.2. *Philosophical arguments*   185
        3.3. *The intuition of income-contingent repayments*   186
    4. Other Features of Student Loans   188
        4.1. *Basic design elements*   188
        4.2. *Market interest rates*   189
        4.3. *Private money*   189

13. Financing Higher Education: The Options   191
    1. Lessons from Economic Theory   192
        1.1. *Market forces in higher education: Who should make the decisions?* 192
        1.2. *Who should pay?*   194
        1.3. *The resulting system*   195
    2. Lessons from International Experience   198
        2.1. *The USA*   198
        2.2. *The UK*   201
        2.3. *The Netherlands*   206
        2.4. *Sweden*   207
        2.5. *Australia*   208
        2.6. *New Zealand*   211
        2.7. *Conclusions from country experience*   212
    3. Conclusions   215
        3.1. *Misleading guides to policy design*   215
        3.2. *A strategy for higher education finance*   220

14. Twenty-First-Century Education Issues   223
    1. Private Funding   223
        1.1. *The classification problem*   223

1.2. *Approaches to private finance* 225
1.3. *Examples* 231
2. Student Loans and International Labour Mobility 233
3. Rationalizing the Funding of Tertiary Education 234
4. Individual Learning Accounts 236

Part 5. The Welfare State in a Changing World

Introduction to Part 5 239

15. The Welfare State in Post-Communist Countries 241
   1. The simple analytics of transition 241
      1.1. *The old order* 241
      1.2. *The effects of transition* 242
      1.3. *Resulting reform directions* 246
   2. Insurance: Assisting Labour-Market Adjustment 247
      2.1. *The problem* 247
      2.2. *Policy directions* 248
   3. Pensions 252
      3.1. *The problem* 252
      3.2. *Policy directions* 253
   4. Education 258
      4.1. *The challenge of transition* 258
      4.2. *Policy directions: Adapting education to the needs of a market economy* 260

16. The Welfare State in a Changing World 263
   1. Is the 'Crisis' a Crisis? 263
   2. A Continuing Welfare State 270

References 273
Index 287

List of Tables

7.1. A simplified Pay-As-You-Go system 119

8.1. Essential elements in pension reform 127

13.1. Spending on higher education, selected OECD countries, 1995 199

13.2. Higher education funding in different countries 213

14.1. Illustrative operation of private finance 228

15.1. Real GDP in Central and Eastern Europe, the Baltic countries, and the CIS in 1999 compared with 1989 244

15.2. Unemployment rates, selected transition countries, 1998 245

15.3. Poverty rates, selected transition countries, 1987–8 and 1993–5 246

15.4. Age dependency ratio and system dependency ratio, selected countries, 1996 253

List of Figures

2.1. Rational choice in the Fisher model   12

3.1. Stylized distribution of gains and losses by socioeconomic group   44

10.1. The efficient level of output   163

12.1. Trajectory of income-contingent and mortgage loan repayments   187

15.1. Science and mathematics test performance of children in selected
      transition and industrial economies   261

'When a man sets out upon any course of inquiry, the object of his search may be either light or fruit—either knowledge for its own sake or knowledge for the sake of good things to which it leads . . . there will, I think, be general agreement that in sciences of human society . . . it is the promise of fruit and not of light that chiefly merits our regard . . . That is true of all social sciences but especially true of economics.'

A. C. Pigou, *Economics of Welfare*, 1920

Chapter 1

Introduction

1. CORE ARGUMENTS

Of the many purposes of the welfare state, two stand out:

- as a series of institutions that provide poverty relief, redistribute income and wealth, and reduce social exclusion (the 'Robin Hood' function);
- as a series of institutions that provide insurance and offer a mechanism for redistribution over the life cycle (the 'piggy-bank' function).

The redistributive purpose of the welfare state is enormously and enduringly important, and, not least for that reason, there is a large literature on the topic. The piggy-bank function, in contrast, has received relatively little attention and is not widely understood. This book is intended to redress the balance. Building on economic theory, it develops three central arguments that apply to industrial countries and to post-communist and middle-income developing countries: the welfare state has an important piggy-bank function that is additional to and separate from poverty relief; secondly, and consequentially, the welfare state is here to stay; thirdly, the welfare state will adapt to economic and social change.

THE WELFARE STATE AS PIGGY BANK. Even if all poverty and social exclusion could be eliminated, so that the entire population were middle class, there would still be a need for institutions to enable people to insure themselves and to redistribute over the life cycle. Though private institutions are often effective, they face predictable problems, and attempts to address those problems inescapably involve state intervention. Thus the welfare state exists not only to relieve poverty, but also to provide insurance and consumption smoothing. That does *not* mean that the state is necessarily the main—still less the only—actor, nor that its role is immutable either over time or across countries. The configuration can vary in ways that are one of the main subjects of this book.

The argument that the welfare state has an efficiency function is important. The resulting gains to well-being are potentially enormous and affect the entire population. Thus it should not be surprising that Falkingham and Hills (1995) (one of the few pieces of research to tackle the topic) estimate that between two-thirds and three-quarters of UK welfare-state spending is life-cycle redistribution, with only a third or less on poverty relief. In quantitative terms, it might therefore be argued that the piggy-bank aspect is *the* key function of the welfare state.

The argument is important, secondly, because it offers guidance about how most effectively to pursue key equity objectives—for example, access to food and to health care. Food is generally sold at market prices, and the poor are given access through targeted income transfers that enable them to pay those prices. With health care, in sharp contrast, access in most countries is through free or subsidized medical treatment, not just for the poor but for the generality of the population. As discussed in more detail at the end of Chapter 2, the choice of these very different instruments is not accidental: the conclusion of the efficiency arguments about market-versus-state also illuminates the equity question of cash-versus-kind.

The welfare state's efficiency function also casts a new light on arguments about middle-class 'capture'. These tend to suggest that receipt by the middle class of welfare-state benefits is *necessarily* an adverse feature. This book suggests that the issues are more subtle than that. Finally, the argument sheds new light on the view that universal benefits foster social solidarity. This might well be the case; but it is no longer the only argument for universal benefits.

THE WELFARE STATE IS HERE TO STAY. The book's second central argument flows directly from the first: the welfare state is here to stay. The reasons for its existence, including risk and uncertainty, will continue to apply, as evidenced by discussion in later chapters of a series of twenty-first-century issues. The pressures discussed below (which apply equally to private institutions), if anything, strengthen the importance of insurance and consumption smoothing. If insecurities, as some writers argue, are greater than in the past, it may be that state institutions are *more* necessary.

One piece of muddled thinking—the failure to distinguish structure from scale—should be nailed immediately. Structure is concerned with whether an activity is more efficiently conducted in the public or the private sector; as argued throughout the book, the issue is primarily microeconomic, focusing on the extent of market failures and the ability, or lack of it, of government to address them. Scale, in contrast, is concerned with the optimal level of spending on an activity; it is largely a macroeconomic issue, particularly of fiscal sustainability. Fiscal pressures are an argument for fiscal containment, not *per se* an argument for privatization. Analogously, global competition may exert downward pressure on the scale of spending on the welfare state, but that is not an argument for dismembering it.

THE WELFARE STATE WILL ADAPT. Neither of the previous arguments implies that the welfare state will be static. Its form—as in the past—will adapt to changes in the world within which it operates: declining job security has implications for the nature of unemployment insurance; declining family stability implies, for example, pensions for individuals rather than, as in the past, for husbands on the assumption that this would also cover wives; demographic change will tend to exert downward pressure on benefit levels; and increasingly easy international transmission of information and capital (so-called globalization) may create pressures to convergence.

Parallel to these largely global forces, a series of country-specific objectives and constraints will also influence the future shape of the welfare state. The economic, political, and institutional requirements of particular policies are a recurring theme in the chapters about reform options, and of particular salience when discussing the reforming post-communist countries: some forms of health finance depend critically both on political will and on administrative capacity; private pensions have major private-sector prerequisites but are also dependent on effective government and continuing political support; student loans depend on the capacity to collect repayments. Thus the welfare state will adapt: some adaptations, particularly responses to the universal pressures in the previous paragraph, are fairly predictable; others, particularly those connected with different country objectives and different configurations of constraints, will show significant variation.

EFFECTIVE REFORM RESTS EQUALLY ON GOOD POLICY AND EFFECTIVE IMPLEMENTATION. A fourth argument is different in kind from the others: it applies far more widely than reform of the welfare state; and it is not rooted in theory but is deeply practical. Effective reform has two co-equal ingredients: the need for well-designed policy is obvious; in addition, that policy has to be implemented effectively. It is sometimes forgotten that the essence of reform is not in words on paper or in ministerial speeches, but in institutions—job information systems, walk-in medical clinics, pension payments, schools—that work well. Bad implementation of a potentially good reform not only leads to outcomes that fail to achieve its objectives, but can also discredit the underlying policy.

Effective implementation has two roots. First, as just discussed, any reform has institutional prerequisites. In their absence, a simpler reform, which respects country-specific constraints, needs to be adopted or the reform postponed until institutional development allows. Secondly, the best-designed policy will fail for lack of political support, or if it cannot be administered. Effective reform depends simultaneously on three very different sets of skills: the ability to design a coherent policy strategy; the ability to engender political support that is sufficiently wide, deep, and durable; and the ability to put into place effective administration. The word 'simultaneously' is key: the world is littered with policies that failed because they were designed by policy-makers who then handed them on to implementers. Effective reform requires all three skills from the beginning of any proposed reform, not least to head off proposals that are politically inept or administratively impossible. In the absence of this tripod, reform will generally fail to achieve its objectives.

In short, the welfare state is here to stay, because the fundamental reasons for its existence will continue to apply. Its structure and scale will continue to adapt. Such adaptations are not automatic manifestations of 'crisis' but, at least as much, are rational responses to a changing world.

2. THE WELFARE STATE AND ITS OBJECTIVES

Like many widely used terms, the welfare state is hard to define. There are at least three complications (for fuller discussion, see Glennerster 1997a: ch. 1). First, welfare derives from multiple sources: from paid work; through private activity such as saving and insurance; through voluntary welfare; and via the state. Secondly, modes of delivery vary widely. A service can be publicly *funded*, publicly *produced*, neither, or both. Thirdly, the boundaries of the welfare state are not well defined: expenditure that is generally not included in welfare-state spending—for example, for public health and environmental policies—is very similar in purpose to that on activities that are included.

Welfare is thus a mosaic, with diversity in both its source and the manner of its delivery. Nevertheless, the state at national or subnational levels is much the most important single agency in industrialized countries. Throughout the book, 'welfare state' is used as a shorthand for state activities in three broad areas: income transfers, health promotion and health care, and education.

The objectives of the welfare state are wide-ranging (for fuller discussion, see Barr 1992). *Productive efficiency* is concerned with generating the maximum output from given input—for example, building a school with as few workers as possible standing around waiting for something to do. *Allocative efficiency* is a broader concept.[1] It includes productive efficiency, but also considers whether the school should be built in the first place, or whether social welfare would be higher if the resources were used instead to build a hospital or community centre, or whether the land should be used for a park and the money saved used to reduce taxes. The concept embraces both using a given volume of resources efficiently (static efficiency) and using resources to promote output growth (dynamic efficiency).

Efficiency is thus multidimensional. In macroeconomic terms it is concerned with the division of resources between spending on the welfare state and on

---

[1] Formally, allocative efficiency requires that resources are used in such a way that any reallocation makes at least one person worse off. See e.g. Stiglitz (2000: ch. 3) or Varian (1999: ch. 1).

other areas. It is inefficient to spend nothing on health care, since people would die unnecessarily; equally, it is inefficient to spend the whole of national income on health care, since people would then die of starvation. A particular aim is to avoid distortions that lead to cost explosions, an example discussed in Chapter 4 being uncontained medical spending. In microeconomic terms, allocative efficiency concerns, for example, the division of education resources between primary, secondary, and tertiary education. There is also a concern with incentives. High payroll taxes (for example, to finance an overgenerous pension scheme) may discourage work effort, impede new employment, and/or reduce the growth rate.

Efficiency also has an intertemporal aspect that is particularly relevant to this book. Individuals' well-being is increased if they have a mechanism for redistributing to themselves across the life cycle (consumption smoothing), pensions being a particularly important example. Well-being is also increased if individuals have a mechanism for insuring against risk—for example, of becoming unemployed or experiencing ill health.

Alongside these efficiency objectives, the welfare state also has equity aims. The purpose of *poverty relief* is to ensure that nobody falls below some minimum standard of living. Other equity objectives may include *reducing inequality*, *strengthening social inclusion*, and *increasing social cohesion*.

Some of these objectives have been accorded much greater prominence than others. In particular, the large literature on the welfare state has mainly concentrated on poverty relief and reducing various dimensions of inequality. This book concentrates on consumption smoothing and insurance.

3. ORGANIZATION OF THE BOOK

There is no intention of exhaustive coverage. Topics included are those that are central to the welfare state's efficiency function and/or that raise particular issues for the twenty-first century. Discussion is largely restricted to *funding* rather than to methods of *delivering* benefits. Finally, though discussion includes a range of countries, such discussion is intended only to illustrate the theoretical arguments; the book is in no sense a comparative study.

The theoretical spine of the book is imperfect information, risk, and uncertainty. Chapter 2 starts by setting out a simple model, the Fisher model, in which a rational person faces a lifetime budget constraint and has to decide how to divide her consumption between her younger and her older years so as to maximize her lifetime well-being. She can transfer consumption from her younger to her older self by saving, for example, to finance her retirement; or she can transfer consumption from her later years to her earlier years by borrowing, for example, to finance her education. A central assumption in the simple model is certainty. As a result, people's voluntary choices are efficient and there is no role for the welfare state except for the lifetime poor.

Relaxing the assumption of certainty has enormous implications. First, there is risk, creating a need for insurance. Secondly, there is uncertainty (a situation where risk, though it exists, cannot be assessed), suggesting that there may be gaps in private insurance, in turn suggesting a potential role for the state. Thirdly, and pervasively, there is imperfect information. Consumers are not well informed—for example, about health care or about complex financial instruments such as private pensions. Insurers are badly informed—for example, about the riskiness of an applicant for unemployment insurance.

Risk, uncertainty, and imperfect information transform the intellectual landscape by undermining the automatic efficiency of unconstrained market outcomes. The following chapters explain how they underpin the welfare state as piggy bank in three broad areas: insurance, pensions, and education.

INSURANCE. In the face of risk, insurance can improve a person's well-being. But uncertainty and other forms of imperfect information on the part of insurers mean that in important areas private insurance will be inefficient or non-existent. Part 2 of the book discusses the resulting problems for voluntary, competitive actuarial insurance, and the state's role in facilitating institutions that offer some protection against risk. Chapter 3 explains why private unemployment insurance is a mirage. Chapter 4 discusses technical problems with medical insurance, including analysis of solutions in a number of countries. Chapter 5 looks at two major twenty-first-century issues: the impact of genetic screening on insurance, and long-term-care insurance.

PENSIONS. Uncertainty and imperfect information also create difficulties for consumption smoothing. Part 3 discusses pensions—that is, redistribution from middle years to later years. Consumers may be imperfectly informed about private pensions; and private-pension providers face uncertainty, for example, over future rates of inflation. These and other problems create a role for the state, though with considerable controversy about its exact form. Chapter 6 sets out the economics of pensions (an area that is simpler than much writing makes it out to be). Chapter 7 exposes a series of myths—views about pensions that are widely held but usually wrong. Chapter 8 sets out options facing policy-makers, with reference both to economic theory and to experience in a range of countries. Chapter 9 discusses two twenty-first-century issues: the wide range of policies in the face of demographic change; and designing pensions in an era of international labour mobility.

EDUCATION. Pensions redistribute from middle years to later years. Analogously, investment in education, discussed in Part 4, redistributes from middle years to earlier years. Again, information problems are pervasive. Consumers, particularly children, may be badly informed; and lenders are badly informed about the riskiness of applicants for student loans, creating a major capital market imperfection. Chapter 10 sets out the core issues in the economics of education. Chapter 11 discusses the presence (and absence) of information problems, reaching very different conclusions for school education and tertiary education. Chapter 12 discusses the design of student loans in the face of the capital market imperfections just mentioned. Chapter 13 looks at the options for financing higher education suggested by economic theory, and reviews selected international experience. Chapter 14 turns to twenty-first-century issues: the role of private funding in higher education; the design of student loans in an era of international labour mobility (for example, the expansion of the European Union); rationalizing the funding of tertiary education; and the development of individual learning accounts.

The final part of the book discusses the welfare state in a changing world. Chapter 15 applies the arguments of earlier chapters to a group of countries—the postcommunist reformers—where change has been particularly rapid. Chapter 16 discusses 'globalization' and other pressures on the welfare state, arguing that their effects, though important, are not apocalyptic.

As noted in the Preface, readers with particular interests should read Chapters 1 and 2, after which the other chapters can be read selectively in any combination. The book's central conclusions can be gleaned from Chapters 1 and 16, and from the concluding sections of various of the chapters.

In sum, the assumption of certainty suggests that voluntarism and private institutions will be efficient; in that world, there is no need for the welfare state except for the lifetime poor. The failure of that assumption, bringing in imperfect information, risk, and uncertainty, is the central reason why the welfare state has a major and continuing role in facilitating insurance and consumption smoothing—the welfare state as piggy bank.

PART 1

ECONOMIC THEORY

Chapter 2

The Market and Information

This chapter sets out the economic theory that underpins the rest of the book. It starts (Section 1) with a simple model—the Fisher model—of rational consumer choice over the life cycle. Subsequent sections relax the underlying assumptions, discussing imperfect information in the goods market (Section 2) and insurance markets (Section 3). Section 4 summarizes the implications for policy.

1. THE WELFARE STATE WITH PERFECT INFORMATION

THE SIMPLE FISHER MODEL shows the options available to an individual over time. The horizontal axis in Figure 2.1 shows a person's potential consumption in period 1 (her younger years), the vertical axis that in period 2 (her older years). Suppose she has an initial endowment shown by point a: she can consume C_1 units in period 1 and C_2 units in period 2. However, she can increase her options by trading with other individuals—that is, by saving or borrowing. For example, she could save $C_1-C'_1$ units of consumption in period 1 in exchange for C'_2-C_2 units in period 2, thus moving to point e.[1]

Thus a person with an initial endowment of C_1 in period 1 and C_2 in period 2, faces a lifetime budget constraint $b-b$. The consumption pattern that maximizes lifetime utility is shown by point e, which the person attains by saving $C_1-C'_1$ when younger, making possible consumption of C_2' when older. Similarly, with an initial endowment of d on the same budget constraint, the person could move to e by borrowing in period 1.

This simple model is based on a series of assumptions, including a well-behaved utility function, rational behaviour, certainty, and competitive markets. The assumption of certainty is critical. First, it implies perfect information:

---

[1] If the interest rate were zero, she could save (say) 1 unit in period 1 and consume an extra unit in period 2. If her initial endowment shown by a comprises 7 units in period 1 and 3 units in period 2, she could, by borrowing 3 units, consume 10 units in period 1 and 0 in period 2 or, by saving 7 units, could consume 0 in period 1 and 10 units in period 2, or anywhere in between. Thus her consumption opportunities are shown by a budget constraint with a slope of −1. If the interest rate is 10%, the budget constraint becomes steeper. For each unit she saves in period 1, she receives 1.1 units in period 2. By saving she can therefore move from a to e. Thus the budget constraint $b-b$ goes through the initial endowment point, a, with slope determined by the interest rate. For a simple introduction, see Auerbach and Kotlikoff (1998: ch. 2) and, for fuller discussion, Varian (1999: ch. 10).

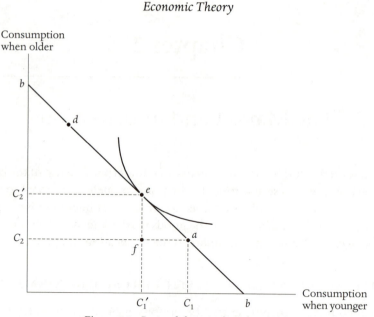

Figure 2.1. *Rational choice in the Fisher model*

consumers are well informed about the quality of the goods and services they buy; for example, people are assumed to be able to make well-informed choices between different pension schemes, different medical treatments, and different educational activities. Secondly, the assumption rules out stochastic outcomes such as risk (where the probability distribution of outcomes is known) and uncertainty (where it is not). The absence of risk means that there is no need for insurance; it also means, for example, that lenders do not have to form a view about the riskiness of applicants for student loans. The absence of uncertainty rules out common shocks such as inflation.

THE CASE FOR THE MARKET. In a world of certainty, there is therefore little need for a welfare state.

- Insurance is unnecessary, since there is no risk.
- People provide for their old age through voluntary saving, and finance their education by borrowing in perfect capital markets. Thus consumption smoothing takes place through voluntary action using private institutions. With perfect information and no external shocks, such behaviour is efficient.
- Transient (i.e. temporary) poverty is also dealt with by borrowing or saving. If the poverty line in period 2 is shown by C_2' in Figure 2.1, someone with an initial endowment of a is poor in period 2, but can deal with the problem by saving in period 1, thus moving from a to e. Dealing with poverty for

someone who is not lifetime poor is more akin to consumption smoothing than to traditional poverty relief.

- The only reason for a welfare state in such a world is to provide poverty relief for a person who is lifetime poor—for example, someone with an initial endowment of *f* in Figure 2.1, whose income is not enough to keep him or her above the poverty line in both periods.

Introducing risk into the model does not change things, since individuals can buy actuarial insurance. For example, a person who does not know how long he will live can convert his pension savings into an annuity. Where individuals and insurers are well informed, such outcomes are efficient.[2]

RELAXING THE ASSUMPTIONS. The rest of the book is concerned with relaxing the certainty assumption. Discussion includes:

- imperfect information in product markets, insurance markets, and capital markets;
- risk and uncertainty, particularly in a context of imperfectly informed insurers;
- external shocks—e.g. demographic change.

Risk and uncertainty imply the need for insurance (Part 2 of the book); and all three factors have major implications for consumption smoothing from middle years to later years to finance pensions (Part 3) and to younger years to finance investment in human capital (Part 4).

2. IMPERFECT INFORMATION IN THE GOODS MARKET

This section summarizes the implications for market allocation of imperfect information and a range of other technical problems.[3]

2.1. *Types of intervention*

Before discussing why the state might intervene, it is useful to outline the methods by which it might do so—regulation, finance, public production, and/or income transfers.

Regulation in some instances, may have more to do with social values than economics (for example, regulation of shop opening hours). But much regulation is

---

[2] These results could be modelled with an overlapping generations model. Brooks's analysis (2000) of pensions uses four types of people for pensions. A full analysis of the welfare state, including borrowing to finance education, would need at least five types.

[3] Many of the key articles in the literature on imperfect information and other market failures are collected in Barr (forthcoming: vol. i).

directly relevant to the efficient and/or equitable operation of markets, especially where consumer information is imperfect. Regulation of *quality*, mainly on the supply side, includes hygiene laws relating to the production and sale of food and pharmaceutical drugs, and consumer protection legislation more generally. Regulation of *quantity* more often affects individual demand—for example, the requirement to attend school, compulsory social-insurance contributions, and mandatory automobile insurance. *Price* regulation includes minimum wages. There can also be regulation of *total expenditure*—for example, global budget caps for medical spending.

Finance involves subsidies (or taxes) applied to the *prices* of specific commodities or affecting the *incomes* of individuals. Price subsidies can be partial (for example, tuition fees at public universities) or total (for example, free primary education). Similarly, prices can be raised by a variety of taxes, particularly in areas that the state wishes to discourage (for example, a tax on tobacco). Income subsidies raise different issues which are discussed shortly.

Though regulation and finance modify market outcomes, they leave the underlying mechanism intact. More drastically, the state can take over the supply side by producing goods and services itself—for example, school education and (in some countries) most health care. Alternatively, the state can commission and direct private-sector activity—for example, weapons procurement. The distinction between finance and production emerges throughout the book.

The previous interventions all involve direct interference with the market mechanism. Income transfers do not interfere directly, but enable recipients to buy goods of their choice at market prices—for example, elderly people receive a pension with which they buy food.

2.2. *Information and other problems*

As a precursor to information problems, it is useful to clear the intellectual undergrowth by briefly summarizing an earlier literature on market failures.

Older arguments
Markets are efficient only if a number of conditions hold.[4]

PERFECT COMPETITION arises where there are many buyers and sellers, free entry into and exit from the industry, and a homogenous product. The assumption can fail in various ways. A monopolist maximizes profit by restricting output below the efficient level. Solutions include regulation—for example, the imposition of a maximum price, or a per-unit subsidy (to encourage larger output) clawed back by a lump-sum tax.

---

[4] For fuller discussion, see Stiglitz (2000: ch. 4).

No EXTERNAL EFFECTS. This assumption is violated when an act of person A imposes costs or confers benefits on person B, for which no compensation from A to B or payment from B to A takes place. If I am inoculated against a communicable disease, this reduces my chances of catching it, and also benefits others because it prevents them catching the disease from me. Social benefits therefore exceed my private benefits, and the market output will typically fall below the efficient output. The same effect operates in reverse: where an activity imposes an external cost on others (pollution, for example), markets generally lead to output above its efficient level.

A range of solutions exist. Coase (1960) shows that, where the law assigns unambiguous and enforceable property rights, the market itself can resolve the problem through negotiation between the parties concerned. However, this may not be possible. Property rights may not be enforceable (water pollution), or the numbers involved may rule out negotiation (traffic congestion). A second way of dealing with externalities (Meade 1952) is through merger of the affected activities. Where neither solution is possible, intervention may be justified through regulation (for example, mandatory water standards) or an appropriate tax on the activity generating the external cost (for example, a tax on gasoline).

No INCREASING RETURNS TO SCALE. Increasing returns to scale arise when doubling all inputs more than doubles output. An implication is that competitive pricing generates long-run losses. Two forms of intervention are possible: paying firms a lump-sum subsidy equal to the loss associated with competitive pricing, or taking the industry into public ownership and paying an identical subsidy. The appropriate intervention is, therefore, subsidy or public production, or both.

No PUBLIC GOODS. Public goods in their pure form exhibit three technical characteristics: non-rivalness in consumption, non-excludability, and non-rejectability. Private goods are rival in consumption in the sense that one person's consumption is at the expense of another's—for example, if I buy an apple, there will be one apple less for everyone else. Excludability means that I can be prevented from eating the apple until I have paid for it. Rejectability implies that I do not have to buy the apple. Not all goods display these characteristics, the classic example being national defence: the arrival of a person from another country does not reduce the amount of defence available to everyone else (non-rivalness in consumption). Nor is it possible to exclude the new arrival by saying that the bombs will be allowed to fall on him until he has paid his taxes (non-excludability). Nor can he reject the defence on the grounds of pacifist beliefs (non-rejectability). Similar considerations apply wholly or in part to roads, broadcast signals, and public parks. Public health, too, has important public-goods attributes: if the water supply is purified, or clean-air legislation enforced, nobody can be excluded from the benefits; and the structure of laws and, more generally, the rule of law have important public-goods characteristics.

It is a standard result (the classic article is Samuelson 1954) that public goods create one of two problems. The market may be inefficient—for example, if the good is priced at average cost. Alternatively, the market may fail to produce the good at all. In the latter case, if the good is to be provided, it will generally have to be publicly organized. This will involve public funding, but not necessarily public production. For instance, the state may mandate and pay for a water purification programme, but the work might be carried out by a private firm.

The main conclusion is how thin is the 'old-style' economic justification for large-scale, publicly organized welfare-state services.[5] Imperfect competition, externalities, and increasing returns to scale may justify regulation or particular types of subsidy. Only public goods offer a strong efficiency case for public production. The only other *efficiency* argument for extensive public provision is if it is believed that an externality is so strong that it justifies compulsory and/or subsidized consumption of a good by the entire population: examples include publicly organized sewerage in response to nineteenth-century British cholera epidemics and, it can be argued, might also include broader aspects of public health, and basic education. In these cases, the externality is so large that the public-goods analysis applies.

The question, then, is how to explain pervasive public involvement in all countries in insurance and consumption smoothing. One route, discussed in Section 4, is through public choice; the other is through information failures.

Arguments based on imperfect information

Consumers and firms need to be well-informed in at least three ways: about quality, about price, and about the future. A later literature explores these assumptions and the effects where one or more fail.[6]

PERFECT INFORMATION ABOUT QUALITY. Consumers are well informed about many products. However, they might be badly informed—for example, about the quality of a school, or about the appropriate type of medical treatment. Producers might be poorly-informed about the quality of a worker applying for a job, or about the riskiness of an applicant for a loan or for insurance. New (1999, 2000) distinguishes two separate problems: an information problem can be resolved by supplying the relevant information; with an information-*processing* problem,

---

[5] Other than public goods, it is not possible, for example, to justify large-scale interventions from Bator's (1958) anatomy of market failure.

[6] The quality literature has its roots in classic articles by Arrow (1963) and Akerlof (1970).

in contrast, the necessary information is so complex that, even if it is supplied, economic agents are not necessarily able to make rational choices. New distinguishes three situations in which, even if they are given the necessary information, people might not be able to choose rationally:

- where the benefits of a good or service occur only a long time in the future, where the problem might be regarded as in some sense a failure of imagination;
- where a good or service has a very small potential for harmful consequences for an individual, where the problem is an inability to process very small probabilities;
- where a good or service requires complex information to be digested and processed, where the problem is lack of technical ability.

In the face of such problems, several solutions are possible. The market may develop institutions to supply information: it is possible to buy consumer magazines; equally, one can pay to have a professional survey of a house. When a person buys such products or services, what she is buying is information. In other cases the state may respond with regulation—for instance, hygiene laws for food. This is generally appropriate where the information is sufficiently non-technical for the consumer to understand it. Where information problems are serious and where, as discussed above, there is a long-time horizon, where the relevant probability is very small, or where the necessary information is too technical to be readily understood by the average consumer, the market will generally be inefficient, and public production may be a better answer. We return to the issue in Section 4.

PERFECT INFORMATION ABOUT PRICES. A second strand of the literature analyses the effects of imperfect information about prices and wages. Again, the market may supply the necessary information—for example, car magazines containing price guidelines, or web sites that make it possible to search for the lowest price. Equally, it is possible to have a house or a piece of jewellery professionally valued. If such solutions do not suffice, the state may intervene with regulation requiring sellers to publish prices.

PERFECT INFORMATION ABOUT THE FUTURE. As well as information about quality and price, individuals also need accurate expectations about the future in order to make rational choices over time, this being the decision analysed by the Fisher model. The assumption is broadly true of food (since people know that they will need to eat tomorrow, next week, next month); it is not true of medical care, because they do not know whether or when they will suffer health problems. In principle, the market can cope with risk through insurance, but insurance may be inefficient or impossible.

3. IMPERFECT INFORMATION IN INSURANCE MARKETS

3.1. *Actuarial insurance with perfect information*

The term 'insurance' is used by different people to mean different things: as a device that offers individuals *protection against risk*, or as an *actuarial mechanism*. The first defines insurance in terms of its objective, the second in terms of a mechanism by which that objective might be achieved. Even where institutions are not insurance in the second sense, they might still be regarded as insurance in that they offer protection against risk.

A risk-averse person is someone who prefers a lower income with certainty to an income that is higher on average but with greater variation. Many students, for example, would prefer a definite scholarship of £5,000 rather than face a lottery with a 50 per cent chance of £12,000 but a 50 per cent chance of nothing.

Risk-averse people buy insurance voluntarily because it increases their welfare. If I have to rely on savings to finance my old age, I need to save enough to cover my *maximum* life span. In contrast, if I can insure by buying an annuity, I need to save enough to cover only *average* life expectancy. The difference between the two figures is large. If I need £20,000 per year (roughly UK national average income in the early 2000s), to live comfortably and retire at 65 allowing a maximum age of 110 the necessary pot of savings (ignoring interest) is £900,000 (i.e. 45 × £20,000). On the other hand, if life expectancy at 65 is fifteen years, the necessary pot if I can buy insurance is only about one-third as large. When a person buys insurance, what he or she is buying is certainty.

The supply of insurance has an easy intuition. Suppose that there are 100 of us; that we decide to fly to Paris to see a football match, that each of us has a suitcase whose contents are worth £1,000, and that we know from long experience that on average 2 per cent of suitcases get lost. Thus each of us faces a potential loss, L, of £1,000, which occurs with a probability, p, of 2 per cent. In those circumstances, it would be possible to collect 2% × £1,000 = £20 from each of the 100 people, i.e. £2,000 in total; when we arrived in Paris, we would find which two people had lost their suitcase, and pay each £1,000 in compensation.

More formally, the actuarial premium for the ith individual, π_i, is defined as:

$$\pi_i = (1+\alpha)p_i L \tag{2.1}$$

where $p_i L$ is the individual's expected loss, and α is the loading the insurance company charges to cover administrative costs (for example, sending an expert to assess the damage) and competitive profit. π is the price at which insurance will be supplied in a competitive market.[7]

---

[7] For fuller discussion, see, in ascending order of difficulty, Burchardt and Hills (1997: ch. 1), Stiglitz (2000: ch. 12), Barr (1998a: ch. 5), Culyer (1993), and Rees (1989).

The price of insurance thus depends on (*a*) the degree of risk and (*b*) the size of the potential loss. Car insurance premiums are high for a driver who is young, or who lives in a high-crime area (both factors leading to a higher probability of loss); and they are high for someone who drives a Rolls Royce or Mercedes (because the potential loss is large). A middle-aged person with a good driving record driving a small, elderly Ford pays a much lower premium.

This, broadly, is the way in which private insurance operates. Note that thus far there is no need for state intervention. As discussed earlier, a rational risk-averse person facing a known risk (for example, about how long he will live) will buy actuarial insurance, which the market can and will supply. Thus the simple Fisher model extends easily to this case.

3.2. *Information problems*

Insurance along the lines of Equation (2.1) is efficient only if a number of conditions hold. Where they fail, private insurance may be inefficient or impossible.

INDIVIDUAL RISK, NOT COMMON SHOCK. Insurance requires a predictable number of winners and losers; in other words, the probabilities in Equation (2.1) are independent. This condition holds for individual risk such as age at death or the likelihood that one's car will be stolen. With a common shock, in contrast, if one person suffers a loss, so does everyone else. As discussed in Chapter 7, an inflationary shock can adversely affect all pensioners. Actuarial insurance is not able to cope with this problem: common shocks are uninsurable.

RISK, NOT CERTAINTY. Insurance addresses risk. Thus p_i in Equation (2.1) must be less than one. If $p_i = 1$, it is certain that the insured person's car will be stolen; hence, there is no possibility of spreading risks. As a result, Equation (2.1) simplifies to:

$$\pi_i = (1+\alpha)L \tag{2.2}$$

and the insurance premium exceeds the insured loss. In those circumstances there are no welfare gains from joining a risk pool. Thus medical insurance for the elderly is problematic, because the probability of requiring medical care is very high; for the same reason, actuarial insurance cannot cover medical problems that the individual already has at the time he or she applies for insurance, for whom the probability of ill health equals one. Pre-existing conditions, in short, are generally uninsurable.[8]

---

[8] The problem has both efficiency and equity aspects. It creates inefficiency in the sense of a missing market—risk-averse individuals who would like to buy insurance but are unable to do so. For the same reason, there is also inequity.

The two conditions just discussed relate to the fundamental nature of insurance—what it is and what it is not. The remaining conditions show how insurance can fail for reasons explicitly related to imperfect information.

RISK NOT UNCERTAINTY. If p_i in Equation (2.1) is unknown, the insurer cannot calculate a premium, making actuarial insurance impossible. In other words, insurance can cope with risk (where the probability is known) but not with uncertainty (where it is not). The problem can arise, first, where the insured event is rare (for example, early satellite launches); with few observations, any estimate of the probability will have a large variance. The probability might be unknown, secondly, because of complexity. Thus actuarial insurance against future inflation is difficult or impossible, because the probability of different levels of future price increases cannot be predicted.[9] Equally, there is no way today of estimating the extent of risk from exposure to BSE ('mad cow disease'). The problem can arise, thirdly, where the insured event has a long time horizon. An example discussed in Chapter 5 is the probability that someone aged 25 today will require long-term care in extreme old age.

A further condition is that all agents—the person buying insurance and the person selling it—must be equally well-informed. Where the condition fails— the problem of asymmetric information—actuarial insurance is inefficient or non-existent. There are two classes of problem: adverse selection and moral hazard.

ADVERSE SELECTION. Efficiency requires that high-risk individuals pay a higher premium than low-risk individuals. Thus the efficient premiums for people with a low and high risk of loss, p_L and P_H, respectively, are:

$$\pi_L = (1+\alpha)p_L L \tag{2.3}$$
$$\pi_H = (1+\alpha)p_H L. \tag{2.4}$$

With automobile insurance, for example, someone who is twice as risky pays roughly twice as high an insurance premium.

Adverse selection arises where the purchaser can conceal from the insurer the fact that he is a bad risk, and is thus an insurance-market manifestation of 'lemons' (Akerlof 1970). The individual knows he is a 'lemon' (that is, a bad risk), but can conceal the fact from the insurer, hence the description of adverse selection as 'hidden knowledge'.[10] Private insurers in the USA, for example, believe (rightly or wrongly) that elderly applicants for medical insurance are dispropor-

---

[9] As discussed in Chapter 7, the government can issue indexed bonds to deal with inflation; that, however, is not private insurance, but tax-funded state intervention to assist private insurance.

[10] Akerlof's competitive analysis was extended by Rothschild and Stiglitz (1976) to cover strategic behaviour by firms. For further discussion, see, in ascending order of difficulty, Atkinson (1989: ch. 7) reprinted in Barr and Whynes (1993: ch. 2), Culyer (1993), and Rees (1989).

tionately people who have something to hide. The problem can also arise if health care is an important part of employer benefits: firms with the best health-care packages will tend to attract workers with health problems, thus reducing the firm's competitiveness.

The problem is not that people differ in their riskiness, but that insurers are less well informed than the buyer about the applicant's risk status. Insurers can respond in two ways, though, as discussed in more detail in Chapter 4, Section 2, in the context of medical insurance, neither approach is a complete solution. One option is to seek a 'pooling equilibrium' in which the insurer charges a common premium, $\bar{\pi}$, based on average risk, $\bar{p}$. Two potential problems result: the outcome might be inefficient because low risks, who have to pay a higher-than-actuarial premium, buy an inefficiently small amount of insurance and, conversely, high risks an inefficiently large amount; or the market may fail entirely as low risks opt out. A second way in which insurers attempt to get round adverse selection is to try to separate high and low risks through self-selection (a 'separating equilibrium') by offering policies that incorporate incentive structures whereby a customer's choice reveals his or her true probability—for example, by offering only limited cover for the first year of the policy.[11] Two problems can result: such a separating equilibrium might not exist; or, where it does, it is inefficient.

A third possible approach is to enforce a pooling equilibrium by making insurance compulsory. Thus low risks are not able to reduce the amount of insurance they buy nor to opt out; and high risks are not able to buy an inefficiently large amount of insurance. If preferences do not differ greatly across individuals, the welfare loss from such compulsion may be small.

MORAL HAZARD. A second class of asymmetric information, moral hazard, arises where the insured person can influence the insurer's expected loss, $p_i L$, without the insurer's knowledge (hence the characterization of moral hazard as 'hidden action').

Pauly (1974) analyses individual expenditure on a preventive activity, z, which reduces the probability of the insured event. The efficient level of z is where its marginal cost is equal to the marginal reduction in insured losses. But, if the individual bears none of the cost of inaction and the insurer cannot monitor a person's preventive activity (hidden action), the individual's incentive is to spend little or nothing on z. Inefficiency arises because, if monitoring is not possible, people behave differently if they are insured. Four cases should be distinguished.[12]

1. Endogenous p_i, but at substantial psychic cost. An example is suicide: the probability is endogenous, but only at high cost to the individual. Because

---

[11] See Ravallion and Datt (1995) for analysis of such self-selection in different contexts.
[12] For fuller discussion of moral hazard, see Stiglitz (1983), Rees (1989) or Culyer (1993).

individuals cannot insure against the psychic cost of death, insurance is incomplete. Moral hazard in such cases is not a problem.

2. Endogenous p_i, with no substantial psychic cost. If people are insured they might drive less carefully. This is the Pauly result. My extra spending on z (for example, maintenance of the brakes on my car) reduces my premium by only an infinitely small amount: the main beneficiaries are other insured people who now pay slightly lower premiums. As a result of this type of externality, individuals face incentives to underinvest in preventive activities. In this case, moral hazard causes inefficiency, since people take less care than if they had to bear the full loss themselves.

3. Endogenous p_i, with substantial psychic gains—for example, voluntary pregnancy. Here the insured outcome is not an undesired exogenous event but deliberate choice. Individuals face no psychic cost, and can control the probability, p_i, in Equation (2.1); this is very different from an unwelcome exogenous event—the problem insurance is meant to address. In this case, the insurance company can calculate neither the expected loss nor the actuarial premium. Cases of this sort are generally uninsurable for individuals.[13]

4. Endogenous L at zero or low cost (the 'third-party-payment problem'). In this case, the endogenous variable is the size of the insured loss, L. The problem is illustrated by contrasting the amount of champagne people drink if they have to pay for it themselves with their consumption of champagne provided free by the airline. In the case of medical insurance, if the insurer pays all costs, neither patient nor doctor is constrained by the patient's ability to pay. The marginal private cost of health care is zero for both doctor and patient, even though social cost is positive. Moral hazard in this form leads to inefficiently high medical spending.

Thus moral hazard creates incentives to overconsumption on the demand side (cases 2 and 3) or on the supply side (case 4). The problem is fundamental: the more complete the cover and the lower the psychic loss from the insured event, the less individuals have to bear the consequences of their actions and the less, therefore, the incentive to behave as they would if they had to bear their losses themselves.

A number of devices try to reduce the problem, either through regulation or through incentives. Inspection (that is, regulation) is frequently used for damage claims. The insurer inspects the damage and pays benefit only in respect of what it regards as the true insured loss. This mechanism can work well for such claims as automobile repairs, but is less useful in cases such as medical intervention,

---

[13] The problem can sometimes be sidestepped in group schemes, where the insurer can impose a pooling solution.

where urgent action is needed. Incentive mechanisms share the cost between the individual and the insurer: frequent claimants (for example, accident-prone car drivers) pay higher premiums; deductibles make the insured person pay the first £X of any claim; with coinsurance the insured person pays x per cent of any claim. None of these, however, faces the individual with the full marginal financial cost of making good the loss.

In analytical terms, adverse selection and moral hazard are both examples of imperfect information. If the insurer could read the thoughts of his customers, there could be no hidden knowledge nor hidden action. There is a clear link between such asymmetric information and the principal–agent problem. If the principal (the insurer) is risk neutral and the agent (the insured) risk averse, it is Pareto efficient if the agent is fully insured by the principal. But the agent then has no incentive to exert effort (in this case, to take risk-avoiding measures), since his income no longer depends on that effort. The incentive can be partially restored if the agent's income is tied to the final outcome, but only at the price of deviating from Pareto optimality. The problem is solved if the principal has sufficient information to monitor the agent's behaviour.

3.3. *Social insurance as a response to information failure*

Arrow argues that, where markets fail, other institutions may arise to mitigate the resulting problems: 'The failure of the market to insure against uncertainties has created many social institutions in which the usual assumptions of the market are to some extent contradicted' (Arrow 1963: 967). In other words, institutions (public or private) may arise that are insurance in the sense of protecting against risk, even if they are not insurance in a narrow actuarial sense.

There is an interesting contrast between Arrow's arguments and those of Hayek (1945). The starting point for both writers is asymmetric information. To Hayek the fact that different people know different things is an argument in favour of markets: we go to a doctor or lawyer precisely because they have specialist information that we do not. Hayek argued that the market makes beneficial use of such differences by allowing gains from trade to be exploited. Arrow showed that the market is an inefficient device for mediating important classes of differences in knowledge between people. Lucas, in discussing unemployment, reached an identical conclusion:

Since . . . with private information, competitively determined arrangements will fall short of complete pooling, this class of models also raises the issue of *social insurance*: pooling arrangements that are not actuarially sound, and hence require support from compulsory taxation. The main elements of Kenneth Arrow's analysis of medical insurance are readily transferable to this employment context. (Lucas 1987: 62, emphasis in original).

Social insurance thus derives from two sources. The need for insurance arises because in industrialized countries employment is largely a binary phenomenon: a person is either employed or unemployed, either working or retired. Thus the risks against which social insurance offers protection are to some extent a social construct. Secondly, in the face of extensive information failures, actuarial insurance cannot cover contingencies such as unemployment, inflation, and important medical risks. Social insurance is one response.

The institutions of social insurance are modelled on private institutions. Benefits are conditioned on a contributions record and on the occurrence of a specified event, frequently related to employment status, in that one of their major purposes is to replace lost earnings.

Social insurance, however, differs from private insurance in two strategic ways. First, membership is compulsory, thus preventing exit by low risks. A pooling solution is, therefore, an option. As a result, it is possible (though, as discussed in Chapter 8 in the context of pensions, not essential) to break the link between premium and individual risk. The extent to which the relationship is actuarial shapes the nature of the social-insurance contribution—is it a tax or an insurance premium? The core analytical difference is whether the contribution is seen as a one-way transaction (that is, a tax) or a two-way exchange. With actuarial insurance, the transaction is two way: the individual pays the price in exchange for insurance cover. Thus, if social insurance is close to actuarial and if the amount of cover people are compelled to buy is broadly what they would choose voluntarily, the contribution will be seen as an insurance premium rather than a tax. In contrast, social insurance will have the same behavioural effects as a tax if it is seen as a tax, which is more likely if the scheme is not actuarial but strongly redistributive.

The second way in which social insurance differs from private insurance is that the contract is usually less specific, with two advantages. First, protection can be given against risks that the private market cannot insure; this is the central topic of the chapters in Part 2. Secondly, the risks can change over time. Atkinson (1995: 210) points out that 'the set of contingencies over which people formed probabilities years ago may have excluded the breakdown of the extended family, or the development of modern medicine, simply because they were inconceivable'. Thus, in sharpest contrast with actuarial insurance, social insurance can cope not only with *risk* but also with *uncertainty*.

4. IMPLICATIONS

4.1. *Market success*

The assumption that consumers and firms are well informed about the nature of the product and about prices is plausible for some goods, less so for others.

Assuming away problems such as imperfect competition, externalities, and public goods, markets are generally more efficient

(a) the better is consumer information;

(b) the more cheaply and effectively it can be improved;

(c) the easier it is for consumers to understand available information—i.e. where there is an information problem, rather than an information-processing problem;

(d) the lower are the costs faced by someone who chooses badly, and

(e) the more diverse are consumer tastes.

Food, by and large, conforms with these conditions. Taking them in turn, people generally know what constitutes a balanced diet; food prices are well known, not least because food items are bought frequently; and people know roughly how much food they will need today, tomorrow, and next week. Knowledge about food can be improved reasonably cheaply—for example, through public information campaigns about healthy diet. It is no accident that the incidence of cigarette smoking has fallen dramatically among large sections of the adult population. Thirdly, such information—for example, 'you can increase your life expectancy by eating more fruit and vegetables and fewer animal fats'—can easily be understood. Fourthly, for many aspects of quality, the costs of mistaken choice are low: if a new local restaurant produces soggy vegetables or wilting salad, customers go elsewhere. Finally, tastes in food are enormously diverse, making allocation by a central planner impossibly complex.

This, however, is not the whole story. There are some aspects of quality that consumers do not know. Has the food been produced hygienically? What are the ingredients in products like breakfast cereals? Are milk, cheese, and the like fresh? The state therefore has a critically important role as regulator: hygiene laws relating to the production and sale of food; regulations requiring ingredients to be listed; and the requirement to put 'sell-by' dates on packaging. Food illustrates how private markets can be helped by effective state intervention. A national food service would be enormously inefficient. The other extreme—complete deregulation—is equally unpalatable. Problems with salmonella, E coli, BSE, and so on illustrate graphically the problems that arise if the state does not take its regulatory role sufficiently seriously.

Clothing, too, conforms with criteria (a)–(e) and is therefore best left to the market. It can, however, be argued that people are less well informed about the quality of clothing than about food, not least because they buy clothes less frequently. Yet there is virtually no regulation of the quality of clothing. One reason is that with food, though the costs of a mistaken choice of restaurant may be low, other forms of mistaken choice can be very costly—for example, food poisoning and, in the extreme, death; with clothing such costs are much lower. The exceptions—safety clothing and crash helmets—precisely for that reason *are* heavily regulated.

Consumer goods such as televisions, washing machines, kitchen appliances, and personal computers fit into the same pattern. The market supplies considerable amounts of information through consumer magazines, newspaper articles, and consumer programmes on radio and television; such information is cheap, and consumers can understand it; and aggrieved individuals can seek legal redress. Minor consumer ignorance is ignored where the costs of mistaken choice are small. Regulation of quality concentrates on situations where the potential costs of poor quality are high—for example, electrical appliances that might catch fire.

Cars raise two sets of issues: their production, and their use. On the production side, the arguments are similar to those for consumer goods, a key feature being the extent of consumer information about quality. In particular, consumers cannot easily check that a car's brakes and steering are safe, and its tyres well designed. Given the high costs of mistaken choice, regulation of such safety features is stringent and continually evolving. So far as the use of cars is concerned, regulation mainly addresses the costs my driving might impose on others if I drive unsafely (for example, drink-drive laws), or if I operate a car in unsafe mechanical condition (worn tyres, faulty brakes), or if it is unacceptably noisy or polluting.

Similar arguments apply to insurance. Risks such as accidental damage to one's car, loss of luggage, theft, and fire damage conform with the necessary conditions discussed earlier and can therefore generally be dealt with through private insurance. State intervention is, for the most part, not necessary.

In such cases, for theoretically precise reasons, the state's role is to regulate to protect consumers where (*a*) they are not sufficiently well informed to protect themselves and (*b*) the costs of mistaken choice are high. Beyond that, however, matters should be left to the market. These are cases of market success.

4.2. *Market failure and government failure*

Much of the discussion in subsequent chapters addresses market failure, so discussion here is brief.

As discussed in Chapter 4, medical care does not conform well with the criteria outlined above: consumer information is often poor; people generally require individual information, so that the process will not be cheap (violating (*b*)); much of the information is highly technical (violating (*c*)); and the costs of mistaken choice can be high. Similarly, as discussed in Chapter 11, school education can raise similar problems: parents may not be well informed; improving their information may not be cost effective; and the costs to a child's educational and emotional development of bad choices can be enormous.

Separately, insurers might be badly informed in the ways described in Section 2. As discussed in Chapters 3, 4, and 5, this leads to private insurance against important employment and medical risks being inefficient or non-existent. Similarly, as discussed in Chapter 7, the fact that inflation is an uninsurable risk has important implications for the role of the state so far as pensions are concerned.

Thus markets can be inefficient, and so can insurance markets. But government can also be inefficient: it can be well-meaning but ineffective; or it can be corrupt; or it can be effective and non-corrupt but pursue objectives incompatible with efficiency. The government failure literature points to two distorting influences of the last sort. Public agencies may partly be run for the benefit of the bureaucrats who run them (Niskanen 1971). Such 'organizational slack', it is argued, occurs because politicians cannot fully monitor the actions of utility-maximizing officials. Thus, it might be argued, there is continuing upward pressure on the scale of publicly organized health care or education.

A second source of potential inefficiency is the response of government to the electorate in the form of coalitions of voters or through pressure groups. Writers such as Buchanan and Tullock (1962) and Tullock (1970, 1971) argue that most transfers from the rich are captured by the middle class through their electoral power as median voters or acting as interest groups and, as a result, that the middle-class receives a disproportionate share of the benefits of the welfare state. Other arguments stress the role of interest groups, which can affect outcomes either directly (for example, the poverty lobby) or through their influence on regulation. Regulators may be 'captured' by those whom they are supposed to regulate. It is sometimes argued, for example, that regulation of the medical profession is an entry barrier that allows the extraction of monopoly rent.

For one or more of these reasons, it is argued, the size of the public sector may be inefficiently large, or its composition distorted to meet the needs of the bureaucracy, powerful interest groups, or voters in marginal constituencies. The core of the argument is that government actions are based on the self-interest of people within government rather than on maximizing social welfare.

Though this is not the place for detailed assessment (see Mueller 1997), a number of counter-arguments should be noted. First, even in their own terms, these arguments should not be overstated. Writers such as Friedman (1962) and Hochman and Rodgers (1969) offer explanations of tax-financed redistribution that do not rely on electoral coercion. Interest groups may enhance efficiency (it is argued, for example, that pressure groups like Friends of the Earth make it politically easier for governments to introduce pollution taxes). Regulation is not inevitably a source of monopoly rents, but often serves to protect imperfectly informed consumers.

The power of bureaucrats can be overstated and their motivation misunderstood (Dunleavy 1985, 1991). Organizational slack should not be exaggerated: it is reduced by competition between agencies; increases in department size can be monitored; voters may be able to vote with their feet against high local taxation (Tiebout 1956); and, depending on the internal structure of rewards within the public service, bureaucratic utility maximization can just as easily lead to *less* government.

Nor do the government failure arguments necessarily apply equally everywhere. Tullock's claim (1971) that benefits go disproportionately to the middle class may be more true of the USA than elsewhere. In Germany and Sweden, for instance, the lowest-income quintile in the mid-1980s received net transfers of about 10 per cent of GDP.

The important contribution of the public-choice literature is the idea that analysis of government should treat its activities as endogenous. It does not, however, follow that the social-welfare outcome of the political market place is necessarily inferior to that of conventional markets. Markets can be efficient or inefficient; so can governments. Neither market failure nor government failure is an overriding argument: market failure is no automatic reason for intervention, any more than government failure is an automatic reason against. As Le Grand (1991*a*: 442) concludes:

a study of government failure does not imply that governments always fail, still less that markets always succeed. Whether a particular form of government intervention creates more inefficiency or more inequity than if that intervention had not taken place is ultimately an empirical question. . . . Governments sometimes succeed, a fact that should not be lost to view in the current glare of the market's bright lights.

4.3. *State intervention: When, why, and how*

The market versus the state was one of the titanic debates of the last century, manifested most fundamentally in the ideological conflict between 'capitalism' and 'communism'. Depending on political perspective, markets were seen as 'good' and state intervention 'bad', or vice versa. The issue was thus a political football.

Ideology, however, is only part of the picture; market failure is another, and government failure another. These efficiency considerations, the subject of this chapter, have a twofold importance. They give an analytical handle for the choice between different instruments—unrestricted market allocation, market allocation modified by regulation, subsidy or income transfers, or central planning in one form or another—to achieve efficiency. If the assumptions in Sections 2 and 3 hold, efficiency is generally best achieved by the market. Where market failures are small and/or where government capacity is limited or corrupt, this conclusion may continue to hold. Where market failure is costly and government is effective and non-corrupt, intervention will generally increase efficiency.

A second reason—though largely outside the remit of this book—why the efficiency arguments are important is the light they shed on how best to pursue equity goals.

- Where the efficiency arguments point to market allocation, distributional objectives are generally best achieved through income transfers to the poor. Earlier arguments suggest that markets for food, subject to some regulation, will be efficient. Thus it is not surprising that most food in most countries is allocated through markets and sold at market prices, with access pursued through income transfers. We generally do not give pensioners free food, but pay them a pension sufficient to pay market prices, and similarly with transfers to the poor.
- In contrast, where the *efficiency* arguments point towards public funding of a particular good or service, *equity* goals are likely to be achieved more effectively by in-kind transfers. We do not generally give income transfers to poor people to enable them to buy medical care at market prices. The efficiency arguments (discussed in detail in Chapter 4) point towards health care that is free or heavily subsidized for the entire population, thus also largely addressing issues of access for the poor.

Thus the answer to the efficiency question also offers important guidance about how best to pursue equity objectives. It is no accident that almost all countries have some sort of national health service, but none a national food service.

PART 2

INSURANCE

In the world described by the Fisher model at the start of Chapter 2, there is no risk, so individuals need no insurance. In a world with risk, insurance can improve people's well-being; and in many cases the market can provide insurance efficiently without state intervention. As discussed in Chapter 2, however, this is not always the case: imperfect information or other technical problems in insurance markets may make private insurance inefficient or impossible.

The chapters in Part 2 discuss a number of these cases. There are many potential examples, including sick pay (that is, income replacement during temporary, health-related absence from work), disability insurance (that is, income-replacement for people whose health problems rule out work for an extended period or permanently), and widowhood. This section concentrates on two central risks—unemployment and ill-health—where technical problems in insurance markets create a continuing need for state activity.

Chapter 3 discusses unemployment insurance. Private insurers face a series of problems, of which moral hazard is the most intractable. It is, therefore, not surprising that private insurance connected with unemployment—for example mortgage protection policies—is offered on only the most restrictive of conditions, and that no private policies offer cover remotely comparable to that of state schemes.

The wide-ranging and well-known problems of medical insurance are explored in Chapter 4. A key conclusion is that attempts to adapt private arrangements to accommodate these problems end up looking remarkably like social insurance, in the sense that premiums are not based on individual risk and insurers are not allowed to exclude high-risk applicants. A second key conclusion is that different strategies for financing health care have different but largely predictable problems.

Chapter 5 discusses two issues that will assume increasing salience: the impact of genetic screening on insurance markets, and problems of long-term-care insurance.

Chapter 3

The Mirage of
Private Unemployment Insurance

Insuring against unemployment may be regarded like any other form of insurance. . . . Because the risks of unemployment differ widely so should the premia. . . . National insurance contributions should depend upon the unemployment risks faced by individual contributors. In the longer run, the supply of unemployment insurance should be left to the private sector and the insurance industry. (Beenstock and Brasse 1986: 97–8)

In agrarian societies, all family members work in the fields. Thus nobody is unemployed, though they may be underemployed. In industrial societies, in contrast, employment has become largely a binary phenomenon: workers are either employed/self-employed or they are unemployed. Thus unemployment, as pointed out by Atkinson (1995: ch. 11), is a risk that in important respects is a social construct rooted in labour market institutions. Retirement pensions are similarly a social construct (Hannah 1986) to the extent that—at least during the latter part of the twentieth century—the not-retired/retired distinction in industrial societies tended to be binary.

How should industrial societies deal with unemployment? It is sometimes argued that the risk is no different from that of a car accident or burglary, and should therefore be insured in the same way. From this viewpoint, social insurance—where contributions are generally not related to risk—is like automobile insurance in which a young man driving a Ferrari pays the same premium as a middle-aged person driving a Ford. Instead, it is argued, unemployment contributions should be calculated according to Equation (2.1), with the premium actuarially related to (a) the person's risk of being unemployed and (b) the chosen benefit level. Unemployment insurance, in short, should be organized like car insurance or burglary insurance.

Though beguiling, this argument is false, because it takes no account of information problems. Private markets plus competition do not necessarily lead to more efficient outcomes than publicly organized institutions. It is equally the case that state organization is not necessarily efficient. The trick in any particular context is to choose the least inefficient set of institutions.

To oversimplify, we can divide insurance into two sorts. In the first, private markets can often supply insurance efficiently and, on the demand side, insurance can be left to voluntary individual decisions, burglary insurance being a case in point. In other cases, however, technical problems arise and, for reasons discussed later, there may be an efficiency case for making insurance compulsory. Where the technical problems are serious, insurance must be publicly organized, though the resulting institutions cannot be actuarially based, but are social insurance in the sense discussed in Chapter 2. Additionally, because insurance is compulsory, breaking the link between premium and individual risk does not cause major inefficiency.

Unemployment insurance, this chapter argues, is an example of the latter case, for which actuarial insurance is not a useful model. Section 1 briefly discusses the objectives of unemployment insurance. Section 2 discusses a series of information and other problems; Section 3 looks at the operational problems private unemployment insurance would face. The concluding section draws out the implications for policy. Three overall results emerge: the argument for private unemployment insurance does not stand up in theoretical terms; practical examples of private unemployment insurance are not evidence of the feasibility of private insurance (if anything, the reverse); and there are also serious operational problems.

1. OBJECTIVES

From the viewpoint of the individual, the objective of unemployment insurance is exactly that—insurance. By joining a risk pool, a person can buy protection against income loss caused by the loss of his or her job. For someone who is risk averse, the purchase of insurance is welfare improving.

Unemployment insurance also contributes to social welfare more broadly. The labour market should give incentives for workers to work effectively and to move into the job in which they are most productive (static efficiency); it should also encourage workers to acquire new skills in the face of unfolding technology, thus contributing to dynamic efficiency.[1] Too much security blunts these incentives to efficiency, the most dramatic example being the declining (and in some countries eventually negative) growth rates in the latter days of communism. A significant cause (though not the only one) of the increasing unviability of communist central planning was that job security and pay were almost entirely divorced from the quality of a worker's performance. Equally, however, too little security hampers efficiency: inadequate protection against the lack of a job blunts the incentive to risk taking. Well-designed unemployment benefits are, therefore essential to the efficient operation of the labour market.

---

[1] Static efficiency is concerned with making the most efficient use of existing resources, dynamic efficiency with policies to promote the growth of those resources.

Unemployment benefits also have an equity function. They should provide a worker and his or her family with an adequate standard of living. If the formula is weighted towards lower incomes, the benefit offers both insurance and poverty relief.

2. INFORMATION PROBLEMS

2.1. *The simple model*

As discussed in Chapter 2, the actuarial insurance premium for the ith individual, π_i, is defined as:

$$\pi_i = (1+\alpha)p_i L \tag{3.1}$$

where $p_i L$ is the individual's expected loss, and α is the loading that the insurance company adds to cover administrative costs and its competitive profit.

In the context of the labour market, p_i is the probability, at a given point in time, that the ith individual will be unemployed, where p_i varies *inter alia* with the individual's skills, geographical location, sex, and race. For some purposes it is useful to distinguish between

θ_i = the probability that the ith individual will enter unemployment, and
τ_i = the probability that the ith individual will leave unemployment.

The long-run relationship between θ_i, τ_i, and p_i is given by:[2]

$$p_i = \frac{\theta_i}{\theta_i + \tau_i} \tag{3.2}$$

For many purposes it is possible to discuss matters in terms of the simple probability, p_i.

2.2. *The technical conditions*

Actuarial insurance, as discussed in Chapter 2, is feasible and efficient where the relevant probabilities are independent, known, and less than one, and where

---

[2] Suppose the labour force is $LF_i = L_i + u_i$, where L_i = the number of employed people and u_i = the number of unemployed. The flow of new unemployed people is given by

$$\Delta u_i = \theta_i L_i + \tau_i u_i.$$

The general solution is

$$u_i = \frac{\theta_i}{\theta_i + \tau_i} LF_i + Ae^{-(\theta_i + \tau_i)t}$$

and, as $t \to \infty$, $u_i \to \theta_i/(\theta_i + \tau_i)$. See Beenstock and Brasse (1986: 35).

there is no significant adverse selection or moral hazard. To what extent does un-employment fit this model?

INDEPENDENT PROBABILITIES. For insurance to be feasible, insurers need a rea-sonably predictable number of winners and losers—that is, probabilities must be independent. In practice, θ_i and τ_i cannot be predicted in advance, and will change over the duration of any insurance contract in line with domestic and for-eign macroeconomic performance—events that are external to the insurer and to the individual buying insurance. The fact that θ_i and τ_i are stochastic (that is, are not known constants, but vary along a known probability distribution) need not be a problem for private insurers so long as the probabilities change only gradually and the stochastic term has a zero mean. Thus, the risks of having a car accident or of being burgled have risen over time, and insurance companies have responded by revising upwards their estimates of the relevant probabilities.

Unemployment, however, is more complex. First, both the probability, p_i, and the loss, L, in Equation (3.1) can be high, leading to a large actuarial premium, π_i. As a result, a 50 per cent premium increase will have a greater distributional effect than a 50 per cent increase in the (generally much smaller) burglary insurance premium. Secondly, and for present purposes more importantly, unemployment probabilities can change suddenly and semi-permanently, as after 1973 in the West, or after 1989 in the former communist countries. Thirdly, unemployment can be self-reinforcing (that is, the stochastic terms are correlated). Thus the clo-sure of a pit or a large local factory will increase the likelihood of unemployment among a much wider group of people than those directly affected. This is not true of other local events like a car crash, which is likely, if anything, to make people more careful, and hence to *reduce* the likelihood of further crashes.

For these reasons, unemployment is not just a random phenomenon. It tends to occur in waves; in other words, it has a strong element of common risk. Thus it is highly questionable, to put it no more strongly, whether the relevant proba-bilities are sufficiently independent and sufficiently well behaved for actuarial in-surance to be viable. Private companies offering unemployment insurance might have survived in the advanced industrial countries during the 1950s and 1960s, but it is hard to see how they could have coped subsequently.

PROBABILITY KNOWN AND LESS THAN ONE. The insurer needs to know the rele-vant probability in order to calculate the insurance premium. However, if the probability equals or approaches one, that premium will equal or exceed the in-sured loss, so that nobody will buy insurance. The average probability of being unemployed, $\bar{p}$, is roughly equal to the aggregate unemployment rate (though subject to problems of how unemployment is defined and measured), and hence is normally between 4 and 10 per cent. For some groups, however, the relevant probability is too much a certainty for insurance to be possible. Examples include unemployed school-leavers with no premium record (whose exclusion from cover is analogous to that in medical insurance policies for pre-existing conditions), and the long-run unemployed—for example, a 55-year-old, unskilled black man living in an area with long-run high unemployment. No private scheme could cover such individuals.

No ADVERSE SELECTION. Insurance can cope with high- and low-risk people by charging each a premium related to his or her risk. That, however, depends on the insurer knowing each person's risk status. Could an applicant conceal his or her risk status from the insurer? Up to a point the answer is no, since an applicant's previous employment record (which is in principle verifiable) offers some information. This argument, however, is not watertight. Adverse selection can cause problems for people with only a short employment history (teenagers or people returning to the job market after an extended period outside the formal labour force). In addition, the past is not a complete guide to future behaviour; indeed the presence of a problem that does not yet manifest obvious symptoms (for example, potential problems with substance abuse) will increase the likelihood that a person will take out insurance.

One way of limiting the inefficiency caused by adverse selection is to make insurance compulsory; and we shall see later (Section 3.1) a second efficiency argument in favour of compulsion on completely different grounds. The problem is how compulsion would work. If insurance were private, schemes would be set up with membership limited to low-risk individuals—for example, the British Medical Association would have a scheme for its members, as would the Law Society. If so, what would happen to the worst risks, for whom the relevant probabilities might be too high for insurance to be viable?

2.3. *Moral hazard*

Adverse selection arises where the insurer is imperfectly informed about the individual's risk status (hidden knowledge); the worry for the insurer is that only applicants who know that they are at risk of unemployment will apply. Moral hazard arises from a different type of information problem—where the insurer cannot monitor people's behaviour (hidden action). The objective is that a person remains unemployed for the efficient duration—that is, for the period he would have remained unemployed if he had faced the cost of unemployment himself, for example, out of saving or through borrowing on a perfect capital market. The worry for the insurer is that, because a person is insured, he or she will remain unemployed for longer than the efficient duration.

MODELLING MORAL HAZARD. Influences on θ and τ are of three sorts. First is the general economic situation, including macroeconomic variables domestically and internationally; if the probabilities are well behaved (as with car insurance), private insurers adapt by varying premiums over time. Second are factors specific to the individual, but observable, such as his or her skills, health, and previous employment experience. Private insurance deals with this, as in equation (3.1), by charging premiums that vary with individual risk. Thirdly, there are factors specific to the individual that are unobservable. These can give rise to moral hazard, in that once an individual is insured, there is in principle a temptation to *become* unemployed by manipulating θ_i, or to *remain* unemployed by manipulating t_i.[3] I shall argue that the *possibility* of moral hazard (to a large extent irrespective of whether or not it actually occurs) makes unemployment a risk that private insurance cannot cover.

Beenstock and Brasse (1986), drawing on Flemming (1978), attempt to model the way in which a private insurer might address moral hazard. They postulate that moral hazard is stronger the higher the replacement rate (that is, the higher the ratio of unemployment benefit to net income when in work), and model the probabilities θ_i and τ_i, upon which the premium is based, as:

$$\theta_i = \theta_0 + F(B_i / W_i) \qquad F' > 0$$
$$\tau_i = \tau_0 + G(B_i / W_i) \qquad G' < 0 \tag{3.3}$$

where $B = $ the level of benefits when unemployed
$\qquad W = $ net wage income when in work.

Thus, by assumption, as the replacement rate rises, the probability of becoming unemployed, θ_i, rises and the probability, τ_i, of leaving unemployment falls. The idea is that people with higher replacement rates are more prone to moral hazard and should, therefore, pay higher premiums, thus covering the additional costs resulting from their behaviour. Insurance companies, it is argued, will thus be able to break even despite the presence of moral hazard.

CRITICISMS of this approach are twofold. First, as argued later, insurance companies might not be prepared to offer cover against unemployment, however the premiums are calculated. Secondly, basing premiums on Equation (3.3) is generally inefficient, because the equations are an aggregate for a cohort as a whole, and tell us nothing about the individual. This is shown most easily by rewriting Equation (3.3) in linear form,

$$\theta_i = \theta_0 + m_i \frac{B_i}{W_i} \qquad m_i \geq 0$$

$$\tau_i = \tau_0 + n_i \frac{B_i}{W_i} \qquad n_i \leq 0. \tag{3.4}$$

---

[3] A special case of manipulating τ_i is outright fraud, where an individual has found paid work but continues to draw benefit.

Premiums based on moral hazard modelled along the lines of Equation (3.4) will be efficient if

$m_i = n_i = 0$ for all i—i.e. where there is no moral hazard; or
$m_i = \bar{m}$ and $n_i = \bar{n}$ for all i—i.e. where there is no variation in individual behaviour across the group.

However, where m_i and n_i in Equation (3.4) vary across individuals but premiums are based on a probability for the *group*, there is an incentive for each individual to remain unemployed for an inefficiently long time (that is, for longer than if he or she had to finance his or her unemployment out of savings, or by borrowing on a perfect capital market), since most of the cost of any additional duration will fall on the premium payments of others. There is an exact analogy with the third-party-payment problem with medical insurance. Probabilities based on Equation (3.3), being averages for the group, allow insurers to cover their costs; but the procedure is inefficient where the probabilities θ_i and τ_i vary across individuals on the basis of unobserved characteristics. The unobserved characteristics arise because the insurance company cannot distinguish two very different cases:

- the individual is unemployed because no job has been offered despite assiduous search;
- the individual is unemployed because, being insured, he is less assiduous in searching for/accepting a job than would be the case if he faced the full marginal cost of longer unemployment.

The first case describes what, so far as the individual is concerned, is a genuinely exogenous event; the second is an example of moral hazard. The problem is that imperfectly informed insurance companies are not able to separate the two cases.

The difficulty emerges clearly in comparison with other types of insurance. An event like a house burning down has two characteristics: it is a once-and-for-all event; and monitoring (that the house has indeed burned down) is easy.[4] Illness can be prolonged (in other words, is a continuing event), but monitoring is feasible, not least because checks do not have to be continuous. Unemployment, in contrast, is often prolonged; and in addition, monitoring is far from effective and is necessary more or less continuously over the entire duration of unemployment. Thus the attempt to charge actuarial premiums requires not only the calculation of θ_i and τ_i, but also faces substantial transactions costs (α in Equation (3.1)) in the form of continuous monitoring through a large and intrusive inspectorate; such a system,

---

[4] It is true that the cause of a fire is often an accident that the householder could have avoided; and the same can be said of car accidents. However (and crucially), the householder does not *want* a fire, nor does a driver want an accident, and to that extent moral hazard is only a limited problem.

though technically possible, is costly in terms of resources and intrusive in terms of liberty. Nor are such costs a complete solution, since premiums based on Equation (3.3) are generally inefficient.

IMPLICATIONS. Moral hazard prevents insurers from calculating the actuarial premium, making private unemployment insurance difficult, and probably impossible. Any publicly organized system of unemployment compensation will, of course, face the same problems, but is better able at least partially to address them. First, any publicly organized system of contributory unemployment benefit will be social insurance, in the sense discussed in Chapter 2, Section 3.3, not actuarial insurance. Secondly, the design of the insurance policy, notwithstanding its imperfections, at least has democratic legitimacy, since it is embedded in legislation. That legislation has two potential advantages relative to private schemes. There is freedom to set the level and structure of benefits to maximize the incentive to return to work.[5] In addition, judgements by public officials about a person's entitlement to benefit, not being influenced by the interests of shareholders, may be less biased. However, judgement is not perfect, so the need for an appeals procedure remains. Even with the best appeals procedure, however, no scheme can cope entirely efficiently with moral hazard, in the sense of ensuring the people remain unemployed for the optimal duration—long enough to allow efficient job search, but not inefficiently extended because of moral hazard.

The conclusion is twofold. Private unemployment insurance faces enormous problems; no publicly organized scheme will be entirely efficient, but a well-designed scheme will be less inefficient than competitive private schemes.

2.4. *The inapplicability of private-sector examples*

Certain types of private cover against unemployment do exist. However, they strengthen rather than contradict the argument that private unemployment insurance is not feasible.

MORTGAGE PROTECTION POLICIES make an individual's mortgage repayments while he or she is unemployed (for a survey and analysis of such policies in the UK, see Burchardt and Hills 1997). For present purposes such policies have three key characteristics. First, they are open, by and large, only to the best risks. Owner-occupiers tend to have more secure jobs and so face a lower probability, θ, of becoming unemployed. They are also more mobile (since, at least in the UK, owner-occupiers are less affected than renters by housing market rigidities), hence reducing the probability, τ, of remaining unemployed. Most companies

---

[5] There is a large literature debating whether replacement rates do or do not have strong incentive effects; for surveys, see Atkinson and Micklewright (1991) and Atkinson and Mogenson (1993).

seek further to pinpoint the best risks through restrictions on who may buy a policy: all insurers impose an age restriction, many require a recent work history, and one-third exclude self-employed people. Insurers reduce the risk they face even further because under most policies premiums can be changed month by month, and yet further because policies have a maximum payout period, thus capping the insurance company's loss.

A second set of restrictions is designed to guard against adverse selection. Some insurers allow a person to buy a policy only at the time that she buys the house, on the basis that she is unlikely to buy a new house if she knows that her job is at risk. In addition, most policies do not pay out for claims arising during an initial 'qualification period'—for example, unemployment starting during the first three months of the policy. Thirdly, some policies do not pay out for an initial period of unemployment (for example, the first thirty or sixty days of unemployment).

Finally, owner-occupiers tend to be among the better paid and so face lower replacement rates. This acts to reduce moral hazard, a point reinforced where the person in question has not only a high money income but also substantial job satisfaction.

Mortgage protection policies are thus limited to the best risks, impose restrictions to minimize adverse selection, and sidestep the worst problems of moral hazard. Such policies are genuinely private insurance. Their existence suggests the possibility of limited private unemployment insurance for professionals such as doctors and lawyers, but offers no basis whatever on which to generalize to a system of private unemployment insurance for everyone.

CREDIT LOAN INSURANCE is available from most banks. The policy makes repayments on personal loans in the face of sickness or accident, and some policies have extended cover to unemployment. However, the arguments about mortgage protection insurance apply equally here. In addition, benefits are limited in size (the maximum benefit is the total outstanding loan). Finally, sickness and accident are, by and large, insurable risks; unemployment was possibly added as an afterthought, and such cover might be possible for the same reasons that mortgage protection insurance is possible. Again, however, there is no basis for generalizing to the population at large.

TRADE UNION COMPENSATION FOR THE UNEMPLOYED. Some trade unions have unemployment compensation schemes. In a typical scheme, members qualify by contributing for a year or more; benefit has a limited duration, and may decline after x weeks of unemployment; a longer period of contribution may entitle the worker to longer benefits; and the rules of such schemes generally allow the trade union considerable discretion in changing the contribution and benefit regimes. Thus Beenstock and Brasse (1986: 78) conclude that 'in none of the trade union accounts that we have examined is there any explicit recognition of sound economic/actuarial principles in matching claims to contributions. Rather, union provident schemes, like national insurance benefits, operate on a pay-as-you-go basis.'

Even the one suggested advantage is fraught with difficulties: 'trade union schemes have a built-in system of checks and balances that effectively removes the problem of moral hazard. The local union branch office is in the best possible position to verify a member's claim' (Beenstock and Brasse 1986: 79). This implies that a local official could withhold benefits or, in the extreme, threaten expulsion from the trade union. A number of issues follow: would we wish any private-sector official to have such powers; how would horizontal equity be preserved when different local officials in a given scheme give different decisions, or when the rules of schemes differ across trades unions; and would we wish to modify our answers if the union were a closed shop, so that expulsion from the union was equivalent to expulsion from the profession?

Thus trade-union schemes should not be characterized as actuarial insurance with risk-rated premiums; rather, they should be regarded as a form of decentralized social insurance for members of the union concerned. Earlier argument suggests that no other result is possible.

3. OPERATIONAL PROBLEMS

Alongside these various technical problems, private unemployment insurance faces a series of practical difficulties: compulsion and its enforcement; protecting individuals; and the calculation of the relevant probabilities.

3.1. *Compulsion*

Two questions arise: should insurance be compulsory and, if so, how would compulsion be enforced? The standard argument for voluntarism is that it is efficient for individuals to make their own decisions so long as they bear fully the resulting costs. Thus a person should be free not to insure against income loss due to unemployment; if he then loses his job and starves, that is his prerogative.

Quite apart from equity issues, the voluntarism argument in this case is flawed in efficiency terms, because it overlooks the external costs that non-insurance imposes on others: upon taxpayers if an uninsured person is given social assistance; and more broadly if the uninsured person is left to starve. In the latter case, the external costs of non-insurance fall, for example, on dependent children, or emerge through any resulting increase in crime, or—in the extreme—through the costs of disposing of dead bodies, or the health hazard if they were left where they fell.

The market itself cannot eliminate the externality, not least because of the large number of agents involved. Nor is it clear how a Pigovian tax/subsidy would improve matters.[6] Making insurance compulsory removes the inefficiency caused by non-insurance; however, to the extent that individuals have different degrees of risk aversion, it does not wholly eliminate inefficiency, since some people may be obliged to buy more insurance than they would voluntarily have chosen. There is a fairly exact analogy with compulsory car insurance, where, quite correctly on efficiency grounds, compulsion is limited to cover in respect of damage to third parties.

How would compulsion be enforced? With automobile insurance, enforcement in the UK is through the need to obtain a new road fund licence annually.[7] With private unemployment insurance, employers could be required to inspect their employees' insurance certificates; or they could be obliged to organize insurance for all their employees. Either method involves a fair amount of bureaucracy, and some people would still escape the net.

3.2. *Protecting Individuals*

QUALITY CONTROL. It is not just insurers who are imperfectly informed. Information problems arise also on the demand side of the market. As discussed in Chapter 2, Section 4, regulation to protect consumers is justified in efficiency terms where people are not sufficiently well informed to protect themselves and where the cost of any resulting mistaken choice is high. Private unemployment insurance faces just such problems. Contracts are complex; and by the time a person is denied benefit because of an imperfectly understood exclusion clause it is too late to do anything to put the problem right.

At least two sorts of regulation are therefore needed. First, there has to be regulation about acceptable terms and conditions in the design of insurance policies, including the types of exclusion that are or are not permissible. Regulating the design of contracts is no simple matter, given continuing innovation by insurers intent on guarding against adverse selection and moral hazard. Regulation is needed, secondly, on how the resulting policies are implemented. If anything, the problem is even harder: since moral hazard by definition arises out of the insurer's imperfect information, attempts to withhold benefit because someone

---

[6] Where an activity creates an external benefit, an unrestricted private market will supply an inefficiently small quantity. One way of restoring supply to its efficient level is to pay a so-called Pigovian subsidy. Analogously, a Pigovian tax discourages excessive supply in the present of an external cost (for fuller discussion, see e.g. Stiglitz 2000: ch. 9).

[7] A new road fund licence is issued only on production of a valid certificate of insurance. The licence must then be displayed on the car and so, at least to some extent, is visible proof of insurance. Even so, non-insurance is not unusual.

Insurance

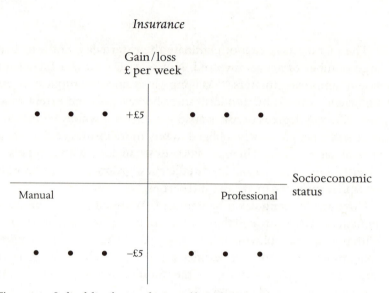

Figure 3.1. *Stylized distribution of gains and losses by socioeconomic group*

remains unemployed for 'too long' are often impossible except on the basis of individual judgement.

DISTRIBUTIONAL EFFECTS OF RISK-RELATED PREMIUMS. A separate set of issues concerns the distributional effects of private insurance. The starting point is to consider the correlation between risk-related premiums and a series of socioeconomic variables such as wage, marital status, number of children, region, and so on. Beenstock and Brasse (1986) report a correlation between premium and wage of −0.22; they interpret this low correlation as showing that risk-related premiums have no undesirable distributional effects. Even if true overall, however, this finding is only an average across all individuals. It does not follow that no individuals or subgroups will suffer adverse distributional effects. The point is illustrated in Figure 3.1 for a hypothetical distribution of gains and losses of individuals by socioeconomic group. The scatter of gains and losses gives rise to a correlation of zero, but clearly many individuals, including some in the lowest socioeconomic groups, suffer substantial losses.

Nor is it enough to look only at the immediate distributional effects. The labour market has already adjusted to different risks of unemployment. People who are unlikely to lose their jobs (for example, civil servants) are paid less than otherwise because of low unemployment risks. Nevertheless, many such individuals remain among the higher paid, and would systematically be advantaged by risk-related unemployment insurance premiums. Similarly, the lower paid with higher unemployment risks would systematically be disadvantaged.

Aggregate statistics like the correlation coefficient do not tell us what we need to know. What is necessary is a study of the effects of risk-related premiums on individuals, based on microdata. Burchardt and Hills (1997: 26–30) conduct precisely such a study for mortgage-protection insurance. In comparison with tax funding, they find that risk-rated premiums disadvantage the lower part of the income distribution and benefit people with higher incomes, and that the effect is strong.

HOW WOULD INDIVIDUALS BE PROTECTED AGAINST RISING PREMIUMS? In the UK, social-insurance contributions increased sharply between 1973 and 1980, mainly because of rising levels of unemployment. If premiums in a private scheme double, there is no major problem, so long as the absolute size of the premium is small (cover for a small elderly car in a rural area) or where the policy can be cancelled (by reverting to public transport). Nor is there a major problem with rising social insurance contributions, because they are related to a person's income. With private unemployment insurance, however, premiums for many people are large, compulsory, and unrelated to individual income, so that the result of any sharp increase would be poverty and/or arrears in premiums. The problem is aggravated because risk-related premiums would vary widely; Beenstock and Brasse (1986) estimate nearly a fifty-fold difference in the premium between the most advantaged and least advantaged for a given level of benefit. Thus individuals would need protection from poverty in respect of the high *level* of premiums and also in respect of any rapid *change* in premiums. The latter, in particular, would not be easy.

Other issues are mentioned only as questions. How would individuals be protected whose insurance company went bankrupt, or whose employer failed to take out an insurance policy? Even with social insurance there have been cases of employers collecting the contribution and simply pocketing it. In such cases, once the innocence of ex-employees was established, benefit was paid. Could private insurers be relied on to do the same?

3.3. *Calculating the relevant probabilities*

Risk-related premiums require estimation for each individual or group of the probabilities θ_i and τ_i of entering and leaving unemployment, respectively. Two questions arise: how possible/accurate is such estimation; and how worthwhile is the exercise?

Stern (1982), estimated inflow probabilities, examining the effect on θ of differences in one personal characteristic (for example, age) holding constant all other personal characteristics (region, occupation, industry, family composition, education, and housing status). This was a major exercise, and even so was very approximate. Greater accuracy requires letting all relevant personal characteristics vary simultaneously and acquiring up-to-date information on individuals. Given the lag in collecting microdata, estimates of θ in practice are likely to be costly, out of date, and of only limited accuracy.

Outflow probabilities were calculated by Arulampalam and Stewart (1995), who estimated the conditional probability of leaving unemployment for two male cohorts, one in 1978, previously analysed by Narendranathan, Nickell, and Stern (1985), and one in 1987 at a time when unemployment was twice as high. This approach has the advantage of considering all the variables simultaneously. A key finding is that constraints on the demand side, measured by the local unemployment rate, have a stronger effect for the latter cohort. As with the estimates of θ, however, the results of necessity are based on data that are several years old.

Is the endeavour welfare improving? At least four sets of problems arise. Gathering data is costly, and the resulting estimates not wholly accurate. The results are also out of date, since microdata take time to collect, so that we do not know current probabilities, let alone future ones. Finally, estimation omits unobservable characteristics: if moral hazard affects individual behaviour, these will be related to the duration of unemployment, and will therefore bias the estimates of θ and (particularly) τ.[8]

The question is whether the costs of data collection and analysis plus those of correcting inaccurate predictions are worthwhile. In particular, are these costs more than offset by the efficiency gain from charging risk-related premiums? Though ultimately the question is empirical, the exercise is unlikely for at least two reasons to be cost-effective. First, the efficiency gains will tend to be small, mainly because, for the reasons discussed earlier, insurance is compulsory, thus reducing the potential efficiency gains of a move to risk-related premiums. Secondly, the transactions costs of implementing risk-related premiums is high (that is, α in Equation (3.1) is large); and, the higher is α, the greater the efficiency gains necessary if risk-rated premiums are to increase efficiency overall.

4. CONCLUSIONS

4.1. *Theoretical arguments*

Private unemployment insurance faces three sets of problems. First, because of moral hazard, unemployment is uninsurable for most if not all employed people. Problems are even greater for the self-employed, for whom not only τ_i, the probability of leaving unemployment, but, to a much greater extent than for those on wages and salaries, also θ_i, the probability of entering unemployment, are en-

---

[8] In most estimation methods, omitted independent variables give rise to biased estimators.

dogenous. The situation should be contrasted with an insurable event that is wholly outside individual control, such as developing a kidney infection. Unemployment, it should be clear, is a very different animal.

Secondly, unemployment insurance faces substantial, and at times insuperable, difficulties because unemployment can occur in large waves; thus individual probabilities can be interdependent. The point is worth emphasizing: with the possible exception of the twenty-five halcyon years between 1948 and the first oil shock in 1973, industrial countries faced substantial waves of unemployment over the course of the twentieth century, and so, latterly, have the post-communist countries.

A third problem is that there are gaps in coverage for some groups, notably unemployed school-leavers and the long-term unemployed.

Precisely because of these difficulties, examples of private unemployment insurance are hedged about by substantial restrictions, and none offers a basis for generalization. Precisely because of these difficulties I have yet to find an example of private, actuarial insurance offering protection remotely equivalent to the state scheme. It has been suggested that the existence of state-organized unemployment insurance cuts the ground from under any private initiative. The difficulty with this argument is that state pensions are usually more generous than unemployment benefits, yet private pensions exist in all advanced industrial countries, often on a large scale.

4.2. *Policy implications*

What are the policy implications of these technical arguments? Two issues arise: how should insurance premiums be priced; and should the insurance be organized publicly or privately?

PRICING. Are actuarial premiums (*a*) possible, (*b*) necessary, and (*c*) desirable? It is *possible* for social insurance to have contributions closely related to individual risk. The UK between 1948 and 1975 had a flat-rate weekly contribution based on the average risk; and it would be possible to have flat-rate contributions at different rates for different risk groups (£10 per week for a 55-year-old construction worker, £1 per week for a 30-year-old doctor). In addition, it would be possible to charge the employer a risk-related premium.

Such arrangements are not, however, *necessary*. Compulsion, in the form of government determination that each worker will have a set quantity of insurance, can be justified on efficiency grounds; and, once quantity has been externally set, price differences largely lose their efficiency function.

Are actuarial premiums *desirable*? In the case of unemployment, actuarial premiums for employees contribute neither to efficiency nor to vertical equity. And the need to introduce additional cash benefits to offset any adverse distributional effects could lead to a situation where the poorest people, being the worst risks, pay the highest social insurance contributions and receive higher cash benefits to enable them to pay those contributions. The efficiency case for risk-rated premiums for employers is, however, stronger.

PRIVATIZATION. It is perfectly possible to have more private administration of unemployment benefits. The Swedish system of unemployment insurance, for instance, is notionally a private-sector activity organized mainly by trades unions. But, though its administration is private, over 90 per cent of the funding is public, the system is hedged by extensive regulation, and individuals without cover are eligible for tax-financed, non-contributory benefits. The system is, therefore, more usefully regarded as a public scheme whose administration has been hived off to the private sector. In such cases, private institutions act, in effect, as agents of the state. All this, however, is very different from 'real' privatization, which would require *all* unemployment insurance benefits in respect of *all* employees to be supplied by the private market, at least for an initial period of unemployment. This chapter has argued that unemployment for technical reasons is not an insurable risk, and that in consequence no private insurance company would offer cover against unemployment except in the most restricted circumstances. Large-scale privatization is, therefore, impossible. The private schemes discussed in Section 2.4 offer no empirical contradiction.

4.3. *The bottom line*

The following options are feasible.

- Social-insurance contributions could be more closely related to individual risk than currently in most countries.
- Greater private-sector involvement in the administration of unemployment benefits is possible.
- It might be possible to have limited private insurance for professionals (lawyers, doctors)—that is, for those groups who need such protection least.

However, we should be clear about the resulting institutions.

- Not least because moral hazard affects all schemes, whether public or private, no scheme available to the generality of the population could be actuarial insurance in the sense that automobile insurance or burglary insurance is actuarially based.
- Such insurance could not be private in the sense of being organized in the private sector, and with relatively little state intervention via regulation or subsidy.

- The calculation of the necessary probabilities of entering and leaving unemployment would be costly, and the results out of date and not very accurate.
- Given that membership is compulsory, the efficiency gains from risk-rated employee contributions are questionable.
- Though distributive matters are not the primary focus of this chapter, the introduction of risk-rated premiums would substantially disadvantage poorer people.

Finally, these conclusions rest on technical arguments about what is and what is not an insurable risk, and have little to do with ideology. Unemployment compensation is publicly organized in all the advanced industrial countries, because unemployment is a risk against which the private market is unable to provide systematic protection. Foreseeable twenty-first-century developments do nothing to change this conclusion.

Chapter 4

Problems with Medical Insurance

Economics is about improving well-being, of which life itself—its quantity and quality—is central. For precisely that reason, health care arouses strong emotions; it is also—and increasingly—very costly. Its finance and availability are therefore both economically and politically salient.

This chapter starts by discussing objectives. Section 2 sets out the major information problems that arise with health care and—separately—with medical insurance, and the problems that result. Section 3 considers the strategies that economic theory predicts could work well, and those for which it predicts disaster. Section 4 draws together the conclusions. Though focused mainly on the finance of health care, and in particular on insurance, discussion is at times broader, since the central issue of information has wide ramifications.

1. OBJECTIVES

THE PRIMARY OBJECTIVE. The argument starts from a very simple proposition: *the primary aim of health policy is improved health*. What matters, in other words, is longer life expectancy (reduced mortality), improved quality of life (reduced morbidity), and the sharing of those gains equitably across the population. In strict analytical terms, therefore, health care is important not for its own sake (in other words, is not a primary objective), but only as an instrument of improved health.

A second proposition is that good health has many sources, of which medical care is only one. Overall living standards are a key determinant: rising wealth over the twentieth century was associated with increased life expectancy; and cross-sectionally, richer countries today have longer life expectancy than poorer countries. More controversially, Wilkinson (1996) argues that there is a strong association between greater income inequality and poorer health outcomes: it is not just the *level* of income that determines health outcomes; for a given average level of income, a wider *dispersion* of that income is associated with poorer health outcomes. That finding, however, is much contested; see the various papers in Kawachi, Kennedy, and Wilkinson (2000). A second major determinant of health is individual choice about diet (healthy eating) and lifestyle (exercise, avoiding smoking, and so on). A third determinant is the individual's personal circumstances. These include the general external environment (for example, pollution or its absence) and the person's individual environment, such as the type of job (or *having* a job). There is evidence (though the matter is controversial) that higher unemployment is causally related to poorer health outcomes, including premature death (Morris *et al.* 1994; Benzeval *et al.* 1995: ch. 8); and large-scale studies of British civil servants (Marmot *et al.* 1991; North *et al.* 1993) suggest that work-related health problems are caused less by stress than by feelings of lack of control over their working lives.[1] A fourth determinant is the quality and availability of health care. Finally, a person's health is affected also by his or her inheritance—for example, physical and emotional strength. Note that only this last is beyond the reach of public policy.

This suggests a third proposition, explored below: health policy should focus not only on health care, but also on other causes of health that are amenable to policy intervention.

UNPACKING THE PRIMARY OBJECTIVE. Achieving the primary objective involves using resources efficiently and equitably. Allocative efficiency (sometimes also referred to as *external efficiency*) aims to produce the quantity, quality, and mix of health interventions that bring about the greatest improvement in health. It embraces the total amount spent on health care and also the way those resources are used. It follows from earlier discussion that policy should range widely to consider *all* sources of health. Health policy needs, first, to consider the efficient division of health spending between primary medical care and hospitals; between preventive interventions (vaccination campaigns, pre-natal care) and curative interventions; and between spending on health care and spending aimed at the other determinants of health—for example, public information campaigns designed to encourage healthier lifestyle choices. Health policy also involves broader aspects of policy design. The Ministry of Finance might impose 'sin taxes' on unhealthy products like tobacco; the Education Ministry could include health education in the school curriculum (for example, there was widespread ignorance under communism about the ill-health effects of smoking);[2] and action on environmental factors such as access to clean water is crucial (it is argued that such action would do more to increase life expectancy in sub-Saharan Africa than any reform of health-care systems).

The efficient mix of policies will obviously depend on a country's economic development: the efficient use of health resources in a poor country would place heavy emphasis on clean water, education about basic hygiene, simple preventive

---

[1] The studies found that junior civil servants, who generally face less stress than their seniors but have less control over their working lives, experienced poorer health outcomes.

[2] For fuller discussion of health and health care in the transition countries, see Preker and Feachem (1994), Shapiro (1995), and World Bank (1996: ch. 8).

medical care, and basic curative care; a wealthy country can afford to spend more on more advanced and expensive curative interventions.

Efficiency therefore matters. If health-care resources are used inefficiently, they will fail to produce the maximum health gain; if no extra resources are available to fill the gap, inefficiency means that some people have shorter lives or less healthy lives than they would with better use of existing resources; if extra resources are made available, inefficiency in the health sector deprives people of better schools or roads, or higher personal consumption, and such deprivation could be avoided with better use of health-care resources.[3]

Equity is concerned with the distribution of health outcomes—for example, with lower life expectancy of poorer people or of minorities; it is also concerned with the distribution of health *care*—for example, with constraints on access to medical care by poorer people. As a practical matter, policy tends to be concerned more with the latter because of its high political visibility.

2. INFORMATION PROBLEMS

To what extent will market allocation achieve these objectives? Section 2.1 discusses fairly briefly the pervasive information problems that affect health care. Section 2.2 discusses equally pervasive, but different, information problems with medical insurance.

2.1. *Health care*

HOW WELL INFORMED ARE CONSUMERS? As discussed in Chapter 2, Section 4, markets are more efficient (*a*) the better is consumer information, (*b*) the more cheaply and effectively it can be improved, (*c*) the easier it is for consumers to understand available information, (*d*) the lower are the costs if someone chooses badly, and (*e*) the more diverse are consumer tastes.

Discussing these aspects in turn, consumers are often badly informed. People can be unknowingly ill. Diagnosis is often complex and technical; people may be poorly informed about what types of treatment are available; and there is uncertainty about the effectiveness of different interventions. And frequently an individual does not have time to shop around if her condition is acute (contrast the situation with a car repair, where there is time to acquire information).

Can information be improved? Knowledge such as first aid can be improved cheaply. However, a person with a medical problem generally requires information based on individual consultation with a medical expert, which is inherently more costly than provision of information that is more generally applicable. In

---

[3] For fuller discussion, see Eddy's conversation (1992) with his (medical doctor) father.

that sense, medical care is more like an individually tailored product (for example, a made-to-measure suit) than like a standard, mass-produced product (for example, a car).

Can people understand medical information? Much medical care is technically complex. In the extreme, it would be necessary to train everyone to be a doctor. Because of that complexity, people do not necessarily understand information even when it is offered. Thus there is not only an information problem but, as discussed in Chapter 2, Section 2.2, also a major information-processing problem.

Mistaken choice is costlier and less reversible than with many other commodities. If I buy a shirt that turns out to be low quality, I learn at relatively low cost that I should in future go to another provider. Mistaken decisions about medical-care providers can be vastly more costly. The argument is illustrated most graphically by unregulated backstreet abortion, but applies much more broadly.

To a considerable extent, therefore, consumers are poorly informed about the quantity of treatment they need and about the quality of the care they receive; and, even if information were available, health care is inherently a technical subject, so that there is a limit to what consumers can understand without themselves becoming doctors. The problem is exacerbated by the existence of groups who would not be able to make use of information even if they had it, such as victims of road accidents. All these information problems create an overwhelming case at a minimum for wide-ranging regulation, including medical qualifications, the testing, production, and sale of pharmaceutical drugs, and the quality of medical treatment.

HOW USEFUL IS COMPETITION? Competition has two generic advantages: it gives producers incentives to respond to consumer choice; and it creates downward pressures on cost. However, responsiveness to consumer choice is not welfare improving if a person is too badly informed to make a rational choice; equally, the ability to buy a lower-quality product at a lower price is welfare improving only if the choice is well informed. Thus the advantages of competition are contingent on the quality of information. Where people are well informed, the advantages of competition are real and major. Where the information problem is relatively small and/or consumer tastes highly diverse, consumer choice, albeit imperfect, will generally be more efficient than decisions by someone acting as the person's agent making decisions on his or her behalf. Major information problems, however, call seriously into question the advantages of competition.

2.2. *Medical insurance*

How should health care be financed? Imperfect information arises in at least three ways. First, nobody knows how much health care they will need. That fact, combined with the scale of the potential loss, means that for most people, insurance will be welfare-improving. As discussed in Chapter 2, Section 3, a competitive insurance company charges a premium,

$$\pi_i = (1+\alpha)p_iL \tag{4.1}$$

where p_i is the probability that the insured event will occur, L is the size of the loss against which the individual insures, and α is the insurance company's mark-up to cover administrative costs and competitive profit. Is this the appropriate mechanism for releasing these welfare gains?

A second type of imperfect information then arises: medical insurance policies are complex financial instruments. Thus a person buying a medical insurance policy is not necessarily well informed: he will not necessarily understand what it covers and what it excludes, how the contract can be altered or ended, and whether the conditions for such alteration or termination are symmetric between the individual and the insurer. Though not insurmountable, such complications certainly point to a need for regulation of competing medical insurance policies.

The third set of information problems afflicts insurers. As discussed in Chapter 2, Section 2, private insurance operates efficiently only if a series of conditions holds: the relevant probabilities must be independent, less than one, and known; and there must be no substantial problems of adverse selection or moral hazard. Problems can arise under each heading.

Independent probabilities

Insurance can cover individual risk but not a common risk. With a common shock, at its extreme, everyone suffers a loss, and insurance collapses. The condition that probabilities are independent generally holds for medical risks: if I break a leg, this does not influence the probability that you will require medical attention. However, the condition fails during a major epidemic—voluntary actuarial medical insurance would not survive something like the Black Death; nor could it cope with AIDS on the scale found in many African countries.

Probability less than one

Insurance can deal with risk but not with certainty. Where someone is certain to make a claim, the insurance premium will equal or exceed the insured loss, in which case nobody will buy insurance. The condition that the relevant probability is less than one holds for many afflictions—for example, a broken leg or developing a kidney complaint. However, it fails for a person who has a chronic medical problem prior to taking out insurance: a diabetic applying for medical insurance by definition has a 100 per cent chance of developing diabetes. In addition to such pre-existing conditions, the condition fails, or comes close to failing, for elderly people, who have a high probability of requiring medical treatment. Finally, genetic screening has a major impact, by accurately predicting future medical problems. This last issue, which is potentially devastating both in a medical context and for insurance more broadly, is discussed in detail in Chapter 5.

Probability known
The insurer needs to know the relevant probability in order to calculate the insurance premium. For the most part, this condition holds. However, it fails in areas too complex for accurate assessment of the relevant probabilities—in other words in the case of uncertainty. BSE ('mad cow disease') has already been mentioned. Another example is AIDS, which faces two sorts of uncertainty: there is no way of predicting how widespread the disease will become, creating uncertainty about the probability p_i in Equation (4.1)); equally, there is no way of knowing how much treatment will cost, creating uncertainty about the size of L. The condition also fails where there is a long-run time horizon to the insurance contract—that is, where someone pays a premium today in respect of a potential benefit in the future. An example that affects increasing number of people is long-term-care insurance, discussed in Chapter 5.

No adverse selection
Where people are differentially risky, the efficient insurance premiums for low- and high-risk people are:

$$\pi_L = (1+\alpha)p_L L \qquad\qquad (4.2)$$
$$\pi_H = (1+\alpha)p_H L \qquad\qquad (4.3)$$

where p_L and p_H are the probability of making a claim for low- and high-risk individuals, respectively. Thus differing degrees of risk cause no problems where the insurer knows who is low and who high risk. Adverse selection arises where a person knows that he is a bad risk but can hide the fact from the insurer.

Medical insurers try to guard against the problem in a number of ways. First, and most obviously, they require a medical check-up before a policy is issued, but this is not a complete solution because investigations, however thorough, give only a partial picture. Secondly, insurance proposal forms require the applicant to list 'all relevant facts', with the threat that benefit will be denied if it can be shown that relevant information was deliberately withheld. Not the least of the problems with this approach is demonstrating that any withholding was deliberate.

POOLING EQUILIBRIUM. In principle an insurer could get round the problem by putting all its clients into a single pool and charging everyone a common premium based on the average risk,

$$\bar{p} = [\theta p_H + (1-\theta)p_L] \tag{4.4}$$

where p_H and p_L are as above, and θ and $(1-\theta)$ the proportions of high- and low-risk individuals buying insurance. Thus the common premium is

$$\bar{\pi} = (1+\alpha)\,\bar{p}L. \tag{4.5}$$

The key feature of such a pooling equilibrium is that the insurer does not need to know p_H, p_L, or θ, but merely the average outcome, $\bar{p}$.

There are two problems with this apparent solution. First, it is inefficient. It would not be inefficient if both the insurer and the insured were ignorant about the true probabilities. In this case, however, the insured person is assumed to be well informed about her true risk status. Thus a low-risk individual who is charged a premium higher than the efficient premium dictated by her true risk, π_L, will buy less insurance than with an individually tailored premium. Conversely, a high-risk individual will generally buy an inefficiently large amount of insurance. The first problem, therefore, is inefficiency. A second problem is instability: if an insurer offered a common premium, $\bar{\pi}$, a competing insurer could bid away the low-risk group. For example, Blue Cross–Blue Shield, the main US non-profit insurer, originally charged everyone in the same locality a premium based on the average risk (so-called community rating). That, however, meant that commercial insurers could offer policies based on a lower risk to younger people in the locality, thus taking away the best risks and leaving Blue Cross–Blue Shield with a worse risk pool. In the face of such pressures, Blue Cross–Blue Shield was forced to move to premiums based on individual risk.

SEPARATING EQUILIBRIUM. Insurers also try to get round adverse selection by offering policies that incorporate incentives to encourage self-selection by low- and high-risk groups. Suppose that as an insurer I worry that applicants are disproportionately people who know they have a problem, I could offer medical insurance that offered only limited cover for the first year of the policy. There are at least two problems with this approach. It might not be possible to devise such a policy (that is, a separating equilibrium might not exist). Secondly, where such a policy does exist, it is inefficient; the restriction of cover in the first year, designed to screen out bad risks, denies full cover even to good risks.

Adverse selection—either in reality or because insurers fear it is a reality—gives insurers an incentive to recruit good risks and avoid bad risks—so-called cream skimming. Attempts to screen out high risks lead to gaps in coverage for low risks, who can buy only partial cover and, in the extreme, no cover. In the face of adverse selection, the market is either inefficient or fails entirely.[4]

No moral hazard

PROBLEMS of moral hazard can arise in two ways. A patient might be able to influence the probability p_i in Equation (4.1), or she might be able to influence the cost of treatment, L.

A person with full insurance might influence p, first, by taking fewer health precautions; this is the issue (case 2 in Chapter 2, Section 3.2) addressed by Pauly (1986). The problem might be less acute than it appears inasmuch as insurance can cover the financial loss connected with ill health, but does not cover the associated utility costs of discomfort, inconvenience, and so on. As a result, people bear some of the costs themselves, reducing the incentive to underinvest in precautionary activities. Elective medical care raises a separate series of problems: in some situations a person's consumption of medical services is not a random, unwelcome exogenous event (which is what insurance is designed to address) but an act of deliberate choice. Some such cases (hair transplants, 'nose jobs', and the like) raise no significant social policy problems. However, the decision to consult one's family doctor has a significant elective element; and pregnancy is often a deliberate choice. Such elective medical care (case 3 in Chapter 2, Section 3.2) is not well covered by voluntary policies. Moral hazard of this type can create uninsurable risks and hence gaps in coverage.

A second set of problems arises out of third-party-payment incentives, where the patient can influence L. This is case 4 in Chapter 2, Section 3.2. The incentive is seen at its simplest by contrasting the way people behave when faced by a conventional menu with the way they behave in an all-you-can-eat for $9.99 restaurant. The roots of the problem are that (*a*) the insurer is largely divorced from the decisions of doctor and patient, and (*b*) the doctor is paid a fee for service. In the simplest case, the doctor is regarded as the patient's agent: if insurance covers all costs, health care is 'free' to the patient, and the doctor is not constrained by the patient's ability to pay. Both patient and doctor face zero private costs, even though the social costs are positive, and often large; thus both face an incentive to prescribe/consume all health care that yields *any* private benefit. As a result, an inefficiently large volume of health care is prescribed.

In more complex cases, the doctor is regarded as the agent for *two* principals— the patient and the insurer. In this case (see Blomqvist 1991), there is twofold information asymmetry: the doctor is better informed than either the patient or

---

[4] The classic articles on adverse selection are Akerlof (1970) and Rothschild and Stiglitz (1976). For further discussion, see Dasgupta and Maskin (1986), Hellwig (1987), and, for a less technical summary, Atkinson (1989: ch. 7) reprinted in Barr and Whynes (1993: ch. 2).

the insurer. Thus there is even greater potential for inefficiency as imperfectly informed insurers seek to contain prescribing by doctors.

A third potential problem is transactions costs. The strategies insurers adopt to
address adverse selection and moral hazard can be administratively costly. If
transactions costs are on that account high, some risk-averse individuals will
choose not to insure. This is not inefficient if high transactions costs are inevitable. But it *is* inefficient if a different system could avoid them; for example,
private medical insurance in the USA has high accounting costs, which are
avoided, or at least greatly reduced, where health care is financed through taxation or social insurance.

Policy-makers have tried two strategic approaches to contain rising medical expenditure: market solutions are based on incentives; regulation is used mainly in
publicly funded systems.

Incentive-based mechanisms. Considerable effort has gone into devising
methods to contain medical spending in the face of third-party incentives—
methods such as cost sharing, preferred providers, or prospective payment
mechanisms such as health maintenance organizations or diagnosis-related
groups.

Cost sharing. One approach seeks to limit demand by limiting cover: premiums
can rise disproportionately with the degree of cover a person wants; and there
can be less-than-full cover through deductibles (where the insured person pays
the first $X of any claim) or coinsurance (where the insured person pays x per cent
of any claim). The cost-sharing approach faces a number of problems. First,
charging on a scale sufficiently large to produce efficiency gains can conflict with
equity objectives. Secondly, if consumers are imperfectly informed, as discussed
in Section 2.1, the efficiency gains from charging prices cannot simply be taken
for granted: with a large co-payment, a person may choose not to consume
medical care, even though, were he well informed about the ramifications of his
medical situation, he would have made a different choice. Thirdly, even at face
value, the approach is imperfect: except for small claims, deductibles do not face
patients with the *marginal* cost of treatment; and, if the co-insurance rate is (say)
25 per cent, patients face a marginal cost that is only 25 per cent of the true cost.
Not least for these reasons, though co-payments are widespread in the OECD for
such things as pharmaceutical drugs and, in many countries, for hospital beds,
the charges are usually small and/or have a ceiling on total out-of-pocket payments by any individual during a year (that is, there may be a trade-off between
the rate of co-payment and limits on total out-of-pocket expenditures).

Cost sharing can also take place between levels of government. For example,
both Australia and Canada replaced open-ended federal transfers to lower levels

of government by block grants, thus facing lower levels of government with the full cost of additional spending.

Cost sharing seeks to contain demand by patients. A different approach proceeds via the supply side. With cars, the insurer has the right to inspect damage before specifying what repairs it will pay for—that is, to control spending through regulation. Medical insurers generally have no such option: there may be no time for such action, and there is also a potential conflict with clinical freedom. In addition, with car repairs there is a close causal relationship between repair and improved mechanical performance; the connection between medical treatment and improved health is looser, making it difficult to specify contractually what treatment is covered. If insurers seek to contain medical spending on the supply side, they therefore have to design incentive structures that act as a countervailing force to third-party-payment pressures.

Preferred providers. One such incentive is competition: insurers can restrict patients to certain preferred providers, who then face competitive pressures to retain the insurance company's approved status. Not least because of measurement problems, it is hard to test the proposition that competition exerts downward pressure on costs. Certainly, competition did not prevent a cost explosion in the USA, so that writers like Fuchs (1988) have expressed doubts about its value as a device to contain costs; on the other hand, European experience suggests that regulated competition might help to contain medical spending (OECD 1992, 1994; Glennerster 1998*b*; Saltman *et al.*, forthcoming). Even if it does not exert downward pressure on spending, competition may have other advantages—for example, increasing the patient friendliness of medical services.

A further form of incentives is through prospective payment. The basic idea is simple. Like any cost-plus contract, open-ended, retrospective reimbursement imposes the entire risk on the payer, giving suppliers no incentive to economize. If, in contrast, suppliers are paid *ex ante* (for example, a prepayment of $X for a hip replacement), they face strong incentives to use resources carefully. Again, though appealing on the face of it, there should not be undue optimism: prospective payments are, in effect, a form of price control; but expenditure depends on price *and* quantity: thus controlling price is no automatic guarantee of controlling expenditure. Two examples of prospective payment are widely used in the USA: health maintenance organizations and diagnosis-related groups.

Health maintenance organisations (HMOs). Individuals pay a lump-sum annual contribution to a 'firm' of doctors (the HMO), which agrees to provide the contributor with medical services. The HMO may provide treatment directly, or buy services from other providers, or both. The HMO's income is the contributions of its members, which is a prospective payment to cover all medical costs. That income pays for health care, including the salaries of the doctors. Any surplus (like that of any firm) can be distributed to the doctors as higher pay, or to members as lower contributions, or ploughed back into the HMO to improve its service. The idea is not new. Early European health insurance had all the characteristics of HMOs, and by the mid 1930s covered between one-third and half the population in some countries (Abel Smith, 1988).

An important theoretical advantage of HMOs is that the doctor provides both health care *and* medical insurance. The HMO is thus analytically equivalent to merging the activities of doctor and insurance company, thus internalizing the externality caused by third-party payments.[5] As a result, doctors face an incentive to economize.

HMOs have become widespread and evidence (Manning *et al.* 1987; New-house 1993; Robinson and Steiner 1998) suggests that they have indeed exerted some downward influence on medical spending. Once more, however, they are no complete solution. First, though they ameliorate one strategic insurance problem—exploding costs—they do nothing to deal with another—uninsurable risks, for example, pre-existing medical conditions. In particular, since the costs of treatment fall on the HMO's income, HMOs have a strong incentive to seek out the best risks. The same incentive to cream skimming arises in any prepayment system; and anecdotal evidence suggests precisely that tendency, an effect that is becoming stronger as the US population ages.

There is a second reason for caution: the fact that HMOs exert downward pressure on spending in comparison with retrospective third-party reimbursement does not mean that they necessarily provide the efficient quantity of treatment. The behaviour of an HMO will be influenced by its precise institutional arrangements. Enthoven (1999) distinguishes 'Delivery System HMOs'—in essence HMOs run by doctors—from 'Carrier HMOs', which, in essence, are owned and controlled by an insurance company. In the former, doctors' decisions are likely to take account both of medical need and of the cost-effectiveness of different forms of intervention, thus moving closer to an efficient level of spending than with third-party reimbursement. With Carrier HMOs, in contrast, the insurer offers employers a comprehensive package of medical services and contracts with a variety of fee-for-service medical providers to deliver them. From the viewpoint of employers, this is an HMO-type arrangement—a single entity handles both insurance and the delivery of health services; but the incentives facing the doctors providing the services closely resemble those of third-party reimbursement. This latter type of HMO is thus less likely to restrict spending to its efficient level.

---

[5] Uncontrolled third-party payments drive up costs. The costs of my profligate consumption fall mainly on *other* peoples premiums: the third-party-payment problem is thus a type of externality. One way of dealing with an externality is to internalize it, in this case by merging the activities of doctor and insurer (the classic article is Meade 1952), thereby forcing doctors to face the cost of the treatment they prescribe. An HMO does exactly that.

Diagnosis-related groups (DRGs) are another form of prospective payment, initially devised by US Medicare as a way of controlling publicly funded reimbursement of medical care for older Americans. Hospital inpatient cases are classified into different types, and hospitals paid a fixed price per case, depending primarily on its DRG. Once more, the idea is no panacea. Like any classification system, costs vary *within* each category, giving hospitals an incentive to select cheaper cases of each type. Pressures therefore grew for more refined DRGs. That, however, gave incentives to 'DRG creep', where hospitals classified as 'severe' as many cases as possible. The issue faded somewhat as government responded by reducing the inflation adjustment to reimbursement rates by the extent to which the case mix index rose, so that real reimbursement was rolled back as the relative share of severe cases increased. Though that solution contained expenditure, it meant that the most scrupulous hospitals were punished for their virtue.

None of these approaches to containing costs, whatever their sophistication, is a complete solution. This should be no surprise. All are grappling with two largely intractable problems. First is the recurring theme of imperfect information, in this case on the part of insurers about the behaviour of the insured. This problem is compounded because health is hard both to define and to measure; nor is the causal link between treatment and improved health always clear. Both reasons make it difficult to specify contractually what treatment is covered for different medical conditions.

REGULATION of medical spending is a second approach to containing costs. Publicly organized medical insurance faces the same problems of moral hazard as private insurance, and in part has to rely on the same dubiously effective instruments such as cost sharing, preferred providers, or prepayment. However, publicly funded systems have a further range of options: regulation of medical spending. The logic is simple: total spending = price × quantity. Successful cost containment must (*a*) control total spending directly, or (*b*) control price *and* quantity, or (*c*) use price control to reinforce an overall spending constraint. Control of medical fees (that is, price control) with open-ended budgets only partially contains costs, because of the incentive for doctors to increase output to compensate for lost income. This is what happened with medicare in the USA (Evans 1974; Evans *et al.* 1989). Canada, in contrast, managed to avoid the worst of the medicare cost explosion because it adopted both price control *and* a global budget ceiling. European countries, too, have developed systems that combine price and expenditure control (Abel Smith 1984, 1985; OECD 1992, 1994; Mossialos and Le Grand 1999).

Whatever the system, successful methods of restricting supply to around its efficient level all include the imposition of budget limits either on public expenditure (Britain, Sweden) or on insurance disbursements (Canada). This is an important result, because the demand for health care is increasing with advances in medical technology and also because of ageing populations.

Conclusions

Economic theory thus predicts that conventional medical insurance will face two strategic sets of problems largely, though not entirely, because of information problems facing insurers.

- *Gaps in coverage* arise *inter alia* for chronic pre-existing medical problems, for the medical needs of the elderly, and for medical care connected with individual choice such as primary health care and pregnancy.
- *Inefficiency* includes uninsured risk-averse individuals, who face inefficiently high transactions costs, and uncontrolled increases in medical spending in the face of third-party incentives.

As discussed in the next section, though ameliorative actions are possible, none is a complete solution.

3. FUNDING HEALTH CARE: THE OPTIONS

This section briefly assesses three strategies for organizing medical care: private funding of privately produced medical care, as in the USA; public funding of public production, exemplified by the UK; and public funding of private production, illustrated by Canada. Discussion is deliberately broad brush, with no pretence at either detail or completeness; nor is there any attempt at formal comparative analysis. The purpose is simpler: to put flesh on the theoretical arguments of the previous section, to draw out the *strategic* conclusions to emerge from the theory, and to derive policy conclusions.[6]

3.1. *Private funding plus private production*

The USA's strategy of private funding plus private production faces exactly the problems predicted in the previous section. Up to the early 1960s, the system was based on private production financed by private medical insurance. But, as medical costs rose and the insurance industry become more competitive, gaps in coverage increased, as did the cost of medical insurance. Partly as a response, medicare (for the old) and medicaid (for the poor) were created in the mid-1960s. The modification they introduced was simple: the poor and old continued to

---

[6] For fuller discussion of arrangements in different European countries, see the various country reports emanating from the European Observatory on Health Care Systems, which can be downloaded from http://www.observatory.dk, and, for assessment, Mossialos and Le Grand (1999).

receive private treatment, but their medical bills were paid out of federal/state funds.

The effect of these unlimited third-party payments was entirely predictable: public spending on health care rose sharply to the point where it became the fourth largest item of federal spending after income support, defence, and debt interest (the classic article is Evans 1974; see also Aaron 1991). Private spending, too, increased sharply, since privately funded medical care also faced third-party incentives.

The US response has evolved over the years. A public response was the use of diagnosis-related groups in the administration of medicare and medicaid. A private response was the growth of HMOs. The 1990s saw the emergence of *managed care* (Enthoven, 1993, 1999; Robinson and Steiner 1998), in which private outcomes are subject to extensive management and regulation. The approach is also being applied to the public sector: in 1997 about three-quarters of US states used managed care for medicaid. Earlier discussion pointed to two complementary approaches to containing costs: regulation and the use of incentives. Managed care has both ingredients. Regulation takes the form of intensive management of medical provision—in other words, a form of private regulation. Over the years, the USA has increasingly moved from a system in which doctors had free rein to a management-controlled industrial model. Incentives, as discussed earlier, are based around prospective payment.

A major conclusion of the theoretical discussion in the previous section is that voluntary actuarial individual insurance faces two strategic problems: gaps in coverage—for example, in respect of chronic health problems, the elderly, and pregnancy/childbirth; and inefficiency, both through uninsured risk-averse individuals and through unintended and uncontained increases in medical spending. The US health-care system faces both sets of problems.

In assessing the US system, it is useful to adopt four criteria—cost containment, access, waiting lists, and consumer choice—which are taken up in the subsequent assessment of other strategies.

COST CONTAINMENT. In the late 1990s, US medical spending, at 16 per cent of GDP, was by a considerable margin a larger fraction of GDP than in any other country. At the same time, medical spending in the UK was about 7 per cent of a smaller GDP. Yet, in terms of broad outcomes such as infant mortality and life expectancy, the USA, despite its much higher spending, did no better than the UK. 'High and rapidly increasing health expenditures create serious problems for our society. They strain public finances: government now pays 46% of the health care bill. A lot of this is at the expense of education and other important public goods. They reduce growth in real wages for working people' (Enthoven 1999: 1–2).

Even after accounting for the USA's high income (it is well established that richer countries spend a higher fraction of GDP on health care than poorer countries) and the age structure of its population, a residual remains, which can be explained largely by third-party-payment incentives, though also by other factors, such as high administrative costs necessitated by individual billing,[7] and defensive medical practice in the face of potential litigation. Note that most public spending is in precisely those areas where the theory predicts private insurance would have gaps: Medicare (for the elderly), Medicaid (for the poor), veterans' benefits (in part for chronic health problems), and maternity and child welfare.

ACCESS. Despite high public spending in a notionally private system, gaps remain. High and rising medical spending 'price health insurance out of reach for families of moderate means and taxpayers who would like to help them: 43 million people in this country are now uninsured and the number is growing. According to a recent survey of uninsured Californians, affordability is by far the reason cited most frequently for not buying health insurance' (Enthoven 1999: 2).

In addition, access to quality care was far from equal. 'Somewhere in America might be found the world's best medical care. But the merits of that claim might not be apparent to the families of hundreds of Californians who have died of inappropriate or equivocal open-heart operations . . . especially if their widows are being hounded for payment because their deceased husbands did not have insurance' (Enthoven 1989: 49).

WAITING LISTS. Given the high level of medical spending in the USA, waiting lists have not typically been a problem. Anecdotal evidence, however, suggests that HMOs, facing harder budget constraints, are rationing treatment more stringently and, in consequence, waiting lists are starting to appear.

CONSUMER CHOICE is generally not a problem, since medical care is supplied by a wide range of competing providers. The system thus creates incentives to consumer friendliness. However, in this context, too, financial pressures are starting to restrict patient choice.

A further US problem is how to finance medical training. Historically, teaching hospitals had higher charges for patients, making it possible to cross-subsidize training. Here, too, attempts to contain costs are starting to bite (see Aaron 2000).

TOWARDS A SOLUTION. Can the problems of high spending and unequal access be solved? The arrangements offered by Stanford University show both what is possible and the scale of the necessary intervention. The system has five key features.

---

[7] For estimates of administrative costs, see Himmelstein and Woolhandler (1991). They conclude that, if US administrative spending had been brought down to the average of OECD countries that fund medical care through social insurance, the resulting savings in 1987 would have been around $50 billion.

(*a*) The university contracts with a number of insurers, mainly HMOs.[8]

(*b*) To be allowed to join Stanford's 'club', each insurer must offer a policy with three elements: an agreed core package of health care available to all its members; a structure of premiums that can differ with family size, etc., but must be unrelated to a person's medical risk; and universal access— that is, the insurer must accept all applicants.

(*c*) The university operates a system of redistribution such that plans that attract a higher-than-average risk group receive transfers.

(*d*) Employees can choose which plan to join.

(*e*) The university contributes a fixed sum to each person's medical insurance, broadly equal to the cost of the cheapest of the approved policies.

Under elements (*a*) and (*b*) the university acts as agent for badly informed consumers to ensure that insurance contracts are transparent and contain no hidden snags. Element (*b*) rules out cream skimming and ensures that nobody is excluded from cover, and elements (*b*) and (*e*) together ensure that everyone can afford cover. Element (*c*) protects insurers from adverse selection. Element (*e*) helps to contain costs, since the individual employee faces the *entire* marginal cost of joining a more expensive scheme. This is efficient; it is also politically feasible, since individuals can choose which scheme to join, a scheme limited to a single medical provider, for example, being cheaper than one with unrestricted fee for service.

Such an arrangement is therefore a genuine strategy.[9] The interesting question is what sort of a strategy it is. Viewed from a US perspective, this is a private scheme hedged by sufficient regulation and transfers to deal with market failures. However, the scheme can equally be described as a system of decentralized social insurance, its key features being central regulation, universal coverage, premiums unrelated to individual risk, and the existence of transfers to schemes with a disproportionate number of high risks.

The latter perspective on the Stanford scheme points to a powerful conclusion: that any strategy for addressing the problems of actuarial medical insurance leads inescapably to institutions with the major characteristics of social insurance. It is noteworthy that the finance of health care in the Netherlands and Germany, discussed in Section 3.3, has many similarities to the Stanford scheme. Thus there are pressures to convergence between two very different conceptions: private insurance supported by necessary regulation and subsidy ends up as decentralized

---

[8] A fee-for-service, free-choice-of-provider plan, originally included, was dropped when it became too expensive. One of the current HMOs includes a preferred provider plan; thus members have comprehensive HMO coverage, but can also choose any provider in the world and take some of their insurance with them.

[9] This should not be surprising, since Alain Enthoven, a Stanford faculty member and one of America's leading health economists, chaired the committee that designed the scheme. The Stanford arrangements were subsequently emulated by Harvard and the University of California.

social insurance; nationwide arrangements that allow decentralization but only on the basis of universal access end up looking remarkably similar.

Thus it should not be surprising that the USA is alone among industrial countries in using competitive private insurance as the major instrument for financing medical care. Elsewhere, two models predominate. Social insurance (as discussed in Chapter 2, Section 3.3) abandons the model of actuarial insurance because it does not fit health care very well. Alternatively, medical care can be financed via the tax system.

3.2. *Public funding plus public production*

Notwithstanding a series of reforms over the 1990s,[10] the UK National Health Service strategy has remained broadly unchanged: health care is publicly produced and is largely funded from general taxation. Several of the Scandinavian countries have a broadly similar strategy.[11] The approach genuinely (albeit of necessity imperfectly) gets to grips with the market failures discussed in Section 2.

The strategy has four cornerstones. Two deal with demand-side problems.

- Treatment is decided by doctors, thus addressing the problems of consumer ignorance discussed in Section 2.1.
- Health care is (mostly) tax financed and (mostly) free at the point of use. This approach avoids gaps in coverage by abandoning insurance even as a fiction; and because health care is free at the point of use, the poor are not excluded. Thus medical care is universally available.

On the supply side:

- There is little fee for service, reducing third-party incentives.
- Health care is explicitly rationed, in part by administrative means and in part by the existence of a global budget constraint for the national health service. The idea, at least in principle, is to restrict consumption to its efficient level, an objective whose achievement is assisted by the absence of fee for service.

Thus the strategy is defensible in both efficiency and equity terms, both theoretically and in terms of the four criteria used previously.

COST CONTAINMENT. The UK national health service is cheap by international standards. UK medical spending is below the average for a country at its income level, but UK health outcomes are broadly equal to the European average. The reasons include the fact that medical providers generally have no financial stake

---

[10] On the reforms, see Le Grand *et al.* (1998), and, for broader assessment of the national health service, Le Grand and Vizard (1998) and Emmerson *et al.* (2000).

[11] For discussion of Scandinavia, see the relevant country reports from the European Observatory on Health Care Systems (http://www.observatory.dk).

in their decision and hence have no incentive to overprescribe. It can be argued that the national health service is *too* successful on this count: budgetary pressures can create incentives for *under*-treatment; and there are extensive waiting lists for treatment.[12]

ACCESS. Access is good: treatment is free, however long or serious the medical event, and no-one is denied access because of low income. The fact that access is generally good does not, however, mean that it is equal. There is a large and controversial literature about whether, and to what extent, middle-class patients receive more care than patients from lower socioeconomic groups.[13] Despite action over the years, there is also continuing unequal access by region.

WAITING LISTS are politically highly salient, figuring prominently in recent election campaigns and political discourse more generally.

CONSUMER CHOICE is another problem area. The national health service came to show most of the problems of a supply-side monopoly, including inflexibility and a limited ability to accommodate consumer preferences.

Various attempts are being made to address the latter two problems. Public spending on health care was increased in the early 2000s, an explicit purpose being to reduce waiting lists. Devices such as a Patient's Charter attempted to make the service more responsive to consumers. Perhaps more fundamentally, attempts were made to improve efficiency and responsiveness by introducing competition through quasi-markets. An assessment by Le Grand, Mays, and Mulligan (1998: 129) concludes that:

Perhaps the most striking conclusion . . . is how little overall measurable change there seems to have been related to the core structures and mechanisms of the internal market. Indeed, in some areas where significant changes might have been expected, there were none. For instance, there seems to have been no difference between fundholders and non-fundholders in referral rates for elective surgery, despite the fact that one set of [doctors] was making referrals from a fixed budget for which they were responsible, and the other set were not.

3.3. *Public funding plus private production*

Canada's strategy is like that in the UK in the sense that most health care is publicly funded, but like the USA in that health care is privately provided.

As with the UK, the strategy holds together.

---

[12] For detailed discussion of whether the national health service is underfunded, see McGuire (1996), Dixon (1997), and Harrison *et al.* (1997*a*, *b*).

[13] See Culyer and Wagstaff (1993), Le Grand (1991*b*, 1992, 1995), and Powell (1995).

- Health care is publicly funded and free at the point of use. Funding is organized at a provincial level, partly from provincial resources (taxation and, in some provinces, social insurance contributions) and partly through transfers from the federal government. As with the UK system, this approach avoids gaps in coverage by abandoning the insurance mechanism; and the poor are not excluded.
- Since medical care is privately provided, fee for service is widespread. This creates the familiar third-party incentives. For that reason:
- There is stringent regulation of total medical spending. With public funding such regulation, though not easy, is at least feasible.

Germany has a similar strategy, though the details of funding are very different. There are about 450 sickness funds, most of which derive their contributions from payroll deductions. Though in a strict legal sense they are private entities, they collect what are, in essence, social-insurance contributions, in that contributions are unrelated to individual risk and nobody is excluded. Medical fees are negotiated at provincial level and medical spending is subject to a provincial global budget. Thus German funding can be regarded as a form of decentralized social insurance, which pays for mainly privately produced medical care.

The system in the Netherlands is in many ways a nationwide counterpart to the Stanford scheme discussed in Section 3.1. About two-thirds of the population are covered by sickness funds broadly similar to those in Germany. About 34 per cent of the population voluntarily buy individual or group private insurance, which generally provides cover similar to that offered by the sickness funds. Private insurers are permitted to charge risk-rated premiums. However, to ensure that risk rating is compatible with access, legislation requires insurers to accept older people and high-risk individuals for a standardized benefit package at a fixed price. There is a system of transfers to compensate insurers with a high-risk pool, financed by a mandatory surcharge on the premiums of all other privately insured individuals. Once more, the modifications necessary to ensure that private insurance does not have gaps in coverage results in a system that has all the characteristics of social insurance.

Nor is social insurance restricted to Europe. Japan's system has much in common with German arrangements except that the system is national. Medical fees are the outcome of negotiations between doctors, the Ministry of Health and the Ministry of Finance, and medical spending is subject to a global budget constraint (see Campbell and Ikegami 1998).

The four criteria used previously reveal a pattern of outcomes different from either of the earlier strategies.

Cost containment. The Canadian strategy of publicly funded fee-for-service production encounters the obvious problem of third-party-payment incentives, and therefore over the years has faced continuing pressures on medical spending—an inescapable problem for any country with this type of arrangement. In (former West) Germany medical spending rose from 6.4 per cent of GDP in 1970 to 9.4 per cent in 1975, and many other countries have faced similar pressures. With the exception of the USA, most have addressed the issue with a fair degree of success, but only through stringent regulation of medical spending (for a recent survey, see Mossialos and Le Grand 1999).

The core of any successful strategy, in sharp contrast with arrangements in the USA, is that funding is not open-ended; in other words, there is a budget cap rather than open-ended funding in the form of tax deductions for medical insurance or medical spending. Canada illustrates the point. Most medical care is tax funded at the provincial level, supported by federal block grants. Each hospital has a global annual budget. Doctors' fees are negotiated between government and medical associations at the provincial level, and charges above these standard fees ('extra billing') are in practice forbidden under federal law. Total spending on doctors has been controlled at different times in various ways. One mechanism (also used in Germany) is through a budget cap for provincial spending on doctors' fees backed up by a contract under which agreed fees are retrospectively reduced if the treatment provided by doctors collectively exceeds a pre-negotiated volume.[14] Another mechanism is to combine a provincial budget cap with a ceiling on the income each individual doctor can earn from the province. The imposition of budget constraints in this way controls doctors' *incomes* rather than their *actions*, thus, in contrast with managed care, leaving doctors largely autonomous in treating their patients.

Canada, in short, combines price control with expenditure control. Though medical spending is under continual pressure, government has, as a practical matter, managed to keep it under control.

ACCESS. As with the UK system, health care being publicly funded means that nobody is excluded on the grounds of poverty. Access is therefore good.

WAITING LISTS. Canada spends significantly more than the UK on health care. Waiting lists are therefore not a problem.

CONSUMER CHOICE is not a problem either: medical care is supplied by competing providers. As in the USA, however, tighter budgets are beginning to constrain choices.

---

[14] In other words, if doctors prescribe twice as much of a given treatment as previously agreed, the fee for that treatment will retrospectively be halved, leaving total spending unchanged.

4. CONCLUSIONS

OPTIONS FOR FUNDING AND DELIVERY ARE LIMITED. Economic theory (Section 2) and international experience (Section 3) both point to conclusions that, except in the USA, are no longer controversial.

- *Funding.* There is a strong message—the major vehicle for health finance should be public funding through taxation or social insurance. Such arrangements can be administered by central government (as in the UK), by provincial government (as in Canada), or by parastatal institutions (as in Germany). Systems that rely primarily on private finance face problems of gaps in coverage and exploding costs.
- *Delivery.* There is no similar strong message about delivery. There are successful systems with health care produced mainly publicly (the UK, Scandinavia), mainly privately (Canada), or via a mix.
- *Compatible packages.* Policy-makers do not have complete freedom to mix and match. One compatible package is public funding plus public production; another is public funding plus private production *plus* stringent regulation of medical spending.

THERE IS NO PERFECT SOLUTION. None of the resulting strategies—however well designed—will be remotely as efficient as private markets where the necessary conditions hold. Where those conditions fail badly, as with health care, there is a major problem. As a result, no system of health finance is perfect; the objective for policy-makers is to choose the strategy whose faults are least objectionable for the society in question.

IMPERFECTIONS ARE PREDICTABLE. A third strategic conclusion is that the problems with any country's system of health care are a predictable consequence of that country's chosen strategy for addressing market failures.

- Public funding plus public production, as in the UK and Scandinavia, is a genuine strategy. Its particular strengths are its ability to contain costs and promote access. The approach is relatively weaker on consumer choice, and may face problems with waiting lists.
- Public funding plus private production—for example, in Canada or Germany—is an alternative strategy. It scores well on access, consumer choice and the absence of waiting lists. Its besetting problem is it vulnerability to third-party incentives and hence to upward pressures on medical spending. A key lesson is that no country should consider this strategy unless policy-makers are confident that they have both the political and the administrative capacity to make the necessary cost-containment measures stick.

- The US strategy of private funding plus private production faces exactly the problems the theory predicts. In the face of diverse and competing funding sources, third-party incentives have not been contained, leading to a major cost explosion. Despite heavy public spending, gaps in coverage remain. And access to quality care is unequal. These outcomes are entirely predictable, should come as a surprise to no one, and will not be resolved short of a new strategy based on some sort of social insurance combined with regulation of total medical spending. The economic strength of that conclusion, however, is largely offset by its political frailty.

Chapter 5

Twenty-First-Century Insurance Issues

The design of insurance-type arrangements to address unemployment was a continuing part of economic and social policy discourse for most of the twentieth century; and discussion of medical insurance assumed increasing importance over the latter part of the century. This chapter discusses two newer issues that will become increasingly salient: genetic screening and its likely impact on insurance against a range of risks; and problems with insuring against the need for long-term care.

1. GENETIC SCREENING

For many years, tests have been able to predict medical problems even where they do not yet show any symptoms—for example, early asymptomatic mutations in the colon show an increased probability of colon cancer. Genetic screening broadens the range of such tests, making it possible to tell if an individual has a predisposition towards medical problems such as muscular dystrophy, cystic fibrosis, or Huntington's disease. With clinical advances almost, it seems, on a daily basis, the range of these tests is increasing rapidly, so that it will become possible to test for a predisposition towards early coronary heart disease, breast and bowel cancers, asthma, and Alzheimer's disease. Such testing has major implications for insurance. The first part of this chapter explains the problems. Section 1.2 discusses different approaches to solving them. Section 1.3 suggests possible ways forward.

1.1. *Problems*

Harper (1992) points to a number of ways in which genetic testing is particularly powerful:

- *Independence of age*. Since an individual's genes remain largely unchanged over his or her life, the test result will be the same at any point in the individual's life. Thus, the result will be as apparent early in life as later.
- *Independence of clinical state*. The test result will usually be the same whether the person already has the disorder, or will develop it a long time in the future. Thus the disorder can be detected a long time in advance.

- *Independence of tissue.* Since genes are present in all body cells, the gene for a serious brain disease can be isolated from a simple blood sample. Such non-invasive tests increasingly make it possible to test for disorders for which no tests were previously available.
- *Stability of results.* A single blood spot provides enough cells for many tests, allowing repeat tests. The sample also lasts for many years, allowing retesting at a later stage.

Because of its power, particularly its ability to predict so long in advance and the increasing range of disorders about which it offers information, genetic screening raises important issues for insurance. The starting point is to analyse the case of voluntary insurance. On the demand side, the individual can choose whether or not to take out a policy, and how much cover to buy. On the supply side, insurers face no constraints other than the tax laws and financial market regulation; they have complete discretion about whom they cover, which risks they cover, and the premiums they charge. In addition, and critically, insurance companies are allowed to ask for the results of genetic screening.

The economics of insurance was set out in Chapter 2, and more fully in the medical context in Chapter 4. A competitive insurance company of the sort described above charges a premium,

$$\pi_i = (1+\alpha)p_i L \tag{5.1}$$

where p_i is the probability that the insured event will occur, L is the size of the loss against which the individual insures, and α is the insurance company's mark-up to cover administrative costs and competitive profit. Thus a competitive insurance premium depends on the degree of risk and on the size of the insured loss: the effect on premiums if a person's riskiness increases depends not only on how much the risk, p_i, changes, but also on how expensive it is to treat the resulting disorder, L, if the risk eventuates. Clearly it is expensive to insure a risk to which a high probability attaches. But insurance can be expensive even where the risk is small, if any resulting treatment is expensive.

In the clearly defined circumstances discussed in Chapter 2—in particular where the relevant probability is less than one, known equally to both parties, and outside the control of the insured person—voluntary insurance is both possible and efficient. Suppose, now, that genetic screening is introduced that can tell a person that he or she has a predisposition to condition X (for example, Alzheimer's disease). In discussing the problems that arise—uninsurable risks and adverse selection—it is useful to distinguish three cases, in which the test tells the person that

    (a) he already has X, or is certain (or virtually certain) to get it;
    (b) the predisposition increases the relevant probability significantly;

(*c*) the predisposition increases the relevant probability only slightly.

UNINSURABLE RISKS. In case (*a*), genetic screening shows that the person already has the disorder, or will have it. In such cases, private insurance becomes impossible because the actuarial premium equals or exceeds the loss against which insurance is sought (in this case the cost of treatment). For such reasons, pre-existing conditions are generally uninsurable in private markets. As a result, the individual cannot buy cover for that condition. Suppose an advance in genetic screening makes it possible to show for certain that an applicant for insurance will at some point in the future develop cancer; in that case genetic screening has turned a risk (which is insurable) into a certainty (which is not). Advances in genetic screening, in other words, are like a fungal infection creating more and more uninsurable conditions—the more, and more powerful, the tests, the fewer the events that insurance can cover.

Alongside uninsurable conditions, where insurance is provided by the employer (as frequently in the USA), there is also an impediment to labour mobility: a person moving to a new job will generally have to have a medical check-up, which will reveal any pre-existing condition; either the insurer will refuse cover, in which case the person is locked into his or her old job, or it will offer cover only at an increased premium, in which case the prospective new employer is likely to turn the applicant down.

Kenneth Arrow (1994: 10) refers to this problem as the Information Dilemma. 'The dilemma is stark. Improved prognosis is frequently beneficial to the patient or potential patient. . . . But in the . . . system of medical insurance, prognosis may be costly to the patient in terms of medical insurance premiums, denial of coverage, and inability to get new jobs.'

ADVERSE SELECTION. A second type of problem arises if individuals, because of genetic screening, have better knowledge of their risk than the insurer. This will happen if individuals are allowed to withhold screening results. In the extreme, the individual is perfectly informed and the insurance company uninformed; for the individual, this is like betting on a horse race when the result is already known. Individuals who know that they are high risk will disproportionately apply for insurance. The resulting adverse selection is an insurance-market manifestation of Gresham's Law—bad risks will drive out the good.

As discussed in Chapter 2, attempts by insurers to address adverse selection cause inefficiency. If an insurer cannot distinguish high-risk from low-risk applicants, it has to base premiums on the average risk (a pooling equilibrium). This is not a problem where (case (*c*)), genetic screening shows only a very small increase in a person's chances of getting X: insurers do not know who is low- and who is high-risk and hence charge everyone the same premium; but the difference in probabilities is small and so, in consequence, is the resulting inefficiency.

Case (*b*), in contrast, raises major difficulties. The first problem that results is inefficiency: a low-risk individual pays a premium that is higher than the actuarial premium and therefore tends to buy less insurance than is efficient; a high-risk individual, conversely, pays a premium that is less than commensurate with his or her risk, and thus buys more insurance than is efficient. Where the problem is serious, low-risk individuals may choose not to insure at all. A second problem with such a pooling solution is instability: a competing company could offer cheaper policies aimed at low-risk groups—for example, people who could demonstrate 'clean' results to genetic tests—thus leaving the original company only with the poor risks.

A second approach is a separating equilibrium, in which the insurer attempts to devise policies that only low-risk people would buy—for example with only limited cover for certain conditions. As discussed in Chapter 4, Section 2.2, it might not be possible to devise such a policy, in which case adverse selection makes insurance impossible. Alternatively, where such a policy can be devised, it will generally be inefficient, because the restrictions on cover designed to screen out the bad risks also reduce the cover offered to good risks.

Thus genetic screening affects the viability of insurance in at least two ways: it creates a new and rapidly growing group of uninsurable conditions; it also has a major bearing on the ability of individuals to obtain cover, a problem of concern both to the individual and of broader relevance to social policy. Neither problem is new, but genetic screening greatly increases the number of people affected.

1.2. *Approaches to a solution*

The pervasiveness of the potential problems suggests a number of questions.

- Is an applicant obliged to volunteer the results of any screening to the insurer?
- Is the insurer allowed to ask for the results of such screening, or explicitly forbidden to ask for such results?
- Is the insurer allowed to require the applicant to be screened?
- Is the insurer allowed to charge higher-risk individuals a higher insurance premium?

In addressing these questions, I make two value judgements. A person might be high risk for two very different reasons: because of personal choice (for example, unhealthy diet and lifestyle increase the risk of heart disease), or because of something beyond his control (for example, coming from a family with a history of heart disease). The first value judgement is that individuals should be able to acquire at least a measure of protection against risks that they acquire through no fault of their own, in other words, which are not the result of individual choice.

Secondly, the terms on which individuals can buy insurance against such risks should not depend on the timing of the insurance policy—that is, on whether or not the policy was in force at the time that the risk became apparent. This means *either* that the insurance company should not be allowed to ask for the results of genetic screening *or*, if insurance companies are allowed access to such information, that the terms on which individuals can buy cover is invariant to those results.

The following paragraphs discuss approaches to genetic screening in terms of who bears the cost of any increase in identified risk. The individual might bear the cost (for example, in the form of a restriction on the amount of cover he can buy); or the cost might fall on the pool of policyholders with a given insurer (for example, if insurers are not allowed to ask for the results of genetic screening); or the costs could be spread more broadly, across the pool of policyholders of all insurers collectively, or across all taxpayers.

POLICY 1. NO INSURANCE COVER. The insurance company can refuse to cover the individual against X, where genetic screening shows that he or she has already contracted X or is predisposed to it. Thus the individual is forced to self-insure. This violates the value judgement that individuals should be able to acquire a measure of protection against risks which are not the result of their own actions.

POLICY 2. THE AMOUNT OF COVER THE INDIVIDUAL CAN BUY IS RATIONED. The acceptability of this solution depends in part on where the ceiling is placed: does the individual receive genuine protection, or is he or she left significantly exposed? If the ceiling is high enough, this option may be viable.

POLICY 3. THE INDIVIDUAL PAYS A HIGHER PREMIUM. In Policies 1 and 2, the costs were imposed on the individual by limiting the quantity of insurance he or she can buy. Alternatively, the costs can take the form of a higher premium. In this case, individuals are obliged to disclose the result of genetic screening, and those with a predisposition to X pay a higher premium that matches their higher risk. This avoids insurance market distortions, but faces higher-risk individuals with higher costs. As discussed earlier, the additional cost to the individual would be substantial either if the degree of risk rises significantly or if the costs of dealing with X are high. In case (*c*) discussed earlier (where genetic screening reveals only a very small increase in the relevant probability), no problem arises unless X is a very expensive condition to treat. In case (*b*) (a significant increase in the probability), the increase in premium might be substantial, so that individuals might not be able to afford cover; in such cases, Policy 3 is equivalent to Policy 1.

Thus far, the costs of additional risk all fall on the individual. In the next group of policies, risks are shared across the pool of insured individuals.

POLICY 4. COSTS ARE BORNE COLLECTIVELY BY THE POLICYHOLDERS OF THE INSURANCE COMPANY. This is the case where insurance companies are forbidden to take account of the results of genetic screening. The company therefore has to charge a premium based on the average risk; thus higher-risk individuals (that is, those with a predisposition to X) are subsidized by those without such a predisposition.

Arrow (1994) gives a simple example of how this would work. Suppose that medical insurance costs £2,000, and that a test exists that can detect a predisposition to a medical disorder that affects 1 per cent of the population. If the disorder occurs, it lasts for one year at an average cost of £10,000. Averaged across the population, the extra cost is £100 (1 per cent of £10,000). In such circumstances, therefore, the insurance company could in principle cover the risk by charging all its clients a premium of £2,100.

There are two potential problems with this approach. First, if insurance is voluntary, there will be a tendency to self-selection by high-risk individuals, driving up insurance premiums. This will tend to drive out the low risks (the case of Gresham's Law discussed earlier). The problem, then, is the number of uninsured low-risk individuals, for whom the result is similar to Policy 1. The result is both inefficient and inequitable.

Secondly, even where there is no such effect, this policy is feasible only where all insurance companies have broadly the same mix of risks. In the example above, the premium of £2,100 charged by a particular company assumes that the insurer faces a risk pool that is broadly representative of the population as a whole. Difficulties can arise in a number of ways.

- Any company with a disproportionately risky pool (for example, an insurer in a part of the country to which elderly people retire) would have to charge higher and higher premiums. The company could go bankrupt, leaving a large pool of people with uninsurable pre-existing conditions. Thus the system could be unstable.
- This type of arrangement also gives incentives to cream skimming (that is, attempting to avoid covering high-risk people), because the insurer receives the same premium whether a person is high or low risk. As is well known, covert secondary discrimination can be very subtle. Even if companies are forbidden to refuse applicants, they can still take actions that minimize applications from high risks.

Thus, even if Gresham's Law does not apply, potential problems remain of bankruptcies of companies with an adverse risk pool, instability, and cream skimming.

POLICY 5. COSTS ARE BORNE COLLECTIVELY BY THE POLICYHOLDERS OF ALL INSURANCE COMPANIES. A way of getting round the problems of Policy 4 is to impose a levy on all insurance policies that cover conditions like X, and to use the proceeds to pay benefits to those who ultimately contract the disease; thus the risk pool is now all people who insure against X, whichever company they insure with. This policy has much to commend it. It protects individuals (because people's ability to buy insurance is not influenced by whether or not genetic screening shows a predisposition to X), and also protects insurers against the effects of an adverse risk pool. Under this arrangement, people with a predisposition to X, as a group, receive a subsidy from those with no such predisposition; a case can therefore be made on horizontal equity grounds of imposing a ceiling (at a reasonably high level) on the amount of cover they can buy.

POLICY 6. THE COSTS ARE BORNE BY TAXPAYERS GENERALLY. In this final case, risks are pooled not just across the insured population but across the citizenry as a whole. In essence, the state would underwrite the cost of treating X. Again, there is a case for a ceiling.

Policies 5 and 6 are not uncommon. Automobile insurers in the UK maintain a financial pool to compensate any of their members who is involved in a car accident with someone who (illegally) is not insured. Even more relevant, as discussed in Chapter 4, Section 3.3, the finance of medical and long-term care in the Netherlands incorporates a pooling arrangement for its private medical insurers to ensure that older people and high-risk people are not excluded from cover, and also elements of tax funding.

1.3. *Preferred options*

Two approaches stand out, one where the additional costs of insurance are small, one where they are larger.

THE INDIVIDUAL PAYS A HIGHER INSURANCE PREMIUM, COMMENSURATE WITH HIS OR HER HIGHER RISK. This approach (Policy 3) is satisfactory where the additional costs to the individual are sufficiently small not to penalize those with a predisposition to X. This requires *both* that the increase in probability is small *and* that the costs of treatment are relatively low.

A CEILING ON COVER PLUS CROSS SUBSIDY. A ceiling on cover (Policy 2) may well be warranted where a group receives a systematic subsidy from another group. Given the instability and the incentives to cream skimming of a cross-subsidy within the pool of a single insurance company (Policy 4), the preferred option is to combine Policy 2 with Policy 5. For all but the smallest problems, therefore, a promising approach is a levy on all insurance policies covering condition X, combined with a fairly high ceiling on cover.

This approach has much in common with the Stanford University arrangements for medical insurance (see Chapter 4, Section 3.1). It avoids instability and incentives to cream skimming, with the additional major advantage that the individual's ability to acquire insurance cover is not disadvantaged by the emergence of new information about his or her medical prognosis. Thus there is no incentive against seeking such information.

In conclusion, the answers to the questions posed earlier are as follows:

- Since insurance cover does not depend on the results of genetic testing, it is an open question whether individuals should be obliged to volunteer the results of such tests.
- Insurers, however, should not be forbidden from *asking* for the results of genetic screening, since the individual's cover is not affected by the answer.
- Since, for various reasons, individuals may prefer not to be screened, insurers should not, however, be allowed to *require* an applicant to be screened.
- So far as cover up to the ceiling is concerned, insurers should not be allowed to charge higher-risk applicants a higher premium. For cover above the ceiling, individual pricing should be allowed.

2. LONG-TERM-CARE INSURANCE

One of the purposes of the welfare state is to make sure that those who are not able to look after themselves are cared for. Three groups of people are particularly vulnerable. There is an obvious public interest, first, in action to ensure children are well cared for, both as a universally held value judgement, and because thriving children grow up to contribute to a thriving economy. Secondly, it is necessary to make sure that disabled people receive adequate care. The finance of such care can, in principle, be organized through insurance, though some of the technical problems discussed in earlier chapters may arise with voluntary individual policies. As a result, private cover tends to be incomplete, expensive, or both, and in many countries disability benefit is therefore included as part of social-insurance arrangements. Thirdly, many frail elderly people require long-term care.

This part of the chapter concentrates on the third of these issues. Child care has more in common with consumption smoothing than with insurance. Disability insurance is widespread and—for the most part—not a potential crisis area.[1] Long-term care, in contrast, is not well covered by insurance and is becoming

---

[1] Spending on disability pensions has risen very rapidly in some countries. However, that is a problem that can largely be addressed by making sure that disability benefits are not used as a mechanism for dealing with unemployment. For fuller discussion of disability and social exclusion, see Burchardt (2000).

increasingly problematical. Care can be in a person's home or in a residential setting, and a person may need personal care (for example, help getting dressed),
nursing care, or both. Section 2.1 sets out a range of information problems, and
Section 2.2 discusses the potential role of social insurance.

2.1. *Information problems*

In the UK in the past, many people who could no longer care for themselves were
looked after within the extended family; with fragmented family structures and
increased women's labour-force participation, policy can no longer rely on this
approach. Alternatively, people were cared for by the national health service,
hence care for the most part was paid out of taxation. However, the number of
older people is growing, and changes in the finance of the health service together
with fiscal constraints have exerted downward pressure on taxpayer support. As
a result, people have been forced to sell their homes to finance the costs of long-
term care, and the fact that so many elderly people are owner-occupiers has made
the problem politically salient. In the face of these problems, a Royal Commission reported in 1999 (UK Royal Commission 1999a).

   Not everyone needs long-term care; and nobody knows in advance how much
care (if any) he or she will need, or for how long. Thus there are potential gains
from pooling risk. In principle, therefore, the solution is insurance. Suppose that
one in six people in the UK requires long-term care, and that where a person requires care, she typically does so for six years. Thus a representative individual
needs care for one year (that is, one-sixth of six years), and could therefore buy insurance for a single premium equal to the cost of one year's care. In contrast, if no
insurance is available, instead of saving to cover the *average* duration, self-insurance means that a person has to save enough to cover the *maximum* duration. If a
person thinks she might need care at age 80 and might live to be 100, she has to
save enough to pay for twenty years' care—twenty times the relevant premium if
insurance is possible. The welfare gains from insurance are thus glaringly obvious. The question, therefore, is whether needing long-term care is a risk that can
be covered efficiently by voluntary individual policies.

Consumer information problems
On the demand side, policies, being long term, are inescapably complex, calling
into question the quality of consumer information. First, what type of care will
be covered: will the policy cover only residential care, or also domiciliary care
(that is, care in a person's own home); will a person be entitled to residential care
on the basis of general infirmity or only on the basis of clearly defined ailments?
How will the answers to any of those questions change with advances over the
years in medical technology? Secondly, on what financial basis is care provided:

will the insurer be allowed to increase premiums if a person becomes more risky; what ceiling will there be on the monthly cost of care; will there be a maximum duration over which benefit is payable? Will those figures change over time in line with changes in general prices, changes in the cost of care, or changes in wages? Thirdly, how well specified is the contract: does the wording allow insurers to change the basis of cover; does the wording make clear the circumstances in which an individual can make choices; what arrangements are there to deal with any disagreements between the policyholder and the insurer? Complication arises, fourthly, because people may not know how much cover they actually have. If public funding becomes more generous, people with extensive private insurance end up with an inefficiently large amount of cover. Conversely, cuts in public funding may leave people underinsured; and if such underinsurance occurs relatively late in life, top-up private cover is expensive.

In the face of such complexities, Burchardt and Hills (1997: ch. 6; see also Burchardt 1997) found that even an academic study such as theirs was unable to find the necessary data for a proper assessment of policies, calling seriously into question the ability of individuals to make informed choices. At the barest minimum, there is need for regulation so that policies all cover at least a basic package.

Insurance problems

On the supply side, insurers face many of the problems discussed in Chapter 2, section 3.

UNCERTAINTY arises in two forms: insurers may not know the relevant probability and/or what the costs of care will be. On the first, what insurers know is the probability that applies to *today*'s frail elderly. What they need to know is the probability distribution of care for *future* cohorts of elderly. Those probabilities may change over the course of a contract that has a long time horizon (a person aged 30 buys a policy under which he might not make a claim for over fifty years). The probability of requiring care might get smaller because of medical advances that help people to care for themselves (for example, tablets that deal with arthritis) or because of technical advances with the same effect (for example, cheap robots that can do household chores for housebound arthritics). On the other hand, medical progress, by extending life, might increase the likelihood of requiring care. All available evidence suggests that today's young have a longer life expectancy than someone who is currently middle-aged. What is not known, however, is whether a person's dependent period will on average be longer or shorter than currently. The relevant probability cannot be known this far in advance; and even the *direction* of change is not clear. Over such a long time horizon, therefore, the issue becomes one of uncertainty rather than risk.

A connected problem is an uncomfortable tension between encouraging people to buy a policy at a younger age or an older age. With younger people, the range of uncertainty facing the insurer is greater but so are the gains from risk pooling. With older people, conversely, uncertainty is less but, since some people now have a high probability of requiring care, the opportunity of risk pooling is reduced.

Uncertainty about the cost of care is a separate problem. It is well known that the relative cost of services rises over time.[2] But over the very long term the ability to form a view about the costs of care becomes very questionable.

For both reasons, there is a considerable 'funnel of doubt' about the future costs of long-term care. The Royal Commission's sensitivity tests suggest that costs could vary by a factor of two (£21 billion to £39 billion) in 2031, and by a factor of nearly three (£28 billion to £76 billion) in 2051 (UK Royal Commission 1999b: table 5.1; see also Nuttall *et al.* 1995). In the face of such uncertainty, voluntary private insurance becomes highly problematical.

INDEPENDENCE. A further technical problem is that the relevant probabilities may not be independent. A medical advance that does not prevent or cure disability but prolongs life once a person has become disabled affects the probability of *all* policyholders.

ADVERSE SELECTION. The issue is identical to that for medical insurance: the person buying insurance, knowing that he is a bad risk, might be able to conceal that fact from the insurer. It does not matter whether such asymmetric information is a reality; the efficiency of insurance markets suffers when insurers *think* they are a reality. Evidence from the USA (Sloan and Norton 1997) suggests that adverse selection, whether real or perceived, is a problem.

MORAL HAZARD arises in two ways. If someone has full insurance that covers the costs of long-term care, he or she is more likely to demand care since the cost to him or her (at the time of use) is zero. This is the third-party-payment problem familiar from medical insurance. As discussed in Chapter 4, Section 2.2, a range of instruments exists to contain costs in such circumstances.

A second aspect, however, is very different from health care. The third-party incentive increases the likelihood that a person will demand care. But in this case, the incentive applies not only to the policyholder but also to his or her family. Insurance cover changes the balance of probability as between care from family members and care by others. To guard against being put into residential care against one's will, it could therefore be rational not to insure (Pauly 1990; Sloan and Norton 1997).

---

[2] The relative price effect (also referred to as excess medical inflation in the context of medical care) measures the extent to which the price of services tends to rise faster than prices generally. There are two reasons: the price of labour tends to rise faster than the general price level (i.e. real earnings rise); second, services like health care and education have a higher than average direct labour content (see Baumol, 1996). The argument applies at least as much to care services.

Thus not only consumers, but also insurers are imperfectly informed. Insurers therefore design policies that reduce their exposure to risk in several ways. Premiums err on the side of safety so far as p in Equation (5.1) is concerned. There is a cap on the total payout per year (though not usually on the number of years), thus limiting L. Insurers attempt to counter adverse selection by requiring full disclosure of an applicant's medical history, where a failure to disclose a 'relevant' fact invalidates the policy even where the insurer has not specifically asked for the fact. Attempts to guard against moral hazard include contracts that offer cover against tightly defined criteria, rather than for a more general 'need for care'.

It is therefore not surprising that the UK Royal Commission Report (1999b: 93) concludes that:

Left to grow without intervention, there seems little reason to think that private insurance will become more important in the UK than it has become over a 14-year period of development in America. At present only 4%–5% of Americans have taken out long-term care insurance, while 10%–20% could afford to do so and 80%–90% could not afford the cost in any event.

Burchardt and Hills (1997: 45), more fundamentally, conclude that 'it must be questioned whether private insurance is a suitable way to meet the security needs of a large part of the elderly population'.

2.2. *Preferred options*

THEORY. There are powerful arguments for a strategy based on the sort of social-insurance arrangements discussed in Chapter 2, Section 3.3.

- These are not risks that fit the actuarial mechanism very well. With social insurance, in contrast, as discussed in Chapter 2, Section 3, the contract need not be fully specified, making it easier to adapt to uncertainties connected with changing social and medical circumstances.
- The costs of residential care are much lower than for pensions, because on average people require care for a much shorter period than they require a pension.
- The arguments for pre-funding precisely parallel those for pensions (see Chapter 6, Section 2). It is not the size of the pot of money that matters, but the size of the pile of output.

Thus far the argument is clear. Beyond that, however, complications arise (see also Glennerster 1998a). The first set of problems is technical, concerned mainly with the difficulties of quantifying the extent of a person's disability: does a person experience sufficient problems to warrant care; and, if so, how severe is the problem?

A second set of problems is behavioural. In theory, the efficient quantity and quality of care are those that I would rationally choose if I had to pay for that care myself out of accumulated savings or by borrowing in a perfect capital market. That, however, boils down to self-insurance, whose high welfare costs were discussed earlier. With insurance, the individual has to pay only a fraction of the cost, or none at all. This creates incentives to inefficiency in two ways: over whether or not to seek care at all; and, if so, over the quality/cost of that care.[3] Both factors, as with any third-party-payment incentives, tend to drive up consumption, and hence expenditure.

Both sets of problems are difficulties equally for private insurance and for social insurance. Social insurance, nevertheless, has advantages. It can adjust to changing realities (that is, to uncertainties) and hence today's premium need not err on the side of caution to guard against tomorrow's possible problem. In addition, social insurance can impose restrictions (assessment criteria, a ceiling on benefit) that, if they are the outcome of democratic politics, have some legitimacy—almost certainly more legitimacy than restrictions imposed by private insurers mandated to consider the interests of their shareholders.[4]

The starting point is to remind ourselves of what is being insured—the extra costs associated with long-term health problems. The word 'extra' is central: long-term-care insurance is not intended to cover the ordinary costs of day-to-day living, which people normally meet out of their own income.

This line of argument suggests that long-term-care insurance should cover two sorts of additional cost, connected with clinical-need and 'hotel' aspects of care, respectively. Insurance should cover the full cost of meeting clinical need, broadly defined to include medical care, nursing care, and other care (for example, help getting dressed), however severe those needs and whatever the duration of the resulting care—all costs that people living independently do not incur. The assessment of such needs—for example, can a person walk unassisted—is in principle a technical issue relating to matters largely beyond the person's control.[5]

Insurance should also cover some 'hotel' costs, but with two sorts of restriction. It should normally cover only the *extra* costs of day-to-day living (for example, food costs might be higher because of the need to pay someone to cook it, rather than doing one's own cooking), but not the underlying costs. The only case where insurance should cover the full 'hotel' costs is for people whose income is so low that they would be entitled to income-tested housing benefit if liv-

---

[3] The two aspects are analogous to the distinction between (*a*) the labour-market-participation decision and (*b*) the decision, having decided to participate, about hours of work.

[4] There is a parallel with the discussion in Chapter 7, Section 1.5, of Pay-As-You-Go pensions; because the state can change the level of the pension over time, it is possible to argue that a simple conversion of pension promises into explicit debt overstates that debt.

[5] This discussion abstracts from the difficulties of measuring clinical need. Note, however, that such measurement is necessary, however the costs of long-term care are financed.

ing in their own home, the principle being to create a level playing field between people living independently in their own home, those receiving care in their own home, and those receiving residential care. The second restriction is that insurance should cover the extra costs of good-quality food and shelter, but not those of care in a stately home serving gourmet food and vintage wines. Thus there should be a ceiling on the monthly amount of cover connected with 'hotel' costs.

Thus social insurance pays all costs connected with clinical need plus unavoidable extra costs of an agreed standard of 'hotel' care. Beyond that, the person faces the costs of additional 'hotel' care him or herself.

PRACTICE. The UK government is moving towards the sort of arrangement just described, where, at least in principle, people pay the 'hotel' aspects of care while the state pays for the costs of additional care. The policy, however, takes a narrow view of what 'care' involves, in particular whether it covers care needs broadly, including personal care, or only medical and nursing care (for fuller discussion, see UK Department of Health 2000).

Long-term-care arrangements in other countries are assessed by the UK Royal Commission (1999b: ch. 6) (see also OECD 1996), which looks in detail at four countries: Australia, Denmark, Germany, and New Zealand. The following discussion focuses on Germany, which has the most explicit social-insurance arrangements. The system, introduced in the mid-1990s, makes long-term-care insurance compulsory.

Contributions, for about 85 per cent of the population, are rolled in with their medical insurance, which is organized by sickness funds financed by a payroll contribution. Thus contributions are related to a person's income, not to his or her degree of risk. The contribution for long-term care is 1.7 per cent of a person's earnings (up to a ceiling), shared equally between worker and employer. Official estimates suggest that this will have to rise, to about 2.4 per cent by 2040. A noteworthy feature is that the contribution is payable not just by workers, but also by pensioners (shared 50:50 between the pensioner and the pension fund), thus muting the demographic sensitivity of the finance of long-term care. The contribution covers the long-term-care needs of the contributor and also those of his or her immediate family.

Benefits are of three sorts: home care services; a home care cash allowance, which allows a person to buy his or her own care; and institutional care. Each of these is paid at three levels, corresponding to three different levels of assessed need for care. The home care cash allowance can be used either to buy in private care or to reimburse informal carers. Informal care is also encouraged in other ways (for details, see UK Royal Commission 1999b: 186–7).

The system has significant advantages: it provides cover for the entire population, with contributions based on ability to pay; the contributions mechanism protects the system, at least to some extent, from demographic change; the system provides help, not previously available, to informal carers; it has widened and deepened the market for care; the benefits (and the restrictions on benefit) have democratic legitimacy; and the system is piggy-backed onto an existing administrative system, thus contributing to administrative efficiency. For all these reasons, the system appears to be politically popular.

Other features can be regarded as advantages or disadvantages, depending on viewpoint. Since the scheme provides only capped benefits within each category, beneficiaries may face additional out-of-pocket expenditures. If the ceiling on benefit is realistic, this feature can be argued to contribute to efficiency. Secondly, the scheme pays at least some families to provide care they would have provided anyway. From that perspective, such benefits are a deadweight cost; on the other hand, the benefit to informal carers is a gain.

Genetic screening will inescapably involve state intervention to make sure that people can find insurance cover. Similarly, long-term care raises a series of technical problems that private insurance cannot solve alone. In both cases state involvement is inescapable, will probably grow, and, if properly designed, will contribute to people's well-being.

PART 3

PENSIONS

In the world of certainty described by the Fisher model at the start of Chapter 2, people provide for their old age through well-informed saving decisions, and those voluntary choices are efficient. Once the analysis is extended to allow for risk, uncertainty, and imperfect information, pensions based on voluntary saving are no longer necessarily efficient, opening up the possibility that state intervention might improve well-being by providing or facilitating mechanisms for moving consumption to old age.

Chapter 6 starts with the simple economics of pensions, and then turns to discussion of the problems of risk, uncertainty, and imperfect information. Consumers are imperfectly informed, not least about complex, long-run contracts, necessitating, at a minimum, stringent regulation of financial markets. Insurers are badly informed in a variety ways, suggesting that social insurance might have a role. Consumers, insurers, and government all face uncertainty, through demographic shocks (for example, population ageing), and macroeconomic turbulence (for example, an oil crisis). At a minimum, such shocks suggest a role for the state in addressing inflation; they also suggest a potential role for consumption smoothing across generations.

In the face of these problems a large literature on pension reform has grown up, generating considerable controversy. Rather than survey this literature, Chapter 7 instead summarizes the core issues by focusing on ten rather persistent myths about pension design that have clouded discussion, many of them centred on the debate about the respective merits of funded pensions (in which today's pensions are paid out of previously accumulated contributions) and Pay-As-You-Go arrangements (in which today's pensions are paid out of today's contributions). Analysis of pensions needs to draw on microeconomics, macroeconomics, financial economics, and an understanding of the theory of social insurance. Many of the myths are based on analysis that is incomplete because it omits one or more of these components.

Chapter 8 sets out the wide range of options for pension design, drawing on economic theory and the experience of selected countries. The options vary in the form and extent of state involvement, but even the most private-oriented arrangements require continuing government involvement, notably to ensure macroeconomic stability, to enforce contributions, and to regulate financial markets; and if reducing uncertainty is an objective—addressing inflation, pooling risks within a generation and across generations—the role of the state is to that extent larger.

Chapter 9 discusses two sets of issues that will be increasingly discussed in the future: the realities of the ageing population for pension finance, and designing pensions that are compatible with national and international labour mobility, fragmented family structures, and international pressures.

Chapter 6

The Economics of Pensions

This chapter establishes three themes that recur in subsequent chapters: the centrality of output to the macroeconomic viability of pensions; the pervasive uncertainties and (separately) the pervasive risks faced by pension schemes; and consumer information problems.

1. OBJECTIVES

From the viewpoint of the individual, the primary purpose of retirement pensions is income security in old age, an objective with three elements. First, there is consumption smoothing: pensions transfer consumption from productive middle years to retired older years. The purpose of invalidity pensions (paid to a person whose poor health makes work impossible) is insurance. Both mechanisms contribute to efficiency. A third purpose is poverty relief.

Pension systems may also have a series of secondary objectives—in other words, objectives of public policy that are not direct objectives of the pension system itself. One of these is economic growth. Excessive public pension spending may contribute to high tax rates, and thus may hinder growth. Conversely, it is suggested that accumulating pension funds can contribute to growth, an argument assessed in Chapter 7, Section 1.3. A further objective is to minimize distortions in the labour market.

2. THE CENTRALITY OF OUTPUT

THE SIMPLE ECONOMICS OF PENSIONS.[1] The macroeconomics of pensions is crucial for two reasons: completeness and simplicity. A central point to emerge from the analysis of Chapter 7 is that microeconomic analysis of pensions (for example, the effects of imperfect information, risk, and uncertainty) is dangerously incomplete unless set in its macroeconomic context. Secondly, the economics of pension schemes can be confusing because it tends to focus on financial aspects such as analysis of portfolios of financial assets. I shall try to simplify matters by concentrating on the essential economic issues—the production and consumption of goods and services.

---

[1] For excellent parallel discussion, see Thompson (1998).

There are two (and only two) ways of seeking security in old age. It is possible, first, to store current production by storing part of current output for future use. Though this is the only way Robinson Crusoe could guarantee consumption in retirement, the method in practice has major inefficiencies. First, it is costly: storing tins of baked beans is expensive because it gives up the potential return to financial savings; and there are direct costs of keeping a steak frozen for thirty years. A second problem is uncertainty: how many tins of baked beans should I store, what new goods might become available, what old goods might turn out to be harmful (BSE-infected beef, pharmaceutical drugs that turn out to have side effects), how might my tastes change, and how might my constraints change (for example, future medical problems might mean that I can no longer drink wine)? Thirdly, though some services can be stored by storing the physical capital that embodies them (it is possible, for example, to store housing services by being a home-owner), it is not possible to store services deriving from human capital; for example, I cannot store a young doctor to provide medical services in my old age. Organizing pensions by storing current production on a large scale is therefore a non-starter.

The alternative is for individuals to exchange current production for a claim on future production. There are two broad ways in which I might do this: by saving part of my wages each week I could build up a pile of *money* that I would exchange for goods produced by younger people after my retirement; or I could obtain a *promise*—from my children, or from government—that I would be given goods produced by others after my retirement. The two most common ways of organizing pensions broadly parallel these two sorts of claim on future output. Funded schemes, where pensions are paid from a fund built over a period of years from the contributions of its members, are based on accumulations of financial assets; Pay-As-You-Go (PAYG) schemes, where pensions are paid (usually by the state) out of current tax revenues, are based on promises.

FUNDED AND PAY-AS-YOU-GO SCHEMES. In a funded scheme, contributions are invested in financial assets, the return on which is credited to its members. When an individual retires, the pension fund will be holding all his or her past contributions, together with the interest and dividends earned on them. This usually amounts to a large lump sum, which is converted into an annuity—that is, a pension of £X per year. Funding, therefore, is simply a method of accumulating money, which is exchanged for goods at some later date.

Funded schemes take many forms, of which two in particular should be distinguished. Under a *defined-contribution* scheme (also called individual funded accounts), the contribution rate is fixed, so that, for a given life expectancy at retirement, a person's pension is determined only by the size of the lump sum accumulated during working life. Under a *defined-benefit* scheme, usually run at a firm or industry level, the firm promises to pay an annuity based on the employee's wages either at retirement or averaged over some longer period. Both types of scheme are discussed in greater detail in Section 3. An implication of a funded scheme is that a representative individual, or a generation as a whole, gets out of a funded scheme no more than he has put in; with funding, therefore, a generation is constrained by its own past savings.

Pay-As-You-Go (PAYG) schemes are usually run by the state, based on the fact that the state has no need to accumulate funds in anticipation of future pension claims, but can tax the working population to pay the pensions of the retired generation. From an economic viewpoint, PAYG can be looked at in several ways. As an individual contributor, my claim to a pension is based on a promise from the state that, if I pay contributions now, I will be given a pension in the future. The terms of the promise are fairly precise: they are given in each country's social-security legislation. From an aggregate viewpoint, the state is simply raising taxes from one group of individuals and transferring the revenues thereby derived to another. State-run PAYG schemes are thus direct transfers of title to consumption from younger to older people.

The major implication of the PAYG system is that it relaxes the constraint that the benefits received by any generation must be matched by its own contributions. Samuelson (1958) and Aaron (1966) showed that with a PAYG scheme it is possible in principle for *every* generation to receive more in pensions than it paid in contributions, provided that real income rises steadily; this is likely when there is technological progress and/or steady population growth.

THE CENTRALITY OF OUTPUT. Given the deficiencies of storing current production, the *only* way forward is through claims on future production. Those claims can be organized through PAYG, through funding, or through both. Whichever method is used, *what matters is the level of output after I have retired.* The point is fundamental, and emerges repeatedly in Chapter 7: pensioners are not interested in money (that is, coloured bits of paper with portraits of national heroes on them), but in consumption—food, clothing, heating, medical services, seats at football matches, and so on. Money is irrelevant unless the production is there for pensioners to buy.

3. UNCERTAINTY AND RISK

3.1. *Uncertainty and risk facing pension schemes*

With risk, the probability distribution of potential outcomes is known or estimable; with uncertainty it is not. The distinction is critical, as discussed in Chapter 2, Section 3.2, because actuarial insurance can generally cope with risk but not with uncertainty. Pension schemes face both problems.

Uncertainty arises in at least three ways.

(a) *Macroeconomic shocks* can have adverse effects on output, prices, or both. Since funding and PAYG are merely different ways of organizing claims on future output, it should not be surprising, as discussed in Chapter 7, Section 1.1, that a fall in output has adverse effects on either sort of scheme. On the other hand, purely inflationary shocks adversely affect funded schemes more than PAYG schemes.

(b) *Demographic shocks*, as discussed in Chapter 7, Section 1.1, also affect all pension schemes.

(c) *Political risks* affect all pension schemes, because, as discussed in Chapter 7, Section 3, all pension systems are dependent—albeit in different ways—on effective government.

Risk. All pension schemes face these common shocks. Private funded schemes face further risks.

(d) *Management risk* can arise through incompetence or fraud, which imperfectly informed consumers (Section 4) generally cannot monitor effectively.

(e) *Investment risk*: pension accumulations held in the stock market are vulnerable to stock-market fluctuations. At its extreme, if a member of a defined-contribution scheme is required to retire on his or her sixty-fifth birthday, there is a lottery element in the value of his or her pension.

(f) *Annuities market risk*: for a given pension accumulation, the value of an annuity depends on remaining life expectancy and on the rate of return the insurance company can expect over those years. Both variables face not only risk but also significant uncertainties.

3.2. *Risks facing individual pensioners*

Given these uncertainties and risks, a separate question is how they are shared. With a defined-contribution scheme, the contribution rate is fixed, so that a person's pension is an annuity whose size, given life expectancy and the rate of interest, is determined *only* by the size of her lifetime pension accumulation. Insurance protects the individual against the risks associated with longevity but leaves her facing all the uncertainties ((a)–(c)) and risks ((d)–(f)) associated with varying real rates of return to pension assets.

Under a defined-benefit scheme, often run at a firm or industry level, the firm pays an annuity based on the employee's wage and upon length of service. A key design feature is the way wages enter the benefit formula. In older schemes, pension was often based on a person's wage in his or her final year (or final few years) of work, a typical formula being one-eightieth of final salary per year of service. That arrangement, however, has distortionary effects. For example, as discussed in more detail in Chapter 9, Section 2.3, a pension based on a person's final salary creates labour immobility. The trend has therefore been to base benefits on a person's real wages averaged over an extended period. Whichever way wages are calculated, a person's annuity is, in effect, wage indexed until retirement. The employee contribution is generally a fraction of his or her salary, so that the employer's contribution becomes the endogenous variable.

In a defined-benefit scheme, the risk of varying rates of return to pension assets therefore falls on the employer and, as a result, can be shared in different ways. If the pension fund does badly, the cost of making good the pensions promise can fall on the industry's current workers: the firm could pay lower wages (or smaller wage increases) and transfer the savings to pensioners. Alternatively, the cost can fall upon the firm's shareholders and the taxpayer through effects on profits. Thirdly, the cost can be transferred to the firm's customers in the form of higher prices. Finally, the cost could be transferred to the firm's past or future workers, shareholders, or customers, if the company uses surpluses from some periods to boost pensions in others.[2]

With social insurance, exemplified by state-run PAYG schemes, risk is shared yet more broadly. The costs of adverse outcomes can be borne by the pensioner through lower pensions, by contributors through higher contributions, by the taxpayer through tax-funded subsidies to pensions, and/or by future taxpayers through subsidies financed by government borrowing.

The issues raised by risk and uncertainty are taken up in more detail in Chapter 7, particularly Section 2.2.

4. INFORMATION PROBLEMS

The advantages of consumer sovereignty rest on the assumption that the individual is well informed or, at a minimum, is better informed than the central planner. Imperfect information creates problems for pensions generally and private pensions in particular.

Individuals are imperfectly informed, first, because of uncertainty in the face of the common shocks just discussed. In this context, individuals are not well informed about the future because nobody, including government, is well informed.

Individuals are imperfectly informed, secondly, in the face of risk. For example, people do not know how long they will live, and hence do not know how long a period their pension will have to cover. This need not be a major problem for market solutions so long as the relevant risks can be covered by actuarial insurance.

---

[2] For detailed comparison of defined benefit and defined contribution schemes, see Bodie *et al.* (1988).

A third type of imperfect information applies particularly to defined-contribution schemes. Private pensions are complex, based on an array of financial institutions and financial instruments. Two sorts of imperfect information are usefully distinguished: some problems can be improved by public education, others are inherent (these were referred to in Chapter 2, Section 2.2 as the information problem and the information-processing problem, respectively).

IGNORANCE THAT CAN BE REDUCED BY PUBLIC EDUCATION. Even in the OECD countries, many people are ignorant about financial markets. A report by a large UK bank pointed out that 'lack of investment growth is a significant risk even if the fund is secure. However, there is little evidence that this basic truth has been understood. The concept of risk remains foreign to most people [in Britain], or understood only in the context of the risk of theft or fraud' (National Westminster Bank 1997: 19).

According to a UK government Green Paper on pension reform, 'Few people really understand pensions. Few know about their own pension provision and the action they need to take to improve it' (UK Department of Social Security 1998: 27). Alongside the efficiency issues raised by consumer ignorance, there is also a distributional point, in that those who are least well informed are disproportionately the least well off.

There is widespread consumer ignorance even in the USA, arguably the country with the greatest public knowledge about, and interest in, financial markets. Orszag and Stiglitz (2001: 37) quote the Chairman of the US Securities and Exchange Commission as stating that over 50 per cent of Americans did not know the difference between a bond and an equity.

IGNORANCE THAT IS LARGELY INHERENT. Even financial sophisticates cannot necessarily be regarded as well-informed consumers.[3]

[M]ost current personal pensions are difficult products for people to understand. People find it hard to know whether a pension offers them a good deal and are unable to make easy comparisons between them. There are complex charging structures, with different types of charges and quite different effects depending on how long the pension is held for. . . .

Individuals have limited power in the pension market. Personal pensions are complex. Individual consumers have no real power to negotiate with pension providers. Shopping around effectively is difficult. When they join, they have no influence on the terms of their contract and no power to press for improvements after they have joined.   (UK Department of Social Security 1998: 51)

---

[3] At a conference in 1993 about the UK Maxwell scandal, an eminent Professor of Finance reflected on the fact that she did not regard herself as a well-informed member of the UK university teachers' pension scheme, nor even a *potentially* well-informed consumer.

Given the high potential cost of mistaken choice, imperfect information creates an efficiency justification for stringent regulation of pensions for reasons of consumer protection in an area where consumers are insufficiently well informed to protect themselves. Scandals in the UK (see UK Pension Law Review Committee 1993; UK Treasury Select Committee 1998) illustrate the need for tightening regulation even in advanced industrial countries.

Chapter 7

Misleading Guides to Pension Design

Over twenty years ago, in a paper called 'Myths my Grandpa Taught Me' (Barr 1979), I addressed a particular myth—that funded schemes are less vulnerable to demographic pressures than Pay-As-You-Go schemes. This chapter returns to that earlier myth, and to a range of newer ones emerging from a noisy debate about pension design, largely motivated by population ageing throughout the OECD (see e.g. Disney 2000). Like many myths, those discussed here have an element of truth. That element is often just enough to give a semblance of plausibility but, on closer inspection, is sufficiently tenuous to be a misleading guide to policy. The following discussion examines three sets of myths (see also Orszag and Stiglitz 2001): those concerning the macroeconomics of pensions (whose essential part in the argument was stressed in Chapter 6), those concerned with pension design, and those concerning the role of government.

1. MACROECONOMIC MYTHOLOGY

1.1. *Myth 1: Funding resolves adverse demographics*

'Some degree of pre-funding is desirable in an old age security system. This helps to insulate the system from demographic shock' (James 2001: 63).

The facts of demographic change are well known. There were large birth cohorts in the late 1940s and in the mid-1960s in many countries, including most of the advanced industrial countries and many of the post-communist countries.[1] The earlier cohort will retire from 2005 onwards and the later cohort from about 2020 onwards. Thus there will be many people of pensionable age. These facts are not controversial. What is controversial is what they imply for the finance of pension schemes.

Consider a balanced PAYG scheme, where:

$$sWL = PN \tag{7.1}$$

where $s =$ the PAYG social security contribution rate
$W =$ the average real wage

---

[1] The 1948 peak was sharp but fairly short; the mid-1960s peak was not as sharp but lasted longer, and is therefore quantitatively more serious.

$L =$ the number of workers
$P =$ the average real pension
$N =$ the number of pensioners.

In such a scheme, current contributions of the workforce exactly cover current pension payments.

To show the effects of adverse demographics, suppose that a large generation of people of working age in period 1 is followed by a smaller generation in period 2—broadly the phenomenon just described. As a result, the smaller period 2 workforce has to support the large generation of retired period 1 workers. It is helpful to consider separately the cases of static output and growing output.

STATIC OUTPUT. Suppose that, because of a decline in the birth rate, L halves. Other things being equal, a PAYG scheme can remain in balance in various ways, of which two are relevant in the present case (other options are discussed shortly).

- Halve the average pension, P, imposing the entire cost of the demographic shock on pensioners. This is problematical, because it breaks the promise made to pensioners and because of its potential adverse equity effects, including pensioner poverty.
- Double the contribution rate, s, imposing the entire cost on workers. This is problematical, not least because of its potential adverse effects on work effort.

It is sometimes argued that funded schemes get round this problem: period 1 workers build up pension savings; the savings of a representative worker exactly cover his pension stream;[2] if there is a large number of period 1 workers, this is not a problem, it is argued, because each worker accumulates enough to pay for his or her own pension.

The problem with this argument is that, though it is true in nominal terms, it is false in real terms, as demonstrated in Barr (1979). To see why, note that the underlying problem caused by demographic change is a fall in output. This affects a PAYG system by shrinking the contributions base, WL, correspondingly reducing the pensions bill that can be supported by a given contributions rate. With funding the mechanism is more subtle, but equally inescapable, operating through a mismatch between demand and supply in either the goods market or the assets market. The mechanism merits explanation. Discussion starts with a closed economy; subsequent extension to a global economy does not change the result.

If a large generation of workers is followed by a smaller generation, there will be a large accumulation of pension funds belonging to the older generation at a

---

[2] i.e. the present value of his pension stream exactly equals the lump sum he has accumulated by the time he retires.

time when the workforce is declining. The large older generation will seek to draw down its accumulated savings to finance its desired level of consumption in retirement. That desired level of spending will exceed the desired pension contributions of the smaller younger generation. If output does not rise, the resulting disequilibrium manifests itself in either of two ways:

(a) Suppose that pensioners seek power over future production by building up piles of money, for example, bank accounts or government bonds. Desired pensioner consumption (that is, the amount that the large generation of pensioners wishes to spend out of its accumulated savings) is greater than the amount the smaller generation of workers wants to save. This leads to excess demand in the goods market, causing price inflation, and thus reducing the purchasing power of period 2 annuities.

(b) Suppose, instead, that pensioners seek power over future production by accumulating non-money assets such as equities. In that case, pensioners finance their consumption by selling their financial assets. Given the imbalance in the size of the generations, however, desired asset sales by pensioners exceed desired purchases of assets by workers. Excess supply in the assets market reduces asset prices, reducing the value of pension accumulations and hence the value of the resulting annuity.[3]

Under either outcome, pensioners do not get the real pension they expect. Funded pensions face similar problems to PAYG schemes, and for exactly the same reason—a shortage of output. In strict economic terms there is little difference between the two approaches. The main difference is political: with funding the process whereby demographic change reduces pensions is less transparent, and hence might be preferred by politicians, since that way bad news would be seen to arise through market outcomes rather than political decision.

GROWING OUTPUT. Returning to Equation (7.1), with static output the problems of PAYG could be resolved by halving P, by doubling the contribution rate, s, or by a combination of the two. An alternative solution arises where output, and hence the average wage, W, doubles, but P remains constant. Though this implies a fall in the replacement rate,[4] P/W, pensioners—crucially—get the real pension they were promised, and hence can afford the level of period 2 consumption they chose in the context of the simple Fisher model discussed in Chapter 2. Thus Equation (7.1) holds, the PAYG scheme remains in balance, and there is no need for either a reduction in pensions or an increase in contributions.

---

[3] Heller (1998) also makes this point. A simulation exercise by Brooks (2000) based on a stochastic overlapping generations model with stocks and bonds shows the general equilibrium effects on asset returns of demographic change, demonstrating more formally how this result emerges.

[4] The replacement rate shows benefits (in this case pensions) as a fraction of wages when in work.

Equally, increased output is a complete solution for funded schemes. Cases (*a*) and (*b*), above, now play out as follows.

(*a*) *Goods market*: a decline in the savings rate at full employment increases aggregate demand; but if aggregate supply has increased sufficiently, there is no excess demand for goods and hence no inflation. As with the PAYG case, though the replacement rate, P/W, falls, period 2 pensioners get the real pension they expect.

(*b*) *Assets market*: higher output generally implies that workers will have higher wages; if period 2 workers want a pension of (say) 50 per cent of their previous wage, their demand for assets to hold in their pension accumulation will increase in proportion with their wages. At its simplest, L halves but W doubles, so that the demand for assets equals desired sales by pensioners. Hence there is no deflation of asset prices. Again, period 2 pensioners get the real pension they expect.

POLICIES IN THE FACE OF DEMOGRAPHIC CHANGE. Thus the central question—and the reason for the emphasis on output in Chapter 6—is how to make sure that output grows, and the part that funding does (or does not) play in bringing this about. In principle, output can be increased in two ways.

One approach is to increase the productivity of each worker, thus increasing W in Equation (7.1). Policies to this end include (*a*) more and better capital equipment—for example, robots—and (b) improving labour through more education and training. A second approach is to increase the number of workers from each age cohort, thus increasing L in Equation (7.1). Such policies include (*c*) policies to increase labour supply—for example, by married women by offering better childcare facilities, (*d*) raising the age of retirement, (*e*) importing labour directly—for example, through more relaxed immigration rules,[5] and (*f*) importing labour indirectly by exporting capital to countries with a young labour force.

What impact does funding have on these policies? It clearly has no bearing on (*b*)–(*e*). The evidence on the effect of funding on capital accumulation via policy (*a*) is controversial, and is the main topic in Section 1.3. The effect of funding on (*f*) also requires discussion. The emphasis on output is because what matters to pensioners is consumption, not money. However, pensioners are not restricted to consumption of domestically produced goods, but can consume goods made abroad so long as they can organize a claim on those goods. It does not help British pensioners to build piles of pound notes if there are no British workers producing anything. However, if British workers use some of their savings to buy Australian factories, they can in retirement sell their share of the factory's output

---

[5] Though this would have to be phased in carefully to prevent another demographic crunch in 30–40 years time.

for Australian money to buy Australian goods, which they then import to Britain. This is an example of policy (*f*).

This approach can be effective, but is no panacea. The policy breaks down if Australian workers all emigrate to California; in that case Australian factories remain idle, and so both UK pounds and Australian dollars are useless. Thus, the age structure of the population in the destination of foreign investment is important. Secondly, if large numbers of British pensioners exchange Australian dollars for other currencies, the Australian exchange rate might fall, reducing the real value of the pension. Thus the ideal country in which to invest has a young population *and* products one is likely to want to buy.

Accumulating assets in countries with younger populations is thus a useful way to maintain claims on future output. Overseas investment by pension funds is one way to implement this policy. But there are other ways of accumulating foreign assets: I could, for example, hold part of my saving in Australian equities or mutual funds; and, as discussed in Chapter 14, Section 2, it might be beneficial to invest in human capital in countries with younger populations. Funding *per se* is not paramount—what is paramount is saving.

The conclusion to which this leads is threefold.

- In the face of demographic problems the key variable is output.
- Policy should consider the entire menu of policies which promote output growth directly.
- From a macroeconomic perspective the choice between PAYG and funding is secondary.

In sum, the argument that funding insulates pensioners from demographic change should not be overstated.

1.2. *Myth 2: The only way to pre-fund is through pension accumulations*

Since the effects of demographic change are, in broad, terms, predictable a long way in advance, it is desirable to have a long-term planning horizon. It is argued that moving towards funded pensions is exactly such a move. It is not, however, the only one.

CUTTING FUTURE SPENDING. One way to pay for pensions in the future is to find fiscal headroom to do so. Returning to Equation (7.1), we have already seen that one way to maintain the average pension in the face of demographic change is by increasing the PAYG contribution. The argument against this approach is its potential adverse incentive effects, particularly on labour supply. However, it is not public pension spending which matters for incentive purposes, but *total* public spending, which determines the total rate of tax,

$$t = s + v \qquad\qquad (7.2)$$

where t is the total rate of tax, s the PAYG contribution, and v the rate of tax required to finance spending other than pensions.

An increase in s is feasible provided that it is offset by a fall in v—that is, so long as any increase in pension spending (and other age-related spending such as health care and long-term care) is counterbalanced by reduced public spending in other areas. One way to do this is to start to repay public debt now. As a result, in 2025, when the demographic 'blip' is at its worst, public pension spending will be higher and debt-servicing expenditure lower, making it possible to maintain the real value of the PAYG pension without an increase in overall taxes. The title to consumption formerly represented by the stream of interest payments is now transferred to pensioners. On one interpretation, this is an example of consumption smoothing by government.

SETTING ASIDE RESOURCES TO MEET INCREASED FUTURE DEMANDS. An alternative approach is to pre-fund in ways other than pensions. For example, Norway top slices its oil revenues, using the proceeds to build up a fund one of whose purposes is tax smoothing in the face of demographic change. The USA, similarly, has a trust fund in anticipation of future pension spending and Canada a similar arrangement. Another example is Singapore's Provident Fund. However, it is important to be clear that, unless these policies increase output, they are a zero-sum game: with a fixed level of output, pensioner consumption, however financed, is at the expense of consumption by workers.

Thus, if pre-funding is thought desirable (a defensible view), it does not follow that a move towards private pensions is the only instrument for doing so.

1.3. Myth 3: There is a direct link between funding and growth

It is often regarded as self-evident that saving, and hence economic growth, will be higher with funding than under PAYG. The claim in a famous (1974) paper by Feldstein is that the US PAYG social-security system reduced personal saving by about 50 per cent, thereby reducing the capital stock by 38 per cent below what it would have been in the absence of the social-security system. The resonances from that article—particularly the argument that PAYG schemes reduce saving rates—continue in policy debate: 'the core rationale for the multi-pillar recommendation ... [includes] funding to increase national saving' (James 2001: 63).

The claim that funding increases savings and hence output growth requires at least three major qualifications.[6]

---

[6] For fuller discussion, see Mackenzie *et al.* (1997) and Thompson (1998).

INCREASES IN SAVING, IF ANY, OCCUR ONLY DURING THE BUILD-UP OF THE
FUND—in steady state, saving by workers is exactly matched by dissaving by pensioners.

FUNDING MAY NOT INCREASE SAVING EVEN DURING THE BUILD-UP PHASE. In
principle, the issue can be posed simply. Suppose that my mandatory pension
contribution of 100 is moved from a PAYG scheme to a funded scheme. Two illustrative outcomes are interesting:

- My voluntary saving (for retirement or bequests to my children) does not
  change. Thus saving increases by 100.
- I reduce my voluntary saving by 100; thus there is no increase in saving.

On the face of it, therefore, the issue is the extent to which any increase in
mandatory saving is offset by a reduction in voluntary saving. That, however, is
only part of the story. In any switch from PAYG to funded accounts a central question is what happens to the pensions of the older generation, the main topic in
Section 2.4. If they are reduced, consumption will fall, and hence, *ceteris paribus*,
savings will increase. If pensions are not reduced, they will have to be paid from
taxes or debt. Extra taxation will exert downward pressure on saving; extra debt
will be an offset, at least partially, to additional private capital formation. Once
more, analysis of individual behaviour is incomplete if macroeconomic effects
are ignored. Such effects could swamp the behaviour of individuals whose pension contributions are moved from a PAYG to a funded scheme.

It is, therefore, not surprising that there is much controversy, going back to Victorian times, about the effect on saving of a move from PAYG to funded accounts.
I make no attempt to summarize the debate in detail (see Aaron 1982; Thompson
1998; Orszag and Stiglitz 2001). Auerbach *et al.* (1989) and Auerbach and Kotlikoff
(1990) use a seventy-five-period life-cycle general equilibrium model to simulate
the effects of demographic change under different pension regimes. The results
highlight the key role of expectations (which are largely unmeasurable) on retirement behaviour. Gale (1998) argues that the savings offset is larger than previously supposed because of econometric biases in earlier work, suggesting that
the effect of funding on total saving is smaller than previously supposed. Holzmann (1997) reaches a similar conclusion. An IMF study (Mackenzie *et al.* 1997: 1)
concluded:

Studies of the U.S. economy, on which most research has been done, provide some moderately strong evidence that the introduction and development of the public pension plan
have depressed private sector saving, although the extent of this impact has proved hard
to estimate. Studies of other countries as a group have tended to be inconclusive. . . . The
upshot is that *it is not possible to generalize across countries about the impact of the public pension system on saving.* (emphasis added).

Taking the evidence as a whole, there is no robust confirmation that a switch from PAYG to funding increases saving in any country except the USA; and the US evidence is controversial.

AN INCREASE IN SAVING DOES NOT NECESSARILY RAISE OUTPUT. There are not one, but three links in the argument that future output will be higher with funding than with PAYG:

- funding leads to a higher rate of saving than PAYG;
- the resulting higher saving is translated into more and better investment; and
- the resulting higher investment leads to an increase in output.

None of the three links *necessarily* holds. The evidence on the first, as just discussed, is mixed. On the second, increased saving does not necessarily lead to new investment: a British trade union once famously invested part of its pension fund in old masters. More fundamentally, in a world of international capital mobility, domestic investment is no longer constrained by domestic savings. In an open economy, interest rates—a key determinant of investment—are therefore not determined by the flow of domestic saving but by international factors. For a small country (for which world interest rates are given), this breaks the link between any increase in domestic savings and the level of investment.

So far as the third link is concerned, it is important to focus not only on the volume of savings, but also on how those savings are used. The most glaring demonstration that investment does not lead automatically to growth is provided by the latter days of communism, when investment rates were enormously high: 'in 1985 only 25 percent of Soviet industrial output was of consumer goods. The remaining 75 percent was of producer goods' (Estrin 1994: 64). Even in well-run economies it cannot simply be *assumed* that pension-fund managers make more efficient choices than other agents in channelling resources into their most productive use. The UK Government Actuary admitted that he was 'not in a position to judge whether . . . pension fund money is more capable than other money of being deployed in accordance with the long-term national interest' (UK Government Actuary's Department 1978: para. 25).

The link between savings and growth faces further complications in post-communist and developing countries: funding contributes to growth only if it increases domestic investment. In transition countries, however, domestic investment may be low yield and high risk, the exact reverse of what pension-fund managers look for. Thus pensions policy faces a horrible dilemma, discussed further in Chapter 8, Section 2.2: domestic investment puts old-age security at risk; foreign investment puts growth at risk.

All three links have to hold before it can be asserted that funding will lead to greater increases in output than PAYG.

INDIRECT EFFECTS ON OUTPUT. It is argued, separately, that funding contributes indirectly to growth by widening and deepening capital markets. As Diamond (1995) points out, though this is not an argument that applies to the OECD countries, it is potentially relevant in transition and developing countries. However, the broader context is important: though a larger capital market may be a *component* of growth, it is not *on its own* a solution. As discussed in Section 3, the key lesson from Chile (to which the capital-market-widening-and-deepening argument is often applied (Holzmann 1997)) is the effectiveness of reform outside the financial sector.

To summarize a large, complex and controversial literature:

- The magnitude of the impact of funding on growth is controversial. Though there is some empirical evidence that funding contributes to higher savings in the USA, there is no robust evidence of a similar effect elsewhere.
- The issue, in any case, relates only to one of the sources of growth. Hence policies concerned with growth should consider the *entire* menu of policies discussed in Section 1.1, and not focus exclusively on pension funds.
- As Mackenzie, Gerson, and Cuevas (1997: 1) point out, 'It can hardly be overemphasized that the basic objective of a public pension program is not to raise the savings rate, but to provide income security—at the very least, a minimum income—for the elderly.' Increased saving is not the primary objective—what matters is to maximize well-being.

1.4. *Myth 4: Funding reduces public pension spending*

In proposing a radical shift towards defined-contribution funded pensions, the UK Secretary of State for Social Security argued that one of the key advantages of the reform was that 'ultimately the taxpayer and the economy will be relieved of the largest single item of public spending—some £40 billion a year' (quoted in UK Department of Social Security 1997).

Private pensions might make it possible to reduce state pension spending in the longer term, when the new schemes are mature. However, they are no short-term solutions. If workers' contributions go into individual funded accounts, they cannot be used to pay the pensions of older people. Unless government refuses to pay the pensions of the older generation, it has to finance them out of taxation and/or through debt. As a result, the need to finance the transition to a new pension regime generally *raises* public pension spending in the short to medium term. In the words of an IMF study, 'the fiscal costs of undertaking such a shift [to a fully funded scheme] may be very high, and . . . meeting those costs may require, in many cases, an amount of fiscal adjustment that is substantially higher than what would be needed to fix the PAYG system' (Chand and Jaeger 1996: 32–3).

Furthermore, the costs of privatizing a bloated PAYG system are greater than those of privatizing a sustainable scheme. An important conclusion follows: privatization is no solution to fiscal problems. *If the problem is a state scheme that is unsustainable, the only solution is to make it sustainable* by increasing contributions, cutting benefits, or a mixture of the two. Thus a move towards funding, whatever its other merits, should not be undertaken for reasons of short-run expenditure constraint.

1.5. *Myth 5: Paying off debt is always good policy*

'The problem with state schemes is that they are pay-as-you-go. Nothing is saved or invested for the future' (UK Department of Social Security 1997).

The argument runs as follows.

(*a*) Members of a PAYG pension scheme have accumulated rights.

(*b*) Those rights are an unfunded liability and hence can be thought of as implicit debt.

(*c*) The scale of that debt is large; fiscal prudence therefore suggests that it should be reduced.

(*d*) A move towards funding achieves this. The state requires younger workers to join funded schemes and pays the pensions of the older generation through taxation or borrowing. Such expenditure ceases once the older generation has died; accumulated debt, if any, is repaid by current and future taxpayers.

(*e*) Hence a move towards funding is desirable because it reduces implicit debt.

In considering the validity of this argument, it is useful to distinguish a series of questions: what is the nature of pension debt; how should PAYG pensions be represented in the public accounts; is paying off debt necessarily desirable; what are the arguments for reducing public spending; and how can public spending be contained in the face of demographic pressures?

WHAT IS THE NATURE OF PENSION DEBT? Any pension scheme has liabilities and assets. With a fully funded scheme, the gross liability is the present value of promised future pension payments and the gross assets are the holdings of the pension fund. With a defined-contribution system the present value of the liabilities and assets are by definition equal; thus the net present value of the system is zero. An important feature of the system is that liabilities and assets are both explicit.

Under a PAYG system, the gross liability is the present value of promised future pension payments. However, government can change the terms of the promise so as to reduce liabilities—for example, making the basis of indexation less generous (as in the UK in 1980), increasing the retirement age, or lengthening the averaging period used to calculate benefits. In sharp contrast, funded schemes, whose liabilities are explicit, have no such let out. The ability of governments to change the rules breaks the equivalence between implicit and explicit liabilities. Specifically, treating implicit liabilities as though they were explicit may overestimate them.

The gross assets of a PAYG system are the government's right to tax current and future generations. As with liabilities, valuation is not formulaic. It might be argued that the right to levy taxes is not an asset comparable to an explicit pension accumulation: the doubt might be a philosophical antipathy to taxation; it might point to the deadweight costs of taxation; or it might focus on the uncertainty of future revenues. All these factors would tend to reduce the value of the assets. The counter-argument is that, provided government is effective, the tax base will generally be as buoyant as financial assets and is likely to be more robust. Provided one accepts that taxable capacity is adequate to meet pension liabilities, as shown by Equation (7.1), the net present value of the scheme is zero.

For these reasons Nuti argues that:

A fully-balanced Pay As You Go system, in which current pensions match exactly current contributions . . . has zero gross assets; its net present value is negative due to future liabilities to current pensioners and employees, but as long as the system stays balanced this never comes to the surface. That net negative present value is matched, as it were, by a kind of seigniorage that the government obtains from the exclusive right to run a universal and compulsory PAYG pension system. *The 'true' net present value of the PAYG system is zero, in the sense that, if the government wanted to privatise[7] it, transferring its rights and obligations to a private institution enabled to maintain pensions at a level no greater than allowed by current contributions, there would be no need for any public compensation* for the outstanding net negative present value, nor for any recurring future subsidy.   (Eatwell *et al.* 2001: 136–7, emphasis added)[8]

In contrast, a PAYG scheme will have a negative net present value if assets fall short of liabilities—that is, if we believe that future governments will not be able to collect contributions sufficient to pay promised pensions. This outcome could arise because government is ineffective (for example, makes irresponsible promises) or because government is effective but faces adverse demographics. Where a scheme is unsustainable, the *only* solution is to reduce liabilities (where

---

[7] Note that when Nuti uses the word 'privatise' he is referring to a PAYG scheme run by a private entity.

[8] Geanakoplos *et al.* (1999: 80) reach a parallel conclusion: 'We prove that in an ongoing social security system, with or without a trust fund, the net present value of transfers to all generations must sum to zero.'

pension promises are too generous), or to increase assets (where the problem is ineffective collection of contributions), or a mix of the two.

HOW SHOULD PAYG PENSIONS BE REPRESENTED IN THE PUBLIC ACCOUNTS? With a balanced PAYG scheme, gross assets (the right to levy taxes) equals gross liabilities; thus the net present value of the scheme should appear in the public accounts as zero. There are two reasons why this might not be so. First, as discussed earlier, people might take different views about the valuation of the right to levy taxes. Secondly, the scheme might be unsustainable. Under either of these arguments, projected PAYG deficits are a negative item in the public accounts.

Looking at the issue in more detail, consider a benchmark case where the contribution, s in Equation (7.1), is fixed in perpetuity. For a given level of employment, L, and real wage W, total contributions are constant, and are shared across the pensioner population, N. Thus the endogenous variable is the average pension, P, and the costs of demographic change fall entirely on pensioners. There are no fiscal worries: if the scheme is sustainable today, it will remain sustainable. As a mental experiment (to use Atkinson's term), such a scheme could be handed over to a private entity without paying any compensation to the private buyer, and thus has a zero net present value.

More realistically, consider the case where the real value of the pension, P, is fixed in perpetuity. In this case, the real pension is constant, hence total pension spending and so also s are endogenous. The costs of demographic change fall on the working generation. It is useful to consider four different cases.

(a) There is no population ageing. This case is equivalent to that in which s is fixed in perpetuity. The net present value of the scheme is zero.

(b) Population ageing is matched by productivity increases. Thus W rises in parallel with N; again s remains constant and the net present value of the scheme is zero, in that it could be handed over to a private entity.

(c) Population ageing exceeds productivity increases but within fiscal tolerances. Thus s has to increase. If the effect is small and there is fiscal headroom (for example, the UK), assets continue to match liabilities; the scheme remains sustainable and—albeit arguably—can appear on the public balance sheet as a zero item.

(d) There is substantial population ageing with no fiscal headroom. In an arithmetic sense, assets can be increased in line with liabilities by raising the contribution rate in parallel with rising numbers of pensioners. In economic terms, however, the scheme is unsustainable: the assets need to be deflated because the necessary increase in s would have costly adverse incentive effects. Such a scheme clearly has a negative present value.

This line of argument suggests the following conclusions:

- If, in the extreme, we place a zero value on the state's right to tax, gross PAYG pension liability should appear as a negative item in the public accounts.
- Taking tax revenues at face value, the negative entry on the public accounts should relate only to any *increase* in *s* necessitated by demographic change or by promises of future pension increases unmatched by changes in the wage base. Where *s* is constant—cases (*a*) and (*b*)—the net present value of a PAYG scheme is zero.
- A strict approach would contain a negative item even in respect of sustainable increases in *s* (case (*c*), above). A more liberal approach would contain a negative item only for an increase in *s* that is regarded as unsustainable (leaving to one side the definition of 'unsustainable').

IS PAYING OFF DEBT NECESSARILY DESIRABLE? If the net present value of a sustainable PAYG scheme is zero, what is the case for pre-funding? More generally, should all anticipated future needs be pre-funded? I know that I will need to buy food for the rest of my life; but I do not accumulate a food fund, but intend to pay my supermarket bills out of future earnings. The reason for making a pension accumulation is a different one—namely, that I intend to retire—that is, to stop producing goods that I can exchange for other goods. No such accumulation is needed in a world without retirement—that is, where people are immortal, or where they remain healthy and active in the labour force until their death. Such a world is mythical for the individual but is exactly the case for a country, which does not have to take action to anticipate a time when production will cease. The fact that countries are immortal is central: from an economic perspective, it makes pre-funding unnecessary unless it has a positive effect on output, an issue about which, as discussed in Section 1.3, the arguments are equivocal.

If pre-funding does not increase output, paying off debt does nothing to change net wealth. Suppose that I have savings of $20,000 and debt of $5,000; my net worth is therefore $15,000. If I repay the debt, my savings fall to $15,000; my net worth remains $15,000. Repaying debt does not change net wealth, but does mean that one has to tighten one's belt. If there is never any need to repay the debt, the gains from repaying it are not obvious. This, as just argued, is the case with a sustainable PAYG scheme.

Thus it can be argued that the case for paying off implicit debt is not as strong as it first appears. In strict economic terms, the case for a move towards funding rests on its impact on output. Secondly, as discussed earlier, conversion to explicit debt may overstate the size of debt, and hence may repay more than is necessary. Thirdly, if the worry is the state's unfunded liabilities, why is the argument applied only to pensions? In all but the poorest countries, health care and education are largely publicly funded. Governments would not willingly renege on promises to care for the sick and to educate the country's children (these promises can be explicit—for example, constitutional guarantees about access to education). Such commitments are implicit debt in the same way as pensions, and their scale is not dissimilar, yet there is no discussion of pre-funding.

This line of reasoning suggests two conclusions. First, what matters is not the gross magnitude of the future liability but its sustainability. Secondly, the case for minimizing implicit or explicit debt is not strong; here—as elsewhere—the scale of debt should be optimized, not minimized. In those circumstances, what is the case for reducing public pension spending?

WHAT ARE THE ARGUMENTS FOR REDUCING PUBLIC SPENDING? Generational accounting[9] considers pension spending in the context of public spending generally. Kotlikoff argues that government should promote 'generational equity', and should therefore seek to equalize tax burdens across generations. This objective is contentious. First, it is a value judgement and so, like all value judgements, is disputable. Secondly, a range of exogenous inequities—wars, natural disasters, major epidemics, the Great Depression, the collapse of communism—have generation-specific effects; it is by no means clear that equalizing tax burdens is the equitable solution. Thirdly, a definition of equity based on *generations* rather than *individuals* opens an ambiguity; with generations of varying sizes, equal treatment of generations by definition means unequal treatment of individuals, and vice versa.

A very different argument for fiscal sustainability (Barro 1979) is that smoothing tax rates over time minimizes the welfare loss caused by taxation. This is a straightforward efficiency argument that does not rely on normative appeals to inter-generational equity. Note that the efficiency argument does not require the sophisticated generational accounting of the equity argument: what matters is the total size of the tax bill, not the age distribution of taxes and benefits.

HOW CAN PUBLIC SPENDING BE CONTAINED IN THE FACE OF DEMOGRAPHIC PRESSURES? If it is thought desirable to make tax rates more equal over time, how might this be done? As earlier discussion makes clear, a move towards private, funded pensions is not the only way to attenuate the impact of demographic change. One approach to improving the fiscal position is to reduce future spending directly, by reducing the average pension or by raising the official age of retirement. This line of attack can be defended on the Kotlikoff grounds of inter-generational equity. On the other hand, raising the retirement age needs no such defence: the policy is desirable for its fiscal impact; it is also a sensible response to increased life expectancy, reducing pension spending not by reducing

---

[9] See Kotlikoff (1992), Auerbach *et al.* (1999), Kotlikoff and Raffelhueschen (1999), and Cardarelli *et al.* (2000).

living standards in retirement but through a shorter duration of retirement. This approach levels down public spending, maintaining taxes broadly at existing levels, thus imposing relatively more of the cost of demographic change on pensioners.

A second approach, already discussed, is to reduce future spending on things other than pensions—for example, reducing public debt now so as to reduce interest repayments in the future. This latter approach brings forward spending, so that the tax burden is 'levelled up' to a point between present and projected future levels, thus imposing relatively more of the cost of demographic change on current and future taxpayers.

In conclusion, the argument that implicit pension debt should be minimized is too simple. The relevant variable is not public pension spending but total public spending; and the size and time path of that spending should be optimized, not minimized.

2. MYTHS ABOUT PENSION DESIGN

A second set of myths relates to the design of pension systems.

2.1. *Myth 6: Funded schemes have better labour-market incentive effects*

'The core rationale for the multi-pillar recommendation [includes] . . . defined contribution to provide good labor market incentives, especially regarding the age of retirement' (James 2001: 63).

SIMPLE ANALYTICS. Labour-market distortions can (*a*) affect retirement decisions and (*b*) influence labour-market responses earlier in life. So far as the retirement decision is concerned, what matters is that pensions should be related *at the margin* to individual contributions, and that contributors and beneficiaries should perceive this to be so. The argument is important. It is open to policy-makers to have a pension formula that is redistributive in the sense that worker A, with twice the earnings of worker B over his working life, gets a pension that is higher than B's, but less than twice as high. However, if either A or B retires early, his pension should be actuarially reduced relative to the pension he would have received at age 65.

Earlier labour-market decisions depend not just on the marginal relationship between contributions and benefits, but on the relationship between total contributions and benefits. In this latter case, labour-market distortions are minimized where contributions bear a fully actuarial relationship to benefits, and are seen to do so. This is the case with private defined-contribution schemes. It is also the case with state schemes that pay benefits strictly proportional to a person's lifetime contributions, an example being the Swedish 'notional defined-contri-bution' scheme, discussed in more detail in Chapter 8, Section 3.2.[10]

In contrast, badly designed schemes, whether private or public, can cause labour-market distortions. Gruber and Wise (1999), reporting on a study of eleven industrial countries, find a strong relationship between the design of pub-lic pensions and early retirement. They examine the fact that, where people delay retirement, most countries increase pensions by less than the actuarial amount, thereby creating an incentive for people to leave the labour force at the age at which their pension wealth is maximized. Gruber and Wise call this 'the tax force to retire', and find a strong correspondence between that variable and the labour-force departure of older men.

Such distortions also exist in private schemes. It is well known (see Campbell 1999; Burtless and Quinn 2000) that employer, defined-benefit schemes can cre-ate labour immobility,[11] and also give incentives to retire at the time when pen-sion wealth is at a maximum. Note that publicly organized defined-benefit schemes, being universal, do not impede labour immobility, since members can change jobs without changing to a new pension scheme.

COMPLEXITIES. The simple case assumes rationality. In consequence, labour sup-ply is independent of debates about PAYG and funding—what matters is the in-centive structure of pensions, not the mechanism by which their finance is organized. As an empirical matter, however, reality and perception can diverge: people may perceive a contribution to a private scheme as a contribution (hence causing no distortions), while perceiving contributions to a state pension—even an actuarially organized state scheme—as a tax. The converse, too, could hold, if people had confidence in a state scheme but little or none in private schemes. To the extent that there is a divergence between reality and perceptions, the conclu-sions of the simple case may not hold.

The simple case also implicitly assumes that pensions are the only labour-mar-ket distortion. A general equilibrium analysis would take explicit account of other influences on the labour market, notably the presence of progressive in-come tax. Such analysis has yet to be conducted, though an early foray by Peter Diamond reported by Orszag and Stiglitz (2001) suggests that the comparison be-tween defined-contribution and defined-benefit schemes is complex, and with no clear outcome.

Finally, the simple case assumes that all that matters is labour supply. Again, however, it is necessary to keep one's eye on the ball. Analogous to earlier argu-ments about saving, what matters is not labour supply but economic welfare. It

---

[10] A strong relation between contributions and benefits can have particular benefits in countries with a large grey economy, where incentives can to some extent substitute for enforcement in assisting compliance with contributions and taxes.

[11] This topic is discussed in more detail in Chapter 9, Section 2.3.

may be, for example, that a defined-benefit scheme reduces labour supply at the margin; but if the loss of utility resulting from lower output is more than offset by the utility gain resulting from greater security, then defined-benefit arrangements are welfare improving notwithstanding reduced labour supply.

The conclusion to which these arguments lead is twofold.

- Badly designed pensions—whether public or private—can affect labour supply adversely.
- Labour supply should be seen in the broader context of welfare maximization.

2.2. *Myth 7: Funded pensions diversify risk*

Pensions face a series of uncertainties and risks. The future is an uncertain business, and no pension scheme can give certainty. In the face of these problems, it is argued that 'the principal advantage of a multipillar pension scheme lies in risk diversification. Not all of the population's retirement portfolio will be held hostage to political and demographic risk' (Holzmann 2000*a*: 21). Before discussing whether this is so, it is necessary to discuss in more detail the uncertainties and risks outlined in Chapter 6.

The first group of problems, broadly, are uncertainties arising out of common shocks—problems that apply to all pension schemes.

MACROECONOMIC SHOCKS. Two cases need to be distinguished: an output shock and a purely inflationary shock. Output shocks affect all pension schemes—with PAYG by shrinking the contributions base (or the rate of growth of the contributions base), with funding by reducing the value of the financial assets on which funds are based. Given the centrality of output discussed in Chapter 6, this conclusion should not be surprising. In contrast, where the shock is inflationary (that is, a purely monetary phenomenon), there is little or no effect on PAYG pensions: if prices double, nominal earnings will double, and thus also the nominal yield of social-security contributions, making it possible to double nominal pensions. In real terms nothing has changed.[12]

There is a sharp contrast with defined-contribution schemes. It is important to distinguish pensions in build-up and pensions in payment. Defined-contribution schemes can generally cope with inflation during the build-up of pension rights, and with a given rate of *anticipated* inflation once the pension is in payment. But they do not cope well with unanticipated post-retirement inflation. The reason is simple. At retirement, a pensioner receives an annuity whose present value equals his pension accumulation. For a given remaining life expectancy, the size

[12] This simple argument deliberately abstracts from complications such as the fact that inflation erodes pensioner purchasing power continuously, whereas pensions are increased only periodically.

of the annuity depends on the size of the accumulation and the *real* rate of return facing the seller of the annuity. Two cases need discussion: certainty and uncertainty.

If inflation is 5 per cent each year with certainty, it is an easy matter to offer an annuity that rises in nominal terms by 5 per cent each year. Inflation is no problem.

With uncertainty matters are more complex. Inflation is a common shock and therefore uninsurable. In addition, since future rates of inflation are unknown, inflation raises issues of uncertainty rather than risk and so—for a completely separate and additional reason—cannot be covered by actuarial insurance.[13] A possible escape route where inflation is purely domestic is to hedge through an internationally diversified portfolio of pension assets. Another escape route, from the insurer's perspective, is to offer limited indexation. If the limit is 5 per cent, then, so far as the insurer is concerned, the situation is similar to the certainty case, in the previous paragraph—the risk of inflation beyond 5 per cent is transferred to the pensioner.

The conclusion is that, once pensions are in payment, private, funded schemes can cope with limited inflation (in other words, can offer indexation up to some pre-specified level). But they face major problems with inflation beyond that level. The point is much more than academic. The price index in Britain in January 1974 was 100; in September 1978, in the wake of the first oil shock, it was 200. With 5 per cent indexation, pensions would have increased from 100 to about 133, rather than to 200. Pensions in payment would have lost one-third of their purchasing power. At least three points are noteworthy: private defined-benefit schemes—in contrast with PAYG schemes—are vulnerable to purely monetary phenomena; any loss is permanent—in contrast with pensions during build-up, there is no opportunity to make up any of the lost ground; and people are retired today for many more years than previously.

The fact that inflation is an uninsurable risk does not mean that nothing can be done. It is possible to hedge the risk to some extent by holding a range of assets, perhaps including foreign assets. Empirically, however, hedging against unanticipated post-retirement inflation is generally incomplete, expensive, or both. A complete solution—particularly in countries with less well-developed financial institutions—is for the state to deal with the inflation element of pensions, for example, by issuing indexed bonds. This introduces an unfunded element into the

---

[13] As discussed in Chapter 2, insurance is efficient only if a number of technical conditions are met, of which two are relevant in this case: (*a*) the relevant probabilities have to be independent; and (*b*) the probability distribution of outcomes has to be known. In the context of pensions, if one member of a pensioner generation experiences inflation, they all do, violating (*a*); and future inflation rates are unknown even over a five-year period, let alone over the much longer periods relevant to pension schemes, thus violating (*b*). For both reasons, inflation is an uninsurable risk.

scheme, alongside any existing unfunded elements such as the tax advantages pension funds may enjoy.

DEMOGRAPHIC SHOCKS affect PAYG schemes, again, via effects on the contributions base—other things being equal, the smaller the generation of workers the smaller the contributions base. With funding, as explained in Section 1.1, the shock operates through inflation in the goods market and/or through deflation of the financial assets in pension funds.

POLITICAL SHOCKS. As discussed in Section 3, below, all pension systems depend critically on effective government.

In addition to these uncertainties faced by all pension schemes (indeed, by all economic activity), private pensions face additional risks.

MANAGEMENT RISK. The issue of imperfect consumer information was highlighted in Chapter 6. If government is ineffective, *any* pension scheme will be at risk. Even with effective government, however, individual pension funds may be badly managed. Management may be honest but incompetent; or it may be deliberately fraudulent. For both reasons, pension funds require substantial regulation to protect consumers.[14]

INVESTMENT RISK. Even if managed with complete probity and high competence, pension funds face the risk of differential pension portfolio performance. With defined-benefit schemes, these risks fall on the industry and hence, as discussed in Chapter 6, can be shared broadly across the industry's current workers, shareholders, and customers, or spread across past or future generations.

Under a defined-contribution scheme, two people with identical earnings and contributions records may end up with very different pensions. 'Benefits depend on the returns to assets (which are stochastic and with the right stochastic process in dispute) and on the pricing of annuities (which is also stochastic and also subject to dispute about mortality trends as well as future rates of return)' (Diamond 2001: 76). Consider individuals A and B with identical lifetime contributions profiles: if A retires when the stock-market index stands at 5,000, and B retires six months later when the stock market has fallen to 4,000, B's pension will be 20 per cent lower than A's. Burtless (2000), comparing the pension received by different cohorts of workers who differ only in respect of the year in which they retire after a forty-year working life, finds substantial variations—for example, a replacement rate of 80 per cent for a worker retiring in 1972 had collapsed to just over 40 per cent for one retiring in 1974. This outcome may be more than a short-term phenomenon; depending on its duration, a stock-market downturn could ad-

---

[14] See UK Pension Law Review Committee (1993) and UK Treasury Select Committee (1998) for official discussion of how to tighten the regulation of private pensions in the UK.

versely affect an entire cohort. Miles (2000), in a simulation of 1 million non-overlapping thirty-year return histories, using historical data on European stocks, shows that 'some age cohorts would earn very low, and possibly, even negative returns. . . . These findings on the risk faced by pensioners are at odds with the position taken in much of the literature and suggests that the benefits of funded schemes tend to be overstated' (Royal Economic Society 2000: 13).

Up to a point, these risks can be reduced. The average return to pension funds is boosted by keeping costs low: for example, by collecting contributions through payroll deductions and by limiting advertising expenditure. A second approach might be to require funds to be run on fairly simple lines—for example, as index (i.e. tracker) funds, rather than actively managed, thus reducing or eliminating the lower tail of pension fund performers. Thirdly, if people are obliged to convert on the day they retire, and if they are obliged to retire on their sixty-fifth birthday, the value of their pension is to a significant extent a lottery. To reduce the resulting inequity, it is therefore essential to allow flexibility over the timing of conversion of a person's lump sum into an annuity.[15] For all these reasons, government proposals about 'stakeholder pensions' in the UK are designed explicitly to reduce costs and risk (see UK Department of Social Security 1998, and, for a critique, Agulnik and Barr 2000). This solution, however, is a zero-sum game: it does nothing *per se* to increase output; and, at a given level of output, the gain in pensioner consumption from selling pension accumulations at the top of the market is at the expense of worker consumption.

Having adopted these various strategies, the remaining investment risk is inherent in the logic of individual funded accounts. The extent of that risk should not be underestimated: the problem is not just the substantial variance of outcomes but, in addition, the fact that the mean outcome is uncertain.

ANNUITIES MARKET RISK comes on top of investment risk. Under a defined-contribution scheme, the annuity a person can buy with her lump sum depends on (*a*) her expected duration of retirement—that is, her remaining life expectancy at the time she retires, and (*b*) the interest rate the insurance company expects to earn over the lifetime of the annuity, in particular the rate of interest on long-term government bonds. There is significant uncertainty about both variables. On the first, a major health breakthrough could lead to insurance company failures. Separately, the return—even on 'safe' assets like long-term government bonds—varies, so that a person who retires during a recession, with low interest rates, may receive a significantly lower annuity than someone who retires during a period of higher interest rates. In Chile, for example, 'the collapse of long-term interest rates in the past two years has had a dramatic effect on annuity rates. By way of example, 100,000 units of capital would have secured a life-long annuity of

---

[15] In the UK, personal pensions can be converted into an annuity at any age between 50 and 75.

8,000 per annum in July 1998. For the same 65-year old man, by October 1998, 100,000 units of capital would only have secured an annuity of 5,800 per annum' (Callund 1999: 532).

A further problem is that in many countries, even advanced industrial countries, the annuities market is thin: with competing providers, each company has only a small share of the market, and hence only a few people in each age group. Thus the opportunity of economies of scale is largely lost and, consequently, transactions costs are high. This reduces the value of an annuity, quite independently of interest-rate fluctuations.

DOES A DIVERSIFIED PENSION SYSTEM REDUCE RISK? What, then, of the proposition that a multipillar pension scheme diversifies risk? The proposition holds only if those risks are negatively correlated or, at a minimum, are orthogonal to each other. Applying this criterion to the risks above, economic risk and demographic risk, as discussed in Section 1.1, are common to both funding and PAYG. Funded schemes, in addition, face management risk, investment risk, and annuities market risk. Nevertheless, the variance in wages and real asset returns are not fully correlated (see e.g. Holzmann 2000a: annex); equally, political risks (for example, unsustainable PAYG systems) and investment/management risks may be independent. These issues, ultimately, are empirical. Because of citizens' perceptions, funded schemes in some countries at some times in their history might have greater legitimacy; in other countries, however, state PAYG pensioners have been better protected than recipients of private pensions—for example, the UK in the 1970s (though not over the 1990s).

These arguments point towards two conclusions. First, the risk-spreading argument is more complex than its apparent plausibility suggests, and is not always and automatically right: private pensions may or may not diversify risk; they certainly introduce additional risks. Secondly, if we *do* accept the argument, we should be clear that it is a defence as much of the state pension as of private pensions.[16] Thus the risk-diversification argument is logically incompatible with the view (World Bank 1994a; James 1998) that the PAYG state pension should be minimized.

2.3. Myth 8: Increased choice is welfare improving

Holders of individual funded accounts face all the uncertainties and risks just discussed, as well as the consumer information problems discussed in Chapter 6. Two issues stand out: the benefits from consumer choice; and the administrative costs connected with the exercise of that choice.

---

[16] Merton (1983) and Merton *et al.* (1987) argue that a mixed system, with an unfunded state pension tied to earnings growth and a diversified, funded component tied to stock-market performance, can reduce risk relative to a fully-funded system.

The conventional advantages of competitive market allocation are that it gives suppliers an incentive to respond to consumer choices, and that it exerts downward pressure on costs. An increase in the range of choice, however, is desirable only where consumers are sufficiently well informed to make choices, which the discussion of Chapter 6 calls into question; and, if competitive forces push down prices, consumers, for the same reason, are unable to assess whether quality is low (for example, whether a pension fund has poorly qualified managers), and if so whether they want the lower-quality product at the lower price. The counterargument to the proponents of competitive pension provision is that the advantages of competition are contingent on perfect information. For fuller discussion of the key role of information, see Loewenstein (1999).

The scale of uncertainty, risk, and other consumer information problems does not *necessarily* rule out consumer choice as welfare improving, but should be seen as a counterpoint, most particularly in poorer countries where citizens have little financial market experience.

The cost of allowing choice, in particular administrative costs, is an equally relevant part of the argument. Constrained choice, for example, in a state scheme, opens up the possibility of administrative economies of scale; with little constraint on choice—for example, with individual funded accounts from competing providers—those economies of scale are lost. It may be argued that competitive pressures will act to keep costs down. But, as Orszag and Stiglitz (2001: 35) remind us, competition 'only precludes excess rents; it does not ensure low costs. Instead, the *structure* of the accounts determines the level of costs' (emphasis in original).

The issue is important because the power of compound interest (one of the main arguments used in support of funded accounts) applies equally to administrative costs. The US Advisory Council on Social Security estimates that, under plausible assumptions, the *additional* administrative costs of a decentralized system absorb about 20 per cent of the value of a pension accumulation over a forty-year career (Orszag 1999: 33). Thus it should not be surprising (see e.g. Diamond 1998a) that individual funded accounts in Chile have high administrative costs, and that the same is true for such pensions in the UK.[17]

Additionally, a significant element of administration takes the form of a fixed cost—the cost of maintaining a pension account is related to such variables as the duration of the account and the frequency of deposit, but not to the size of each deposit. Administrative costs thus bear most heavily on small pension accounts, and hence on low earners. This point may not be overriding in OECD countries but is immensely significant in poorer countries.

---

[17] Murthi *et al.* (1999) present preliminary results that suggest that fees and other administrative costs absorb over 40% of the value of individual accounts in the UK. For broader discussion of administrative costs, see the report of the Panel on Privatization of Social Security (1998: 25–35).

The conclusion is that increased individual choice is not necessarily welfare improving.

2.4. *Myth 9: Funding does better if real returns exceed real wage growth*

Samuelson (1958) and Aaron (1966) show that the rate of return to a mature PAYG scheme is the sum of the population growth rate, n, and real wage growth, w. Suppose that the return on the stock market is i. If

$$i > n + w \tag{7.3}$$

(where all variables are net of administrative cost), workers on the face of it do better if they put their contributions into a funded scheme. Put another way, for a given contribution funded schemes provide a higher pension than PAYG. 'In contrast to the 2.6-percent equilibrium return on Social Security contributions, the real pretax return on nonfinancial corporate capital averaged 9.3 percent over the same . . . period . . . [As a result], forcing individuals to use the unfunded system dramatically increases their cost of buying retirement income' (Feldstein 1996: 3).

A straightforward comparison between rates of return, however, does not compare like with like. A full analysis needs to include (*a*) the costs of the transition from PAYG to funding, (*b*) the comparative risks of the two systems, and (*c*) their comparative administrative costs.

Financing the transition: the equivalence proposition
The following analytics draw on Orszag (1999), a non-technical summary of an important series of results originally established by Breyer (1989) (see also Homburg 1990), which have recently been applied to the US debate by Geanakoplos, Mitchell, and Zeldes (1998, 1999) and Belan and Pestieau (1999). The conclusion is that, if proper account is taken of the costs of transition from a PAYG to a fully funded scheme, there is generally an equivalence between the return to two schemes.

DESIGNING A SYSTEM FOR A BRAND NEW WORLD. The argument that pensioners are better off under funding if the real return to assets exceeds real wage growth is, indeed, true in a brand new world, and is therefore potentially relevant to a country (for example, India) with a small public pension scheme. However, note the important qualification that it is only later generations, with a full contributions record, who get the higher return, not the first generation, who do not have enough time to build such a record.

That, however, is not the issue in most countries. What is being discussed is a move from an existing PAYG scheme towards funding. In that case, it is necessary to include the transition costs of the change, in other words, to look at funding not only from the viewpoint of the funded pensioners, but from that of the economy as a whole.

CONSTANT BENEFIT RULES; TRANSITION COSTS FINANCED BY PUBLIC BORROWING. To illustrate the argument, consider the simplified example in Table 7.1, taken from Orszag (1999: ch. III), with static output and no population growth, in which a generation pays $1 in contributions when it is young and receives $1 in pension when old. In period 1, the $1 pension of older generation A is paid by the $1 contribution of younger generation B. In period 2, when generation B is old, its pension is paid by the contributions of younger generation C.

Table 7.1. *A simplified Pay-As-You-Go system*

Period	Generation			
	A	B	C	D
1	+$1	−$1		
2		+$1	−$1	
3			+$1	−$1
4				+$1

Source: Orszag (1999: 9).

Assume that the real rate of return on assets, i, is 10 per cent, and imagine that we are generation C. As members of the PAYG system, we pay $1 in contribution in period 2 and receive $1 pension in period 3; the real rate of return is zero. If, in contrast, we sign up for an individual account, we would save $1 in period 2 and get back $1.10 in period 3; the real rate of return, it appears, is 10 per cent.

The flaw in the argument is that if generation C contributes to individual funded accounts, generation B's pension must come from some other source. If that source is government borrowing, and if the interest on that borrowing is paid by the older generation, generation C receives a pension of $1.10 but has to pay interest of 10 cents on the borrowing that financed generation B's pension. The real return—as under the PAYG scheme—is zero. The lower return on the PAYG system in this case is not the result of some inherent flaw, but precisely the cost of the initial 'gift' to generation A: 'falling money's worth in this model is *not* due to the aging of baby boomers, increased life expectancy, or massive administrative inefficiency, but rather to the simple arithmetic of the pay-as-you-go system' (Geanakoplos *et al.* 1999: 86, emphasis in original).

If, instead, the interest payments are made by the younger generation, generation C does indeed enjoy a 10 per cent real rate of return. However, generation

D receives a zero real return: when young it would make $1 of pension contributions as well as repaying 10 cents interest; in retirement it receives $1.10 in pension. The higher return to generation C is paid by requiring all future generations to earn a zero real return on a larger base ($1.10 rather than $1).

This result is the subject of simulations by Geanakoplos, Mitchell, and Zeldes (1998, 1999) and is demonstrated formally by Breyer (1989) and Belan and Pestieau (1999) (see also Pestieau and Possen 2000). There is a precise equivalence between the two schemes if the move to a funded scheme is considered not in isolation but alongside the cost of financing the change—a cost wholly and exclusively the result of the gift to the first generation. If there is a move to individual funded accounts, the higher return to equities is exactly offset by the interest payments on the debt required to pay the pensions of the transition generation; if, in contrast, the system stays PAYG, the present value of the lower return under PAYG over all future generations is equal to the introductory gain of the first generation of pensioners.

As a result, generation C and onwards are not made better off by a move to individual accounts. As Belan and Pestieau (1999: 118) put it:

> privatisation which involves moving from an unfunded to a fully funded scheme is neutral if public borrowing is used to finance the retirement of the transition generation. In other words, a pension privatization that leaves the mandatory contribution rate equal to the payroll tax of the former public system, and that does not alter the terms of eligibility or magnitude of retirement benefits under the old system, will have no impact on the disposable income and wealth of individuals who move from the old system to the new.... In effect, the privatization simply converts an implicit government obligation to future retirees into explicit debt'.

Geanakoplos, Mitchell, and Zeldes (1999: 139–40) reach exactly the same conclusion for exactly the same reasons.

CONSTANT BENEFIT RULES; TRANSITION COSTS FINANCED BY TAXATION. What happens if we relax the assumption that the transition is financed by public borrowing? Returning to Table 7.1, suppose once more that we are generation C in period 2. We put our contribution of $1 into an individual funded account, and the $1 pension of generation B is paid out of a budget surplus. As members of generation C, we receive a pension of $1.10, a 10 per cent real rate of return; generation D, similarly, makes a contribution of $1 and receives a pension of $1.10. The real return is 10 per cent because, with tax funding, generation C and its successors do not have to pay interest on additional public debt.

It is critical to note, however, that the identical result could be achieved by injecting some partial pre-funding into the PAYG system. Suppose that, in period 2, the $1 of generation C is paid as pension to generation B, and *in addition* $1 is invested in a social-security trust fund. Generation C then receives a pension of

$1.10, $1 from PAYG financing, 10 cents from the proceeds of the trust fund; the real return is 10 per cent. The same is true for succeeding generations.

The conclusion is that the higher return results not from any move to individual funded accounts, but from the injection of an extra $1. From another perspective, 'paying back' the gift to the first generation makes it possible to increase the real rate of return to subsequent generations of pensioners. This does not, however, mean that the transition is costless. If output is fixed, an increase in the real return to pension contributions benefits pensioners, who thereby can consume more in old age, but that increase is at the expense of consumption by workers. Thus the move is a zero-sum game, and hence no claims for Pareto improvement are possible.

No benefits to the transition generation. Yet another way of financing the transition is to throw generation B out of the lifeboat by not paying their pension at all. That way, it is true, generation C and onwards enjoys a 10 per cent real return. But those gains by subsequent generations are at the expense of generation B, on whom the entire cost of transition is concentrated. Put another way, the cost of the gift to generation A is offset by the negative gift to generation B.

The fundamental point is that, once the gift to the first generation under a PAYG scheme has been made, there is a cost that future generations cannot escape. As Diamond (1998*b*; quoted by Orszag 1999: 26) puts it, 'The creation of individual accounts does not change the history that leaves Social Security with unfunded liability.'

Thus there is a zero-sum game between the first generation and subsequent generations. The burden of the gift to the first generation can be placed entirely on the transition generation of pensioners (generation B) by reneging on PAYG promises; or entirely on the generation of workers at the time of transition (generation C) by financing generation B's pension out of taxation; or by spreading the burden over succeeding generations by financing the transition through public borrowing. It is possible to alter the time path of the burden, but not its total. Again, the only way out of the impasse is if a move towards funding leads causally to higher rates of growth,[18] an issue on which, as discussed in Section 1.3, controversy continues.

Other aspects of comparison

Risk. The costs of financing the transition is one element in the comparison between PAYG and funding. A second element is risk, considered in detail by Geanakoplos, Mitchell, and Zeldes (1999). As discussed in Section 2.2 all pensions face uncertainty arising from macroeconomic, demographic, and political shocks. Holders of individual accounts, in addition, face management risk,

---

[18] Holzmann (1999) makes just such an argument.

investment risk, and annuities risk. PAYG pensions avoid the latter group of risks; and well-run schemes, by offering fully indexed pensions, also give protection against inflation. This is not the place for detailed discussion of the treatment of risk. All that needs to be said is that the real return both to PAYG and to funded schemes needs to be adjusted downwards to account for risk. In countries with effective government, the volatility of the tax base is less than that of the stock market and, to that extent, even at face value the gain from a switch to individual accounts is less than it appears.

ADMINISTRATIVE COSTS. Finally, the comparison between PAYG and individual accounts has to consider any differential in administrative costs. As already discussed (Section 2.3), the evidence that the administrative costs of individual accounts are higher—often considerably higher—than PAYG schemes is well established.

Thus it is possible that a full comparison—depending on country and circumstance—might show that a move to individual accounts might leave generation C and onwards with a *lower* level of welfare than staying with PAYG. The conclusion is *not* that moving to individual funds is necessary a bad policy, merely that the desirability of such a move cannot be established by a simple comparison of rates of return.

3. THE ROLE OF GOVERNMENT

3.1. *Myth 10: Private pensions get government out of the pensions business*

A final myth concerns the role of government, whose importance is now recognized by the 'Washington consensus'.

I argue that the failures of the reforms in Russia and most of the former Soviet Union are not just due to sound policies being poorly implemented. I argue that the failures go deeper, to a misunderstanding of the foundations of a market economy. . . . For instance, reform models based on conventional neoclassical economics are likely to under-estimate the importance of informational problems, including those arising from the problems of corporate governance; of social and organizational capital; and of the institutional and legal infrastructure required to make an effective market economy. (Stiglitz 1999, abstract)

Capitalism is revealed to require much more than private property; it functions because of the widespread acceptance and enforcement in an economy of fundamental rules and safeguards that make the outcomes of exchange secure, predictable, and of reasonably widespread benefit. Where such rules and safeguards, such institutions, are absent, what suffers is not just . . . equity, but firm performance as well. . . (Nellis 1999: 16)

Effective government is essential whichever approach to pensions is adopted. The problem of government failure is most obvious in the case of PAYG schemes built on fiscally irresponsible promises, coupled with an inability to collect contributions. Results include inflationary pressures and political instability. However, private pensions are also vulnerable. Fiscal imprudence leads to inflation that can decapitalize private funds; and inability to regulate financial markets creates inequity, and may also squander the efficiency gains that private pensions are intended to engender. As Thompson (1998: 22) puts it,

It is . . . too early to know how effectively the new systems based on the defined contribution model will be insulated from irresponsible behavior. Politicians are not the only people who are prone to promise more than they can deliver. The defined contribution model requires sophisticated oversight and regulation to ensure that one set of problems resulting from public sector political dynamics is not simply traded for a different set of problems derived from the dynamics of private sector operations.

In contrast, effective government is essential for both state and private schemes. Governments throughout the OECD are putting into place cost-containing measures in the face of demographic prospects (see UK Department of Social Security 1993). Reform in Canada and Sweden in the later 1990s and earlier reform in the UK are prime examples. Government capacity, similarly, is essential for effective private schemes. As Diamond (1995: 94) points out,

One advantage of investment in private assets is the potential contribution to the development of capital markets. This was a major benefit from the Chilean reform. But the capital market development did not come automatically from the introduction of the privately managed mandatory savings scheme. Extensive development of capital market regulation was a critical part of the privatization.

Two other issues should be considered in this context. It is sometimes argued that funded schemes are safer from government depredations than PAYG pensions. This is not necessarily the case. Governments can, indeed, break their PAYG promises; but equally they can reduce the real return to pension funds, either by requiring fund managers to hold government financial assets with a lower yield than they could earn on the stock market or by withdrawing or reducing any of the tax privileges the fund might have (the UK budget of July 1997 is an example of the latter).

A separate argument considers the role of government if things go wrong. It is argued that political pressure on government to repair ravages to a state scheme will be stronger than those to put right adverse outcomes in private schemes. Where there is an explicit government guarantee (as in Chile), this argument is obviously false. Though ultimately the matter is empirical, the argument might fail more broadly: the larger the share of the population with private pensions, and the greater the fraction of pension income deriving from private sources, the greater the pressure on government in the face of disaster. Just as PAYG is argued to represent implicit debt, so can it be argued that mandatory private pensions have a strong implicit state guarantee.[19]

The conclusion is that effective government is therefore critical:

- to ensure macroeconomic stability, which underpins well-run PAYG schemes and which is necessary to protect pension funds, which are sensitive to unanticipated inflation;
- to ensure regulatory capacity in financial markets for reasons of consumer protection.

Thus there is an inescapable role for the state in pensions even if one distrusts politicians.

---

[19] Heller (1998) distinguishes contingent and conjectural liabilities.

Chapter 8

Pension Design: The Options

1. LESSONS FROM ECONOMIC THEORY

The analysis of the previous two chapters points towards a number of positive conclusions that should particularly inform policy. These are summarized in Section 1. The following two sections discuss pension design, distinguishing factors that apply to *all* reforms, over which policy-makers have little choice, from those features over which policy-makers have explicitly to make choices. Discussion is organized in this way not only for logical but also for operational reasons. When advising governments, it is helpful to distinguish those areas where international organizations such as the World Bank and the IMF can legitimately thump the table (for example, in asserting that public pension spending must be compatible with economic growth) from those where they should tread carefully to avoid usurping the rights of sovereign states. These two very different aspects of advice are the subject matter of Sections 2 and 3, respectively. Section 4 draws together the main conclusions deriving from Chapters 6, 7, and 8.

THE CENTRAL VARIABLE IS FUTURE OUTPUT. As discussed in Chapter 6, Section 2, the possibilities for storing current output until old age are limited. Thus the only way to organize pensions on a large scale is through claims on future output. PAYG and funding are simply different ways of organizing such claims. Two implications follow. First, it should not be surprising that the two approaches fare similarly in the face of output shocks in general or demographic change in particular. Secondly, since future output is uncertain, all pension schemes, however organized, face uncertainty.

THERE IS A LARGE RANGE OF POLICIES TO INCREASE OUTPUT. As discussed in Chapter 7, Section 1.1, policies to increase output include those that increase the productivity of each worker, thus increasing real wages, W in Equation (7.1), and those that increase the number of workers from each cohort, thus increasing L.

A RANGE OF POLICIES CAN CONTAIN FISCAL PRESSURES. The fiscal position can be improved by reducing future pension spending directly. This can be achieved either by reducing the average pension, P in Equation (7.1), or by reducing the number of pensioners, N. Excessive reliance on the former may aggravate pensioner poverty and/or create political pressures. A better policy is to reduce N by raising the age of retirement, a desirable policy, it can be argued, in both fiscal and social-policy terms. This approach imposes the burden of adjustment on pensioners.

A second approach notes that what matters for incentive purposes is not public pension spending but total public spending. Higher pension spending in the future is possible if fiscal headroom can be increased by reducing some other spending. The example discussed earlier (Chapter 7, Section 1.2) is to reduce public debt now, thus reducing interest repayments in the future. This policy levels up taxation to a point between present levels and those that would apply in the future in the absence of any policy change. The cost of change is thus spread across generations of taxpayers.

A third way to contain the future burden of taxation is to set aside resources now to meet projected pension spending. Examples noted earlier include building up a surplus on the state PAYG scheme, as in the USA and Canada. Policies under this head may also include private pension accumulations.

The three approaches can, of course, be combined—for example, paying off some debt to allow fiscal smoothing, and raising the retirement age to share the burden with pensioners.

It follows from the previous paragraphs that there is a large range of policies to contain demographic pressures. The topic is take up in more detail in Chapter 9.

PENSIONS SHOULD BE DESIGNED WITH LABOUR-SUPPLY INCENTIVES VERY MUCH IN MIND. In contrast with the controversy over the incentive effects of pensions on saving and growth, the evidence on labour-market incentives is strong. Badly designed schemes—whether public or private, funded or PAYG—can create strong adverse incentives, both during working life and in respect of the age of retirement. Pensions should be designed to avoid such incentives, both through good design and through policies to ensure that perceptions (for example, of an actuarial relationship between contributions and benefits) accord with reality. Given the demographic prospects, pensions should offer encouragement to later retirement.

2. ESSENTIAL ELEMENTS IN PENSION REFORM

2.1. *Public-sector prerequisites*

The key prerequisites—public sector and private sector—for effective pension schemes are summarized in Table 8.1.

FISCAL SUSTAINABILITY OF THE STATE SCHEME. State pension promises must be fiscally sustainable in both the medium and long run. Sustainability is important,

Table 8.1. *Essential elements in pension reform*

Essential elements	Essential for state scheme	Essential for private schemes
Public-sector prerequisites		
Fiscal sustainability of state scheme	✓	
Political sustainability of pension reform package	✓	✓
Administrative capacity to enforce taxes/contributions	✓	✓
Capacity to maintain macroeconomic stability	✓	✓
Effective regulatory capacity		✓
Private-sector prerequisites		
Sufficiently well-informed population		✓
Adequate public trust in private financial instruments		✓
Financial assets		✓
Financial markets		✓
Private technical capacity		✓

because a central goal of policy is to increase living standards through economic growth. Whatever the debates about the effects of taxation on growth, there is no debate that beyond a certain point the deleterious effects of high taxation are devastating, as manifested, for example, by the growth experience of the transition countries during the latter days of communism. Thus public spending, and within that public pension spending, must be compatible with economic growth.

This emphasis on containing state pension spending is not intended as an attack on pensioners. Nor is it a statement that state pension spending in the long run should necessarily be minimized (as opposed to optimized). The World Bank's 1996 *World Development Report* (ch. 7) correctly talks about 'rightsizing' government, and makes it clear that economies can function well with governments of different sizes—but only within fiscally sustainable limits.

POLITICAL SUSTAINABILITY OF THE PENSION REFORM PACKAGE. Political sustainability has several essential ingredients. The first is strength of political will: there has to be sufficient political will to carry through the reform process. Thus domestic ownership of reform is important. A second aspect is the breadth of political support. It is not enough for the top echelons of government to understand the reform proposal. The idea and its implications must be understood throughout government *and* administration. Without that breadth of shared understanding, the original plan risks being implemented badly or, at worst, actively subverted by lower levels of government or administration. Equally vital, thirdly, is the duration of political support. Pension reform—whether large-scale reform of the state scheme or the introduction of private pensions—is not an event but a process. Reform does not end when the legislation is passed, but needs continuing commitment from government, both for technical reasons, to ensure necessary adjustments to reform proposals as events unfold, and for political reasons, to sustain continuing political support. Reform that is regarded as a single, once-and-for-all event runs the risk of neglect, discredit and eventual reversal.

The achievement of fiscal and political sustainability requires government capacity of the following three sorts.

ADMINISTRATIVE CAPACITY TO COLLECT TAXES AND ENFORCE CONTRIBUTIONS. Public pensions require government to be able to collect contributions; private schemes require government to have the capacity to enforce contributions. A country that cannot implement even a simple payroll tax cannot run a pension scheme. The issue then becomes one of how to organize poverty relief in a context of limited fiscal and administrative capacity, a topic with a huge, and entirely separate, literature.[1]

THE CAPACITY TO MAINTAIN MACROECONOMIC STABILITY is necessary to foster economic growth, as well as for long-run stability of PAYG finance. It is also of fundamental importance for private pensions, which are sensitive to unanticipated inflation.

EFFECTIVE REGULATORY CAPACITY. Effective regulation of financial markets is critically important for private pensions, to protect consumers in areas too complex for them to protect themselves. There should be annual statements giving details of a person's pension accumulation, predicted pension, and administrative charges. For this purpose it is essential that annual statements have a common format, and are based on common definitions of rates of return, inflation, and so on. Such transparency is essential to ensure that the claims of competitors are directly and precisely comparable. Chile sets a good example to more advanced countries, by requiring information to pensioners to be issued in a standard way; the UK government intends to introduce standardized annual statements from 2001.[2]

Such policies require tightly drawn-up regulatory procedures *and* a body of people with the capacity and will to enforce those procedures. The latter task is

---

[1] For discussion of poverty relief, see Ravallion (1996) and, for discussion in the context of transition countries, Chapter 15, Section 2.

[2] Hidden charges for private pensions have been a besetting problem in the UK. As an example of what is needed, credit-card companies in Western countries are all required to use the same definition in their promotional literature of the interest rate they charge customers, thus making it easy for people to see which company is offering the best rate. In contrast, the price structures of airlines and telephone companies are not comparable.

more difficult than it looks: precisely because private pensions are such complex instruments, regulators need to be highly skilled—the sort of skills with a high price in the private sector. There are at least three strategic problems: that the regulatory regime collapses (or is ineffective); where that problem is avoided, that the regulatory regime becomes *de facto* state control, with the pension provider acting, in effect, as an agent of the state; or, where that problem is avoided, that the management and regulation of pension funds crowds out other demands for scarce human capital.

These public-sector prerequisites are relevant, for the most part, both to state and private pensions. Private pensions have additional private-sector prerequisites.

2.2. *Private-sector prerequisites*

A SUFFICIENTLY WELL-INFORMED POPULATION. A number of points, though obvious, need to be stressed. First, private pensions require that both government and citizens are well informed about the operation of financial markets. In some less-advanced reforming countries there is still a belief, even at high levels in government, that, if a fund is 'private' and the money 'invested', a high real rate of return is inevitable, with no understanding either of the nature of the risk, or of the connection between financial variables and real variables such as national output and employment levels. Nor should this be regarded as a patronizing remark about poorer countries. The discussion in Chapter 6, Section 4, made clear the depth of ignorance about financial-market institutions even in countries such as the UK and USA.

ADEQUATE PUBLIC TRUST IN PRIVATE FINANCIAL INSTRUMENTS. Alongside knowledge about private financial instruments is a separate issue of public trust. Specifically, does the public trust the private sector at least as much as it trusts government?[3]

FINANCIAL ASSETS AND FINANCIAL MARKETS. Equally obviously, private schemes require financial assets for pension funds to hold and financial markets for channelling savings into their most productive use. Some apparent solutions are blind alleys. If pension funds hold only government bonds, this appears to address the lack of other financial assets. However, the resulting schemes are, in effect, PAYG, since the interest payments and subsequent redemption both depend on future taxpayers. Thus there is no budgetary gain, no channelling of resources

---

[3] Kazakhstan introduced a funded scheme based on government bonds in the late 1990s. Many people initially stayed in the government accumulation fund. Considerable pressure was put on people to move out of the government fund: a draft law in mid-2000 proposed that there should be no state fund, and that people would not be allowed to take a job until they had chosen their private fund.

into productive investment, and considerable extra administrative cost. It is sometimes argued that schemes based on government debt will encourage development of private financial assets—that is, that supply will create its own demand. This may, indeed, have happened in some countries. However, the root of private financial assets is progress in the private *real* economy (competitive markets, effective corporate governance, effective regulation, and the like). Though the market for public debt can be a useful benchmark market for the private sector, the logical priority of developments in the real economy is ignored at policymakers' peril.

Another apparent solution is to use the pension savings of a poorer country to buy Western financial assets. Bulgarian savings would go into (say) German firms, Bolivian savings into US firms, or Philippine savings into Japanese firms, thus getting round the absence of domestic financial assets and financial markets. The obvious argument against this approach is that it forgoes the growth of domestic investment and domestic employment that is part of the argument used in favour of private pensions. To get round this problem, it is argued (for example, by Kotlikoff and Seeger 2000) that poor countries should buy low-risk Western assets, offset by an inflow of Western capital better able to accommodate high-risk investments. In evaluating this argument (see also Holzmann 2000*b*), it is necessary to consider four aspects: the source of such funds, their volume, their composition, and their duration.

Kotlikoff and Seeger (2000) argue that the World Bank could '[use] its lending power to provide capital inflows that offset any short-term capital outflows'. However, international financial institutions offer loan capital not equity participation; thus a major stock-market crash would not exonerate Bulgaria, Bolivia, or the Philippines from repaying the loans that financed their purchases of foreign assets. The argument thus amounts to a poor country borrowing from the World Bank to finance the purchase of Western financial assets, rather than for domestic investment. This seems curious, to put it no more strongly. An alternative source of capital inflows are Western firms (for example, Volkswagen in Skoda) or Western venture capitalists. Further questions then follow.

Would Western capital inflows be large enough to offset capital outflows? The evidence, not surprisingly, is that inflows are determined by real, not monetary, factors. The countries with the largest per capita foreign direct investment are those that are doing best—for example, Hungary and Poland. Western capital flows are dictated by expected profit not by the unmet needs of a poor country's pension system. At best, the two are unrelated; more likely, they are inversely related.

Will Western capital inflows support industries with long-term growth potential? It is an oversimplification to consider investment only in aggregate terms; its composition in terms of static and dynamic efficiency is, if anything, even more important. A poor country's desired investment mix will be determined by a medium-term growth strategy, including essential physical infrastructure (roads, telecoms) and essential institutions (a tax system, legal structures). Western capital does not necessarily support such ventures; indeed, the historic *raison d'être* of the World Bank has been to provide loans for such activities precisely because private capital was not forthcoming in sufficient quantity on sufficiently good terms. Separately, Western capital would not contribute to the financing needs of small and medium-sized enterprises, from which most growth emerges.

Equally, the investment needs of a poor country have a medium- to long-term time horizon. Western capital is likely to have a short- to medium-term horizon.

None of this rules out the 'investment-swap' approach. Certainly, if a country meets the prerequisites for private, funded pensions, there is much to be said for at least partial international diversification of pension assets. But the microeconomic arguments call seriously into question the contention that a country needs virtually no domestic financial assets or financial markets. The prerequisites of financial assets and financial markets really *are* prerequisites.

PRIVATE TECHNICAL CAPACITY is essential, given the heavy demands of private pensions. First, does the private sector have the necessary financial-market skills? If not, the risk to the stability of pensions is obvious. Secondly, is private-sector administrative capacity adequate? A lack of capacity runs the risk that excessive administrative costs will erode the investment return to pensioners. Since there is a fixed cost to running an individual account, the issue is of particular concern for small pensions. At worst, deficient administrative capacity puts at risk the viability of private funds. Thirdly, even if private-sector capacity is adequate, is its deployment in managing private pensions its most welfare-enhancing use?

Table 8.1 summarizes the various prerequisites, and serves as a check-list for policy-makers contemplating pension reform and a guide to commentators assessing actual or proposed reforms. The table should serve as a reminder that implementation tends to be harder than policy design and that, not least for that reason, people with the relevant implementation skills need to be brought in from the beginning. If, for example, the objective is to introduce individual funded accounts, those skills include expertise in managing the administration of private pension accounts, practical experience of managing portfolios of financial assets, expertise in designing financial market regulation, and, separately, experience in enforcing it (itself dependent on the rule of law). Such technical expertise needs to be buttressed by political skills to ensure that support is sufficiently strong and enduring, and communication skills to ensure that people have a sufficient understanding of what is being proposed and can therefore give informed consent.

In meeting these prerequisites, advanced transition countries such as Poland and Hungary have the capacity for the sort of sophisticated reforms they are proposing.[4] It was precisely because of the demonstrable failure to meet several of the prerequisites that in 1998 the World Bank—courageously but completely correctly—withdrew its support for proposals to bring in mandatory second-tier private pensions in Russia. Reference to the same criteria calls seriously into question the strategic direction of reform in Kazakhstan, which has introduced private, funded pensions based largely on government bonds.[5]

These, then, are the areas in which policy advisers can legitimately be forceful. We turn now to those areas where advisers should tread with care.

3. POLICY CHOICES

3.1. *Building blocks*

A widely publicized World Bank study in 1994 (World Bank 1994*a*) 'recommended a multipillar pension system—optimally consisting of a mandatory, publicly managed, unfunded pillar and a mandatory but privately managed funded pillar, as well as supplemental, voluntary, private funded schemes. . . . We still conclude that the multipillar approach to pension reform is the correct one' (Holzmann 2000*a*: 12–13).

Taking a step back, the start of Chapter 6 put forward three primary objectives of pension systems: consumption smoothing, insurance, and poverty relief. Rational policy design starts by agreeing objectives and then proceeds to discussion of instruments for achieving them. The World Bank analysis, from this perspective, can be criticized because its categorization scheme focuses on instruments rather than objectives, and thus presupposes the choice, and to some extent also the mix, of instruments.

---

[4] Progress in Poland has been rapid. In January 1990, I was faced with a radical pension privatization proposal at a time when the monthly inflation rate was 80 per cent and when—since there were no financial markets—there was no financial market regulation, thus violating two essential prerequisites of private pensions. At that time I wrote in a World Bank report: 'The need to restructure the state pension scheme [in Poland] is urgent, and clear-cut recommendations for immediate action are [discussed in] Chapter 11. . . . Private pensions, in contrast, raise major issues which require detailed study beyond the remit of this report; moreover, the time scale for phasing in private pensions is longer term. For both reasons, this chapter seeks only to set out some of the central issues. Up to a point it indicates potential problem areas. The reason is not to discourage the development of appropriately designed complementary private schemes, but to counter excessive optimism in at least some quarters in Poland about how much can be achieved, and how soon. . . . The general thrust of the recommendations is that, over the medium term, the system of pensions should evolve into a system with three elements: a basic, state-run social insurance pension; a mandatory system of appropriately regulated complementary private pensions; and a system of voluntary private pensions. The balance between the three elements should be a matter for public debate' (World Bank 1993: para. 277). By 1998 the time for reform was right. For recent analysis, see Lindeman *et al.* (2000).

[5] Pension reform in the post-communist countries is taken up in more detail in Chapter 15, Section 3.

I shall categorize pensions in terms of objectives to avoid such presupposition.

- The first-tier pension is intended primarily to provide poverty relief. It is mandatory. Though normally publicly organized and PAYG, its form can vary widely.
- The second tier provides consumption smoothing and insurance; it can in principle be publicly or privately managed; it can be funded or PAYG; and it may or may not be integrated into the first tier.
- The third tier is private, funded, and voluntary, intended to increase the range of individual choice.

This categorization uses the word 'tier' rather than the World Bank's 'pillar' for two reasons. It is linguistically more apt: pillars can only be effective if they are all in place and all, broadly, of the same size; tiers, more appropriately in this case, are additive, in whatever constellation one wishes. Secondly, the word 'multipillar' has become identified with a particular form of pension reform; my preference is for a more neutral term.

The following questions about pension design far from exhaust the list.

How large should the first-tier pension be? A central question is whether the first tier should be a guarantee, available only (or mainly) to those who need it, or a base on which other pension income builds. In ascending order, the first tier could take the form of a state guarantee to individuals in private schemes, as in Chile, whereby only the least well off receive any state pension. Or the state pension could be awarded on the basis of an affluence test (that is, withdrawn from the best off), an example being Australia.[6] Somewhat less stringently, the first-tier pension could be flat-rate (hence going to all pensioners): it could be flat-rate below the poverty line (many poorer countries), equal to the poverty line (broadly the case in the UK), or above the poverty line (New Zealand). Whatever the design of the first-tier pension, a minimum income in old age can be guaranteed through tax-funded social assistance for those whose income from all other sources leaves them in poverty (most OECD countries).

How redistributive should the first tier be? There is less redistribution the smaller the pension and the greater the proportionality between contribution and benefit. Pensions strictly proportional to contributions bring about no redistribution between rich and poor except to the extent that the rich may live longer. Such proportionality can be achieved either through flat-rate pensions

---

[6] Suppose that there are three income groups, poor, middle income, and rich. The purpose of an income test is to ensure that only the poor get benefits; thus benefits are clawed back rapidly as a person's income rises. The purpose of an affluence test is different—to keep benefits out of the hands of the rich; thus benefits are clawed back less rapidly so that both poor and middle-income people receive benefit. For details, see Australia, Commonwealth Department of Family and Community Services (2000: table 1).

financed by flat-rate contributions or where both pension and contributions are proportional to earnings. A flat-rate pension financed by a proportional contribution will be more redistributive and a flat-rate pension financed from progressive general taxation more redistributive still.

Should there be a second-tier pension? The second-tier pension provides consumption smoothing. A libertarian approach argues for mandatory membership only so far as poverty relief is concerned.[7] Such a scheme would comprise mandatory membership of a minimal first-tier pension plus a third-tier (voluntary) private pension. The argument for a mandatory second-tier pension can be couched in a number of familiar ways: as a merit good (in other words, paternalism); because of myopia; because imperfectly informed younger people will make suboptimal choices from the perspective of lifetime utility maximization; to ensure insurance against unknowable events;[8] or to avoid moral hazard in the presence of a generous first-tier pension.[9] The issue has a significant normative dimension: an individualistic perspective points towards a voluntary third-tier pension, a paternalistic viewpoint towards mandatory consumption smoothing (for fuller discussion, see Agulnik 2000*a*).

If it is thought that there should be *some* compulsory consumption smoothing, a second question is whether compulsion should be applied only to provision up to some ceiling and, if so, what ceiling.

Should a second-tier pension be payg or funded? In the USA, the first- and second-tier pensions are rolled into one, both tiers being run mainly on a PAYG basis. In Canada, a first-tier state pension provides poverty relief and a mandatory, publicly organized, PAYG second-tier pension provides consumption smoothing. Other countries, in contrast, including Australia and several in Latin America, have privately managed, funded, mandatory second-tier pensions. The UK has a mixed system: the basic state flat-rate pension is mandatory; beyond that it is mandatory to belong either to the state earnings-related pension scheme (which is PAYG), or to an approved occupational scheme (private, funded, frequently defined benefit), or to contribute to an individual funded account.

Should the second tier be defined contribution or defined benefit? The issue here is how broadly should risks be shared. As discussed in Chapter 6, Section 3.2, individual funded accounts leave the individual facing most of the

---

[7] Though Libertarians generally oppose compulsion, it can be justified for the first-tier pension, even in Libertarian terms, because non-insurance imposes an externality. If someone chooses to make no pension provision, the costs of his decision fall on others, either on the taxpayer (if he is bailed out via social assistance) or, if he is not bailed out, on others, such as his family (if they thereby face starvation) or wider society (if he resorts to crime).

[8] This is particularly an argument for social insurance, which can address uncertainty as well as risk.

[9] The argument is that, if there is a minimum guarantee, low-income people will have little incentive to make voluntary provision.

risk, in particular of differential pension fund performance. The individual may also face the inflation risk, though this can be shared partly or wholly with the taxpayer if the state provides indexation. Occupational schemes are often defined benefit, thus sharing risks more broadly.

SHOULD THE SECOND TIER BE MANAGED PUBLICLY OR PRIVATELY? As just discussed, the second-tier pension is publicly managed in some countries—for example, the PAYG schemes in the USA and Canada. Singapore's Provident Fund, a form of compulsory saving scheme, is a publicly managed funded scheme. Many other countries, including Australia and Chile, have privately managed second-tier pensions.

SHOULD OPTING OUT OF STATE ARRANGEMENTS BE ALLOWED? The first-tier pension, which is redistributive, is by definition mandatory. Beyond that, the question is whether people should be allowed to choose whether consumption smoothing should be via a state pension or through private arrangements. In the UK, people can opt out of the state earnings-related pension and instead join a private scheme. In the USA and Canada, in contrast, membership of the state earnings-related scheme is compulsory. Part of the argument against opting out is that it opens up the possibility of adverse selection; part of the argument in favour is that it allows additional individual choice.

TO WHAT EXTENT DOES THE STATE ASSIST WITH INDEXING PENSIONS? Once a person has retired, pensions based on an annuity are vulnerable to unanticipated inflation. A major design question, therefore, is the extent to which government offers pensioners protection against inflation and through what mechanism. To the extent that government does participate, this introduces an unfunded element into funded schemes.

3.2. *Fitting the pieces together*

Pension design is controversial. Of the questions asked above—which far from exhaust the list—controversy swirls in particular round two sets of issues:

- Should the first-tier, mandatory, state PAYG pension be minimal or substantial?
- How should the second tier be organized—in particular, should it be mandatory, private, funded, and defined contribution?

The scale of the disagreement is illustrated by the following two quotes. According to James (1998: 275):

The first pillar resembles existing public pension plans, but is smaller and focuses on redistribution—providing a social safety net for the old, particularly those whose lifetime income was low. . . . this pillar is of limited scope.

The second pillar . . . links benefit actuarially to contributions in a defined contribution plan, is fully funded, and is privately and competitively managed.

A third pillar, voluntary saving and annuities, offers supplemental retirement income for people who want more generous old-age pensions.

In contrast, in the context of the reforming post-communist countries, Eatwell *et al.* (2000: 140–1) argue:

Clearly there is no 'ideal' model for pension reform . . .. however, the arguments developed earlier indicate the following course as being . . . the best approach for a country that has inherited a non-sustainable PAYG system:

• scaling down generosity towards pensioners. . .
• if there is a positive political assessment of the net advantages of a FF [fully funded] system, [this argues for] its introduction. . .
• the promotion of a third pillar of voluntary private savings, preferably with some tax privileges. . . .

The end result is a potential three-pillar system, apparently similar to that advocated by the World Bank (1994). . . . The third pillar of voluntary savings is, of course, always actually or potentially present . . . and cannot be considered as a distinctive feature of any reform. There are, however, very substantial differences between the recommendations listed above and those of the World Bank (1994) in that here:

• the first pillar is strengthened and maintained in its own right and with its own function. . .
• a FF component is introduced not as a technically superior solution but as a primarily political, though entirely respectable, solution . . . .

In many ways the potential range of choice is even wider. Even if each of the issues in the previous section is taken as a simple yes / no choice, the eight questions yield 256 possible combinations, the answers to which will depend on economic variables but also on a country's culture and history.

The following thumbnail sketches of pension systems in different countries are intended neither as detailed descriptions nor in any way as a compendious survey, but as illustrations of the wide range of schemes in the OECD and other successful economies.

CHILE. Under reforms that have become famous, pensions in Chile were privatized in the early 1980s. Employees are required to join an individual private, funded, defined-contribution scheme; workers pay 10 per cent of their earnings, plus a commission charge; there is no employer or government contribution. Workers can choose which scheme to join, and can change schemes. Upon retirement, the worker can buy an annuity or make a series of phased withdrawals. The pension is indexed to inflation, largely (though not wholly) on the basis of government-indexed bonds. There is a minimum guarantee: where a worker with twenty or more years of contributions has only a low pension, the state will bring it up to the guarantee level; the provision is intended to protect low earners, and also to protect contributors against poor performance by their chosen fund and pensioners against bankruptcy of the company paying their annuity. There are also generous, government-funded, transitional arrangements for workers transferring from the old (PAYG) scheme to the new scheme. In short, the second tier is a mandatory, privately managed, individual funded account; there is a residual first tier in the form of a guarantee to recipients of the second-tier pension. It is also open to workers to make additional, voluntary contributions.

The Chilean reforms continue to be widely discussed (for assessment, see Diamond 1996; Callund 1999). They are also controversial. To some, they are seen as a beacon of hope (World Bank 1994a): the reformed system, it is argued, imposed fiscal discipline, promoted savings, and widened and deepened capital markets, and hence contributed significantly to high growth rates in Chile over the 1980s; others are more sceptical (Beatty and McGillivray 1995).

In assessing the Chilean reforms, and the extent to which they may or may not be transferrable to other countries, a number of points are noteworthy.

- Because the system is based on defined contributions, the entire risk above the minimum pension is borne by the individual worker.
- The scheme is individualistic: there is redistribution neither within a generation (there is no redistribution from rich to poor except through the guaranteed minimum pension), nor between generations (pensions are indexed to prices, not wages, so that pensioners do not share in economic growth that takes place after their retirement).
- There are significant gaps in coverage, both because of non-compliance (that is, workers legally required to contribute who fail to do so) and because formal employment embraces only about 65 per cent of the workforce.
- Outcomes are sensitive to compliance rates, and also to real rates of return to pension-fund assets. On the latter, the average real rate of return to pension savings in Chile over the 1980s was 12.6 per cent per year. This is very high, and a key question is whether it is sustainable. Returns were not as high during the 1990s.
- Outcomes are also sensitive to design features. After contributing for a minimum of twenty years workers have some options to draw down their pension accumulation rather than buying an annuity. This can create an incentive to draw down the accumulation to the point where the government guarantee comes into play.
- The fiscal costs of the transition are high, including (a) the cost of pensions for older people who never transferred to the new system, (b) the cost of the transitional contribution for workers who switched to the new system,

(*c*) the cost of indexed bonds, and (*d*) any costs associated with the guaranteed minimum pension. The first two costs will eventually decline; the last two will continue in steady state. It is significant that the reform was introduced at a time when the government budget was running a surplus of over 5 per cent of GDP, giving room for the up-front costs of transition to the new system. Recent estimates (Arenas de Mesa and Marcel 1999: 4) show 'a fiscal imbalance of 6.5% of the GDP in the period 1981–98. The available projections indicate that this fiscal pressure is far from receding.'

SINGAPORE has a system in which workers and employers contribute to a Central Provident Fund (see Asher 1999). The Fund is run by the government, and each account attracts an interest rate decided by government.[10] It offers workers consumption smoothing not just for old age, but also for housing and medical expenditures. As such it offers no guarantee of old-age security. Singapore, like Chile, thus relies almost exclusively on a defined-contribution second-tier pension: most risk is borne by the individual worker, and the scheme is individualistic in the sense of embodying no redistribution. In sharp contrast with Chile, however, the fund is publicly managed.

SWEDEN introduced a 'notional defined-contribution' scheme in 1998 (Sweden, Federation of Social Insurance Offices 1998). The reforms have the following broad shape.

- The basic state pension remains PAYG, financed through a social-insurance contribution of 18.5 per cent of a person's earnings, of which 16 per cent goes into the public scheme.
- Though this year's 16 per cent contribution is used to pay this year's benefits, the social-insurance authorities open a notional (or virtual) individual account, which keeps track of contributions, just as for a 'real' fund. Specifically, each worker's cumulative account attracts a notional interest rate reflecting average income growth.
- At the time a person retires, she will have accumulated a notional lump sum. The resulting pension is calculated on the basis of the size of the lump sum, combined with expectations about the lifetime of the current cohort of retirees and output growth over the estimated period of retirement.
- The basic arrangements are adjusted in that there is a safety-net pension for people with low lifetime earnings, periods spent caring for children carry pension rights, and there is a ceiling on contributions.
- The remainder of a person's contribution (2.5 per cent of earnings) goes into a funded scheme: the individual can choose to place it in a privately managed individual account or in a government-managed savings fund.

---

[10] The process is *ad hoc* and far from transparent.

- The individual can choose to retire earlier or later, the pension being actuarially adjusted.

The idea of notional defined-contribution pensions is for social-insurance pensions to mimic an annuity, in that the pension a person receives (*a*) bears an explicit relationship to contributions, (*b*) is based on lifetime contributions, and is adjusted for (*c*) the life expectancy of the cohort and (*d*) economic developments. Individuals can respond (*e*) by adjusting their age of retirement. The introduction of element (*c*) is an important innovation.

Thus Sweden has a defined-contribution scheme with a safety-net guarantee, and is therefore a publicly organized, PAYG analogue of Chile. There are important arguments in favour of these arrangements.

- They simultaneously give people choice *and* face them with efficient incentives. For example, they assist choice about retirement by allowing people to choose their preferred trade-off between *duration* of retirement and *living standards* in retirement, but face them with the actuarial cost of those decisions.[11]
- The strong connection between contributions and benefits, as discussed in Chapter 7, Section 2.1, may assist labour-market efficiency.

These two advantages are common to the Swedish and Chilean approach. The Swedish approach has additional points that, depending on viewpoint, can be regarded as advantages.

- The scheme avoids the risks specific to private defined-contribution schemes.
- The scheme is individualistic to the extent that it is defined contribution; but the various credits (for example, for caring for young children) introduce an element of social solidarity.
- Being PAYG, the scheme avoids the transition costs of a move to funded arrangements.

These arguments point to something that is often overlooked—that there is much flexibility *within* PAYG schemes. Many of the problems of state social-insurance systems are not inherent in the social-insurance mechanism, but are soluble.

---

[11] The good feature of the Swedish scheme is that the pension formula takes account of the life expectancy of the cohort. However, the endogenous variable is not the minimum permissible age of retirement but the size of the pension. In a world of rationality and perfect information this would not be a problem; but, if people have a personal discount rate higher than the discount rate used for actuarial adjustment of the pension, they will continue to retire as soon as possible, with progressively larger actuarial adjustments. In the limit, this pulls everyone down to the minimum pension. I am grateful to Lawrence Thompson for this point.

AUSTRALIA is like Chile in the sense that its second-tier pension takes the form of mandatory membership of an individual funded account, but unlike Chile in that it has a much more fully articulated first tier (the Age Pension). The distinctive features of the latter are (*a*) that it is funded from general taxation and (*b*) is subject not to an income test (designed to restrict benefits to the poor), but to an affluence test, which has the more limited purpose of clawing back benefit from the rich. As a result, all but the best off receive at least some state pension. Since it is funded from taxation and is larger for less well-off Australians, the first-tier pension is strongly redistributive. The second-tier pension, like that of Chile and Singapore, faces the pensioner with the risk of differential pension portfolio performance and incorporates no significant redistribution.

NEW ZEALAND has a relatively generous universal flat-rate pension system (New Zealand Superannuation), supplemented by voluntary, funded, defined-contribution pensions. The flat-rate pension is PAYG, funded from general taxation, and included in a person's taxable income. Pensionable age is being increased from 60 to 65. The rate of pension is increasing towards a target of 65 per cent of average weekly earnings by 2001; once that target has been achieved, it is intended that pensions will be indexed to wage growth. There is some discussion of establishing a government-operated fund partially to pre-fund future pension spending.

Interestingly, a proposal to replace the state pension with mandatory, private, individual funded accounts along the lines of Chile was heavily defeated in a referendum in 1997; 80.3 per cent of the electorate took part, with 91.8 per cent of voters rejecting the proposal.

THE UK has a low flat-rate PAYG state pension. Under a 1980 reform, the pension was tied to changes in prices rather than wages. As a result, the state pension fell steadily as a percentage of average earnings. Someone whose only income is the basic state pension is eligible for income-tested social assistance—in other words, the state pension is below the poverty line. Superimposed on the basic pension is mandatory membership of a second-tier pension: people can choose whether to join the state earnings-related pension, an occupational (usually defined-benefit) pension, or an individual, defined-contribution pension.

THE USA has an earnings-related PAYG state scheme that is generous relative to a minimalist view, though not in comparison with a number of European countries. The scheme is redistributive: individual A, with twice the earnings of individual B, receives a pension that is larger than B's, but less than twice as large.[12]

---

[12] The pensions formula is applied to a person's indexed monthly earnings averaged over the thirty-five years with the highest earnings (call this W). The formula in 2000 was as follows:

$W < \$531$:   0.9$W$ *cont./*

Though it is possible to retire earlier, full pension is paid when a person retires aged 65, rising gradually to 67.[13] Many people also belong to a company or industry pension scheme and/or to an individual defined-contribution pension, such membership being voluntary so far as government is concerned. The US state scheme thus embraces both first- and second-tier pensions. Private schemes form a voluntary third tier.

4. CONCLUSIONS

The main lessons from economic theory were summarized in Section 1. More broadly, Chapters 6, 7, and 8 suggest the following conclusions.

TWO KEY VARIABLES. Effective pensions policy rests on two central factors.

- Policy depends critically on effective government, which is a prerequisite for well-run pensions, however they are organized (Ross 2000 reaches a similar conclusion). It is not possible to get government out of the pensions business.
- The key economic variable is output.

DEMOGRAPHIC CHANGE: A PROBLEM, NOT A CRISIS. Demographic change creates problems but, from an economic perspective, not insoluble ones. Policies range widely and can be used more or less in any combination. They include increasing output, reducing the average pension, increasing the age of retirement, adopting policies now to reduce future non-pension spending, and setting aside resources to meet future needs. Chapter 9 discusses these policies in more detail.

THE DIFFERENCE BETWEEN PAYG AND FUNDING IS SECOND ORDER. The debate between PAYG and funding concentrates on a very narrow part of the pensions picture: from a macroeconomic perspective the choice is secondary; the connection between funding and growth is controversial; and the issue, in any case, relates only to one of the sources of growth. There may, however, be important political-economy differences, depending on country and historical context.[14] It is argued, for example, that the political economy of raising the retirement age may be easier with a private scheme. In contrast, it can be argued that a state scheme that combines poverty relief and consumption smoothing, by embracing middle-class voters, will retain electoral support.

$531 < W < $3,202:	$0.9(\$531) + 0.32(W-\$531)$
$3,202 < W < $6,050:	$0.9(\$531) + 0.32(\$3,202-\$531) + 0.15(W-\$3,202)$
$W > $6,050:	$0.9(\$531) + 0.32(\$3,202-\$531) + 0.15(\$6,050-\$3,202)$

---

[13] If someone retires aged 62 with a full contributions record, her pension is 80 per cent of what it would be if she delayed retirement till age 65.

[14] For a political-economy analysis of PAYG schemes, see Cooley and Soares (1999).

Whatever the political arguments, the gains in terms of economic welfare of one pension arrangement as opposed to another is equivocal. Since PAYG and funding are simply different financial mechanisms for organizing claims on future output, this should not be surprising.

A GIVEN SET OF OBJECTIVES CAN BE ACHIEVED IN DIFFERENT WAYS. There is no one-to-one relationship between instruments and objectives.

Consider a scheme whose objectives include mandatory consumption smoothing with some redistribution and risk pooling. The USA achieves this through a mandatory, publicly organized PAYG pension embracing both poverty relief and consumption smoothing, and with the redistributive formula described earlier. The UK achieves a broadly similar objective for a significant fraction of pensioners through a combination of a flat-rate PAYG state pension broadly equal to the poverty line, together with privately organized, funded, defined-benefit occupational pensions. The pattern of replacement rates at different income levels is not, of course, identical in the two countries, but the pattern of retirement income has significant similarity.

Alternatively, consider a scheme whose objectives include actuarial, mandatory consumption smoothing with a safety-net provision. The aim in this case is to have a fairly strict separation of consumption smoothing and poverty relief, the latter being the only redistributive element in the scheme. Chile pursues this package of objectives through competitive, privately managed individual funded accounts, with a residual government guarantee. Sweden pursues broadly similar objectives through a publicly organized PAYG notional defined-contribution scheme together with a safety-net provision. The Swedish scheme introduces an element of solidarity in that years spent looking after children are counted as contribution years but, beyond that, is in major respects a public-sector analogue of arrangements in Chile.

THE RANGE OF POTENTIAL CHOICE OVER PENSION DESIGN IS WIDE. The key message of the previous section is not merely that one size does *not* fit all—which was always a foolish proposition—but that, provided government is effective, there is a considerable range of choice.

- The state pension should be *optimized*, not *minimized*. It can be smaller, as in Chile, where it takes the form of a minimum guarantee, or the UK, where it is close to the poverty line, or larger, as in the USA. It can be income tested (Chile), affluence tested (Australia), flat-rate (New Zealand), partially earnings related (USA), or fully earnings related (Sweden). In poorer countries, fiscal constraints point to a relatively small state pension; as countries become richer their range of choice increases.
- Consumption smoothing can be organized through a state PAYG scheme (Sweden), a state-organized funded scheme (Singapore), a mixture of state

PAYG and private, funded schemes (the UK or USA), or almost entirely by private institutions (Chile, Australia). Such pensions can be occupational, defined benefit (frequently in the UK), or individual defined contribution (Australia). In developing economies, capital markets tend to be less well developed, the capacity to regulate weaker, and the population less well informed; with economic and institutional development, the range of choice widens.

The wide range of choice, however, does not mean that countries can pick and mix at will.

- Countries with mature PAYG systems that face population ageing should adopt the range of policies discussed in the next chapter, which address the problem directly. The core policies (*a*) increase output and / or (*b*) reduce the generosity of PAYG pensions—for example, by raising the retirement age. Pre-funding could be one element in the policy mix.
- Countries with large, unsustainable PAYG systems have very little choice: the only solution is to make the PAYG system sustainable, by reducing benefits, by increasing contributions, or by a mix of the two. Since privatizing a PAYG scheme is much more expensive when it is bloated, making the scheme sustainable is essential, whether or not policy-makers wish aggressively to pursue a move towards private, funded arrangements.
- Countries with limited institutional capacity also have little choice. There is a significant element of progression: in the poorest, administratively weakest countries, the issue is how to organize poverty relief; as taxable capacity increases, the next step might be a tax-funded citizen's pension; growing public administrative capacity makes it possible to implement a contributory system; with rising income, growing private administrative capacity, and effective rule of law, private pensions become an option.
- A country with a small public system and relatively solid public and private administrative capacity has the greatest potential choice. Provided it meets the prerequisites discussed in Section 2, there is a genuine choice of balance between PAYG and funded arrangements. This chapter has argued that from an *economic* point of view there is no dominant policy. That being the case, the best choice is that which accords best with the political economy of effective reform. This, in turn, will depend on country specifics.

Chapter 9

Twenty-First-Century Pensions Issues

Paying for pensions in the face of population ageing (Section 1) already absorbs much analytical energy, and will continue to do so. Alongside this largely macro-economic question, the separate issue of how to design pensions in the face of social change (Section 2) will become increasingly important.

1. POPULATION AGEING: ARE PENSIONS AFFORDABLE?

Demographic change arose repeatedly in the previous three chapters. The facts are not controversial: declining birth rates and increasing life expectancy in many countries mean that the population is ageing, so that in the near future the number of people of pensionable age will increase—in some countries sharply—relative to the number of workers. The logic of earlier argument suggests a range of policies. It is open to policy-makers to use some or all of them, and to use them pretty much in any combination.

POLICY 1: INCREASE OUTPUT. A central conclusion of earlier discussion is that what matters is the size of national output, not the size of the pile of money that individuals accumulate. It is true that an individual can build power over future consumption by accumulating financial assets that she sells in retirement to pay for her consumption. A country as a whole cannot do this; what matters is not financial assets but real output.

As discussed in earlier chapters, in a balanced PAYG scheme

$$sWL = PN \qquad (9.1)$$

where $s =$ the PAYG social-security contribution rate
$\qquad W =$ the average real wage
$\qquad L =$ the number of workers
$\qquad P =$ the average real pension
$\qquad N =$ the number of pensioners.

The range of policies to increase output were discussed in Chapter 7, Section 1.1. They include policies to increase the productivity of each worker (thus increasing W) and policies to increase the number of workers from each age cohort (increasing L). Policies of the first sort include (*a*) more and better capital equipment and (b) increasing the quality of labour through investment in workers' human capital. Policies of the second sort include (c) policies to increase labour supply (better childcare facilities, tax policies that do not militate against part-time employment), (d) raising the age of retirement, (e) importing labour directly, and (f) importing labour indirectly by exporting capital to countries with a young population.

There is a major intellectual and policy bloodbath about whether a move from PAYG pensions to funded arrangements does much to improve matters. As discussed in Chapter 7, Section 1.1, funding is irrelevant to policies (b)–(e), and is not fundamental for (f). Thus there are only two reasons why a move to funding might be part of a strategy to address demographic change. First, it might increase output; if so, that would be a major benefit and an important argument for changing the balance between PAYG and funding. As discussed in Chapter 7, Section 1.3, however, both theory and empirical evidence are far from definitive. There is some evidence that funding increases saving in the USA, but that evidence is controversial, and there is no robust evidence from other countries of any similar effect. The argument should therefore be made with caution.

A second reason for a move to funding is political. As discussed in Chapter 7, Section 1.1, unless it leads causally to output being higher than it would otherwise have been, funding does nothing to address the problems of pension finance caused by population ageing. Demographic change puts funded pensions under pressure in exactly the same way as PAYG pensions, and for exactly the same reason—a shortage of output. In the case of funding, however, the effect is less transparent. Thus it can be argued that a move to funding makes it politically easier to 'sell' a reduction in pensions, since politicians can claim that the decline is the result of market forces rather than political decision.

POLICY 2: REDUCE THE AVERAGE PENSION. Depending on circumstances, it may be possible to reduce the size of the average pension, P, in Equation (9.1). The advantage is the direct and immediate effect on pension spending. The disadvantages are that such moves may be politically unpopular, and that they might aggravate pensioner poverty. There are various ways of reducing pensions less drastic than announcing an immediate 10 per cent cut. Government can make the indexation provisions less generous—for example, raising pensions in line with prices rather than wages. Such a measure protects the real consumption of pensioners, but means that pensioners fall further and further behind average living standards. A second method is to change the period over which benefits are calculated. Pensions based on a person's final wage, or his wage over the best three years, will be higher than one based on a longer averaging period; extending the averaging period to (say) twenty years, or to a person's entire working life, thus reduces pensions. Thirdly, as just mentioned, a move to funding might make smaller pensions politically easier, because the mechanism leading to that decline is less transparent than with PAYG arrangements.

POLICY 3: INCREASE THE AGE OF RETIREMENT. An increase in the retirement age simultaneously reduces the number of pensioners, N, *and* increases the number of workers, L, in Equation (9.1). If pensions remain constant, pension spending falls in proportion with the decline in N, while output, and hence the contributions base, increases. It is, of course, true that raising pensionable age is politically sensitive. But various countries have managed to do so: the UK is implementing a phased increase in women's retirement age from 60 to 65 to bring it into line with the retirement age for men; the USA is increasing normal retirement age in stages to 67; and various of the reforming post-communist countries are phasing in later retirement.

In thinking about the 'proper' age of retirement, the historical context is relevant. New Zealand, one of the earliest countries with a state pension, introduced a non-contributory benefit in 1898, not least for reasons of national efficiency, in the face of increased international competition on an economy highly dependent on its exports. In other words, the purpose of the pension was to get allegedly doddering old workers off the farm or factory floor, where they were hampering the efficiency of younger workers. Today workers in industrial countries retire long before they reach that stage, and can thus enjoy a long, active retirement; this outcome is one of the fruits of rising real income and one of the major successes of the twentieth century. It does not, however, follow, that there is anything immutable about a retirement age of 65. As life expectancy increases, it is rational for the retirement age to move upwards.

In many ways, the retirement age is the key variable in addressing demographic change. In economic terms it has a powerful and immediate effect on pension finance. In social policy terms, as discussed earlier (Chapter 7, Section 1.5), it is a rational response to improved health and increasing life expectancy over the twentieth century. State pensions in the twenty-first century should embody an endogenous retirement age—that is, should have a retirement age explicitly related to life expectancy. As a result, longer life (arguably the largest increase in well-being of all) would be shared between working life and retirement.

POLICY 4: TAKE STEPS NOW TO REDUCE FUTURE NON-PENSION SPENDING. Policy-makers worry about the effect of population ageing because of the potential adverse incentive effects of the increase in the social-insurance contribution made necessary by the increase in the ratio of pensioners to workers. However, as pointed out earlier (Chapter 7, Section 1.2), incentives are determined not by the social-insurance contribution rate, s, but by the total tax rate, t, which workers have to pay on any increase in their earnings. It is possible to create fiscal headroom to allow an increase *s* without any increase in *t* by reducing other spending. One way of reducing non-pension spending in the future is to increase repayments on government debt now; thus, in the future, when demographics are at their worst, government spending on debt interest will be lower, freeing resources to pay for pensions.

POLICY 5: SET ASIDE RESOURCES NOW TO MEET FUTURE NEEDS. It is possible to spend more on pensions without any increase in *s*, if some other source of revenue can be found. One way to accumulate resources is through pension funds, but there are others. A country can build a surplus on its state pension (as in Canada and the USA) partially to pre-fund anticipated increases in pension spending. Alternatively, it can top-slice some other source of revenue (Norway does so with oil revenues) to build a fund. However, unless these measures increase output, they are a zero-sum game between workers and pensioners: at a given level of output, if pensioners consume more, workers have to consume less. Thus setting aside resources in advance is only a partial solution unless those resources are used to increase output.

POLICY 6: FLEXIBLE RETIREMENT. In strict economic terms, this approach is a particular case of increasing the retirement age, but merits separate discussion. Labour-market institutions in Western industrial society have significant inflexibilities. As discussed at the start of Chapter 3, there tends to be a binary distinction between employment and unemployment. The same tendency is true of the work/retirement decision: a person is either in the labour force working full time, or retired and not working at all. Separately, there is a convention that a person's peak earnings will tend to be in the later stages of his or her working life.

This approach is not necessarily rational. In some types of job a person's peak productivity is in his or her middle years; and as people age many would like to continue to work, but perhaps at a reduced rate. This suggests a need for more flexible ways of combining work and pension: a person in middle years would work full-time at peak productivity; a very old person would be fully retired; in between there would be no moment at which a person is forced to make a binary choice, but instead a more gradual transition from work into retirement, with flexibility both over hours of work and the wage rate. It would become much more normal, for example, for a senior and highly paid full-time worker to move to a job that was less demanding qualitatively, less highly paid, and/or with working fewer hours. As discussed below, there is already some movement in this direction, but with scope for more. This policy direction, by undoing the social risk, would unambiguously increase well-being: it leads to more efficient use of labour; depending on how pensions are calculated, it reduces pressures on pension finance; and there are major gains in terms of increased individual choice.

Thus there are at least six policy directions that government can follow. The conclusion to which they lead is that population ageing is, indeed, a twenty-first-century problem. But it is a problem with a range of solutions that—depending on economic, political, and social conditions in a country—can be pursued separately or together. In short, there is a problem but, at least in the advanced industrial countries, not a crisis.

2. PORTABLE PENSIONS: THE WELFARE STATE AS SNAIL SHELL

2.1. *The issue*

Social policy in industrialized countries after the Second World War was based on a number of (usually implicit) assumptions:

- The world was made up of independent nation states, so that constraints on economic policy were largely domestic.
- Employment was a binary phenomenon: a person who was active in the labour market would be employed full-time, or would be unemployed.
- The nuclear family was the typical social arrangement, with divorce rare.

These assumptions[1] were not wholly true even in the immediate post-war years, but they were true enough. Over the second half of the twentieth century, three sets of changes made them increasingly untrue in ways that have major implications for policy.

International competitive pressures increased. Nations became more interdependent, reducing (though, as argued in Chapter 16, not eliminating) national autonomy. The change was in part the result of policy developments, particularly the extension of international capital mobility. It was also a direct result of technological advance, in particular instant worldwide communication and the fact that output consists increasingly of information. As a result, much economic output is now binary digits (television programmes, stock-market prices) and hence 'dematerialized' (Quah 1996). These changes have major implications, making international boundaries for certain purposes more porous. Governments can still have independent economic policies up to a point, but not to the same extent as hitherto.

Secondly, labour markets became more fluid, with more entry and exit, both by choice (longer education) and by constraint (higher unemployment); and there is more part-time work, again both by choice and by constraint. These changes make it important to have arrangements that do not distort between part-time and full-time work, that are portable between jobs and between em-

---

[1] In the UK context, these assumptions underpinned the analysis of the Beveridge Report (1942).

ployment and self-employment, and that cumulate easily across different patterns of labour-market activity. Given the internationalization just described, arrangements need also to be able to cope with international labour mobility.

Thirdly, the nuclear family came to have neither the stability nor the numerical dominance it had in the mid-twentieth century. Fluid family structures require arrangements that are based on the individual rather than the family. As an example, husband and wife should each have their own pension, rather than the pension arrangements of one being deemed to cover both.

Though oversimplified, it is possible to summarize these changes as moves towards *individualization* and *internationalization*. The two forces together imply a world in which, to a greater extent than previously, people need to be able to carry their welfare state on their back like a snail shell. Specifically, in the present context, the question is how to design pensions that are (*a*) individual, to accommodate changing family structures, and (*b*) portable between jobs, between types of employment, and between countries, but that nevertheless (*c*) can genuinely address individual risk and uncertainty.

The important distinction between defined-contribution and defined-benefit pensions was explained in Chapter 6, Section 3.2, and discussed in more detail in Chapter 7, Section 2.2. Under the first, the contribution rate is fixed, so that, other things being equal, a person's pension depends only on the size of the pensions pot she has accumulated during working life; thus the individual faces the risk that her pension fund might do badly. With a defined-benefit scheme, usually run at industry level, the pension scheme pays an annuity related to the person's wage and length of service; thus the risk that the pension fund will do badly falls on the industry.

The following discussion assumes a world where people have both a state pension and a private pension. Private, defined-contribution schemes, private, defined-benefit schemes, and state PAYG schemes are discussed in Sections 2.2, 2.3, and 2.4, respectively. The parallel issues faced by student loans are discussed in Chapter 14, Section 2.

2.2. *Defined-contribution schemes*

Current schemes

The major advantage of defined-contribution schemes is that they adapt well to a new world, but at the price of making the individual bear the risk that the pension fund will not do well, thus undermining their core purpose of consumption smoothing.

With a defined-contribution scheme, my pensions pot is genuinely mine. My contributions go into it each year, as do those from my employer. Employer contributions may have a vesting period (five years is common). If I leave before five years, the employer contributions are removed from the pot, but mine remain. After five years all the contributions are mine; if I move to a new job, I continue to pay contributions into the same pot, together with contributions from my new employer. Thus (subject to any vesting constraints) all accrued rights are preserved, hence there are no impediments to labour mobility.

Towards an individual and internationalized world
The analogy with a snail shell is most obvious with individual, defined-contribution schemes. A movement towards individual arrangements in the face of global pressures would have the following broad shape.

INDIVIDUAL PENSION POTS. Everyone would have his or her own individual pension accumulation within a properly regulated regime. Contributions would be put into the pot by the individual, his or her employer(s) and/or government, the last, for example, in the form of tax concessions or, as advocated by Agulnik and Le Grand (1998), a matching grant.

PENSIONS AND FAMILIES. What is needed is a form of pension arrangement that preserves pension rights in an equitable way in the face of fluid family structures. There are several ingredients. Government might make direct payments into a person's pension accumulation in recognition of family responsibilities—for example, a person who stays at home to bring up young children.[2]

Secondly—and essentially if private schemes are to match family responsibilities— half of the husband's pot would be tipped each year into the wife's pot, and half of the wife's pot would be tipped each year into the husband's pot.[3] This arrangement has important advantages: the wife builds up pension rights proportional to the duration of the marriage, and divorce is transparent with respect to pensions, directly addressing the fluidity of family structures. Secondly, a wife's pension rights are protected while she stays at home looking after children, and similarly for a male homemaker. Thirdly, in so far as pensions are concerned, the costs of having children fall on both partners, since, if the wife is not working, the husband does not receive half of her pension accumulation. A number of questions remain, notably connected with cohabitation. One solution might be to require partners to share pension contributions if they are married or if they have a child.[4]

---

[2] In the UK state scheme, a woman who stays at home bringing up young children receives home responsibility protection, under which she is deemed to have paid social-insurance contributions, thus at least partially protecting her right to a state pension. What is being discussed here is the private-sector analogue. The only difference is that the government's transfer is an actual, rather than a deemed, contribution.

[3] This arrangement formalizes recent developments in divorce arrangements in the UK, USA, and elsewhere—namely, that upon divorce part of the husband's pension rights are transferred to the wife.

[4] That said, detailed work would be needed to fine-tune the equity of pension arrangements—for example, where one unmarried partner looks after a child from his or her partner's previous relationship, or as between same-sex partners.

PENSIONS IN AN INTERNATIONAL WORLD are not a problem. If I emigrate to the USA, matters could be arranged so that I have an undistorted choice between (*a*) leaving my pension pot in the UK, eventually to generate a UK annuity, or (*b*) transferring my pension pot to the USA and adding to it in the USA, leading eventually to a US annuity.

Design problems

Thus the good news is that defined-contribution pensions can readily be made compatible with labour mobility, fluid family structures, and internationalism. The bad news is that the individual faces more risk than under a defined-benefit scheme. This is a genuine and major issue. Uncertainty—particularly uncertainty about a large part of one's income in old age, and for potentially many years of retirement—causes major welfare losses. Indeed, it is the size of those losses that leads people voluntarily to buy insurance. However, in this case, insurance is not possible, because what is involved is not risk but uncertainty: the probability distribution of different stock-market outcomes is unknown; the same is true about future levels of inflation; and both variables, particularly for a young person, have a very long time horizon.

The question, therefore, is whether it is possible to capture the advantages of defined-contribution schemes, while avoiding or minimizing the disadvantage of uncertainty. To do so means that the individual needs some sort of guarantee. There are various ways of doing this.

THE FALKINGHAM–JOHNSON APPROACH. Falkingham and Johnson (1995) analyse what they call a Universal Funded Pension Scheme—a funded pension that replaces the PAYG state pension. In their proposals, the state gives a guarantee that the funded pension will pay a pension of (say) 30 per cent of the average wage at retirement. If necessary, the state contributes to the individual's pension pot either at retirement or during working life (for example, for a person who is unemployed or bringing up young children). Contributions of the latter type could be clawed back if, in the end, they turned out to be unnecessary to achieve the promised 30 per cent replacement rate—in other words, there would be a lifetime means test. One of many issues the scheme raises is that the guarantee might encourage pension funds to invest in inefficiently risky pension assets.

A SOCIAL-INSURANCE APPROACH. The argument (which I have not seen anywhere in the literature[5]) is illustrated in terms of a person with a full contributions record through his own work, his partner's work, and/or any government contributions; the target is a pension of 30 per cent of the person's previous wage; and there is a guarantee (discussed below) of 25 per cent of the person's previous

---

[5] A rash statement—counter-evidence gratefully received.

wage; thus individuals who invest in a fund that does badly face *some* of the cost of that decision, and therefore have an incentive to choose well. All these numbers, and those that follow are purely illustrative.

The source of the guarantee in this case is not the taxpayer, but people whose pension funds do best. For example, a small percentage levy could be imposed on this year's income of the pension fund of anyone whose fund this year performed one standard deviation or more above the average for all pension funds. The levy would be used to top up the funds of those people whose funds performed so badly as not to give them even a 25 per cent replacement rate. The levy can be thought of as an insurance premium, since the individual is accepting a lower return in exchange for certainty. The arrangement would probably have to be compulsory, so that what emerges is a form of social insurance.

Note that this arrangement is *not* redistributive from rich to poor but—as is the essence of insurance—from lucky to unlucky—that is, from people (whether rich or poor) whose pension fund does particularly well to those (rich or poor) whose pension fund does particularly badly. Thus the guarantee relates not to income level but to pension portfolio performance. As with all social-insurance arrangements, there is a good case for a ceiling on such transfers to avoid giving help beyond a certain level to a millionaire whose pension fund has had a bad year.

A GUARANTEED MINIMUM RATE OF RETURN. In contrast with the Falkingham–Johnson arrangements, suppose that there is a state pension, the effect of which is to ensure that everyone has an income in old age at least equal to the poverty line. Thus the state pension deals with poverty relief, leaving consumption smoothing to private arrangements. In that case, the simplest way to provide an element of certainty is through defined-contribution pensions with a guarantee of an x per cent *real* rate of return on its assets.[6] The guarantee could have a social-insurance element, but would be financed most simply out of taxation. Again, there is a good case for a ceiling on the guarantee. The effect of such a scheme would be to give certainty with respect to downside risk: a person could make his or her consumption-smoothing decisions assuming an x per cent return; if the pension fund did better than the guarantee, the extra would be a bonus.

2.3. Defined-benefit schemes

Current schemes

Here the balance of advantage is exactly the opposite: defined-benefit schemes give individuals considerable certainty about living standards in old age, fulfilling the fundamental objective of consumption smoothing. That advantage, how-

---

[6] A similar sort of scheme has been advocated and worked through in some detail by Modigliani *et al.* (2000); see also Muralidhar and van der Wouden (1998*a*, *b*).

ever, comes at a price of significant impediments to labour mobility and some inflexibility in the face of fluid family structures.

So far as certainty is concerned, suppose my pension scheme promises me one-eightieth of my final salary per year of service, plus a pension indexed to inflation. If I retire after forty years' work, I know that my pension will be half my final salary and will be immune to inflation. Thus the risk of differential pension portfolio performance and the risk of inflation pass from the individual to the employer, and hence, as explained in Chapter 6, Section 3.2, fall on some or all of the industry's workers, shareholders, or customers, or on past or future workers, shareholders, or customers if the industry uses pension-fund surpluses in one period to finance deficits in others.

There are also disadvantages. First, there are rules about vesting rights, which specify at what stage the accumulated funds becomes the worker's. In the past the vesting period could be long, inhibiting labour mobility. A second problem is the protection of a worker's accumulated rights if he changes job; in the past, those rights received little protection—for example, they were often not indexed—again, inhibiting labour mobility. Both sets of problems have now largely been dealt with in most OECD countries by legal changes that require a fairly short vesting period and significant protection of accumulated rights if a worker moves to another job.

A third disadvantage is harder to deal with, and is best shown by example. Consider the pension scheme described above, with an annual accrual rate of $1/80$th of final salary per year of service; assume that there is no inflation and no transfer of pension rights between different schemes.[7] If I work at the London School of Economics (LSE) for 20 years during which time my salary rises from 100 to 200, I accumulate a pension entitlement of $(20/80) \times 200 = 50$.

Suppose that, after 20 years, I face a choice of staying at the LSE or moving to another job. If I stay, my salary over my last 20 years rises from 200 to 400, and my pension on retirement is $(40/80) \times 400 = 200$. Alternatively, if I move to a different job with a similar increase in pay and a similar pension scheme, my pension accumulation in the new job is $(20/80) \times 400 = 100$.

If I stay at the LSE, I therefore retire on a pension of 200; if I move in mid-career, my final pension, under the stated assumptions, is 150, 50 from my initial 20 years at LSE plus 100 from my final 20 years in the new job. The problem, obviously, is that the design of the pension scheme inhibits labour mobility.

Towards an individual and internationalized world
How might defined-benefit pensions be adapted to a new world?

---

[7] As discussed in Chapter 6, Section 3.2, there are other ways of designing defined-benefit schemes—for example, basing pension on a longer averaging period. These are not discussed here.

LABOUR MOBILITY. The only way to ensure that there is no impediment to labour mobility is through full transferability of accrued rights between pension schemes. Thus a person's pension depends only on his or her earnings record and length of service, but not on the number of job changes. Requiring full transferability between schemes, however, creates problems. If different firms have different pension schemes, an employer with a generous scheme faces a large bill when taking on workers with rights accrued in less generous schemes. The employer might on that account be reluctant to take on such workers, bringing back labour immobility by another route. One way of avoiding the problem is convergence between employer schemes. But one of the major purposes of employer schemes is precisely to enable the firm to attract and retain workers; if a defined-benefit scheme—because pressures make them all similar—cannot achieve that purpose, it is not clear why employers would wish to operate one; in doing so, they face the extra risk of the scheme relative to a defined-contribution scheme, but with none of the advantages. It is not clear that much headway can be made in addressing this problem.

PENSIONS AND FAMILIES. Just as there are non-linearities in dividing pension rights between employers, similarly, there are non-linearities in dividing them between family members. The issue is becoming salient in the UK in respect of accrued defined-benefit pension rights when a couple divorces. If the divorce occurs midway through a career, valuation of the pension accumulation, and hence of (say) the wife's share, is problematical, because it depends, *inter alia*, on what happens to the husband's pay during the second half of his career. An obvious way to deal with this difficulty is to leave the husband's pension untouched and to divide the pension when it is actually paid. That, however, runs counter to the trends towards 'clean-break' divorces, and also raises significant issues of enforcement. Again, there is no easy answer.

PENSIONS IN AN INTERNATIONAL WORLD. Suppose that I move from a UK job with a defined-benefit pension to a similar job in Australia. Again, problems arise over the valuation of my accumulated UK rights. The problem could be solved by transferable rights, but the resulting difficulties, discussed above, are vastly more intractable in an international context.

The conclusion (which I reach with considerable reluctance given their major advantages in terms of certainty) is that private defined-benefit schemes do not fit well with a world of individual entitlements, fluid families, flexible labour markets, and international mobility.

2.4. *State pensions*

Current schemes
In the early 2000s, state schemes, still based on the implicit assumptions discussed in Section 2.1, face predictable problems. Workers with patchy employment records and hence patchy contributions records have only a patchy entitlement to a pension. Non-working wives are entitled to a pension on the basis of their husband's contributions; not the least of the problems of such an arrangement is that it leaves wives stranded without entitlement to a state pension upon divorce in mid-life. Nor do pension rights extend to non-married partners. Separately, state pensions are generally national as opposed to international. A person who lives abroad after retirement can normally have his pension remitted to him. However, there is no international transfer of contributions. If I work for the first twenty years in the UK and the next twenty years in the USA, I end up with incomplete contributions records in both countries.

Towards an individual and internationalized world
How might state PAYG pensions be adapted?

LABOUR MOBILITY. A major advantage of state-organized schemes is that—in sharp contrast with private arrangements—defined benefits do not cause labour immobility. A person changes job but not pension scheme and, as a result, his pension depends on his contributions record, which in turn depends on the size and continuity of his wages, but is entirely invariant to the number of jobs he has held.

PENSIONS AND FAMILIES. Can PAYG pensions be organized on an individual basis? To some extent this is happening already: more and more women spend time in the labour force, and time spent at home looking after young children counts as contribution years. Thus more and more women are entitled to a pension in their own right. One way to ensure that everyone, irrespective of family arrangements and changes in those arrangements, has his or her own pension is through a tax-funded, flat-rate citizen's pension (as discussed in Chapter 8, Section 3.2, New Zealand has such an arrangement). Other measures are more complex. It might be possible to devise arrangements, analogous to those set out in Section 2.2, whereby half of a husband's social-insurance contributions is credited to his wife's account, and vice versa.

PENSIONS IN AN INTERNATIONAL WORLD. Increasing international labour mobility makes it desirable that a person can transfer his or her social insurance contribution record, so that rights to a state pension are transferrable across countries. There is, of course, nothing to stop countries granting reciprocal entitlement to each other's citizens, a development that is already beginning within the European Union. Transfers across a wider group of countries, however, face problems. First, any such agreement needs political will, which may or may not be forthcoming. Secondly, a country with generous pensions might be unhappy about a large influx of people from countries with less generous arrangements. Even more difficult, someone from the USA who moves to the UK midway through her working life, might be profoundly unhappy about transferring rights from a more to a less generous scheme.

2.5. *Conclusion*

There can be a mismatch between two sets of needs, the technical requirements of actuarial insurance, and the aims of social policy. Difficulties arise because the two sets of needs do not always match, and because wishing does not make it so. It is no good criticizing insurance companies for failing to meet social policy objectives, still less ignoring social-policy needs because actuarial insurance cannot cope. What is needed is a bridge between the two sets of objectives, at which this chapter is an early foray.

The preceding discussion suggests two sets of questions.

Can state pensions be adapted to a world with flexible labour markets, fluid family structures, and international competition? The discussion in Section 2.4 suggests that PAYG defined-benefit pensions run by the state are automatically compatible with labour mobility within a country. They can, though only up to a point, be adapted to fluid family structures. Where they fall down (except perhaps eventually within the European Union) is in respect of people who work for extended periods in different countries. The conclusion is that progress is possible, but without any complete solution.

Going down the route of private pensions, how can one combine their advantages in terms of flexibility with an element of social solidarity sufficient to allow them to fulfil their primary purpose of consumption smoothing? The scope for fitting private defined-benefit schemes to new realities is limited: they are likely to be a continuing impediment to labour mobility nationally and internationally; and their equitable division within the family will remain problematical. Defined-contribution schemes can readily be adapted: they are more or less automatically compatible with national and international labour mobility, and they can be divided within the family.

The conclusion to which this points is a system entirely compatible with the range of arrangements discussed in Chapter 8, Section 3.

- A state-organized, defined-benefit scheme should provide poverty relief, and perhaps also an element of consumption smoothing.

- Defined-contribution, private, funded schemes *plus* a guaranteed *real* return would support labour mobility and can be structured to share pension pots equitably and transparently within different types of family arrangement. In the absence of such a guarantee, or where the guarantee is inadequate, the gains in terms of flexibility have to be weighed against the costs of the uncertainty individuals face. In contrast, so long as the guarantee is sufficient, it establishes a realistic, predictable minimum on the real annuity a person can expect, giving a considerable measure of certainty and thus enabling pensions to fulfil their primary objective of consumption smoothing.

PART 4

EDUCATION

In the world of certainty described in the Fisher model at the start of Chapter 2, people finance their education by borrowing in perfect capital markets against their future income, and such voluntary choices are efficient. Once risk, uncertainty, and imperfect information enter the picture, that result no longer holds, and state intervention is needed in a variety of ways to give people a mechanism for moving resources to their younger years. Chapters 10 and 11 point to problems of imperfect information, risk, and uncertainty facing four sets of actors—policy-makers, consumers of education, borrowers and lenders—all of which shape discussion in the chapters that follow.

Policy-makers lack important information. Chapter 10, section 2, explains why it is not possible to quantify the benefits of education, with two implications: policy-makers cannot measure external benefits and hence the efficient level of subsidy; nor is it possible to quantify the efficient level of spending on education.

As discussed in Chapter 11, Section 1, there is an age gradient in the extent to which consumers of education are well informed. The usefulness of consumer sovereignty about school education is constrained by significant information problems, which also raise equity issues. In the face of these problems, the analysis suggests (though the topic is not pursued in detail) that the state will continue to provide the great bulk of finance for school education and, separately, that the state—at national or subnational levels—is likely to continue to be the major provider. In contrast, consumer choice—and hence market forces—is useful for tertiary education, where the consumer is generally better informed than any central planner. This argument is strengthened by the welcome and growing diversity of post-compulsory education and training. These arguments underpin the case for market forces in higher education discussed in detail in Chapter 13.

Imperfect information is also a problem in capital markets, for both borrowers and lenders. As discussed in Chapter 11, Section 2, conventional loans (for example, to buy a house), when applied to investment in human capital, face borrowers and, for different reasons, lenders with significant risk and uncertainty. As a result (Chapter 12, Section 2), conventional loans are both inefficient and inequitable. Though its form and extent may vary, public involvement is necessary to ensure that student loans are efficient and fair (Chapter 12, Section 3) by helping to collect income-contingent loan repayments, and perhaps also by providing the initial loan capital.

Chapter 13, which focuses on higher education, draws together economic theory and the experience of different countries, and discusses how higher education might be organized and funded in ways that are efficient and equitable, taking account of these various information problems, and of other technical problems such as externalities.

Chapter 14 discusses a series of forward-looking issues: methods of bringing private funding into tertiary education; student loans in a context of international labour mobility; extending loans beyond higher education; and developing individual learning accounts.

Chapter 10

Core Issues in the Economics of Education

In thinking about efficient investment and lifetime redistribution, two questions about education finance stand out.

- What is the efficient level of spending on different types of education?
- What is the efficient level of taxpayer subsidy?

This chapter argues that, despite their importance, these questions can be answered, at best, only indicatively.

The first section discusses objectives, the key point being that they are multiple and hard to measure. Section 2 discusses the problems that arise in trying to measure the benefits of education, and Section 3 the resulting problems for assessing the efficient quantity and mix of education spending.

1. OBJECTIVES: WHAT DO WE MEAN BY A 'GOOD' EDUCATION?

Chapter 4 asserted that the objective of health policy is to improve health, and that good health derives from many sources. The objective of education policy, analogously, is to improve educational outcomes. Again analogously, these outcomes derive from many sources: formal education is, of course, one; natural ability is another; good parenting is critical; and there is increasing evidence of the link between childhood poverty and poor educational outcomes.

Improving educational outcomes has both equity and efficiency aspects. Equity is concerned with the distribution of outcomes—for example, whether poorer people end up with fewer qualifications and, as a result, with lower incomes. One of many definitions of equity is that of *equality of opportunity*. This does not mean that everyone (for example) goes to university; it does not even mean that anyone who wishes can go to university. But it does mean that, if two people have identical abilities and identical tastes, they receive the same education irrespective of factors that are regarded as irrelevant such as parental income. This definition of equity at least has the advantage that it apportions scarcity in a just way.

Allocative efficiency (sometimes referred to as *external efficiency*) is concerned with producing the types of educational activities that equip individuals—

economically, socially, politically, and culturally—for the societies in which they live. It embraces the total amount spent on education, and also the division of resources between different types and levels of education. It will depend, *inter alia*, on a country's economic development: in a poor country, efficiency suggests emphasis on basic skills of literacy and numeracy; wealthier countries can afford to spend more on greater diversity of subject matter and on more advanced education. In all these cases, efficiency is concerned with using today's educational resources well (static efficiency), and with using them to promote economic growth (dynamic efficiency).

Efficiency is therefore central. If resources are used inefficiently, they will fail to produce the maximum gain in educational outcomes and, in consequence, will fail to promote growth effectively. If no extra resources are made available, inefficiency means that some people will have less productive (and hence poorer) lives; and if, as a result, growth is lower it means that everyone will be less well off in the future than they might have been. If extra resources are made available, inefficiency in the education system comes at the expense of better hospitals or roads, or higher personal consumption, deprivations that could be avoided with better use of educational resources.

The efficient level of output, Q^* in Figure 10.1, is that at which the marginal social benefit (MSB) of any improvement in the education system equals the resulting marginal social cost (MSC).[1] To quantify efficiency requires measuring the social costs and benefits of education. Measuring costs presents no insurmountable problems. The direct costs of the state educational system and its components are set out in the public accounts. Apportioning overheads is not an exact science, but standard methods exist. For people past school-leaving age costs should include an estimate of forgone earnings.

Measuring benefits is vastly more difficult. To explain why, it is necessary to look in more detail at what is being measured on the horizontal axis of Figure 10.1, in other words the meaning of 'good educational outcomes'. Discussion frequently portrays the issue as mainly technical, but that view is too narrow. First, education is about learning and scholarship, not just about labour productivity. Second, and less well understood, is the purpose of education in transmitting knowledge and skills, *and* attitudes and values. Education is not only technical but also cultural. Part of its purpose is to produce agreement about values.

To make these arguments more concrete, my teaching actively promotes certain values—for example, that what matters is the analytical content of an argument, not the status or gender of the person making it. Contrasting views include: students should never disagree with their teachers; women should listen but not talk; answers get higher marks if they conform with my/the university's/

---

[1] For fuller explanation, see e.g. Stiglitz 2000: ch. 3.

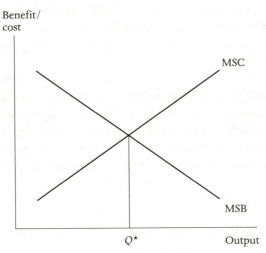

Figure 10.1. *The efficient level of output*

the government's ideology—all values that have been actively promoted in other times and/or countries, and some—for example, the central importance of educating girls as well as boys—still a matter of considerable concern in some countries.

To that extent, education promotes a homogeneity of values. A second set of values, in contrast, promotes diversity—for example, the view that disagreement is no bad thing, indeed that active discussion and debate are fundamental to the health of a free society. Related is the value of free expression in elections, with no subsequent retribution by the winners. In the educational context, the underlying value is that disagreement and debate are not only tolerated but are in many ways the purpose of a good education. As another aspect of diversity, families will have different views about subject matter, the role of discipline, and the place of religion.

A major issue in any society is the dividing line between the promotion of homogeneity and the boundaries of diversity. Freedom of speech is to be encouraged, but many Western democracies make incitement to racial hatred a criminal offence. Diversity and artistic expression are valued, yet many countries have laws about pornography. Inculcating attitudes and values in this way may sound like the educational propaganda of communist education, but with the critical difference that in a free society the values that the educational system seeks to transmit have democratic legitimacy.

Values are important not just because the transmission of culture is a significant activity in its own right, but also because they are an important ingredient in individual productivity—in other words, the technical and the cultural aspects of education can interact. As discussed in Chapter 15, Section 4, education in communist countries included values supportive of central planning and totalitarian government, values that systematically hinder productivity in a market economy.

The conclusion of a very different literature (Ravallion 1996; Barr 1999*a*; Sen 1999) is that it is not possible to quantify a value-free definition of poverty. Analogously, the education package, and hence the meaning of a 'good' education, is multidimensional, will depend on the economic, political, and social structure of the country concerned, and will vary far more than the definition of good health. Thus a definitive measure of the benefits of education is not possible. The next section discusses the problem in some detail.

2. MEASURING THE BENEFITS OF EDUCATION

Attempts to measure the benefits of education face two sets of problems: the difficulties of measuring educational outputs, educational inputs, or the connection between them; and the difficulties of establishing a causal link between education and its outputs. Notwithstanding the very strong presumptive arguments in Section 3, attempts to quantify the benefits of education continue to rest on shaky foundations.

2.1. *Measuring output and inputs*

OUTPUT CANNOT BE MEASURED. Since there is no single definition of a 'good' education, there is no unambiguous measure of output. It is possible to measure test scores, but they are imperfect. First, the connection between test scores and technical skills is by no means simple, so that test results are imperfect even in their own terms. Secondly, even if tests were a perfect measure of technical skills, educational outputs are much broader. There are consumption benefits for the individual, including the enjoyment of the educational process itself. There are investment benefits, such as greater productivity and, connected, higher pay, greater job satisfaction, and increased enjoyment of leisure. Blanchflower and Oswald (2000) show that, holding everything including income constant, education is associated with greater recorded levels of life satisfaction, and also that job satisfaction is typically highest among people with advanced levels of education. A third set of deficiencies of using test scores as a measure of output is that they take no account of a range of external benefits, including shared values. That most of these externalities are unmeasurable does not make them unreal.

EXTERNAL BENEFITS. The external benefits of education merit more detailed discussion because they raise issues that recur repeatedly in later chapters. Education may create benefits to society over and above those to the individual,[2] of which the following examples are conventionally discussed.

Future tax payments are an unambiguous external benefit. If education increases a person's future earnings, it increases her future tax payments. Her investment in education thus confers a 'dividend' on future taxpayers. It is a standard proposition that, in the presence of such an external benefit, the resulting flow of investment will be inefficiently small. A standard solution is an appropriately designed subsidy. For precisely that reason, most countries offer tax advantages for a firm's investment in physical capital.

Production benefits are a second potential external benefit. They arise if education makes someone more productive, and also makes others more productive. Individuals may become more adaptable and better able to keep up with technological change. The economic spin-offs of an occupationally mobile population are relevant in this context. It is not surprising that much 'high-tech' industry occurs in clusters like Silicone Valley, Cambridge (Massachusetts), and Cambridge (England), and education lies at the heart of endogenous growth theory (Romer 1993). Measuring these benefits is difficult, not least, as discussed below, because it is hard to separate the effects of education from other determinants of a person's productivity, such as natural ability and the quantity and quality of physical capital.

Thirdly, education may create cultural benefits external to the recipient in several ways. A common cultural experience (music, art, literature) may foster communication, both at the time and in the future. There may also be neighbourhood effects: taking children to school, for example, brings people into contact and may foster shared attitudes locally. More broadly, there is evidence (Bynner and Egerton 2000) of a link between participation in higher education and participation in political activities, community affairs, and voluntary work. More broadly still, education is part of the socialization process: its function in transmitting attitudes and values, discussed earlier, is a critical part of fostering shared attitudes, thus strengthening social cohesion.

These externalities, particularly the latter two, raise obvious measurement problems. As discussed below, there are also major conceptual problems. Though the externality argument is strong in presumptive terms, satisfactory empirical verification is lacking. Because of the 'tax-dividend' point there is an unarguable external benefit, but it is not possible to show how much.

CONNECTING INPUTS AND OUTPUTS. Even if output could be measured, a further set of problems concerns the connection between educational output and educational inputs, shown by the education production function. The first strategic problem is the difficulty of measuring the inputs: it is possible to measure the

---

[2] For exposition of the theory, see Stiglitz (2000: chs. 4, 16).

quantity of some inputs (teachers' and pupils' time, buildings, equipment, and so on), but there are major problems with variables such as the quality of teachers, the natural ability of pupils, and the quantity and quality of parenting. Secondly, as discussed already, it is not possible to measure output except in terms of test scores. Hanushek (1986) investigates the research on schooling 'and explores what has been learned and where major gaps remain, focussing on production and efficiency aspects of schools, as opposed to the ultimate uses of education' (p. 1142). In other words, he does not discuss external efficiency (that is, the contribution of education to cultural and economic goals) but concentrates on internal efficiency—that is, the effectiveness of the school system in producing educational outcomes such as examination performance. Hanushek (1996) goes into more detail on investment in education, discussing in particular the finding that 'three decades of intensive research leave a clear picture that school resource variations are not closely related to variations in student outcomes . . .' (p. 9). Given the range of missing variables, this result is not surprising.

A third problem in trying to connect inputs and outputs is that the production function itself is hard to estimate. Studies tend to assume (since no other assumption is available) that schools have a single, simple objective—maximizing their pupils' test scores. Though that model is analytically tractable and has a surface plausiblity, it is fundamentally flawed in terms of designing good policy: it implies, for example, that a school should stop teaching children who are not capable of passing tests.

2.2. *Establishing causality: The screening hypothesis*

Even if all these measurement problems were solved, a problem remains. Previous discussion implicitly assumed that education leads causally to increased individual productivity. The screening hypothesis questions the causal link, at least for post-primary education, arguing that education is *associated* with increased productivity but does not *cause* it.[3]

The argument has two parts: first, education beyond a basic level does not increase individual productivity; secondly, firms seek high-ability workers but, prior to employing them, cannot distinguish high-ability workers from low-ability workers, just as insurance companies may not be able to distinguish high and low risks.[4] In that situation, individuals have the incentive to make themselves stand out by some sort of signal. The screening hypothesis argues that post-primary education does exactly that: it gives a signal to prospective employers that it is in the individual's interest to acquire—it signals that he or she is a

---

[3] The large literature on this and other aspects of the economics of education is surveyed by Blaug (1976, 1985) and Glennerster (1993).

[4] See the discussion of adverse selection in Chapter 2, Section 3.2.

high-productivity worker. Just as good health may be due more to a naturally strong constitution than to medical care, so, according to this view, is productivity the result of natural ability rather than post-primary education. If we take the hypothesis literally, it means that there is a private benefit to the individual from post-primary education, but no external benefit.

There are various reasons why the strong form of the hypothesis does not hold. It fails, obviously, where education includes professional training—for example, medicine. It also fails where there is more than one type of job: since skills and job characteristics are heterogenous, it is necessary to match workers and jobs, so that education has a social benefit as a matching device. Whether the hypothesis has *some* validity is an empirical matter. The verdict is undecided and is likely to remain so, since individual productivity, as discussed above, is partly determined by unmeasurable factors such as natural ability and family background.

3. WHAT IS THE EFFICIENT LEVEL OF EDUCATION SPENDING?

In short, it is possible to measure the costs of education, but measuring benefits faces major problems. What, then, can be said about the efficient level of education spending?

3.1. *Quantitative analysis*

If education (*a*) increases individual productivity and (*b*) creates external benefits, the amount of education chosen by an individual in a market system will generally be less than the optimal amount, Q^* in Figure 10.1. One solution, as discussed in Chapter 2, Section 2.2, is to subsidize education by an amount equal to the external benefits it creates. In contrast, if the strong version of the screening hypothesis holds, education has private benefits but no external benefits; in that case, there is no case for a subsidy for post-primary education. Since it is not possible to measure the output, it is not possible to quantify the external benefits; and since we cannot measure causality, it is difficult to establish whether, and to what extent, education has a screening function. Thus attempts to quantify the social benefits of education are problematical, to say the least, with two major implications: it is not possible to quantify the efficient level of education spending, Q^* in Figure 10.1; and it is not possible to establish the efficient level of subsidy for post-primary education.

Notwithstanding these difficulties, many studies attempt to measure the returns to education.[5] Recent papers investigate earnings differentials between

---

[5] For recent UK evidence, see the Education Department's submission to the Dearing Committee (UK National Committee of Inquiry into Higher Education 1997*d*), Glennerster (1997*b*: table 3.8), and Dutta *et al.* (1999). On the USA, see Card (1999).

identical twins with different educational experience in an attempt to control for ability (hence at least partially addressing the screening issue) and for family background.[6] These results are significant advances on earlier work, but still need to be heavily qualified. They measure the money returns to education, but omit non-pecuniary benefits to the individual, such as the consumption value of education and job satisfaction, and a range of broader social benefits—for example, from shared values. As a result, these measures tend to underestimate both private and social benefits to an unknown extent. In addition, to the extent that screening is more of a factor than the estimates pick up, these measures overestimate social benefits (though not private benefits), again by an unknown amount.

For these and other reasons, the causal connection between education and economic growth cannot be quantified. Output growth depends on the increase in the quantity and quality of capital, the increase in quantity and quality of labour, on technological advance, and on a range of other factors. Education as a whole affects only one of these variables, the quality of labour (and according to the screening hypothesis not even that), and more advanced forms of education are connected with technological advance. The estimation problem is to separate the quantitative effect of education on the quality of labour and on technological advance, given all the other influences on output, in a situation where measures of output, inputs, and the production function are highly imperfect, and where causality is problematic. It is, therefore, not surprising that quantitative measures of the link between education spending and economic growth remain problematical.

3.2. *Qualitative arguments*

That does not mean that we can say nothing about the connection between education and growth, but that we need to consider more qualitative analysis. There are three lines of argument that connect education to national economic performance.

HUMAN CAPITAL: ALWAYS IMPORTANT, BUT ARGUABLY MORE IMPORTANT THAN EVER. Alfred Marshall, writing over 100 years ago argued that:

They [the children of the working class] go to the grave carrying undeveloped abilities and faculties; which if they could have borne full fruit would have added to the material wealth of the country . . . to say nothing of higher considerations . . . many times as much as would have covered the expense of providing adequate opportunities for their development.

But the point we have especially to insist now is that the evil is cumulative. The worse fed are the children of one generation, the less will they earn when they grow up, and the

---

[6] On the USA, see Ashenfelter and Krueger (1994); and Ashenfelter and Rouse (1998). For recent UK evidence, see Bonjour *et al.* 2000.

less will be their power of providing adequately for . . . their children; and so on to the following generations.   (Marshall 1961: bk. VI, p. 569)

Thus the argument that human capital is important is an old one. A new twist, due to Thurow (1996), argues that it is an even more important determinant of differential national economic performance today than in the past. The simplest way to make the point starts from a conventional production function:

$$Q = f(K, L, M) \qquad\qquad (10.1)$$

where output, Q, is related to inputs of capital, K, labour, L, and raw materials, M, through the production function f. Considering each of these in turn:

- In the nineteenth century, access to raw materials was critical. A century ago, almost all the largest US firms were involved with raw materials in one way or another. Today, in contrast, value added comes increasingly from other sources: the material component of computers is a trivial part of their cost; the steel used in a modern car costs less than the electronics.
- Historically, countries with a larger capital stock would typically be richer and so, through higher savings, could invest more than poorer countries, thus further increasing their capital stock, the USA being a case in point. With today's global capital markets, domestic investment is less constrained by domestic savings: investment by an entrepreneur in Thailand is not constrained by Thai domestic savings, since he can borrow elsewhere.
- Technology (i.e. the function, f) remains a critical determinant of relative economic performance. Historically, technology tended to be tied to specific countries. Today, not least because information flows are instant, technological advance moves across countries more quickly than hitherto.

Thus f, K, and M are less important explanations of differential economic performance today than in the past. The remaining variable, L, thus assumes increasing importance. In short, a combination of technological advance and international competitive pressures makes education a more important source of economic performance than ever.

THE NATURE OF TECHNOLOGICAL ADVANCE. A connected set of arguments relates to the nature of technological change. First, though it can reduce the need for skills—for example, computers have become more and more user-friendly—most of the impact is to increase the demand for skilled workers; and the overall decline in the demand for unskilled labour has been sharp. Secondly, change is increasingly rapid. Skills learned when young no longer last a lifetime; thus individuals need skills that are flexible enough to adapt to changing technology and that need updating. These changes explain the movement into the 'information age', meaning a need for education and training that is (*a*) larger than previously, (*b*) more diverse, and (*c*) repeated, in the sense that people will require periodic re-training. They also explain the close links between low educational achievement and social exclusion (see Atkinson and Hills 1998; Sparkes 1999).

Thus part of the case for investment in education and training is to ensure that workers have the skills necessary for the application of modern technology. A second part of the case is that investment in human capital—particularly in broad, flexible skills—offers a hedge against technological dynamism. Specific skills may become redundant, but education and training should give people general skills, and therefore saves the resources that would otherwise have to be devoted to retraining labour whose skills had become outdated or, at worst, to supporting workers socially excluded as a result of technological advance. As discussed in Chapter 15, Section 4, a problematic legacy of communist education is the narrow, inflexible skills it gave people.

DEMOGRAPHIC CHANGE. The rising proportion of older people in many countries presages high spending on pensions and other age-related activities such as medical and long-term care. As discussed in Chapter 6, Section 2, the solution is to increase output sufficiently to meet the combined expectations of workers and pensioners. If the problem is that workers are becoming relatively more scarce, the efficient response is to increase labour productivity. Demographic change is thus an argument for additional spending on investment both in technology and in human capital.

For all these reasons, notwithstanding the impossibility of quantifying the efficient level and mix of spending on education, training, and retraining, the qualitative arguments that education contributes to personal and national goals are strong. A recent British inquiry (UK National Committee of Inquiry into Higher Education 1997*b*: para. 6.8) endorsed the 'international consensus that higher level skills are crucial to future economic competitiveness', and went on to quote an OECD (1997*a*) study:

The direction is universal participation: 100 per cent participation with fair and equal opportunities to study; in some form of tertiary education; at some stage in the life cycle and not necessarily end on to secondary education; in a wide variety of structures, forms and types of delivery; undertaken on equal terms either part-time or full-time; publicly-subsidised but with shared client contributions; closely involving partners in the community; serving multiple purposes—educational, social, cultural and economic.

Chapter 11

Information Problems

Information is central to arguments about education. The previous chapter explained why measures of the benefits of education are problematical—an aspect of imperfect information that applies to everyone, including government. This chapter considers (Section 1) whether consumers are well informed in the separate cases of school education and post-compulsory education. A different type of imperfect information—that facing borrowers and, separately, lenders of student loans—is discussed in Section 2.

1. INFORMATION PROBLEMS IN THE MARKET FOR EDUCATION

1.1. *School education: the case against the market*

As discussed in Chapter 2, Section 4, markets are more efficient (*a*) the better is consumer information, (*b*) the more cheaply and effectively information can be improved, (*c*) the easier it is for consumers to understand available information, (*d*) the lower are the costs if someone chooses badly, and (*e*) the more diverse are consumer tastes.

Are consumers well informed about school education? Can information be improved cost-effectively? Will any such information be understood? Children (the immediate consumers) are not well informed. Decisions are therefore generally left to parents. However, parents might themselves not be well informed; in addition, they are likely to differ in the extent of their confidence and articulateness. Parental information can and should be improved, but it does not follow that this approach is necessarily a complete solution. The cost of improving information and its effectiveness in aiding choice will vary considerably across parents. Furthermore, even parents who are generally well informed can be wrong: it is sometimes suggested, for example, that middle-class parents seek out for their children the sort of education they experienced, and thus systematically make out-of-date choices. These problems all suggest that market allocation at a school level will not result in all parents making efficient decisions on behalf of their children.

At least as important, these problems disproportionately affect people from less well-off backgrounds. Thus the case for intervention also rests strongly on equity grounds, in the sense that we might contemplate a very different school system in a world in which all parents were well informed, articulate, and deeply concerned about their children's education.

How high are the costs of choosing badly? A restaurant that provides bad service will go out of business; its former clientele will have suffered nothing worse than a bad meal, and can spend the rest of their lives going out for better meals. School education, in contrast, is largely a once-and-for-all experience. A child who has had a year of bad education may never recover. In addition, a child may face high emotional costs (changing friends, for example) in changing school. A more apt analogy is a restaurant whose food is so bad that it might cause permanent ill health.

All these arguments underpin the case for extensive regulation of school education; the case for public provision is completed if we believe that an important task of the school system is to develop social cohesion—a process that is enhanced if children go through a common educational experience.

The last of the five criteria, however, argues in the opposite direction. There is considerable diversity in consumer tastes. As discussed in the previous chapter, families have different views about subject matter, the role of discipline, and the place of religion. Thus, the education package (and hence the meaning of a 'good education') will depend on the economic, political, and social structure of the country concerned, and will vary considerably. Thus there are inescapable tensions:

- In efficiency terms, what are the respective claims of (*a*) parental choice, given that a 'good education' can mean very different things, and (*b*) public provision aimed at providing a relatively homogenous package of school education in pursuit of common values and social cohesion?
- What is the trade-off between efficiency and equity objectives? If some parents are well informed, what are the respective claims of parental freedom, on the one hand, and equity objectives, on the other? Specifically, should middle-class parents be allowed to make better choices on behalf of their children?

Neither dilemma has a complete solution.

Though these arguments do not lead to a definitive conclusion, a number of factors point towards public production at school level: there are information problems and, separately, information-processing problems, leading to inefficient choices;[1] such problems have a socioeconomic gradient, creating equity

---

[1] Chapter 2, Section 2.2, sets out the distinction (New 1999) between an information problem, which can be solved by ensuring that the necessary information is provided, and an information-processing problem, where, because of complexity or for other reasons, a person cannot necessarily choose efficiently even if provided with all relevant information.

problems; and a strong case can be made for a significant common element in the school education package to foster social cohesion.

1.2. *Tertiary education: The case for the market*

The same criteria lead to very different conclusions when applied to tertiary education. The argument is illustrated here in terms of universities but also applies to post-compulsory education more generally, and to vocational training.

First, information is available, and more can be made available. There are already good university guides, and universities publish detailed information on the Internet. Secondly, the information, for the most part, is sufficiently simple for the student to understand and evaluate. This process is easier because the need to make an educational choice (which course, which subject) can normally be anticipated, so that the student has time to acquire the information she needs, and time to seek advice. The non-urgency of the decision contrasts with finding a doctor to deal with an injury after a road accident.

The costs of mistaken choice are potentially significant, but there are three lines of argument suggesting that individual choice, together with advice and suitable consumer protection, is less inefficient than any alternative. First, the costs of mistaken choice are reduced by modular degrees, which allow students to change subjects and, increasingly, institutions. The costs are also lower because students are older than schoolchildren and, for that reason, the emotional costs of changing subject or institution will generally be less, or at least less long-lasting. Secondly, whatever the costs of mistaken individual choice, a central planner is likely to do even worse. In this respect, too, there is a contrast with school education, which is deliberately designed to be relatively homogenous, as manifested, for example, by a national curriculum of some sort in many countries. Post-compulsory education, in contrast, is properly highly diverse—indeed its diversity is a sign of richness of culture and openness to social and technical innovation. Thirdly, students make choices already.

Though the matter is controversial, it can be argued that the assumption of well-informed (or potentially well-informed) consumers holds for higher education. The many students I have met have generally been impressively well informed—a savvy, streetwise consumer group.[2]

Finally, consumer tastes are diverse, education and training courses are becoming more diverse, and change is increasingly rapid, and global. For all these reasons, students are more capable than central planners of making choices that conform with their own needs and those of the economy. In contrast, attempts at

---

[2] It has been suggested that this is true in some university cultures—for example, the UK and the USA—but that in other countries students are more passive consumers. It remains the case, however, that young adults (or older adults) will generally make better choices than any agent acting on their behalf.

manpower planning are even more likely than in the past to be wrong, largely (though not wholly) because of the increasing complexity of industrial and post-industrial society.

1.3. *Implications for policy*

Two very different strategies for allocating food and health care were outlined in Chapter 2, Section 4. In the case of food, people are generally sufficiently well informed to make choices; nor are there other major market imperfections. This suggests that efficiency should be pursued by market allocation and equity objectives through income transfers—for example, paying pensions to the elderly, who then buy food in the same shops as the rest of us, and at the same prices. With health care, in contrast, there are major information problems in the market for medical care and, separately, the market for medical insurance, suggesting a much greater role for the state.

In considering whether education is more like food or more like health care, there are two important gradients to consider.

- *Age*. As students get older they become better informed. It is clearly right that someone makes educational choices on behalf of a small child. A university student, in contrast, is better informed about his or her needs than anyone else. At some stage in between the balance tips, arguably at the age at which education stops being compulsory.
- *Diversity*. As discussed in Section 1, there are strong arguments for a significant element of homogeneity in what schools offer. Such homogeneity applies both to technical matters (all children should acquire a common package of basic knowledge and skills) and to attitudes and values, to strengthen social cohesion. The higher up the education scale one goes, the weaker the claims for uniformity and the greater the desirability of diversity, particularly of subject matter.

These two gradients both point in the same direction. The capacity of younger children to make choices is limited and the case for uniformity of educational experience stronger, adding weight to the case for a centrally planned package with space for local, cultural, and religious diversity. School education, it can therefore be argued, has more in common with health care than with food.

In contrast, the capacity of young adults to make choices is good and the case for diversity strong. Post-compulsory education is more like food than health care. It is thus completely compatible to oppose excessive reliance on market forces in school education but to support market mechanisms in combination with income transfers for tertiary education and training.

2. INFORMATION PROBLEMS, RISK, AND UNCERTAINTY IN CAPITAL MARKETS

Information problems arise not only in the market for education itself, but also in capital markets. As discussed in subsequent chapters, loans are an important source of finance for investment in human capital. In the world of certainty analysed at the start of Chapter 2, the market provides loans efficiently, and people make voluntary individual choices about how much to invest in their own human capital and how much of that investment to finance by borrowing. This section discusses the major differences that result from relaxing the assumption of certainty, in particular the fact that both borrowers and lenders face risk and uncertainty.

2.1. *Risk and uncertainty facing borrowers*

Students face risk and uncertainty in borrowing to finance investment in human capital. To explain why, it is helpful to start with the example of borrowing to buy a house, a loan that comes close to that in the simple Fisher model in Chapter 2. Such a loan will have a fixed duration (say twenty-five years) and a positive interest rate. A key feature is that a person's monthly repayment is entirely determined by three variables: the size of his loan, its duration, and the interest rate. Apart from adjustments owing to changes in the interest rate, the monthly repayment rate is fixed.

Buying a house is a relatively low-risk activity for an individual.

(a) A person who buys a house knows what he is buying, having lived in a house all his life.
(b) The house is unlikely to fall down.
(c) The real value of the house will generally increase.
(d) If his income falls, making repayments burdensome, he has the option to sell the house.
(e) Because the house acts as security for the loan, he can get a loan on good terms.

For all these reasons, the market provides loans for house purchase with little if any role for the state beyond the regulation of financial markets. The contrast with lending to finance investment in human capital—for example, a university degree—is sharp, with problems of imperfect information, risk and uncertainty.

IMPERFECT INFORMATION. The question behind the discussion in Section 1 is who should be the prime mover in choices about school or university attended, subjects studied, and course content? One of the conclusions is that there is an age gradient, with older students—for example, university students—best placed to make educational choices because they are better informed than anyone else about their own aptitudes and preferences. That line of argument is strengthened by the second gradient, that of diversity, which is much greater at more advanced levels of education, making efficient central planning impossible.

Thus a major conclusion of earlier discussion is that university students are well informed consumers. That conclusion now needs slightly to be qualified by the existence of a third gradient: some schoolchildren (or other potential university students) may not know the benefits of getting a degree. This is particularly a problem for students from poor backgrounds—the very people for whom access is the most fragile, and the very people whose participation governments want actively to foster. Thus the extent to which a person is well informed (element (a)) can have a significant socioeconomic gradient.

RISK AND UNCERTAINTY arise because (b), (c), and (d), though true for housing, are much less true for investment in skills. First, a qualification can 'fall down', in the sense that a borrower may fail his exams. Thus he ends up having to make loan repayments but without the qualification that would have led to increased earnings from which to make those repayments. Secondly, even well-informed students face risk: though the average private return to investment in human capital is positive,[3] there is considerable variance about that average. In addition, as discussed in Chapter 10, even the private benefits of education are hard to quantify, so that the borrower faces uncertainty as well as risk about the return to a particular qualification. Thirdly (element (d)), someone who has borrowed to pay for a qualification and subsequently has low earnings and high repayments does not have the option to sell the qualification, further increasing the borrower's exposure to risk.

For all these reasons, borrowing to finance investment in human capital exposes the borrower to more risk and more uncertainty than borrowing to buy a house. The problem arises for all students, and most acutely for those from poorer backgrounds.

2.2. *Risk and uncertainty facing lenders*

Because of (d), the lender has no security for the loan, leading to a further problem, adverse selection. The effect of these twin problems, in contrast with home loans, is to face lenders with significant risk and uncertainty.

NO SECURITY. If I borrow to buy a house, the house acts as security. If I am unable to repay, the lender can repossess the house, sell it, and take what he is owed. Sep-

---

[3] See UK National Committee of Inquiry into Higher Education (1997*d*) for estimates of rates of return to a degree in the UK.

arately, deliberate default on repayments is not a problem; it is true that I could disappear; but I could not take the house with me. For both reasons, lenders are prepared to offer home loans on good terms. An analogous arrangement with human capital would allow the lender, if I default on my repayments, to repossess my brain, sell it, and take what he is owed. Since slavery is illegal, that is not an option. Thus lenders for human capital have no security. In contrast with lenders for house purchase, they face risk and uncertainty connected with (*a*) whether I will acquire the qualification and (*b*) whether my subsequent earnings record will allow me to repay the loan.

ADVERSE SELECTION. The average rate of return varies across professions; and the variance in the rate of return is much larger in some professions than others. A borrower who wants to become an actor presents considerable risk to the lender: since a large part of the return is job satisfaction rather than money, the average return is low; and the variation in income is considerable, both between one actor and another, and for a given actor over time. For an accountant, in contrast, the mean return is higher and the variance lower. In that sense, from the lender's perspective, an aspiring actor is a 'bad' risk and an intending accountant a 'good' risk. Adverse selection arises because the borrower is better informed than the lender about whether he aspires to a career in acting or accounting.

In principle, insurers can ask questions that elicit the relevant information. A travel insurance company can ask whether my holiday involves skiing or whitewater rafting, charge a premium accordingly, and refuse to pay benefit if my answers were not truthful. The analogue for student loans is to ask people what career they would like, to charge a higher interest rate for aspiring actors, and, quite possibly, to withdraw the loan from a person who said he or she wanted to become an accountant but who subsequently dropped out of his or her degree to become a musician. The analogue is clearly horrendous: it comes close to reintroducing slavery by the back door, since it effectively locks a student into a career; it interferes with student choice and, importantly, with students changing direction over the course of their studies and early career; it also makes the lender, in effect, final arbiter of a person's career choices. The last is deeply damaging, since it is in the interests of the lender to make low-risk loans, while it is in the national interest to encourage the development of flexible skills and new skills.

Thus the case against allowing lenders to seek information about a borrower's career intentions is overwhelming. But that means that the borrower is better informed than the lender about his true career intentions, thus exposing the lender to adverse selection. The resulting inefficiencies, discussed in Chapter 2 and, in the context of medical insurance, in Chapter 4, are well known: there will be an inefficiently small amount of lending, and in the extreme the market may fail entirely.

The implications for policy of risk and uncertainty for both borrowers and lenders are taken up in the next chapter.

Chapter 12

Designing Student Loans

The previous chapter argued that it is entirely consistent to be an enthusiast of market forces in tertiary education but to take the opposite view for school education. This chapter and the next explore in more detail the argument that in the former case market allocation, in combination with state intervention through regulation and subsidy, is more likely than central planning to achieve individual and national objectives. They argue that that conclusion, though debatable in the past, is considerably stronger in a world of mass higher education, rapid technological advance, and international pressures, all of which point to a need for greater occupational mobility.

Chapter 13 discusses the structure of such a system of tertiary education. This chapter discusses in detail one of its core ingredients—the design of student loans. It is useful at the start to distinguish three approaches.

- *Mortgage-type loans* have repayments organized like a mortgage or bank overdraft. Thus the borrower faces repayments of (say) $100 per month for (say) 5 years. Repayments and the duration of the loan are predetermined; the endogenous variable is the fraction of the borrower's income absorbed by loan repayments. These are the conventional loans discussed in the previous chapter.
- *Income-contingent loans* have repayments calculated as (say) 5 per cent of the borrower's subsequent earnings until she has repaid the loan, at which time repayments are 'switched off'. Thus the fraction of a person's income absorbed by repayments is predetermined; the endogenous variable is the length of time it takes to repay. For the reasons discussed below, it is desirable if repayments are collected by the tax or social-insurance authorities.
- *A graduate tax* is similar to an income-contingent loan in that repayments are (say) 5 per cent of the student's subsequent earnings, but fundamentally different in that repayment continues for life (or till retirement). Unlike the previous two cases, therefore, repayments do not cease when the student has fully repaid the loan. Thus the endogenous variable is the total amount a student pays towards the cost of his or her higher education.

This chapter argues that mortgage loans, though they work well for buying a house, have major problems as an instrument for financing investment in human capital, and that, for the latter purpose, income-contingent loans have major advantages. Before turning to such discussion, however, a prior question is why loans are necessary at all.

1. WHY STUDENT LOANS?

Resources for higher education can and should come from taxation, through direct public spending, and perhaps also through tax advantages for students, their families, and/or educational institutions. It is possible to finance a small, elite, high-quality system of higher education more or less entirely from public sources. Today, however, countries have, or are rapidly moving towards, a system of mass higher education. The efficiency reason for doing so is the need for more, more diverse, and more repeated education and training. The equity reason is that access to higher education is severely restricted while the system is small.

Thus the case for a mass system is strong. But a high-quality mass system cannot be funded only from public sources. High taxation creates adverse incentives, particularly in the face of demographic pressures and international competition. Separately, tax funding tends to be regressive. The argument is simple. If taxation is used to fund a commodity consumed only (or mainly) by the poor, the policy is pro-poor. But if taxation is used to fund a commodity consumed only by the rich (for example, mink coats), the policy is regressive. Since higher education is disproportionately consumed by people from better-off backgrounds, the system benefits the best off most.[1]

Both macroeconomic feasibility and distributional equity therefore suggest that a large system of higher education requires public funding to be supplemented on a significant scale from private resources. Private funding can derive from six potential sources:

(a) family resources;
(b) a student's earnings while a student;
(c) a student's future earnings, i.e. loans;
(d) employers;
(e) entrepreneurial activities by universities; and/or
(f) gifts, for example from charitable foundations or bequests in people's wills.

Looking at these in turn, family resources are not bad in themselves, but do nothing to improve access for students from poor backgrounds. Student earnings are generally small. The USA, with high wages, flexible labour markets, and a tradition of student earning opportunities, is an outlier in this respect. In addition,

---

[1] The classic articles, discussing the publicly funded University of California, are by Hansen and Weisbrod (1969, 1978). See also Le Grand (1982: ch. 4).

earning activities compete with study time and leisure and are therefore in competition with the effectiveness of learning and the quality of the student experience. These are not arguments against student earnings, but caution against excessive reliance on this funding source.

Employer contributions, contrary to popular belief, are likely to be small. This is systematic and entirely predictable. In former times, a job, like marriage, was for life. It was therefore rational for an employer to invest in the skills of his workers, since he would reap the benefits of that investment. Today, in contrast, labour is mobile. Thus it remains in the interests of employers *as a whole* to want training to take place, but in the interests of each *individual* employer to leave it to other employers to pay for training, and then to poach the resulting trained person. In short, there is an externality; in consequence, employers will underinvest in training.

Entrepreneurial activities by universities, as a practical matter, frequently yield little net revenue. They certainly need a very different range of skills from those of running the academic side of the institution. At worst, they risk diverting scarce institutional capacity to lower-priority activities. Again it should not be blindly assumed that transplanted US institutions will necessarily flourish in different cultural and economic contexts.

Gifts have analogies with student earning opportunities: they are a useful potential source of funds, but should not be relied on as a *deus ex machina*. They are rarely more than a marginal contribution, except in the USA, which has a culture of giving and highly developed institutions to encourage it. In addition, while gifts may be of relevance to a small number of top universities, they are much less relevant to the generality of universities, and of virtually no relevance to other tertiary educational institutions.

Having ruled out (*a*), (*b*), (*d*), (*e*), and (*f*) as *major* sources of private funds, we are left with loans as the only approach with the potential to yield resources on a large scale and in an equitable way. However, the design of loans is critical. Sections 2 and 3 discuss how repayments should (and should not) be organized, and Section 4 covers other aspects of loan design. Chapter 13 sets out the overall strategy for tertiary education, of which loans are a component.

2. ORGANIZING REPAYMENTS: MORTGAGE-TYPE SCHEMES

Mortgage loans have some advantages. The cost of the loan is transparent to the student. In addition, they might discourage work effort less than income-contingent loans.[2] But mortgage loans have two strategic disadvantages: the information problems discussed in Chapter 11, Section 2, point to major problems

---

[2] The income effect works in favour of labour supply and (in contrast with income-contingent repayments) there is no substitution effect working in the opposite direction.

of efficiency and equity; and mortgage-type loans for human capital are administratively demanding.

2.1. *Efficiency and equity problems*

Chapter 11 concluded (*a*) that some borrowers, particularly from disadvantaged backgrounds, may be badly informed about the value of a qualification such as a degree, and (*b*) that all borrowers face risk and uncertainty, both about the return to their investment in a qualification and because (in contrast with the situation when buying a house) they cannot sell the qualification should their income turn out subsequently to be low. Thus there are technical problems on the demand side of the market for loans and, as a result, borrowing to finance investment in human capital will be inefficiently low.

On the supply side, lenders face risk and uncertainty about the riskiness of an applicant for a loan and will therefore charge a risk premium. A risk premium assessed by a well-informed lender is efficient (analogous to higher automobile insurance premiums for bad drivers). But lenders are not well informed about the riskiness of an applicant, not least because of adverse selection. Thus risk premiums will be inefficiently high, again leading to an inefficiently small amount of borrowing.[3]

A second, and separate, supply-side problem is that lenders will face incentives to cherry pick, in other words, to find ways of lending only to the best risks, a situation entirely analogous to incentives to cream skimming that face private medical insurers (Chapter 4, Section 2.2). An obvious way to do so is to lend only to students who can provide security: for younger people that could mean a home-owning parent; for older students it could mean taking out a student loan using their own home as security. As mentioned earlier the resulting borrowing will be inefficiently low: the interest of lenders is to make secure loans; the national interest is in the optimal quantity and mix of investment in human capital. In a world of perfect information—the simple Fisher model—the two interests coincide; in the presence of imperfect information they do not.

Mortgage-type loans are also inequitable, since these efficiency problems impact most on people from poorer backgrounds, women, and ethnic minorities. People from poorer backgrounds tend to be less well informed about the benefits of a qualification and are therefore less prepared to face the risk of a loan. In addition, these groups tend to have a less well-established credit record. They are therefore less tempting to lenders and thus likely to be on the wrong end of cherry picking.

---

[3] The inefficiency caused by adverse selection is discussed in Chapter 2 and, in the context of medical insurance, in Chapter 4.

2.2. *Administrative problems*

It is sometimes argued that the great advantage of mortgage loans, notwithstanding the problems just discussed, is that they do not depend on tax collection, and can therefore be used in a country without an effective income tax system. That argument is false.

MORTGAGE REPAYMENTS REQUIRE A FAIRLY SOPHISTICATED COLLECTION MECHANISM. Though repayments are not collected by the tax authorities, they still have to be collected by someone. Commercial banks are expert in collecting repayments for loans that are (*a*) short term and (*b*) secured on some tangible asset. On (*a*), however, there are good reasons for wanting student loans to have a fairly long duration: it is efficient if the lifetime of a loan bears a rational relationship to the lifetime of the asset being financed by the loan—hence there are twenty-five-year home loans but three-year car loans; in addition, a longer repayment period makes possible smaller monthly repayments and/or larger loans. Turning to (*b*), there is no security for borrowing to finance human capital. For both reasons, collection by banks is likely to be administratively demanding and hence to require some sort of government guarantee. However:

GOVERNMENT GUARANTEES TO PRIVATE LENDERS CREATE PROBLEMS. If the guarantee is not generous, banks will decline to get involved. But, if the guarantee is sufficiently generous, banks have no incentive to pursue repayments vigorously, not least because they have no desire to alienate people who will become their best customers. The incentive structure is thus inimical to effective collection, leading to high default rates.

A second problem with government guarantees is the classification problem. There are international guidelines for national accounting that determine whether spending is public or private. If students borrow money from banks, but the government guarantee is generous, the government, in effect, takes the risk of default. Thus there is no genuine risk transfer and, under international guidelines, lending by banks to students counts as *public* borrowing. The classification problem is central to discussion of ways of bringing private finance into postcompulsory education, and is discussed in detail in Chapter 14, Section 1.

A PUBLIC COLLECTION AGENCY? One way to get round these problems is to abandon the idea of private collection of loan repayments and instead to have a public collection mechanism. This, however, requires considerable administrative capacity. Even where that administrative capacity exists, the public sector ends up running a student loan collection agency *and* a tax collection system, raising the question of whether resources devoted to collection of mortgage-type student loan repayments would not be used better to bolster the effectiveness of the tax system.

MORTGAGE REPAYMENTS REQUIRE A CAPACITY TO IMPLEMENT AN INCOME TEST. Whether collected by a public or a private agency, mortgage repayments require an income test. The argument is simple. If repayments (say $100 per month) are unrelated to a person's income, a mechanism is needed to protect people with low or no earnings, both for equity reasons and to ensure that the scheme is politically sustainable. But the corollary is that the agency organizing repayments has to administer an income test. This is a difficult task of measurement and enforcement even in an advanced industrial country, let alone in a poorer country that does not have an effective tax system (which was part of the argument for having mortgage-type loans in the first place). An income test, in short, will be administratively demanding and costly. With a mortgage scheme, these costs will be *in addition* to those of the tax system.

In sum, mortgage-type loans, for the well-established reasons discussed in the previous chapter, work well for housing. With lending for human capital, in contrast, the theoretical arguments suggest that they expose both borrower and lender to excessive risk and uncertainty. The outcome is inefficient because it wastes talent and inequitable because capital market imperfections bear most heavily on the least well off. Separately, mortgage loans are considerably more administratively demanding than is generally realized.

3. ORGANIZING REPAYMENTS: INCOME-CONTINGENT SCHEMES

3.1. *Addressing capital market imperfections*

Income-contingent loans reduce the risk and uncertainty faced by borrowers and lenders, and thus improve efficiency and equity.

Collecting repayments as a payroll deduction alongside income tax or social-insurance contributions means that they match ability to pay. Repayments automatically and instantly track changes in earnings. Borrowers with low current earnings make low (or no) repayments; borrowers who do well repay in full, those with low lifetime earnings do not. By reducing the uncertainty facing borrowers, income-contingent repayments avoid the distortions that lead to inefficiently low borrowing, and thus support the efficient level of investment in tertiary education.[4] In addition, properly designed income-contingent loans also protect lenders, and thus open up the possibility of private finance, discussed in Chapter 14, Section 1.

These efficiency arguments are important. Conventional loans (on which mortgage-type student loans are modelled) and student loans are intended to

---

[4] For theoretical discussion, see Grout (1983).

operate in very different circumstances. Loans for house purchase are normally made to people *after* they know their income and assets. Student loans, in contrast, are generally given *before* people know their income and assets; indeed, their entire purpose is to increase them. Of necessity the latter situation is more uncertain than the former, hence the case for income-contingent arrangements.

There are also equity advantages: since repayments are automatically tailored to ability to pay, income-contingent loans make it easier for borrowers from poor backgrounds to participate. If loans cover all living costs and any tuition charges, studying is free at the point of use; and loan repayments, being instantly and exactly related to the person's subsequent income, are, from his point of view, little different from paying tax.

In addition, income-contingent repayments (and hence what a person pays for his or her qualification) are determined not by where a person *starts* but by where he or she *ends up*. This has a strong appeal to social justice.

3.2. *Philosophical arguments*

Another approach to demonstrating that income-contingent loans are efficient and equitable is through a realization during earlier research (Barr 1991) that they are compatible simultaneously with the benefit principle, the ability-to-pay principle, and the social-insurance principle.

Milton Friedman's starting point in his classic book *Capitalism and Freedom* (1962) was the benefit principle—that is, that the person who benefits should pay. He considered the government's role in post-compulsory education and training. He accepted the capital market imperfections just discussed, especially the riskiness of student loans—for example, the lack of any security. He pointed out that

the device adopted to meet the corresponding problem for other risky investments is equity investment plus limited liability on the part of shareholders. The counter-part for education would be to 'buy' a share in an individual's earning prospects; to advance him the funds needed to finance his training on condition that he agree to pay the lender a specified fraction of his future earnings. (Friedman 1962: 103)

On that basis he advocated loans from government, in return for which, 'the individual . . . would agree to pay to the government in each future year a specified percentage of his earnings in excess of a specified sum for each $1000 that he received . . . This payment could easily be combined with payment of income tax and so involve a minimum of additional administrative expense' (ibid. 105).

The ability-to-pay approach, in contrast, starts from a predisposition towards free, tax-financed education, abandoning that model only because of its regressiveness when applied to higher education. Howard Glennerster, writing over thirty years ago (Glennerster *et al.* 1968: 26), pointed out that:

in the United Kingdom, higher education is now financed as a social service. Nearly all the costs are borne out of general taxation . . . But it differs radically from other social services. It is reserved for a small and highly selected group. . . . It is exceptionally expensive . . . [And] education confers benefits which reveal themselves in the form of higher earnings. . . . A graduate tax would enable the community to recover the value of the resources devoted to higher education from those who have themselves derived such substantial benefit from it.

A central theme of this book is the role of the welfare state, of which social insurance is an important part, in assisting consumption smoothing. Pensions redistribute from middle years to post-retirement years; student loans, analogously, redistribute from middle to earlier years. Income-contingent loans are therefore entirely compatible with the idea of social insurance, an approach taken up in greater detail in Chapter 14, Section 1.

3.3. *The intuition of income-contingent repayments*

The power of the income-contingent principle emerges in another guise when the following apparent conundrum is considered. Figure 12.1 illustrates a loan scheme with income-contingent repayments of 2.3 per cent of total earnings per £10,000 borrowed,[5] and with a real interest rate of 3 per cent. Consider a person who leaves university with a loan of £10,000 and a starting salary of £16,000 per year. Suppose that the rate of inflation is 3 per cent; thus he pays an interest rate of 6 per cent (3 per cent superimposed on an inflation rate of 3 per cent). At first glance, the repayment rate is too low. The first year's interest charge is £600 (6 per cent of £10,000); however, his repayment is only £368 (2.3 per cent of £16,000). Thus his repayment does not even cover his interest liability, and his nominal debt increases.

This result is entirely characteristic of income-contingent repayments. With mortgage-type loans, the annual repayment is fixed. Thus, as earnings rise, repayments fall as a fraction of earnings—mortgage repayments are front-loaded. With income-contingent loans, in contrast, what is fixed is not the annual repayment but the fraction of income repaid. As real earnings rise so, therefore, do repayments. Income-contingent repayments are end-loaded, with heavy repayments in later years. A typical pattern, therefore, is for nominal debt to rise in the early years of repayment, then to start to fall, and to fall very rapidly in the final years of the loan.

---

[5] This example draws on the simulations in Barr and Falkingham (1993, 1996); see also Barr and Crawford 1998*a*). Note that the 2.3% repayment rate applies to *total* earnings.

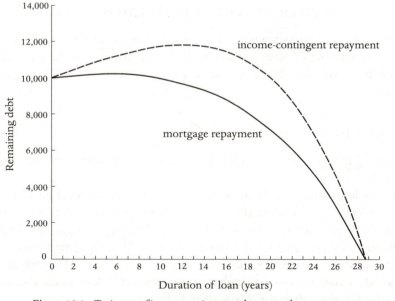

Figure 12.1. *Trajectory of income-contingent and mortgage loan repayments*
Note: For assumptions, see text.

Figure 12.1 illustrates the time path of the two methods of repayment in the case described above. In the early years of the loan, income-contingent repayments (the dotted line) fail to cover interest charges and nominal debt rises. As real earnings rise, however, so do real repayments; the steep slope of the dotted line shows the speed with which the loan is extinguished in the later years of repayment. Under the stated assumptions, the loan is repaid in year 28. For comparison, the darker line shows the time path of mortgage repayments designed to repay the same loan over the same period. Being front-loaded, repayments are larger in the early years and smaller in the later years.[6]

In sum, income-contingent loans have considerable strengths. They address major problems of imperfect information, risk, and uncertainty in capital markets, assist access, and have philosophical advantages, being compatible with the benefit principle, the ability-to-pay principle, and the social-insurance principle. In transition and middle-income developing countries, they also reinforce efforts to strengthen the tax system.

---

[6] Indebtedness under the mortgage scheme increases very slightly in the early years because, in parallel with income-contingent repayments, the loan is assumed to be indexed.

4. OTHER FEATURES OF STUDENT LOANS

The repayment mechanism is a core element of any loan scheme. This section discusses a number of other aspects: basic design elements of the loan scheme, the interest rate that borrowers pay, and arguments for involving private finance.

4.1. *Basic design elements*

Translating the income-contingent principle into a loan scheme raises a series of issues.

At what level of income should a borrower start to make repayments? The case for a relatively high threshold (for example, average earnings) is mainly political; people think that such a system is fairer. That argument, though widely believed, is false. Income-contingency is *automatically* fair. If the repayment rate is 5 per cent of earnings, low earners will make only low repayments. The case for a low threshold is that it makes for a much stronger repayment flow and thus makes the loan scheme more effective. A key issue in loan design is the balance between these economic and political advantages, which pull in different directions.

How large should loans be? If access to tertiary education is an important objective, up-front charges are problematical. Depending on country and the type of educational qualification being discussed, there is therefore a strong case for a loan entitlement that covers all tuition fees and similar costs, and all living expenses. The issue is taken up in Chapter 13.

Repayments based on current income are central. To minimize risk to the borrower, loan repayments should track a person's earnings week by week or month by month, not be assessed retrospectively on the basis of income in a previous year. The only cost-effective method of implementing income-contingent repayments on a current basis is as a payroll deduction alongside income tax or social-insurance contributions.

An effective income-tax system is also central. Earlier discussion of mortgage-type loans stressed the practical problems of collecting repayments. Analogous problems can arise with income-contingent loans, which depend heavily on the effectiveness of the tax system. This dependence raises problems in countries where income-tax collection is leaky and where a large fraction of the population is outside the formal income-tax net. A central question in considering an income-contingent scheme, therefore, is whether the income tax system is sufficiently robust, or can be made sufficiently robust within the near future.

4.2. *Market interest rates*

There are strong reasons why borrowers should pay an interest rate on their loans broadly equal to the government's cost of borrowing. This is higher than the interest charge in loan schemes in many countries, which require a taxpayer subsidy, but, as discussed in the previous chapter, much less than a borrower would have to pay for an unsecured commercial loan, a rate that would contain a risk premium biased upwards by the presence of adverse selection.

A market interest rate, thus defined, has efficiency advantages. With a subsidized interest rate, even if a student does not need to borrow, she faces incentives to borrow as much as possible, put the money into a bank (or government bonds) to profit from the interest rate differential, and repay as slowly as possible. Market interest rates, secondly, have fiscal advantages. As discussed in Chapter 13, Section 2, interest subsidies are very costly.

There are also equity advantages. A general interest subsidy is untargeted. It benefits most those who borrow most. Since it is the middle class who disproportionately go to university, the interest subsidy benefits the middle class most. Instead of spreading interest subsidies thinly across *all* students, a more equitable approach is to charge a market or near-market interest rate and use the savings for *some* students, specifically those for whom access is most fragile, and those whose subsequent earnings are low. In short, market interest rates make it possible to replace an untargeted subsidy by a targeted one.

The case against interest subsidies is thus damning: they are inefficient, expensive, and unfair.

4.3. *Private money*

As argued earlier, the logic of expanding tertiary education makes it inevitable that public funding will need to be supplemented on a significant scale by private funding, an imperative that is all the more acute if quality is to be maintained.

As also argued earlier, the only large-scale and equitable source of private funds is through student loans. However, if students borrow from the taxpayer, there is a net saving in public spending only when the loan scheme is mature—which occurs only when the flow of repayments from former graduates exceeds this year's disbursement to current students *and* has done so for enough years for cumulative repayments to exceed cumulative lending plus accrued interest. Since one of the key objectives of a loan scheme is to allow the student to spread repayment for a long-lived asset over an extended period, it follows that the loan scheme, even if well designed, is unlikely to reach this stage for at least twenty years.

If a way can be found to allow students to borrow from private sources, the upfront costs of the loan scheme no longer fall on the public budget. This may not be a major issue in a well-off country, but is of obvious and acute relevance in fiscally constrained transition and middle-income countries, and may yet become an issue in OECD countries as tertiary education and training expand and demographic pressures increase.

At this stage, however, the classification problem mentioned in Section 2 comes into play. If students borrow from banks, but the banks receive what, in practice, is a complete guarantee from government, there is little or no risk transfer, and the scheme will be classified as public. Thus designing income-contingent loans that bring in private resources immediately is a difficult and not yet wholly solved task. The topic is taken up in more detail in Chapter 14.

Chapter 13

Financing Higher Education: The Options

In contrast with the conclusion about pensions—that there is no dominant policy—this chapter argues that there *is* a dominant strategy for financing higher education. That view, however, is still controversial. At its core lie two—often implicit—debates that are both philosophical and empirical. The first (see OECD 1997*b*) is between two competing stylized models.

- In the 'Anglo-American' model governments act on the assumption that higher education institutions are, and should be, heterogeneous, and therefore encourage diversity of institutions, various forms of provision, and quality comparisons between them.
- In the 'Scandinavian model', also found in other European countries, government acts on the assumption that institutions are homogeneous, and therefore treats them equally and regards all programmes as equal.

The analysis in these chapters is based on two propositions: that the second model, whatever its merits, is incompatible with mass higher education; and that mass higher education is essential in today's world. Thus funding should support a diverse, decentralized system of tertiary education.

The second debate is about ability to pay. Though there is broad agreement that this should be a central ingredient in financial support, there is disagreement about how it should be measured. Should ability to pay be based on current income—in other words, on where people start? The strategy to which this leads is finance—for example, scholarships—based on a student's family income, with more generous support for people whose family are poor (even if the recipients end up becoming rich). Alternatively, should ability to pay be based on future income—that is, on where people end up? The strategy to which this leads is finance based on income-contingent loans or graduate taxes, with more generous support, *ex post*, for people who do not derive much financial benefit from their degree.

This chapter argues that the second approach is the correct one where people are well informed. Support for the generality of students should therefore derive from a mix of tax funding and income-contingent loans. As argued in Chapter 11, Section 2.1, however, there is a socioeconomic gradient in the extent to which students are well informed; many children from poorer backgrounds, for example, never even think of going to university. For such people the first approach is necessary through a range of measures designed actively to promote access.

Section 1 draws out the lessons from economic theory that emerge from the arguments in the previous three chapters. Section 2 tests the arguments against the experience of a number of countries. Section 3 sets out the implications for policy and meets head-on the most frequent counter-arguments.

1. LESSONS FROM ECONOMIC THEORY

1.1. *Market forces in higher education: Who should make the decisions?*

In discussing market forces, three questions are paramount: are consumers of higher education capable of making good decisions (that is, how useful is consumer sovereignty); are universities capable of making good decisions (that is, how useful is producer sovereignty); and who should decide how large the university system should be?

HOW USEFUL IS CONSUMER SOVEREIGNTY? Chapter 11, Section 1, argued that students are sufficiently well-informed to make efficient choices for two sets of reasons: they are generally well informed and/or have the time and capacity to make themselves well informed; separately, higher education is becoming increasingly diverse, making the problem too complex for a central planner. Consumer sovereignty is therefore useful. The same chapter reached very different conclusions for school education.

HOW USEFUL IS PRODUCER SOVEREIGNTY? One aspect — academic freedom — I take as a given. A second aspect — the *economic* freedom of universities — is the subject of heated discussion. With an elite university system of the sort existing in most countries until relatively recently, it was possible, as a polite myth, to assume that all universities were of equal quality, that degrees were worth the same whichever university conferred them, and hence that universities could, broadly, be funded equally (this is the 'Scandinavian model'). With a mass system this myth is no longer sustainable. The characteristics, the quality, and the costs of different degrees at different institutions will vary much more widely than hitherto.

As a result, universities need to be differentially funded to take account both of a particular institution's costs and of the demand for places. In principle this could be done by an all-knowing central planner. The problem, however, is too complex for that to be the sole mechanism. A mass system — and *a fortiori* a mass system in an increasingly complex world — needs a funding regime in which institutions can charge differential prices to reflect their differential costs—in other words, the 'Anglo-American' model.

The conclusion this suggests is that producer sovereignty is not just useful; as higher education expands and the diversity of its activities increases, it becomes essential. As discussed below, this does not means unfettered markets.

HOW LARGE SHOULD THE SYSTEM BE? Why is mass higher education necessary? Is there an investment argument: would expansion of higher education increase the rate of economic growth? Secondly, should there be expansion for consumption reasons—would extra resources add sufficiently to the quality of life (for reasons other than output growth) to make expansion efficient? Though these questions are critically important, they cannot be answered as crisply as the questions about the usefulness of consumer and producer sovereignty.

From the investment viewpoint, several arguments for expanding tertiary education were put forward in Chapter 10, Section 3. First, it can be argued that technological change makes human capital more important than ever as a determinant of national economic performance. The nature of that technological change is leading to rising demand for skilled people and declining demand for the unskilled. Its rate of change requires that individuals are retrained periodically—so-called lifelong learning.

Those arguments are strengthened by international competitive pressures. To keep up with other countries it is necessary to increase the productivity of capital and labour; if higher education contributes cost-effectively to increased productivity, there is an efficiency case for expansion.

A further argument relates to demographic prospects. The efficient response to a decline in the number of workers is to increase the ratio of capital to labour. What is needed, therefore, is investment in technology and in human capital. Expansion of education and training, it can be argued, is therefore necessary precisely *because* of demographic change.

A final argument concerns the downside risk of underinvesting rather than overinvesting. The quote from Alfred Marshal in Chapter 10, Section 3 brings out the high costs of making the wrong investment decisions, given their cumulative impact. The costs of underinvesting in higher education in terms of quantity and quality will be much greater than those of expansion that turns out not to have been strictly necessary.

These arguments create a strong presumption for increasing the resources devoted to higher education (for discussion in a UK context, see Greenaway and Haynes 2000). Definitive quantification, however, is not possible. As discussed in Chapter 10, we cannot determine the effect of higher education on individual productivity, because we cannot measure all the relevant variables. The determinants of individual productivity include measurable attributes such as sex and educational qualifications; they also include vital but unmeasurable factors such as natural ability and the influence of family background. Statistical analysis that is unable to control for the latter faces serious technical problems.

Thus the case for mass higher education is strong; but it is strong only in presumptive terms. We cannot say how much additional investment there should be in total, nor (the subject of Section 1.2) how the costs of that investment should be divided between the individual and the state. This suggests the following stylized facts: (*a*) consumers of higher education are generally well informed; (*b*) producers of higher education are generally well informed; (*c*) the optimal size of the higher-education sector cannot satisfactorily be quantified.

Let us accept (*a*) and (*b*), at least in the weak sense that consumers and producers, if not perfectly informed, are at least better informed than central planners, not least because higher education has consumption as well as investment benefits. This suggests that the way to deal with (*c*) is to divide responsibility into two separate decisions.

- Consumers and producers decide on the size of the sector: students apply to universities; universities decide how many students to accept and what fees to charge; employers decide which graduates they want to employ. These are decisions properly made by the citizenry and by universities.
- Government decides how much it proposes to spend on higher education. This decision is properly the province of government. If public spending falls short of that necessary to meet the choices of citizens and universities, the difference has to be made up with private spending.

In short, the market decides on *total* spending, the government on *public* spending.[1]

1.2. *Who should pay?*

Two questions are relevant: where *can* resources come from; and where *should* they come from?

WHERE CAN RESOURCES COME FROM? Resources should continue to come from the taxpayer. But a high-quality mass system cannot be entirely taxpayer funded. Thus public funds have to be supplemented by private funds. This conclusion is not based on ideology, but on the deeply practical reason that large-scale higher education is vital but is too expensive to rely entirely on public funding. As discussed in Chapter 12, the only source that is both large-scale and equitable is a wide-ranging income-contingent loan scheme.

WHERE SHOULD RESOURCES COME FROM? This is the question of who should pay—specifically, of how much subsidy higher education should receive. The

---

[1] This strategy is presented at its simplest; in practice, as discussed shortly, the government would not merely have a passive role.

conventional theoretical argument is that higher education creates benefits to society over and above those to the individual. In those circumstances it is efficient if the student pays for her private benefit and taxpayers contribute a subsidy equal to the external benefit.

This argument commands almost universal acceptance in qualitative terms. As explained in Chapter 10, Section 2, however, there is no scientifically valid way of measuring the relative sizes of private and external benefits. First, there are valuation problems: the benefits of education include not only higher productivity but also (and all but impossible to measure) direct utility benefits to the recipient and increased social cohesion. Second is the issue of causality. The investment case for higher education rests on the (usually unstated) assumption that it increases productivity. The screening hypothesis argues that education is *associated* with higher productivity, but does not *cause* it.

The following discussion takes it as read that there *is* a case for continuing subsidy, but leaves open its size because there is no definitive way of measuring it, and also because—whatever the scientific arguments—the matter is ultimately one to be decided by politicians and the electorate.

Whatever the size of the external benefit, however, there is one strong result—that higher education creates a private benefit: the typical student benefits personally from a degree, through higher earnings, greater job satisfaction, and/or greater enjoyment of leisure. Thus the theory argues unambiguously that some of the costs should be borne by the student.

1.3. *The resulting system*

The analysis of this and earlier chapters suggests that universities should set fees; students should be entitled to an income-contingent loan covering all tuition charges and all living costs; and borrowers should pay an interest rate broadly equal to the government's cost of borrowing.[2]

EFFICIENCY. The argument for efficiency is that participants are well informed and all relevant stakeholders—students, universities, employers, and government—have an influence on outcomes.

Students pay a part of the cost of their degree and are therefore better placed to demand greater variation in what universities provide. Students will make choices about which university they attend; they will make demands about the type of course they go to; they will also make demands about the structure of the degree—for example, whether part-time or full-time, three years or compressed into a shorter time, taught during the day or in the evening, and so on.

---

[2] This is the system Iain Crawford and I proposed to the UK Dearing Committee, subsequently published as Barr and Crawford 1998*a*.

Employers can influence outcomes indirectly through their choice of employees. They can also have a direct influence through negotiation with universities about course content. In the UK, for example, professional bodies such as accountants and social workers give partial exemption from professional examinations to students graduating from courses whose content takes account of the needs of those professional bodies.

Universities also have the freedom to influence outcomes. The changes in the pattern of demand resulting from a more decentralized system will require universities to respond in ways that are wholly impossible within a centrally planned funding mechanism. Universities have to be free to determine price (that is, the level of tuition fees they charge), quantity (that is, the number of students they accept), and quality (i.e. that is, the types of courses they offer). Thus they will have economic freedom to parallel their academic freedom.

Government retains a major influence. It no longer controls the system as a central planner, but that does not mean that it is powerless—far from it. Government has a direct role in funding, as discussed earlier. It also acts as a facilitator for private funds—for example, through its role in implementing a system of student loans. Its second important task is to promote access in the ways described in the discussion of equity, below, and more fully in Section 3.2.

The third role of government is quality assurance. Part of the task is to ensure that regulation is in place and enforced. Incentives, however, are at least as important—for example, more resources for institutions that produce better outcomes. As discussed in Section 2, several countries are moving in that direction. It is also possible to combine regulation and incentives: a minimalist approach would simply require universities to publish timely, accurate performance data on their web sites—for example, the destination of its recent graduates—thus giving prospective students the information they needed to vote with their feet (see Cave *et al.* 1992).

A fourth role of government is to influence the degree of competition. In a simple-minded model, every student is given a voucher;[3] institutions compete for students; those that attract large numbers flourish and expand, those that fail to attract students go to the wall. Universities, however, are not the conventional firms of economic theory: they do not make a homogeneous product; they do not maximize profit; and the 'product' is not well defined (see Winston 1999). Thus red-in-tooth-and-claw competition is not the best environment for higher education. It is a huge mistake, however, to think that this is the only approach to competition. At the other extreme, government, as in the UK in the late 1990s,

---

[3] Vouchers, paid for out of taxation, are equivalent to money on which is printed 'to be spent only on higher education'. Every student gets a voucher from the state, which he or she can spend to pay for his or her tuition fees. Depending on the scheme, the voucher will pay fees in full, or in part. For further discussion, see Blaug 1984.

could decide how many students would study which subjects at which university, and issue vouchers accordingly. Such a regime simply mimics central planning.

Thus the mechanism of vouchers should be thought of as a continuum, from 0 per cent constrained (law of the jungle) to 100 per cent constrained (pure central planning) or anywhere in between. There are a variety of incentives policy-makers should consider.

- *Promoting subjects*. It can be argued that subjects such as accounting, law, and economics can look after themselves. If a subject like classics needed protection, some vouchers could be tied to the subject. Equally, if government wished to promote a subject, it could offer larger vouchers tied to the subject. As an example, the UK government introduced financial incentives in 1999 to encourage more people to train to become teachers.
- *Promoting institutions* could be organized similarly. For reasons of regional balance there could be vouchers tied to universities in particular parts of the country or to universities that for cultural or historical reasons government wished to favour.
- *Promoting access*. Vouchers do not, as is commonly supposed, have to penalize students from poorer backgrounds. It would be possible—and desirable—to offer larger vouchers to students from poorer backgrounds (for the use of vouchers, more generally, as a redistributive device, see Le Grand 1989). Much of the discussion of methods of promoting greater equity, below, is of this type.
- *Promoting quality*. Would competition degrade quality? There are, of course, incentives in that direction—for example, grade inflation; but there are also adverse incentives in a non-competitive environment—for example, for academics to write books rather than look after their students. Indeed, one of the stronger arguments in favour of competition is that it gives institutions a powerful incentive to look after students. As discussed above, one way to protect standards is to monitor quality and publish the results.

In short, the approach allows intervention to foster both educational and distributional objectives. The degree of competition is a policy variable; different answers are possible for different subjects; and the system can be as redistributive as desired. The resulting system is efficient, because outcomes are determined not by a single, dominant—and often badly informed and ineffective—arm of government, but by the interacting decisions of students, universities, and employers, subject to transparent influence by government. Particularly with complex mass systems of higher education, this approach is much more likely than central planning to achieve individual and national objectives.

EQUITY. The system is also more equitable in two ways. First it allows improved targeting. A move from tax funding towards loans reduces the subsidy to the best off. A move towards market prices (that is, fees set by universities within a regulatory framework) fully supported by income-contingent loans makes it possible to take the large sums currently spent on *general* subsidies and use them instead on *specific* subsidies carefully targeted on groups for whom access is most fragile. Such a move is unambiguously progressive.

The system is more equitable, secondly, because it frees resources to promote access more powerfully and directly than measures that spread subsidies more indiscriminately across the student population. Policies to promote access have at least four ingredients:

- Money measures include targeted scholarships; separately, loans should be available for all students, full-time and part-time, undergraduate and postgraduate.
- Extra personal and/or intellectual support is needed for students from poorer backgrounds once they arrive at university.
- Extra resources are needed to promote access earlier in the education system—for example, through policies that strengthen schools in disadvantaged areas.
- In addition, information and raising aspirations are critical while children are still at school.

These policies are discussed in greater detail in Section 3.2.

2. LESSONS FROM INTERNATIONAL EXPERIENCE

A World Bank study (1994*b*: table 3.1) divides discussion into experience with mortgage-type loans and with income-contingent loans.[4] This section, by and large, follows this classification, looking in turn at the USA, the UK, the Netherlands, Sweden, Australia, and New Zealand.[5] Discussion of each country is brief, to ensure that the strategic pattern emerges clearly.

2.1. *The USA*

BRIEF DESCRIPTION. The US system of universities and colleges is arguably the largest and most diverse of any country.[6] Spending on higher education, 2 per cent of GDP in 1995 (Table 13.1), is higher, often considerably higher, than any other OECD country. A second outstanding characteristic is multiple providers:

---

[4] On international experience, see also Woodhall (1990) and UK National Committee of Inquiry into Higher Education (1997*c*).

[5] The institutions of these six countries are summarized in Table 13.2.

[6] On higher education in the USA, see McPherson and Shapiro (1998) and King (1999). The descriptive data are drawn from UK National Committee of Inquiry into Higher Education (1997*c*: ch. 7).

Table 13.1. *Spending on higher education, selected OECD countries, 1995*

Country	% of GDP
Australia	1.5
Austria	0.9
Canada	1.5
Czech Republic	1.0
Denmark	1.3[a]
Finland	1.3
France	1.1[a]
Germany	1.0
Greece	0.7
Hungary	1.0
Ireland	1.3[a]
Italy	0.8
Japan	0.9
Netherlands	1.3
New Zealand	n.a.
Portugal	1.0
Spain	1.1
Sweden	1.7[a]
Switzerland	n.a.
UK	0.7
USA	2.0
OECD average	1.5
Memorandum items	
Argentina	0.7[b]
Chile	1.6[b]

[a] All tertiary education.
[b] 1996.
Note: n.a. = not available
Source: OECD (1998: table B1.1d).

in the mid-1990s there were over 3,600 higher education institutions, about 1,600 of them public, the rest private. Thirdly, the USA has high participation rates: in 1994, 62 per cent of high school graduates went on to some sort of tertiary education, 22 per cent to a two-year college, 40 per cent to a four-year college. Fourthly, it has mixed funding, of which 60 per cent came from non-governmental sources in the mid-1990s. In the mid-1990s, tuition fees accounted for 27 per cent of the income of universities (41 per cent of the income of private universities, 18 per cent of the income of public universities). Over the 1990s tuition fees rose rapidly, not least to offset declining taxpayer support. Tuition fees are generally set by the university concerned, though state universities are subject to some control by state legislatures for in-state students. A final characteristic is multiple funding sources for students, including loans at federal and state levels, scholarships at federal, state, and university levels, and part-time student employment.

ADVANTAGES. The discussion in Section 1 suggests that the USA gets things broadly right on tuition fees in the sense that, at least for private universities, each university can set its own fee levels. Secondly, there is considerable diversity across the system. This is the 'Anglo-American' model described at the start of the chapter. Thirdly, access is good, at least in terms of aggregate measures like the age participation rate, not least because of the multiplicity and diversity of institutions. Thus a student from a poor background can do a few courses at her local community college and, being successful and enthused, can then transfer to a four-year institution.[7] Fourthly, research capacity is generally good and, at its best, world class. Finally, academic freedom is real.

CRITICISMS. In many ways, therefore, the USA gets its funding of universities broadly right. The problems are largely to do with the way students are funded. First, the system is complex. Indeed, there is no real *system*, but lots of disparate bits, making it difficult for students to understand what is on offer.[8] Secondly, student loans have mortgage-type repayments, notwithstanding that the USA has ample capacity to administer an income-contingent system effectively. Thirdly, loans attract an interest subsidy. As discussed earlier, this tends to benefit the better off, and is also inefficient.

The default rate, fourthly, is uncomfortably high, particularly for students at vocational institutions. This 'leakiness' has two causes: a high default rate, and the fact that students borrow at subsidized interest rates. As a joint result, a significant fraction of lending to students is not repaid, the shortfall being a cost to the taxpayer. As a result, loans bring in much less private money than is at first sight apparent—a problem in which the USA is far from unique.

A final problem is that the US system of guarantees to private lenders almost certainly violates international guidelines about what is classified as public and what as private spending. The USA can get away with such things, but it does not follow that the model can be applied in other countries, particularly transition and middle-income developing countries. The classification issue is discussed in more detail in Chapter 14, Section 1.

There is an apparent conflict between (*a*) the earlier argument that mortgage loans deter access, and the facts that the USA (*b*) has mortgage-type loans but (*c*) a high participation rate. There are a number of reasons why mortgage-type loans are likely to have less of a disincentive effect in the USA than elsewhere. In-

---

[7] A colleague on a recent World Bank mission started out by taking a course in hairdressing at a local community college and ended up as a professor at the prestigious University of California, Los Angeles.

[8] To study the complexity close up, see http://www.finaid.org.

come is different, the USA being a rich country. History is different, the USA having no tradition of free higher education. Attitudes are different: people in the USA, it can be argued, are less risk averse and hence less debt averse than is typical in Europe; and there is less of an elitist attitude towards higher education in the USA, it being a common aspiration for blue-collar workers to send their children to college. Finally, social values are different: arguably, the Americas (North and South) have a more individualistic culture than is typical in Europe, and so give equity a somewhat lower weight.

Though many of these points are debatable, they suggest, at a minimum, that the US experience cannot automatically be transferred to countries with lower incomes and different attitudes. As with earlier discussion of pensions, they illustrate, more generally, the importance of designing policy with due regard to differences in initial conditions.

2.2. *The UK*

Higher education in the UK can be summarized by four central facts.[9]

- In sharp contrast with the USA, the system continues to be centrally planned.
- The system has expanded from an elite system with a 5 per cent participation rate in 1960 to a medium-sized system (14 per cent participation rate) by the late 1980s, to a mass system with a participation rate of about one-third by 2000.
- In the latter years, that expansion came with no parallel increase in university income per student, creating worries about quality. In 1995, total spending on higher education was 0.7 per cent of GDP (Table 13.1), under half the OECD average and, as a fraction of GDP, on a par with expenditure in a middle-income country like Argentina.
- Despite expansion, access remains very skewed: in 1999, 52 per cent of university entrants were from the top two socioeconomic groups, but only 9 per cent from the bottom two (Greenaway and Haynes 2000: table 2). Even worse, there was little improvement in the relative position of poorer families: the fraction of students from the lowest socioeconomic group has remained at about 1 per cent since 1979, while that of the next lowest has increased slightly from 5 to 7 per cent of university students (Greenaway and Haynes 2000: fig. 3).

---

[9] For further detail on the UK, see Barr (1989, 1997), UK Committee of Vice-Chancellors and Principals (1996), Barr and Crawford (1997, 1998*a*, *b*), and UK National Committee of Inquiry into Higher Education (1997*a*, *b*).

Pre-1998: Mortgage loans

BRIEF DESCRIPTION. Under the system prevailing in the 1980s, tuition for UK students was free. Living expenses were paid via a tax-funded grant, based on a parental income test. Thus students with rich parents received little or no grant, it being assumed that the parent would pay the student an equivalent amount (the so-called parental contribution). A student whose parents were poor received a full grant. Historically the grant was enough to live on, but it fell in real terms and by the late 1980s was no longer adequate fully to support a student's living costs.

In 1990 a loan scheme was introduced, in part to address this problem. Under the new system, tuition for UK students remained free. Half of living costs were covered by a tax-funded grant, based on a parental income test, the other half by a loan.

CRITICISMS. The loan scheme was rightly heavily criticized. First, it was hugely and unnecessarily costly in public expenditure terms, putting at risk both expansion (which was the objective in 1990) and quality. The problem had two sources: students borrowed public money, and they paid a zero real rate of interest—that is, there was an interest subsidy. On the government's own estimates (Hansard (Commons), Written Answers, 24 July 1989, col. 441), the scheme would have taken 25 years to break even on a cumulative basis; my own estimate placed the figure at about 100 years (*Financial Times*, 29 June 1989, p. 8). It would have been cheaper to give the money away. As a result, loans brought in no extra money for universities; indeed, increasing student numbers meant that student support crowded out resources for universities, leading to a decline in real funding per student of about 30 per cent between 1990 and 1995 (UK Committee of Vice-Chancellors and Principals 1996: para. 8), and an overall decline between 1980 and 2000 of about 50 per cent per student (Greenaway and Haynes 2000: fig. 4). Thus worries about the quantity of students were converted into worries about the quality of what they were receiving.

The second strategic criticism of the 1990 loan scheme was that it gave little assistance to access. Mortgage repayments had no directly measurable effect, given that (*a*) there was heavy excess demand for entry to what was still an elite system and (*b*) loans were small. However, the continued high taxpayer cost of the system meant that loans could not, for fiscal reasons, be extended to part-time or to postgraduate students, nor for other desirable reforms such as abolishing parental contributions, whose evils are discussed shortly.

Loans were unpopular and did nothing to improve university funding, problems that were both predictable and predicted (Barr 1989, 1991). In the face of mounting funding pressures, the UK Vice-Chancellors in early 1996 threatened to bring in a tuition charge. The government responded by establishing a National Committee of Inquiry (the Dearing Committee).

From 1998: Income-contingent loans
The Dearing Report was published in July 1997 (UK National Committee of Inquiry into Higher Education1997*a*, *b*). The government did not accept its recommendations in their entirety, but instead implemented a modified version, discussed in this section (for fuller discussion, see Barr 1998*b*; Barr and Crawford 1998*b*). The government's response to Dearing had three elements.

- The Report unambiguously recommended a move to income-contingent loans, and the government endorsed this conclusion. Students starting university in or after October 1998 were eligible for income-contingent loans, with repayments collected alongside the borrower's income tax.[10]
- The maintenance grant was abolished, with an income-tested loan entitlement in its place.
- The government broadly accepted the Dearing Report's recommendation of a flat-rate tuition charge of £1,000 (25 per cent of average teaching costs) per student per year, irrespective of university or subject studied, but introduced an income test. Thus students from poor backgrounds pay no tuition fee; students from well-off backgrounds pay the entire fee; and in between the charge is on a sliding scale. The government also expressed hostility to flexible tuition fees.

ADVANTAGES. The introduction of income-contingent loans, with repayments collected alongside income tax, was unambiguous and welcome progress. The introduction of explicit tuition fees is a second advantage, albeit a controversial one. The extent of controversy is slightly surprising: free tuition for *all* undergraduates was a fleeting event, featuring only between 1977 and 1998. Until 1977, fees were payable where income (usually that of the student's parents) was above a certain level. In addition, fees had always been charged for part-time students, postgraduate students, and many students in sub-degree tertiary education. It was only full-time university undergraduates—and then only for the twenty years after 1977—who had been exempt.

CRITICISMS. The arrangements, once more, were rightly criticized. Though ostensibly about UK reform, the arguments about faulty design discussed here are of general application (for fuller discussion, see Barr and Crawford 1997, 1998*b*). They offer a graphic example of problems that arise when policy is made without adequate regard for implementation.

---

[10] Repayments are 9 per cent of a student's marginal income above of a threshold of £10,000 per year.

Continued reliance on central planning was the worst feature. In respect of their UK/EU undergraduate students, universities in England and Wales are told (*a*) how many they may accept and (*b*) what price they may charge. This is a market in which both price and quantity are determined by the central planner. There are draconian financial penalties for universities who undershoot or overshoot their student number targets; and the government made it illegal for universities to charge fees additional to the centrally ordained fee.

Complexity. A student from a poor background pays no tuition fee and is entitled to an income-contingent loan intended to be large enough to cover his or her living costs. The assessment of a student's financial position takes account of parental income for a younger student or of his or her spouse's income. Parental or spouse income has two effects: first, as income rises, the tuition fee rises; once the fee has reached its maximum (£1,000),[11] the effect of additional parental income is to reduce the size of the loan to which the student is entitled. All students, however rich their parents, are entitled to a loan equal to about 75 per cent of the maximum loan *except* that scholarship and similar income, if high enough can reduce loan entitlement to zero. Such complexity has two ill-effects: students, prospective students, and their parents cannot understand the system; and it is a nightmare to administer.[12]

No more resources. Since loans continue to be funded from public revenues, they bring in no more resources in the short run. It is true that loans will bring in private funds on a significant scale once the system is mature. That, however, will take at least twenty years.

In addition, loans continue to attract an interest subsidy. As discussed in Chapter 12, Section 4, interest subsidies are inefficient because they distort individual and family choices, inequitable because they are badly targeted, and very expensive. The last point bears amplification. Barr and Falkingham (1993, 1996), using LIFEMOD, a microsimulation model, find that for every 100 that the government lends, only about 50 is repaid. Of the missing 50, 20 is not repaid because of fraud, early death, and emigration (all of which have a relatively small effect), and mainly because some graduates have low earnings and so never repay their loan in full, and 30 is not repaid because of the interest subsidy. In other words, the interest subsidy converts nearly one-third of the loan into a grant.

As a separate piece of evidence, in 1998 and 1999, the UK government sold tranches of student debt to private buyers. The terms of the deal were not made public, but it is believed that the debt was sold for about 50 per cent of its face value. The government's internal estimates break down the missing 50 per cent

---

[11] The number has been rounded; the actual charge in 2000/1 was slightly higher.

[12] As an example of the complexity from an administrative point of view, see the guidance from the central UK Department for Education and Employment to the Local Education Authorities, who administer the income test (SSIN 28/99, Part 5, on http://www.dfee.gov.uk/ssin/index.htm).

into about 15 per cent because of low income, early death, etc., and 35 per cent because of the interest subsidy. The evidence on the cost of the interest subsidy is compelling. The government did not use LIFEMOD; thus the official estimates and the simulation results reinforce each other.

Potential adverse effects on access. The government's fee proposals pursue an equity objective through a *price* subsidy, in the form of reduced fees for poorer students, rather than an *income* subsidy through scholarships and income-contingent loans. The problem with price subsidies is that they frequently hurt the very people they are intended to help. Access is harmed in several ways. First, student living standards are inadequate because the total of loan and parental contribution remains too low to support an adequate standard of living (for recent evidence, see Callender and Kemp 2000).

Secondly, the system retains parental contributions, which, it is well known, work badly. Barr and Low (1988), using data for 1982/3, found that about half of students entitled to parental contribution received less than they were supposed to, and the shortfall was substantial: students whose parents gave them less than the system supposed received only £53 of every £100 of assessed parental contribution. As a result, one student in thirteen remained below the poverty line even when income from all sources was included. Subsequent work based on 1992/3 data found that 37 per cent of students received less than the assessed parental contribution (UK Committee of Vice-Chancellors and Principals (1996: 14), quoting an official survey).

Thus unpaid parental contributions leave students in poverty. That, however, is only part of the picture. Unpaid parental contributions cause some students to drop out, and the *threat* of unpaid contributions deters an unknown number of students from applying in the first place. In yet other cases, parents pay the contribution, but only if their son or daughter conforms with their wishes: 'we will pay, but only if you do a sensible subject.' Parental contributions thus force young adults into a dependent position. The point is, if anything, even stronger in respect of spouse contributions.

The previous paragraph is *not* an attack on family support for students: where parents wish to help and students are happy to accept, family support should be applauded. The attack here is twofold. First, policy should not be based on an *assumption* that parents will support their children. Such an assumption may, at a stretch, have been valid for an elite system of higher education, regarded as a luxury good for middle-class families; it is invalid for mass higher education as an investment good, and totally inapplicable to a policy of expanding access to groups with no previous experience of higher education. The policy is bad also because it *forces* students into dependence on parental contributions, since there is no option to take out a larger loan in place of unpaid contributions.

A third impediment to access is that the fee contribution is deemed to be paid through the parental contribution, in effect introducing up-front fees that create an enhanced reliance on family resources. No government committed to access should contemplate such a policy.

Finally, all these problems—student poverty, unpaid parental/spouse contributions, and pressure to conform with parental/spouse wishes—are likely to affect women more strongly than men, especially women from particular cultural and ethnic backgrounds, and thus have potential gender and ethnic effects that deter access.

Other inequities. Impediments to access are one source of inequity. There are other ways in which the proposals are inherently unfair. First, they focus on starting point rather than outcomes. Lucky the shopworker's son who becomes a successful barrister, who pays no fees, unlucky the managing director's daughter who pays fees and becomes a social worker. What matters is not where people start but where they end up. Secondly, price does not vary with quality. It is unfair to expect students to pay the same flat fee at Oxford as at a little-known technical college.

In the face of these problems, the UK debate about higher education finance is continuing and fierce.

2.3. *The Netherlands*

STUDENT SUPPORT is generous.[13] There are three components: the basic grant, the supplementary grant, and a student loan. All students receive a basic grant, which is independent of parental income, but is paid at a lower rate if a student is living with his or her parents. Students are also eligible for a supplementary grant based on a parental income test. Interestingly, both grants are made initially as a loan, which is converted to a grant if students meet necessary performance criteria, the most important being that they obtain their qualification within a specified duration. Students are also eligible for a loan, available without an income test, on which they pay an interest rate roughly 2 per cent above the rate on long-term government bonds.

LOAN REPAYMENTS. There are two mechanisms. Under the default system, interest is charged on loan *and* the basic and supplementary grants from the time that they are disbursed (that is, from the first monthly payment in the student's first year). Repayments begin two years after the student leaves higher education. At that time the student's debt is totalled, and monthly repayments calculated such that the loan is repaid over fifteen years—on the face of it a straightforward mortgage-type loan. These repayment terms, however, are imposed only where

---

[13] I am grateful to Ben Jongbloed (1999) for the factual information on which this section draws.

the person has an income above some threshold. A person with a lower income can request to make lower repayments; for very low incomes, repayment is zero. This process has to be repeated each year. Thus people with income below the threshold make income-contingent repayments.[14] Any loan not repaid after fifteen years is forgiven under either repayment method.

Thus student loans in the Netherlands can be thought of in either of two ways: as a mortgage-type system, with abatement of repayment for low earners; or as a system with income-contingent repayments, subject to a ceiling on annual repayments. Viewed from the latter perspective, a number of criticisms can be made: the means test is administratively cumbersome; there is no obvious rationale for the ceiling on repayment; and fifteen years is rather short for loan forgiveness (at the other extreme, there could be no forgiveness, with any unpaid student debt a charge on a person's estate at death).

FUNDING UNIVERSITIES. One interesting feature has already been mentioned—the fact that student funding is performance related, in that the grant is treated as a loan unless the student completes his or her qualification within a pre-ordained time. Universities, similarly, face performance-based funding. They receive a centrally determined, flat-rate tuition fee irrespective of subject or university, but beyond that, under a system introduced in 2000, 50 per cent of a university's teaching budget is based on performance measured in terms of completion rates within a specified time period. On the plus side, these mechanisms create incentives for timely completion for students and universities. On the minus side, they create adverse incentives for universities in two ways: to cream skim by skewing enrolments towards school-leavers, who generally study full time and are more likely to graduate quickly, and to dilute standards of marking at the margin to keep completion rates high.

Total spending on higher education in the Netherlands, 1.3 per cent of GDP (Table 13.1), is midway between the UK and USA, and slightly above the average for the European Union of 1.1 per cent.

2.4. *Sweden*

STUDENT SUPPORT is generous. There is a system of student grants, which meet about 28 per cent of living costs. Students are entitled to a loan for the remainder of living costs. A student is entitled to this package of support for up to six years, but only if he or she maintains at least a minimum level of achievement. Both grant and loan are subject to an income test of the student's income (but *not* that

---

[14] This should be contrasted with the 1990 UK scheme, which had binary repayment rates: below the deferment threshold repayment was zero; above the threshold, students made the full mortgage repayment. This obviously created adverse incentive effects for people with income close to the threshold.

of his or her parents or spouse). These grants and loans are also available to part-time students, and to students in upper secondary school.[15]

Loan repayments are 4 per cent of the total annual income of borrowers, provided that that income exceeds a minimum threshold. Specifically, the student loans agency collects repayments monthly or quarterly, based on the borrower's income two years previously.[16] Interest is computed from the time the loan is taken out. The interest rate is set by government annually (4.1 per cent in 1999). Unpaid debt is written off when a person reaches the age of 65.

These arrangements suggest a number of strategic questions. The first is whether such generous funding is fiscally compatible with Sweden's avowed objective of expanding higher education. Secondly, the 4 per cent repayment rate is proving to be too low, not least because students can borrow for up to six years of study, hence on present projections many students will not repay by the time they reach 65. For both reasons, reform is on the agenda. One option is to increase the grant element. This approach, it is argued, will not add much to public spending; all that is happening is that an implicit grant, in the form of a loan that is not repaid, is being converted into an explicit grant. Another option under consideration is to increase repayments by moving towards arrangements—similar to those in the Netherlands—whereby borrowers repay one-twenty-fifth of their total debt annually, but no more than 5–6 per cent of their income.

FUNDING UNIVERSITIES. Higher education in Sweden is free for all students. Tuition fees are not allowed.[17] University funding is therefore determined almost wholly by government. Expansion has been associated with a drive for greater efficiency. As a result, like the Netherlands (and also Denmark) there is a performance-related element to the amount that each institution gets, based mainly on completion rates.[18] The potential adverse incentives this can create were noted above.

2.5. *Australia*

The 1989 scheme

BRIEF DESCRIPTION. The Australian Higher Education Contributions System (HECS)[19] has become famous. Introduced in 1989, it advanced Australian higher education funding in important ways. First, it established the principle of tuition

---

[15] And also for students in folk high school and municipal adult education.

[16] Swedish citizens living abroad repay one-twentieth of their total debt annually.

[17] There is a small charge paid to the student union for social services, etc.

[18] In Denmark the so-called taximeter funds universities on the basis not only of outcome (i.e. graduation), but also of process, in that funding depends to a significant extent on the number of 'active' students, i.e. students who are passing their exams and actively pursuing their studies.

[19] For further detail, see Chapman (1997), and Commonwealth of Australia (1997, 1998).

fees, by introducing charges of around A$2,000 per student per year, irrespective of subject or university, intended to represent about 25 per cent of the average cost of teaching across all subjects and all universities. Students could pay up-front at a discount, or could attend university free and repay the tuition charge through a loan. The second advance was the introduction of an effective income-contingent loan scheme with repayment collected by the income-tax authorities, this being the first large-scale such scheme to be implemented. As in the UK, students pay a zero real rate of interest. In contrast with the UK, loans pay for tu-ition fees, but do not cover living costs, which have to be financed in other ways, such as from family resources or part-time work. A third advance is that the fees brought in some extra resources: in 1995, total spending on higher education was 1.5 per cent of GDP (Table 13.1).

ADVANTAGES. The Australian scheme has been subject to more research than most other systems (for a summary, see Chapman (1997) and the references therein.) Income-contingent loans brought in significant revenue. In 1995, after the scheme had been running for six years, HECS revenues amounted to 10 per cent of total spending on higher education, and were rising rapidly. If 80 per cent of all lending is repaid, the additional revenue from a charge of 25 per cent of teaching costs will eventually add some 20 per cent to university income.

The administration of the scheme has gone well. The 'cacophony of com-plaints . . . related to the alleged administrative burden . . . in retrospect . . . were seriously exaggerated' (Chapman, 1997: 746). In the mid-1990s, the Australian Tax Office estimated that collection costs were 1 per cent of current annual HECS revenues.[20] As Chapman points out, however, this conclusion depends on the fact that Australia has an efficient tax system.

In assessing the impact of HECS on access to higher education, Chapman (1997) is unequivocal: 'the introduction of HECS does not seem to have had any discernible effects on the socioeconomic composition of the student body' so that 'there is no evidence of HECS diminishing access to higher education of the disadvantaged' (p. 749). This outcome, he concludes, illustrates that 'even a radi-cal movement away from a no-charge system can be instituted without jeopar-dising the participation of disadvantaged potential students' (pp. 749–50).

The main criticism of the 1989 scheme is the fact that students pay a zero real interest rate on their loans; thus loans incorporate an expensive, untargeted subsidy.

---

[20] The Australian tax authorities initially resisted the idea of collecting loan repayments. Once that task had been mandated upon them, they ended up rapidly taking ownership of the scheme, publicizing it, and going round high schools to tell schoolchildren about it.

The 1996 reforms

Reforms in 1996 took a number of wrong turns. Fees were increased and their structure changed, so that they varied by subject but not by university. The student contribution rose from 25 per cent of average teaching costs to 37 per cent, ranging from 26 per cent for agriculture to 80 per cent for law. A second part of the reforms allowed institutions that had filled their quotas of publicly funded students to recruit an additional 25 per cent of students who were free market in the sense that they received no public subsidy for tuition fees, universities could charge whatever fees they wished, but such students were not entitled to HECS loans.

These reforms are inefficient, not least because they retain central planning. The dual system of HECS students, paying an average of 37 per cent of teaching costs, and private students paying closer to 100 per cent, is distortionary. The introduction of private students, paying full fees but with no loan entitlement, was argued to be inequitable by allowing less bright students from wealthy families to get into top universities on the basis of wealth rather than ability.

The West Review

HECS was undoubtedly the right scheme for 1989, when the Australian system was relatively small (a 14 per cent participation rate). However, this centrally planned solution became problematic over the 1990s for two reasons. First the system became larger, more diverse, and more complex. Secondly, as in the UK, student numbers in Australia increased rapidly over the 1990s, leading to funding problems. Faced with similar problems to the UK, the Australian government adopted a similar solution—it established a Review of Higher Education Financing and Policy (the West Committee).[21]

The interim West Report in some ways faced a simpler task than the UK Dearing Report. Australia already had a well-established system of income-contingent loans and, having introduced tuition charges in 1989, faced a less acute funding problem than the UK. It was therefore not surprising that the interim West Report was more radical than the Dearing Report.

- *Fees*. 'Institutions should have the freedom to set tuition fees. . . . Institutions must have the ability to provide a range of courses and delivery options, and to decide the level of resources that are devoted to them. Fee flexibility is also essential to encourage competition . . .' (Commonwealth of Australia 1997: 31).
- *Loans*. 'No student undertaking a first qualification should be required to face the upfront payment of tuition fees. . . . Students should have access to

[21] The two chairmen, Lord (Ron) Dearing, a distinguished retired public servant, and Roderick West, a distinguished retired educator, both men of great integrity and charm, became firm friends over the course of their respective inquiries. For explicit comparison of reform in the UK and Australia, see Barr (1998b).

income contingent loans for the payment of any contribution' (Commonwealth of Australia 1997: 29–30).

These views were carried through to the Final Report (Commonwealth of Australia 1998: 25). The discussion in Section 1 suggests that these were the right recommendations at the right time. Predictably, however, they were politically highly sensitive. As of late 2000, the government had taken no action.

2.6. *New Zealand*

The system in the 1990s
The system in New Zealand[22] can be summarized as follows.

- Universities set fees.
- Fees and living expenses are covered by loans.
- Loans are fully income contingent, with repayments collected by the tax authorities.
- Loans carry a market or near-market interest rate.

When the system was first introduced, student charges covered about 25 per cent of tuition costs. The taxpayer subsidy subsequently fell somewhat below 75 per cent, but remains considerable. There is also a system of income-tested grants for students from poor backgrounds. This is precisely the scheme to which the lessons of economic theory in Section 1 point. It can be argued that in important respects the New Zealand system of higher education finance in the 1990s was the best in the world.

The main criticism of the system is its 'big-bang' introduction, in the sense that deregulation of fees was complete and immediate, with the danger that fees and student indebtedness could rise sharply, without giving people time to adjust to the new arrangements. To give expectations time to adapt, a strong case could have been made for a phased relaxation of government control of tuition fees, accompanied by a parallel expansion of student loan entitlement and scholarship arrangements. New Zealand, from this perspective, can be criticized for adopting the right strategy but phasing it in more rapidly than people could comfortably accommodate and with inadequate attention to the politics of reform.

Subsequent developments had two components. First, as discussed in Chapter 14, a 1998 White Paper advocated treating all tertiary education as an integrated whole and moving towards market forces throughout the tertiary sector. Secondly, changes were made to the loan scheme.

[22] For further detail, see New Zealand, Ministry of Education (1998).

The reforms in 2000

Events in early 2000 seriously undermined the efficiency and equity of the loan arrangements and offer lessons of general interest. A new government introduced several seemingly small changes: full-time students, instead of paying interest from the moment they took out the loan, paid a zero *nominal* rate during their student days; a similar regime was applied to low-income part-time students; and the interest rate that subsequently applied was frozen.

These changes can be heavily criticized (for fuller discussion, see Barr 2000): they are expensive and, like all interest subsidies, badly targeted. Previously, official estimates suggested that, for every 100 lent to students, 90 would be repaid. For lending under the new arrangements it is estimated that only 65 out of every 100 of loan will be repaid. Thus non-repayment increases from 10 to 35 per cent. When fully phased in, official estimates suggest, the three changes will add over NZ\$300 million to a higher education budget that previously stood at NZ\$1.8 billion. What appear to be small changes absorb close to one-sixth of the higher education budget.

2.7. *Conclusions from country experience*

Table 13.2 gives a brief overview of the arrangements in different countries, mainly to show the different ways in which the pieces in the jigsaw are put together.

The strategic conclusions from country experience can be summarized as follows. The USA has a useful model on tuition fees, but still lacks a good loan scheme. The UK, after a bad start with mortgage-type loans, now has an effective loan scheme, but major reform is still needed to reduce complexity, to address the heavy costs of interest subsidies, and to phase in flexible fees. The Netherlands and Sweden, rather like the UK, have loans that (implicitly or explicitly) are income contingent, but both have flat-rate tuition fees fixed by government (in Sweden fixed at zero). Australia has a well-established loan scheme, but has not avoided interest subsidies, and has got into a muddle on fees. New Zealand offers useful lessons on loans *and* fees and, more recently, an example to avoid on interest subsidies.

HELPFUL FEATURES. Earlier discussion suggests a number of useful strategic design features. Where possible, incentives have advantages over regulation in encouraging efficient behaviour by all actors—students, universities, employers, and government. Enforcing regulation can be costly and administratively demanding. Incentives are likely to be cheaper and more effective. Secondly, it is desirable to avoid price subsidies, which are generally costly and regressive. One implication is a move towards market-determined fees; another is a move

Table 13.2. *Higher education funding in different countries*

	USA	UK 1990	UK 1998+	Netherlands	Sweden	Australia	New Zealand to 1999
Fees set by							
Government		Zero	Flat rate[a]	Flat rate	Zero	Multiple flat rate[b]	
Universities	✓[c]						✓
Grants	No	Partial	No	Partial	Partial	Partial, on basis of income test	Partial, on basis of income test
Loans cover							
Tuition fees	Partly or fully	n.a.		Yes	n.a.	Yes	Yes
Living costs	Partly or fully	50%	Partly or fully	Yes	Yes		Yes
Loan repayments							
Mortgage	✓	✓		✓ with income-contingent safeguard			
Income contingent			✓		✓	✓	✓
Interest rate	Subsidized	Zero real	Zero real	Approx. market	Approx. market	Zero real	Approx. market

[a] Fees are flat rate across universities and subject, but are assessed through an income test; thus students from poor backgrounds pay no fee.

[b] Fees vary by subject, but not across universities.

[c] Private universities set their own fees; so do public state universities for out-of-state students.

Note: n.a = not applicable.

towards unsubsidized interest rates for student loans (though any such moves have a major political dimension). Thirdly, income testing should be avoided where possible: it creates a major administrative burden and risks creating adverse incentives.

A fourth lesson suggests developing flexible systems that can evolve. It is highly undesirable to bring in a new system and then have to change it drastically (as with the UK loan system). Any change of system is costly and disruptive. In the face of uncertainty, a rational strategy is to design a system that encourages diversity and is capable of evolving, pointing towards a strategy of market forces plus regulation, rather than one of central planning, which is better suited to a predictable and more static world. The system should therefore include loan schemes that are able to grow, to have their parameters (for example, the interest rate charged to borrowers) changed, and to be extended to further groups of students. Tuition fees should be able to vary across subject and across institution. The amount of public subsidy for higher education should also be capable of varying. University governance should make it possible for course content and degree structures to evolve as circumstances change.

PITFALLS. Economic theory and practical experience point to avoidable problems: (a) fiscally unsustainable public spending; (b) public spending hijacked by the middle class; (c) loans absent, or badly designed, so that they bring in few, if any, extra resources; (d) economic constraints on education providers, which reduce incentives to efficiency; and (e) specific design features that are costly (interest subsidies), administratively demanding (income testing), or both.

These occur in all the countries listed above, though (b) and (d) are less of a problem in the USA and New Zealand, which have variable fees. They also occur elsewhere: an account of Latin America reported that:

Most of the public institutions . . . have argued that low or no tuition fees have provided greater equality of educational opportunity by providing greater access. . . . Such reasoning is simply incorrect . . . the overwhelming public subsidy has been and continues to accrue to students from middle and high-income families.   (Lewis 1999)

IMPLEMENTATION. Alongside policy design, a final, and critical, lesson is the importance of implementation, in many ways the harder part of the task. Discussion here concentrates on student loans, but applies generally. The first question for reformers is whether key institutional prerequisites are in place, including the capacity to collect repayments and a legal system robust enough to enforce them (both points apply equally to mortgage loans and income-contingent loans). If either is significantly inadequate, the idea should be postponed.

If reform gets the green light, it is essential that implementation is taken fully into account at the time the policy is formulated. To that end, the group of people who put together any reform package needs to contain both policy-design and implementation skills. The need for strategic thinking about policy requires little elaboration, since that is what this entire book is about. In the case of loans, it is needed, for example, to ensure that interest subsidies and income testing are not introduced unthinkingly.

Political skills are a second essential. They are needed to communicate why a loan scheme is necessary and how it can help access, or to explain the role and operation of tuition fees. UK experience over the 1990s shows how failure to grasp this point brings students onto the streets. It is also necessary to ensure that political support is continuing. New Zealand is an example of how a reform can be introduced successfully but subsequently at least partly undone.

A wide-ranging set of additional skills address the operational needs of the scheme: the obvious starting point is expertise in running a system with large numbers of loan accounts that remain active over many years; for income-contingent loans, tax expertise is needed to ensure that the scheme is compatible with the operations of the tax authorities; if loans are to be paid using private money, deep financial market expertise is necessary, and so is an understanding of the classification problem;[23] if loans are to be paid to students through banks' networks of cash points, expertise in retail banking is needed. The UK experience shows that attempts to involve banks at a late stage in policy design without any awareness of how they operate can poison relations with private providers for a considerable period. Finally, there has to be sufficient time for any new system to be implemented effectively.

3. CONCLUSIONS

3.1. *Misleading guides to policy design*

It is now possible to see why various arguments against market forces in higher education do not stand up. The arguments that follow are not made on ideological grounds—indeed, I take the imperative to improve access as common ground—but on the pragmatic ones (*a*) that free higher education has failed to achieve its objectives of access and quality, and (*b*) that a different strategy, for example that in Section 3.2, would promote both more effectively.

HIGHER EDUCATION IS A BASIC RIGHT AND SHOULD THEREFORE BE FREE. The assertion that access is a basic right is a value judgement, though one with which (I assume) everyone agrees. But it does not follow that, because something is a basic right, it must be provided free. We all agree that access to food is a basic right; yet the provision of food by competitive suppliers at market prices is uncontentious throughout the industrialized world. The objective is *not* free higher

---

[23] The classification problem is discussed in Chapter 14, Section 1.1.

education but, so far as access is concerned, a system in which no bright person is denied a place at university because he or she comes from a disadvantaged background.

In arguing for free higher education, however, people are reaching towards an important point: though it is not true that higher education should be free, there is a strong case for making it *free at the point of use*. The arrangements set out in Section 3.2 do just that.

IT IS IMMORAL TO CHARGE FOR EDUCATION. The same arguments apply. It is immoral (in my view) if people with the aptitude and desire are denied access to higher education because they cannot afford it; it is also immoral if underfunded earlier education means that they never even aspire to higher education. Similarly, it is immoral if someone is malnourished because he cannot afford a healthy diet. That, however, does not mean that it is immoral to charge for food, meaning that food would be free for everyone, including the rich; rather it is an argument for income transfers to allow everyone to afford a healthy diet.

Making something free for everyone can be justified in efficiency terms where market failures make consumer sovereignty problematic, and in equity terms where consumption is not largely by the better off. School education is an example. Higher education conforms with neither criterion: as argued earlier, consumer sovereignty is useful, and there is a steep socioeconomic gradient in consumption. As a result, taxpayer subsidies are regressive: the taxes of truckdrivers pay for the degrees of old Etonians. In my view *that* is immoral.

Nor has free higher education (as in the UK for most students until 1990) done well in terms of access. As noted earlier, students from the lowest two socioeconomic groups make up broadly the same fraction of undergraduates in the UK in 2000 as in 1979.

ELITISM HAS NO PLACE IN HIGHER EDUCATION. Argument often blurs two separate elements. Many people, including me, agree with the value judgement that *social* elitism is wrong—access to the best universities should not be influenced by a person's social class background. In contrast, *intellectual* elitism is both proper and desirable. The best musicians and the best athletes are chosen precisely because of their abilities, irrespective of whether their background is poor (Pele) or middle class (Tiger Woods). There is nothing inequitable about intellectually elite universities. The equity objective should be a system in which the brightest students are able to study at the most intellectually demanding universities, and that their ability to do so is determined by their ability and wishes, but not by their socioeconomic background.

GRADUATES PAY FOR THEIR DEGREE THROUGH HIGHER TAX PAYMENTS. Graduates have higher earnings and therefore pay more taxes than non-graduates; thus, the argument goes, they already pay for their degree. Economic theory argues that it is efficient if a person pays for his or her private benefit, while the taxpayer pays for any external benefit. If there is no external benefit, people pay the full marginal cost—for example, food. If the benefit is all external to the individual, as with a pure public good,[24] it should be entirely tax funded. These arguments were explored in the context of higher education in Chapter 10, Section 2, and led to two conclusions. First, though they cannot be quantified, qualitative arguments suggest that higher education has external benefits, and hence should be subsidized. Second, and a strong result, is that the private benefit is substantial. In efficiency terms, therefore, there is an overwhelming argument for a student contribution, though no precision about its size.

Because a degree brings private benefit it is, of course, true that someone with a degree has higher earnings than would otherwise be the case, and hence pays higher taxes. Thus a person's investment in higher education confers an external benefit on future taxpayers. The analogue with investment in physical capital is clear. If a firm invests profitably in new machinery, the investment produces an increased profit stream and hence higher tax payments by the firm. Again, there is an external benefit for future taxpayers. The externality is recognized by allowing the cost of the machinery as a deductible expense in calculating the firm's tax liability. That arrangement is justified in theory, universally applied in practice, and unanimously accepted. But nobody has ever argued that, because the firm's investment makes a future profit for the taxpayer, the taxpayer should pay the entire cost of its machinery. For a $1 million machine this would amount to allowing the firm to reduce its tax bill by $1 million in the year in which it buys the machine—in other words, a 100 per cent subsidy on all investment—rather than allowing it to reduce its tax bill over time by $1 million multiplied by the firm's marginal tax rate.

Thus the argument that investment in higher education generates future tax payments that more than cover the cost of a person's degree may well be true. But it is irrelevant. To argue that the tax externality justifies tax-funded higher education is logically equivalent to saying that because Microsoft is enormously profitable and hence pays huge taxes, its investment should be funded entirely out of taxation. Since Microsoft makes a private return, it will invest without any subsidy. Subsidies in excess of external benefits are therefore a deadweight cost and, in the case of higher education, a highly regressive one—it is more efficient and more equitable to use the resources to promote access in more targeted ways.

---

[24] A pure public good is non-rival in consumption, non-excludable, and non-rejectable, an example being national defence. As defined by economists, a public good is *not* the same as a publicly provided good such as health care or school education. See e.g. Stiglitz (2000: ch. 4).

A separate argument is that a graduate and a non-graduate with the same income have the same tax liability. However, the former has received a subsidy from the taxpayer, the latter has not. This is inequitable as well as inefficient.

STUDENTS SHOULD MAKE A CONTRIBUTION VIA A GRADUATE TAX. Some commentators oppose loans, but are prepared to contemplate a higher rate of income tax for graduates—that is, a graduate tax. There are several arguments against this approach. First, there is the 'Mick Jagger problem':[25] Mick Jagger was once an accounting student at the London School of Economics. His enormous financial success has no obvious connection with his time at university, yet with a graduate tax he would repay amounts many magnitudes larger than the cost of his studies. As a value judgement, this is unfair.

A second problem is that a graduate tax, being by definition a tax, rules out the option of students borrowing private money in order to speed up the flow of private resources into higher education. If someone gets her student loan from (say) a bank, repaid via a graduate tax, the resulting system will undoubtedly count as public spending (see the fuller discussion in Chapter 14, Section 1).

A related but separate problem is that, because it is a tax and will be perceived as a tax, this type of arrangement can have adverse effects on work effort. To the extent that loan repayments—even if income contingent—are not seen as a tax, since more rapid repayment hastens the day when the repayment will be 'switched off', loans have weaker adverse incentives.

A fourth problem is that, if the costs of higher education were added to the tax system, they could not, under present arrangements, be recovered from students from other EU countries and certainly not from non-EU students. Loans face no such restriction.

Finally, some people would like to see a graduate tax imposed not only on future students but on past students, so as to increase the inflow of extra resources rapidly. Whatever the desirability of such an arrangement, it is probably not feasible. Legislatures might not tolerate such retrospective legislation. In addition, there is the non-trivial practical problem of identifying who has received tax-funded higher education, and thus no easy way of deciding who should pay the additional tax.

None of these problems on its own is insurmountable. But cumulatively, they suggest that a graduate tax is inferior to an income-contingent loan. That said, there is an important truth underlying the graduate tax argument. While there are problems with an arrangement in which there is *no* relation between the size of a student's loan and the amount he repays, it does not follow that the optimal repayment is 100 per cent of the loan. Chapter 14, Section 1, proposes a scheme in which a cohort of students insures itself through a small risk premium added

---

[25] Lead singer of the Rolling Stones, an immensely successful rock group.

to the interest rate of all students. In this type of social-insurance arrangement, a cohort of students as a whole repays 100 per cent of what they borrowed, but those who do well repay somewhat more. Such an arrangement can be thought of as a graduate tax, but with an upper limit on the total repayment of any borrower. It can equally be thought of as a loan scheme with a social-insurance element.

FEES HARM ACCESS. It is an elementary proposition that raising the price of a commodity will generally reduce the quantity demanded. Thus, it is argued, introducing fees or increasing them will reduce demand, to the particular detriment of the least well off.

The argument is true but incomplete. No sensible commentator would suggest fees *on their own*, precisely because of the resulting harm to access. An important part of the argument for fees is that they free resources for *targeted* action on access. The combined effect is a move up a person's demand curve because of higher fees *and* a rightward shift of the demand curve as the result of (say) a targeted scholarship. If scholarships and similar encouragements are generous, demand increases. Thus fees should be introduced only as part of a strategy for access. A well-designed strategy (see Section 3.2) will do more for access than exclusive reliance on tax funding.

This is not just a theoretical assertion. The poor record of free higher education in promoting access has emerged repeatedly. The social composition of undergraduates in the UK has hardly changed in forty years, and the system is regressive.

LOANS HARM ACCESS. It is true that mortgage loans put access at risk for all the reasons set out in Chapter 12, Section 2. What is being proposed is something fundamentally different. Loans should have income-contingent repayments, thus protecting the student from excessive risk. Secondly, loans should cover all fees and all living costs, thus ensuring that higher education is free at the point of use.

A final point. With income tax, the costs of higher education are paid by the generality of income recipients, including non-graduates, pensioners, and the like. A graduate tax can be thought of as additional income tax paid only by the beneficiaries of higher education and hence, it can be argued, is more equitably targeted. An income-contingent loan can be thought of as a graduate tax that is 'switched off' once a person has repaid her agreed contribution towards the costs of her degree. That contribution can be 100 per cent of the loan or, if the costs of non-repayment are shared by the cohort, more than 100 per cent. In that sense, income-contingent loans can be thought of as, in effect, a form of targeted tax, but in a form that is both more efficient and more equitable than funding via the entire body of taxpayers.

3.2. *A strategy for higher education finance*

The following outline is potentially applicable to all advanced industrial countries and—provided that they can implement an effective income tax—also to the advanced post-communist reformers and to middle-income developing countries. The strategy has three elements: flexible fees, a well-designed loan scheme, and active measures to promote access.

FLEXIBLE FEES. Historically, with a small tertiary system and a limited range of subjects, it was possible for central planners to determine funding levels for different institutions. Recent years have seen two welcome changes: many more students, and considerably greater diversity in what tertiary education offers. As a result, (*a*) the necessary variation in funding is much greater than formerly and (*b*) the problem is now too complex for central planners to get right. Thus flexible fees are necessary both for economic efficiency and to redress underfunding—and the consequent threat to quality—of the best institutions. Flexible fees benefit *all* tertiary institutions, by letting each find its place in the spectrum of institutions.

Some people argue that tertiary education should be entirely funded from taxation. There may be a case for such a policy for sub-university education, but, so far as higher education is concerned, the argument is flawed for the reasons outlined above. University education should be free at the point of use; but it does not follow that there should be no charges. Free tuition is expensive; even more serious, the benefits of free tuition, especially at the university level, accrue to those attending university, who are disproportionately from better-off backgrounds. Thus free tuition is badly targeted; the money could do much more for access if spent in a way that directed resources specifically at those groups for whom access is most fragile. With flexible fees, for example, the balance of taxpayer subsidies could be changed, with more going to access universities where remedial action adds to teaching costs. Lowering tuition charges for higher education in other countries has not improved access. Conversely, introducing the Higher Education Contribution Scheme in Australia in 1989, with tuition charges paid via an income-contingent loan, did not harm access (Chapman 1997).

A WELL-DESIGNED LOAN SCHEME. A first, and fundamental, characteristic of a well-designed loan scheme is that it should have income-contingent repayments. Secondly, loans should be sufficient to cover all tuition charges and all living costs, so that tertiary education is free at the point of use. Income-contingent loans automatically tailor repayments to ability to pay. A further advantage is that repayment is determined not by where someone *starts* but by where she *ends up*.

The third central feature of a well-designed loan scheme is that students should pay an interest rate on their loans broadly equal to the government's cost of borrowing. The essential feature of this arrangement is that, apart from non-repayment because of low earnings, early death, and so on, loans are self-financing. Interest subsidies, as discussed earlier, are inefficient, expensive, and unfair. Given the continuing socioeconomic gradient in higher education, which, though particularly acute in the UK, affects all countries, these subsidies disproportionately benefit the middle class. In contrast, the savings from charging an unsubsidized interest rate make it possible to replace an untargeted subsidy by a targeted one.

Avoiding excessive tuition fee subsidies and charging students an interest rate broadly equal to the government's borrowing rate yield a substantial saving in public expenditure, thus freeing resources for the third leg of the strategy:

PROACTIVE MEASURES TO PROMOTE ACCESS. Income-contingent loans measure ability to pay on the basis of where a person ends up (that is, his or her subsequent income). As discussed at the start of the chapter, this is the best approach for students from better-off backgrounds, who are generally well informed about the benefits of tertiary education. A wide range of proactive measures to promote access is necessary precisely because not everyone is well informed.

Money is clearly central. Measures might include an income-tested grant for university students from poorer backgrounds, thus measuring ability to pay in terms of where a person starts. Parental income, however, is a blunt instrument. Another way of targeting scholarships is through schools in disadvantaged areas; another is to give scholarship money to universities, together with financial incentives to recruit students from poor backgrounds; another is targeting by postcode. There is a need for experiment and innovation. A further source of money is the universities themselves, who will want to use some of their fee income for scholarships. Note that universities' direct interest is not in rich students but in bright students—thus all universities have an incentive to gather resources for scholarships. A second way in which money can improve access is by making loans available to all students, full-time and part-time, undergraduate and postgraduate. To eliminate uncertainty, a central feature of any such system is that a student should know exactly what financial support he or she will be getting before starting university.

A second ingredient in promoting access is extra personal and intellectual support, at least in the early days, for access students to make sure that, once a student starts at university, he gets the support he needs to make the transition.

Action is also needed much earlier. Information and raising aspirations are critical. Many people do not apply to university because they have never thought of doing so. Thus mentoring of schoolchildren by current university students, preferably from similar backgrounds, is important; so are visits by schoolchildren to universities. Action to improve information is vital for access, precisely because students from socially excluded backgrounds will systematically be badly informed. Such information activities need to happen early enough to prevent high school drop out.[26]

Finally, problems of access to higher education cannot be solved entirely within the higher education sector. Thus extra resources are needed to strengthen earlier education, which is where the *real* barriers to access occur.

In sum, flexible tuition charges supported by income contingent loans redistribute from today's middle class (who lose a fraction of their tuition subsidies) to tomorrow's least well off (who, with income-contingent loans, do not repay in full). This is redistributive beyond anything contemplated by successive governments. Reform is therefore at least as much an issue of political will as of policy design.

---

[26] The sorts of schemes that are involved include Saturday Schools, which bring schoolchildren from poor areas to university to study on Saturday morning; summer schools, which do something similar during the summer vacation; visit days, when schoolchildren can visit a university; visits by academics to schools to make the idea of higher education more tangible; visits by current students, ideally from the same or a similar school, to schools in deprived areas; and mentoring of schoolchildren by university students, preferably from a similar background.

Chapter 14

Twenty-First-Century Education Issues

Changes in primary and secondary education are likely to affect the content of what is taught more radically than the way it is organized. In particular, compulsory education will remain largely a public-sector activity. With tertiary education, in contrast, substantial changes are foreseeable. On the delivery side, though outside the remit of this chapter, distance learning and other electronic developments will have a significant impact. Funding will also change: this chapter discusses successively the potential for private finance, loan repayments when workers are internationally mobile, rationalizing the funding of tertiary education, not least by extending loans more broadly than higher education, and individual learning accounts.

1. PRIVATE FUNDING

Earlier chapters argued that human capital is a central determinant of economic performance, and that continuing technological advance necessitates more, more diverse, and more repeated education and training. As discussed in Chapter 12, Section 1, however, the resulting mass system of tertiary education cannot all be funded out of taxation. It is therefore necessary to bring in private funds, notably through student loans. In advanced industrial countries, the money students borrow generally comes from the taxpayer. Since loan schemes take a long time to mature, the flow of private funds (that is, students' repayments) into higher education has been slow.

For poorer countries the question is how to finance student loans when the fiscal capacity to meet their up-front costs is not there—in other words, how to organize a loan scheme in which students borrow private money. Before discussing how such borrowing might be organized, it is necessary to discuss an issue at which earlier chapters hinted repeatedly, the dividing line between public and private spending—what is known as the classification problem.

1.1. *The classification problem*

Devising a system in which students borrow mainly from private sources but where income-contingent repayments are collected by the tax authorities is more difficult than it sounds. International guidelines on national income accounting include detailed discussion of the dividing line between public and private spending. The issue is how to ensure that loans from private sources are classified as private spending under such guidelines.[1]

To simplify a complex problem, four factors are relevant when deciding whether student loans are public or private.

- Who designs the scheme? Does the government set the rules, or the private lender?
- Who decides whether a student is eligible? For example, can a private lender refuse to lend to someone whom he regards as a bad risk?
- Where does the money come from?
- Who bears the risk of default: at the margin does the private lender bear the risk or is there a government guarantee?

If a student takes out a conventional bank loan, it is the bank's scheme (for example, the bank can decide what interest rate to charge); the bank decides whether or not it wishes to lend to the student; the money he or she borrows comes from the bank; and the bank bears the risk that he or she will fail to repay. Clearly this is a private scheme. In contrast, if the government designs a loan scheme, decrees that all students are eligible (even those with a criminal conviction for fraud), provides the money that students borrow, and bears the risk of default itself, the scheme is public.

Problems arise where a scheme meets some of the criteria to be classified as private, but not all. Suppose that a student takes out a loan from a bank, but the government gives the bank a full guarantee. Under international guidelines, the *entire* loan will generally count as public spending. Though on the face of it paradoxical, the logic is straightforward: since the government guarantees repayment, no risk is transferred to the private lender. In taking out the loan, the student is therefore acting as an agent of government, and hence the loan is government borrowing. Though the student nominally borrows from a private bank, all such lending is classified as public.[2]

---

[1] Though there are no internationally binding rules, there are three sources of guidelines for public accounting. The International Federation of Accountants (IFAC) has a wide-ranging advisory role but no mandatory power; see the consultation document International Federation of Accountants (1998), and also www.ifac.org. The IMF publishes Government Financial Statistics (GFS). These relate to fiscal transactions in the *national* accounts, not to the presentation of *government* accounts. The 1986 version is out of date: it is in cash-flow terms, pre-dates most private finance, and therefore does not cover student loans. A new version of GFS is in preparation. The EU has its own guidelines, the European System of Integrated Economic Accounts (ESA95). A new Manual on Government Deficit and Debt was published in January 2000 (Eurostat 2000). The EU is currently moving from a cash to an accruals basis. Its direction is to tighten the definition of what does and does not pass the Maastricht criteria.

[2] For a good, non-technical summary of the issues, see UK Department for Education and Employment (1998*a*), and, for an attempt to grapple with them in a UK context, Barr (1997).

Though there is no mechanical way of assessing whether a particular scheme conforms with the classification criteria, there is increasing agreement about two aspects of any scheme: that what matters is not the letter of any arrangement but its intent; and that the critical element is risk transfer. Thus the fact that a student borrows from a private bank is not on its own sufficient to ensure that the loan is private; it is private only if the lender faces a significant fraction of the risk. It follows that an element of judgement is inescapable. Suppose that government agrees to underwrite losses up to x% of total lending, private lenders bearing the risk of losses above that level. If other relevant criteria are met, if $x = 2$% there would be general agreement that the scheme was private; on the other hand, if $x = 75$% the scheme would almost certainly be classified as public, since risk transfer would be a fiction, not a reality. Clearly, the value of x that tips the scheme from private to public involves judgement. The issue is germane not only to private finance of student loans, but equally to other areas such as transport and investment in hospitals.

1.2. *Approaches to private finance*[3]

This section sets out a mechanism for financing student loans from private sources. Any such loans have to conform with three criteria: (1) they should be income contingent, not least to protect access; (2) the arrangement must conform with the classification criteria; and (3) loans must take a form with which private lenders are comfortable.

There are several elements to fulfilling the third criterion: loans should have secure repayments; lenders should receive a market rate of interest; and the loan should have a fixed duration, which implies mortgage-type repayments. The reliability of the scheme to lenders is doubly important: it is necessary to encourage private lenders; in addition, the more comfortable the lenders, the better the deal they offer borrowers. Thus getting repayment terms right for lenders is a central ingredient in achieving the best possible repayment terms for students.

STRATEGIC APPROACHES. There are two broad strategies for bringing in private funds. With *debt sales*, students borrow public money. Having lent the money, the loans administrator retrospectively sells student debt to a private buyer. This is a well-known technique—for example, sales of credit-card debt are frequent. A second approach is *front-end funding*, whereby students borrow more directly from private sources. The role of the loans administrator in this case is limited to holding the ring and to administering any subsidies and guarantees.

The debt-sale approach has been extensively discussed (Barr and Falkingham 1993, 1996; Barr 1997). Two tranches of student debt were sold by the UK

---

[3] Though I have long advocated a strategy of privately financed income-contingent loans (Barr 1989: 55–7; 1997), the practical implementation outlined in this section is due entirely to the pioneering work of Colin Ward and his team at the UK Student Loans Company.

government in the later 1990s. There has been less exploration of front-end funding, which has two variants. With retail lending, individual students borrow from private lenders; thus student borrowing is individualized. With wholesale lending, the loans administration borrows private money in tranches of (say) £1 billion, which it then lends to students. The following discussion shows how a scheme with front-end funding could operate.

A HERMETICALLY SEALED LOAN FUND. The arrangement has three elements.

A loans administrator. Student loans are administered by a public or quasi-public body, the Student Loans Company.[4]

One or more private lenders. Suppose for simplicity that student borrowing comes from a single source, the Private Lender. It is left open for the time being whether students borrow individually (retail front-end funding) or whether the Student Loans Company borrows wholesale. It is also left open whether the Private Lender is a commercial bank, a merchant bank, a pension fund, or some other capital market institution.

A Loan Fund. On the face of it, income-contingent repayments (criterion 1) and mortgage-type loans (criterion 3) are mutually exclusive. Income contingent repayments encourage access by tailoring repayments precisely to a person's income: to the borrower this means *protection*; to the lender it means *uncertainty*. The solution is to divide the transaction into two parts: (*a*) repayments by students, and (*b*) repayments to the lender, with (*a*) and (*b*) connected by a Loan Fund.[5] The sole purpose of the Fund is to manage the flow of repayments and to reimburse private lenders. Its income comprises students' loan repayments, any borrowing necessary to manage the cash flow, and any guarantees (all discussed further below). Its outgoings are repayments to lenders. A key feature is that income and outgoings are tightly specified by contract in a way that insulates the Fund's financial position from changes in government policy towards student loans. This feature is necessary both as assurance to private lenders and to avoid classification problems.

The following illustration explains the operation of the scheme in terms of an individual student, Anna.

(*a*) Anna applies for her student loan, either to the Student Loans Company directly, or, through the Student Loans Company, to the Private Lender.[6]

---

[4] I am deliberately using UK terminology because it makes clear the nature of the beast as a quasi-public entity, but bound by commercial law, both being important elements in bringing in private finance.

[5] As discussed in more detail in Section 4, this could be integrated with the idea of individual learning accounts.

[6] Since the loan application requires someone to certify that Anna is eligible, there are administrative advantages if the Student Loans Company does the initial processing.

(*b*) Once she leaves university, the tax authorities collect income-contingent repayments and transfer them to the Student Loans Company, which deposits the money into the Loan Fund and credits Anna's account.[7]

(*c*) The Loan Fund makes monthly payments to the Private Lender. These payments incorporate a positive real interest rate and are set at a level that repays the loan in (say) ten years. From the point of view of the Private Lender, therefore, repayments look like a mortgage-type arrangement.

(*d*) If the income-contingent repayments under (*b*) are insufficient to cover repayments under (*c*), the difference is made up by further borrowing by the Student Loans Company. The Loan Fund is critical: analogous to a car battery or a cistern, it is a reservoir that makes it possible for incomings and outgoings to be asynchronous. Thus it is possible for students to make income-contingent repayments while lenders receive mortgage repayments.

(*e*) After ten years, the Private Lender has been fully repaid (the issue of default is discussed later).

(*f*) In the typical case, Anna's repayments into the Loan Fund will not have been sufficient to repay in full. She therefore continues to make income-contingent repayments until she has fully repaid.

An illustrative example. Table 14.1 explains the mechanism at its simplest, ignoring both inflation and interest rates.[8]

Anna takes out a loan of £5,000 per year for each year of a three-year, full-time degree, thus ending up (Year 0) with a debt of £15,000, shown in col. 6. Under the stated assumptions, the mortgage repayments are £1,500 per year over ten years.

In Year 1 she has no earnings (col. 1), hence makes no loan repayments; hence the incomings of the Loan Fund from Anna (col. 2) are zero. The Loan Fund makes her £1,500 repayment to the Private Lender (col. 3), reducing her debt to £13,500 (col. 6).

Suppose that income-contingent repayments are 9 per cent of earnings above £10,000 (the UK arrangements in force in 2000). In Year 2, Anna earns £16,000; thus her repayments are £540 (col. 2). The Loan Fund makes her £1,500 repayment to the Private Lender (col. 3), of which £540 comes from her income-contingent repayment; the rest adds to her Loan Fund deficit (col. 5), which is covered by additional borrowing by the Student Loans Company.

---

[7] In theory, the tax authorities could make the transfer to the Loan Fund directly. There are at least two arguments for an intermediate body like the Student Loans Company: the tax authorities do not normally have the capacity to manage multi-year loan repayment records; and the fact that the Student Loans Company is at arm's length from government and bound by commercial law makes it easier for its borrowing to be classified as private-sector activity.

[8] For more detailed discussion, including positive interest rates, see Barr and Crawford (1998c: annex).

Table 14.1. *Illustrative operation of private finance (£ per year)*

Year	Income	Loan Fund				Cumulative loan balance (initial private loan provider)
		Incomings from income-contingent repayments[a]	Fixed repayments to initial private loan provider	Balance on year	Cumulative loan balance (Loan Fund)	
	(1)	(2)	(3)	(4)	(5)	(6)
0					0	−15,000
1	0	0	−1,500	−1,500	−1,500	−13,500
2	16,000	540	−1,500	−960	−2,460	−12,000
3	16,000	540	−1,500	−960	−3,420	−10,500
4	16,000	540	−1,500	−960	−4,380	−9,000
5	20,000	900	−1,500	−600	−4,980	−7,500
6	20,000	900	−1,500	−600	−5,580	−6,000
7	20,000	900	−1,500	−600	−6,180	−4,500
8	20,000	900	−1,500	−600	−6,780	−3,000
9	25,000	1,350	−1,500	−150	−6,930	−1,500
10	25,000	1,350	−1,500	−150	−7,080	0
11	25,000	1,350		1,350	−5,730	
12	25,000	1,350		1,350	−4,380	
13	25,000	1,350		1,350	−3,030	
14	30,000	1,800		1,800	−1,230	
15	30,000	1,800		1,800	570	

[a] Repayments are 9% of earnings above £10,000 per year.

This process continues until Year 10, at which stage the balance of her debt to the Private Lender (col. 6) falls to zero. At that stage her cumulative Loan Fund deficit is just over £7,000. By now she is earning £25,000 per year. Thus in Year 11 her income-contingent repayment is £1,350 (col. 2), reducing her deficit on the Loan Fund to £5,730.

By Year 15, her income-contingent repayments have reduced her balance on the Loan Fund to zero. Anna has fully repaid her loan.[9]

[9] She is, of course, free at any time to pay off her loan more rapidly, including repaying in full, without penalty.

The mechanism makes it possible to combine private finance with income-contingent repayments, thus fulfilling two of the three criteria. To satisfy the third—the classification criteria—the critical element is risk transfer.

RISK TRANSFER. It is useful to start with the distinction between *default risk* and *social-policy risk*. The default risk has three elements: fraud, emigration, and low lifetime income, the last because of low earnings from whatever cause, including unemployment, disability, or early death. The distinctive feature of default risk is that it lies largely or wholly outside government control. Social-policy risk, in contrast, is directly affected by government policy—for example, increasing the income threshold at which loan repayments start, or offering more generous repayment terms to specific groups such as people caring for children or the frail elderly, or in respect of military service.

The social-policy risk is clearly not something that private lenders can handle. All such risks should be paid by the taxpayer in the form of transfers into the Loan Fund. These repayments are current public spending on social policy, not guarantees to the private lender, and therefore do not fall foul of the classification criteria. Given the tendency for electoral pressures to generate unthought-out and uncosted reforms, there are advantages if such transfers to the Loan Fund have two features: they should take place year by year on a current basis (the contract under which the Loan Fund is established should specify this feature); and they should come from the budget of the department concerned—for example, the interest costs of a repayment holiday during military service should come from the defence budget.

The default risk is different in the sense that it is something to which private lenders are well used. The fraud element is likely to be small in any country with a well-functioning income-tax system. The emigration risk should not be overstated. Under UK arrangements, students make income-contingent repayments while subject to UK income tax; if they are outside the tax net—for example, if they work abroad or emigrate—the loan contract specifies that the loan reverts to mortgage-type repayments. Though the risk of fraud is higher than for domestic repayers, emigration is not a major black hole, as discussed in more detail in Section 2. The third risk—low lifetime income—is quantitatively the largest. Simulations in a UK context (Barr and Falkingham 1993, 1996) suggest that 15–20 per cent of total lending is not repaid for this reason.

Suppose that the overall default risk is 20 per cent. Who should pay? The most obvious solution is the taxpayer in the form of a government guarantee covering the first 20 per cent of losses on the portfolio. In the early years of a new scheme lenders might well require at least that amount and possibly more. This approach is problematical, first, because of its fiscal costs. Even more of a problem, a scheme that incorporates such a large guarantee is likely to be classified as public.

An alternative to a taxpayer guarantee is for the cohort of student borrowers to insure themselves through a risk premium on the interest rate they pay. Under such a social-insurance type arrangement, students pay a risk premium (in other words, an insurance premium) based on their group risk rather than each student paying a premium based on his or her individual risk. Thus the cohort as a whole repays 100 per cent of its debt, high-earning borrowers repaying somewhat more than their individual loan, low earners less. The size of the risk premium will depend on many factors, including the loan repayment formula (more generous repayment terms lead to longer repayment times, increasing the likelihood that someone with a low income might never repay). However, simulations suggest that for a well-designed scheme an extra 2–3 per cent on the interest rate a student pays should cover the default risk.[10]

This arrangement has major advantages. First, it gets students the best possible deal, because it gets round the capital market imperfections discussed in Chapter 11. Specifically, risk is reduced because the asset is the earning capacity of the cohort rather than of the individual; and security is enhanced by using the tax system to enforce repayment. As a result, students can borrow as a cohort on terms vastly superior to those each could get as an individual. Secondly, and equally critically, *the default risk is borne by the private sector*, since it falls on students' repayments, and thus completely avoids any classification problems. The mechanism is robust. The loan contract signed by students would (*a*) allow for a cohort risk premium, but could also include the flexibility (*b*) to adjust the risk premium in the light of evolving outcomes and/or (*c*) to vary the repayment rate.

Particularly with a new scheme, private lenders might still want a government guarantee. There are potential gains to students from such a guarantee, since, in its absence, private lenders would require a higher risk premium. Thus there is a trade-off between risk premium and the size of any guarantee. Given the flexibility of the arrangement outlined above, a small government guarantee would suffice; it would become relevant, if at all, only in the later years of a cohort's repayment and is therefore even smaller in present value terms. A small guarantee of this sort—if the other features of the scheme were appropriate—would not raise any classification problems.

These arrangements have a series of desirable features. The social-insurance element makes possible genuine transfer of risk to the private sector, so that loans qualify as private. In the terminology of Chapter 9, it also enables student loans to combine an individualistic snail shell with social solidarity. The result is a system that combines income-contingent repayments with private finance.

---

[10] During the 1990s, the New Zealand loan scheme (Chapter 13, Section 2.6) charged students 1 per cent above the government's cost of borrowing. According to official estimates, this risk premium covered about half of the default risk.

1.3. *Examples*

PRIVATE BANKS WITH A GOVERNMENT GUARANTEE. The deficiencies of loan schemes of the sort found in the USA should now be clearer. Students take out their loans from a participating private bank (that is, retail front-end funding), banks are responsible for collecting repayments, and banks receive a generous government guarantee. Problems include, first, the fact that banks cannot implement income-contingent repayments on a current basis on anything better than—at best—a rough-and-ready and administratively costly basis. Thus the scheme ends up having mortgage repayments. Secondly, even mortgage repayments have non-trivial collection costs. Thirdly, the more generous the government guarantee, the less the incentive for banks to risk customer relations by aggressively pursuing debt repayment, leading to substantial default. Finally, and critically, such a scheme would not conform with the classification criteria. As indicated in Chapter 13, a country like the USA does not have to worry about such matters, but that does not mean that other countries can do the same.

PRIVATE BANKS WITH SELF-INSURANCE BY THE COHORT. Again, students take out loans from participating private bank (that is, retail funding), but repayments are income contingent, collected by the tax authorities. A Loan Fund matches the flow of income-contingent repayments from students and mortgage-type repayments to lenders, and the cohort of students pools risk through the sort of social-insurance arrangement described above. There might also be a small government guarantee.

Such schemes are complex. First, a loan application would involve both the bank and the student loans administration, since the bank would need confirmation, at a minimum, that the applicant was a bone fide student. Secondly, it would be necessary to monitor the terms of loans to students for reasons of consumer protection. To that end, the loans administration (the Student Loans Company in the earlier example) would set out the broad conditions that any private lender would have to meet—for example, that all students were to be treated as a single risk pool, thus ruling out cream skimming.

There is an analogy between the role of the Student Loans Company and that of a medical insurer inviting competitive bids from doctors or hospitals to become a preferred provider.[11] The Student Loans Company would offer students a list of preferred loan providers and would impose (and enforce) on lenders a series of conditions to protect students and enhance access. Any bank agreeing to those conditions would be so certified. The competitive element ensures that the underlying interest rate would be only slightly above the government's borrowing rate.

---

[11] See the discussion in Chapter 4, Section 2.2.

There are potential gains for students and preferred providers. Students have access to a continuum of financial services, from student loans through mortgages to pensions, from institutions that understand, for example, that a mortgage applicant with outstanding student debt is likely, being a graduate, to be a *better* risk than someone with no student debt but no degree. However, the complexities of the arrangement makes it more plausible as a longer-term option, once private finance for student loans has built up a track record.

CAPITAL MARKET LENDERS WITH SELF-INSURANCE BY THE COHORT. This model is broadly identical to the previous one except that it brings in private finance on a wholesale basis.[12] Students get their loan directly from the Student Loans Company, which raises finance in capital markets. A Loan Fund marries income-contingent repayments by students with mortgage repayments to capital markets. In the early years, borrowing in capital markets is likely to be short term (for example, five years); since it is efficient for student loans to be longer term, the Fund is kept liquid by a rolling programme of borrowing by the Student Loans Company. Thus the income of the Fund for the most part comprises (*a*) borrowing by the Student Loans Company and (*b*) income-contingent repayments. Over time, as the repayment stream grows, the balance of income tips from (*a*) towards (*b*). Further options are possible once the scheme has built up a track record: borrowing might become longer term; or the lender might buy the debt of a cohort of students.

In addition to its overall structure, the contractual details of the scheme are also important for classification purposes. First, though a small government guarantee causes no problem, there can be no additional implicit guarantee, a point that the contract between the Student Loans Company and the private lender should make clear. Secondly, it helps to establish the private nature of the scheme if agency relationships are made explicit. There are two such relationships: the tax authorities are agents acting on behalf of the Student Loans Company; and the Student Loans Company, in turn, acts as agent for the private lender in collecting and processing repayments. It is helpful if the Student Loans Company pays the tax authorities for administering the collection of repayments, the private lender pays the Student Loans Company for administering the loan accounts, and if these matters are all the subject of explicit contractual arrangements.

The scheme has major advantages. It combines income-contingent repayments with private finance. It does so in the simplest way possible, using a guarantee mechanism (self-insurance by the cohort of students) that is flexible and robust, and avoids classification problems. In some ways there is a good analogy with a bank overdraft, except that the overdraft in this case is not that of an individual student to a bank but of a cohort of students to capital markets.

---

[12] In late 2000, Hungary was actively considering a scheme of this sort.

It can be argued that the scheme has social-policy benefits additional to those for students. Student debt might well be attractive for pensions funds, which seek secure, long-term assets to hold. Given the increasing importance of human capital, student loans might therefore be a useful complement to assets based on physical capital. It might be, for example, that the miners' pension fund buys student debt; thus a gnarled, wizened retired miner could be living off the sweat of a young London or Wall Street financial analyst, a pleasing inversion of the usual arrangement.

2. STUDENT LOANS AND INTERNATIONAL LABOUR MOBILITY

This section discusses two approaches to collecting loan repayments when labour is internationally mobile: a simple mechanism that can be implemented relatively quickly, and a more radical solution that requires tax systems to be able to communicate with other tax systems.

A MINIMALIST APPROACH. Within a country, loans should have income-contingent repayments collected by the tax authorities. The loan of a person outside the tax net—for example, working abroad or having emigrated—reverts to mortgage-type repayments.

In some schemes (for example, Australia), borrowers are not liable to make repayments while working abroad. In others (New Zealand, Sweden, the UK), the only effect of a person's residence is to determine whether repayments are income contingent or mortgage. The UK experience suggests that for an efficient loans administration enforcement is not a huge task where the borrower has a known address and job. Most borrowers will comply, and non-compliance can be dealt with through the courts. Enforcement is easier given the speed of communication, the international integration of private finance, and the ability of loans administrations to put a black mark on a person's credit rating.

The main problem of enforcement arises where a borrower's address is not known. Progress is possible with minimal cooperation between tax authorities. If someone with a UK student loan moves to the USA, it would not be difficult for the US tax authorities to notify its UK counterpart that Joe Bloggs, UK national insurance number X, is working in the USA, tax file number Y, and living at the following address. It would then be up to the UK loans administration to pursue repayment. The US tax administration makes no attempt to collect repayment; its only task is to provide information to the UK authorities.

A variety of factors make the task easier than it might appear. Cooperation within the EU already exists, and further strengthening of links is inevitable. Some countries, both within the EU and elsewhere, are already in bilateral discussions; and the US authorities already record the home-country social-insurance number of would-be immigrants. Furthermore, migration tends to be mainly from poorer to richer countries. Thus cooperation of tax authorities within the OECD would deal with the vast bulk of loan repayments.

A MORE RADICAL APPROACH. Chapter 9 discussed pensions as a type of snail shell that people can take with them whichever job they had and in whichever country they lived. In the loans analogue, income-contingent repayments are collected by the tax authorities in whichever country a student subsequently works—for example, the UK authorities collect the loan repayments of immigrants from Ireland and transfer them to the Irish loans administrator. The same would be true when Hungarian lawyers migrate in large numbers to Germany after EU accession, or when Jamaicans emigrate to Canada.

With such an arrangement, loan repayments are transparent with respect to international boundaries. Students are free to migrate, with benefits both for labour mobility and individual freedom. The arrangement also makes it possible to have a loan scheme in developing countries, from which many of the best-educated people emigrate. There are further developmental advantages. It would be possible for the EU or World Bank to establish an International Learning Bank from which students from poor countries would borrow to finance their tertiary education—both those who subsequently stay at home and those who emigrate.

A final advantage makes a further link to earlier discussion of pension finance. One solution to population ageing is to import labour, either directly through immigration or indirectly by investing in countries with a young population. The discussion in Chapter 7, Section 1.1, concerned investment in physical capital, but applies equally to human capital. The sort of arrangement just described provides a financial instrument whereby, for example, middle-aged Europeans can provide student loan capital for young people in the Philippines, with benefits for the young people, for the Philippine economy, and for the European lenders. This new financial asset is the human-capital analogue of internationally diversified investment in physical capital in a pension company's portfolio.

3. RATIONALIZING THE FUNDING OF TERTIARY EDUCATION

Much of the discussion thus far has concentrated on universities. However, many of the arguments apply more broadly to the whole of tertiary education, including sub-degree studies and vocational training.

It can be argued that, the greater the diversity of tertiary education, the stronger the case for treating the system strategically. The argument can be applied both to funding—for example, by extending loans to broader classes of student—and to the structure of qualifications—for example, encouraging modular studies that allow relevant sub-degree courses to count towards a degree.

A New Zealand White Paper (New Zealand Ministry of Education 1998) suggested such a move. It proposed to treat all tertiary education as an integrated whole: 'Through the Universal Tertiary Tuition Allowance, the Government will subsidise all domestic students who enrol in approved courses' (p. 15). 'Students studying for approved courses will be subsidised on the same basis, no matter where they are studying' (p. 16). It also proposed a move towards funding via the student (that is, vouchers) rather than through block grants to universities, thus forcing institutions to compete: 'The number of students subsidised at each provider will be based on actual enrolments' (p. 15). A third component of the strategy concerned the critical role of information and regulation.

The 'contract' between the student and the provider is important. It is up to students to choose wisely and to providers to deliver what they have promised. The Government can support this contract by ensuring that:

- students have access to a diverse range of courses and reliable information about the opportunities open to them, and
- providers have certainty about the rules governing their operation . . . and are accountable for their performance.   (p. 55)

Arrangements of this sort suggest that the arguments in Chapter 13 about tuition fees set by education providers and supported by a system of income-contingent loans could be applied more broadly in the tertiary sector.

At first glance, loans for sub-degree students do not look likely to generate a strong repayment flow. However, many such students study for shorter periods than undergraduates and hence have smaller loans, and take less time out of the labour force to obtain their qualifications, and hence have a longer repayment record. For both reasons, simulation studies based on UK data (Barr and Falkingham 1993: table 5) suggest that students in sub-degree courses who took out a hypothetical income-contingent loan had a better repayment record than university students eligible for the same hypothetical loan. Two results are striking: the extent to which students in further education repay their loans (depending on the interest rate charged and other variables, the simulations suggest that men would repay over 95 per cent of their total borrowing); and the superiority of the repayment flows with income-contingent repayments (because they can extract at least some repayments from relatively low earners) in comparison with those of a mortgage-type scheme.

This suggests investigation of an integrated approach to the differentiated activities that comprise tertiary education, and an integrated approach to funding. In the UK context this means joint consideration of further education and higher education, in contrast with their separate treatment historically, manifested by separate reports in 1997 (UK Further Education Funding Council 1997; UK National Committee of Inquiry into Higher Education 1997*a*, *b*).

4. INDIVIDUAL LEARNING ACCOUNTS

THE IDEA. The list of potential funding sources for post-compulsory education was discussed in Chapter 12, Section 1. They include family resources, the student's earnings while a student, the student's future earnings, employers, and the taxpayer. An individual learning account is a vehicle that draws all these sources into a single entity. As discussed below, it can be applied to tertiary education as a whole or to various of its components. To illustrate with higher education, over the course of a person's childhood, his family could deposit (tax-advantaged) savings into his learning account. At the time he went to university, the state would pay its contributions towards his tuition fees into the learning account. His subsequent employer could also make payments into the account in a variety of ways discussed below. Finally, like any bank account, there would be an overdraft facility in the form of a student loan entitlement. Thus the individual learning account is a receptacle that holds funding from all sources, on which the owner can draw to finance his or her education or training, and is thus a further potential element in the snail shell discussed in Chapter 9.

The idea is based on two principles, both of which accord with the discussion in Chapter 13: the individual is best placed to make choices about the skills he or she wishes to acquire; and the costs of acquiring those skills should be shared. The objective is twofold: to bring private funding into post-compulsory education; and to integrate the roles of the various stakeholders—for example, empowering individuals as consumers of education and training, and giving employers a mechanism for transmitting their priorities to students and education providers.

Perhaps the last is the major novelty. Employers can contribute to a person's learning account in a variety of ways: paying off some or all of a person's student loan as a 'golden hello'; contributing to training costs during a person's career; and/or making regular contributions to a person's learning account as an additional component of his or her pay package. While the first two elements are possible without a learning account, the third is important. As discussed in Chapter 12, Section 1, it is in the interests of employers collectively that training takes place, but in the interest of each individual employer to free ride on training financed by others. One way round this type of externality is for an employer to contribute to training costs only while he employs the person—in effect a user charge for the employee's training. Regular contributions to an employee's learning account achieve exactly that, thereby sidestepping the disincentive to employers to contribute to the costs of training.

Individual learning accounts are a flexible instrument. They can differ in size, ranging from a small account able to pay for a word-processing course to a long-run plan to finance a university degree. They can apply to the different elements of tertiary education. They can also integrate across different financial mechanisms, including other types of tax-advantaged savings and personal pension accumulations, in what has been described as a personal venture capital fund. As discussed below, they can also be integrated with proposals in the UK and USA for capital grants for all young people.

PROS AND CONS. Schemes of this type have been widely discussed in the UK.[13] If they can achieve all that is hoped, they offer an alluring vision:

In theory, this model could lead to a virtuous circle in which education leads to higher pay, higher pay to higher personal investment in education and training, and higher personal investment to higher pay again, with the drawing down from the personal accumulated fund of pensions contributions, employer training funding, and personal input, being more than balanced by the investment allowed by higher earnings and higher tax payments. (Millns 2000: 9).

Achieving that vision, however, will not be easy. Small-scale experiments (UK Department for Education and Employment 1998b, 1999) faced a series of problems: the government contribution of £150 was argued to be too small; the number of participants was also too small to empower them as active consumers; private contributions from individuals and employers were small; and the transactions costs for such small accounts were high.

A further series of issues is more fundamental.

- *How to engage post-16 consumers*: individual learning accounts are intended to increase investment in skills. Lack of demand is not a problem for people who already participate in tertiary education. The issue is how individual learning accounts can promote demand—let alone active consumer behaviour—by those who are currently not participating.
- *How to promote access*: this is clearly related to the previous issue. The evidence is strong that educational exclusion cannot be addressed merely through financial incentives. Thus it is not clear that individual learning accounts *per se* strongly promote access.
- *How to engage employers*, both in terms of financial contributions and as active participants in helping to shape the form and content of courses (see Westwood 2000).
- *How to structure the accounts* so as to make them attractive to private lenders. The discussion of Section 1 makes it clear that this is not easy.

[13] Commission on Social Justice 1994; Robertson 1997; UK National Committee of Inquiry into Higher Education, 1997e; UK Department for Education and Employment 1999; Millns 2000; Robertson and Mason 2000.

- *How to avoid distortions*: if public subsidies to individual learning accounts can be spent only on education, they subsidize only one sort of capital formation, human capital, and thus risk creating a distortion between different types of investment. Not least to create a more level playing field, writers such as Ackerman and Alstott (1999) and Le Grand and Nissan (2000) advocate a capital grant to be paid to all individuals at age 18.

In some ways individual learning accounts close the circle. Pensions are concerned with lifetime redistribution from middle years to later years, investment in human capital with redistribution from middle years to younger years. Individual learning accounts integrate the two sets of consumption-smoothing activities exactly along the lines of the simple Fisher model in Chapter 2.[14] The idea is thus intellectually coherent. However, the jury is still out about whether they should be institutionally integrated.

---

[14] For explicit discussion of integration of individual learning accounts and pensions, see Agulnik (2000*b*).

PART 5

THE WELFARE STATE IN A CHANGING WORLD

The arguments of earlier chapters indicate that the welfare state has a continuing role. Its shape, however, will change as the world within which it operates changes. This last part of the book explores how the welfare state is adapting in the face of two particularly dramatic sets of forces: post-communist reform and so-called globalization.

Chapter 15

The Welfare State in Post-Communist Countries

The transition on which countries embarked when the communist system collapsed in the late 1980s generally had two elements: a move from central planning to market forces, and a move from totalitarian to more democratic forms of government. Among the profound changes that these moves implied was a need radically to reform inherited welfare-state institutions. The difficulty in terms of social policy was to keep the best of the old system while adapting it to a new economic order; the economic difficulty was to keep the system going at all when output was falling rapidly and tax revenues even more rapidly.

Because of the massive economic, political, and social disruption that accompanied transition, the reforming countries fail even more sharply than western countries to conform with the assumptions of the simple Fisher model described in Chapter 2. Information is highly imperfect, as people grapple with all-embracing change. Risk is greater and uncertainty is pervasive, since the major risks—most obviously increasing inequality and falling output—are common shocks. Two conclusions about the welfare state follow. First, except in a small handful of advanced reformers, the state has an even more important role than in the advanced industrial countries, both because problems of imperfect information, risk, and uncertainty are more acute and because private-sector capacity (for example, to organize private pensions or student loans) is absent or scarce. Secondly—and the subject of this chapter—the welfare state needs systematically to change to meet the needs of a market economy.

Section 1 establishes the simple analytics of transition. Subsequent sections, in parallel with the rest of the book, discuss insurance issues, particularly in connection with labour-market adjustment, the reform of pensions, and necessary changes in the education system.

1. THE SIMPLE ANALYTICS OF TRANSITION

1.1. *The old order*

At risk of oversimplification, the old economic order can be characterized in terms of five stylized facts:

(1) Every worker was paid the same, low wage.[1]
(2) Wages were topped up by generous universal benefits such as family al-
     lowances, pensions, and subsidized food, housing, and heating, often pro-
     vided by enterprises.
(3) Work was guaranteed, and jobs were for life.[2]
(4) Resources were allocated by central planning.
(5) Government was totalitarian.

The first three stylized facts largely determine the shape of income transfers.
They imply that the communist system had:

- No unemployment (because of (3)). As a result there was no system of unemployment benefit or, at best, only rudimentary institutions.
- No poverty, at least officially (because of (1), (2), and (3)), and hence little
  poverty relief. Everyone of working age had a job, and wages were topped
  up by social benefits; non-working groups such as pensioners were covered
  by universal social benefits.
- No sophisticated targeting (because of (1)). The flat income distribution had
  important implications. First, benefits were universal: since (to oversimplify) everyone had the same earnings, there was no need for selectivity by
  income level. Secondly, most countries had no personal income tax, its absence being regarded as one of the victories of socialism. Thirdly, governmental administrative capacity was weak, partly because no sophisticated
  targeting was needed and partly because most benefits were delivered by the
  enterprise.

1.2. *The effects of transition*

This was the state of play in the late 1980s. Transition, when it came, had many
effects, of which, for present purposes, three stand out.

(a) The distribution of income and earnings widened. This is beneficial to the
     extent that it is the result of competitive market forces—for example, rising
     wages for skills that the market demands. It is malign to the extent that it de-
     rives from the exploitation of a monopoly position or criminal activity. If we
     can somehow make the latter reasons disappear, the remaining disparity of
     pre-transfer incomes, it can be argued, is a sign of success, since it shows that
     markets are generating incentives conducive to economic growth—one of
     the core purposes of transition. As such, a wider distribution of earnings and

---

[1] 'Key features of the prereform labor market [included a . . .] structure of relative wages characterized by
compressed differentials bearing little relationship to the market value of workers' skills' (Jackman 1998: 123).
[2] 'Very low or nonexistent unemployment' (Jackman 1998: 123).

income is not just a transitional feature but—as in Western countries—a permanent part of the post-communist landscape.

(b) Output fell and, associated, tax revenues fell even more sharply. The scale of the output collapse was larger than anything experienced in the West since the Great Depression and, in some countries, greater still. Even in Poland and Hungary, which were, relatively speaking, the least adversely affected, output fell by around 18 per cent during the first three years of transition. Though growth resumed, the level of output in 2000 in most countries was still below its level in 1989, often considerably so. In the Community of Independent States (CIS),[3] output in 1999 was little more than half of its level ten years earlier (Table 15.1). In only four countries, Hungary, Slovakia, Slovenia, and—pre-eminently—Poland, had output returned to or exceeded it pre-transition level by 1999. There are, of course, major problems in measuring output: statistical information is frequently inaccurate, not least because of the large informal economy; interpreting data is complex when not only absolute but also relative prices are changing sharply; and it is not clear how to value pre-transition output, which was frequently in short supply. That said, there is no argument that output fell massively. Thus this second transition effect remains true in all but a few countries.

(c) Job security ended.

Several results follow directly from these three sets of changes.

OPEN UNEMPLOYMENT. As a direct consequence of (b) and (c), unemployment rose sharply, to over 10 per cent in most of the reforming countries (Table 15.2). The costs of unemployment in terms of forgone output and in personal terms are high. It is noteworthy, however, that unemployment in countries such as Bulgaria and Romania, whose reforms faltered, was not markedly lower than in the most aggressive reformer, Poland.

RISING POVERTY is an inexorable consequence of (a) and (b). As a proposition in pure logic, falling output coupled with a widening income distribution leads to increased poverty. Notwithstanding familiar problems facing attempts to quantify poverty (Barr 1998a: ch. 6; 1999a), empirical evidence overwhelmingly supports the proposition. The World Bank (1999: 6) estimates that the number of people living on less than $4 per day in Central and Eastern Europe and the countries of the former Soviet Union rose tenfold, from 14 million in 1989 to 147 million in 1996. Table 15.3 is based on the same poverty line, and shows the pattern across different countries. Some care is needed interpreting the figures. Richer countries, particularly the Czech Republic, Slovakia, and Slovenia, had few

---

[3] i.e. the former Soviet Union minus Estonia, Latvia, and Lithuania.

Table 15.1. *Real GDP in Central and Eastern Europe, the Baltic countries, and the CIS in 1999 compared with 1989*

Country	Projected real GDP in 1999 (1989 = 100)
CEE and the Baltic countries	
Albania	91
Bulgaria	66
Croatia	79
Czech Republic	95
Estonia	79
Hungary	99
Latvia	60
Lithuania	65
FYR Macedonia	60
Poland	121
Romania	74
Slovakia	101
Slovenia	107
Eastern Europe and the Baltic States	101
CIS	
Armenia	42
Azerbaijan	46
Belarus	75
Georgia	33
Kazakhstan	59
Kyrgyztan	62
Moldova	30
Russia	53
Tajikistan	43
Turkmenistan	53
Ukraine	35
Uzbekistan	89
CIS	53
CEE, the Baltics, and the CIS	77

Source: European Bank for Reconstruction and Development (1999: table 1.1)

people with incomes below $4 per day in either the late 1980s or mid-1990s and, on that measure, experienced little increase in poverty. That does not mean that people in those countries did not experience a fall in income—merely that, *relative to a benchmark of $4 per day*, poverty increased very little. Radical reformers experienced a substantial increase in the poverty headcount, from 6 per cent of the population to 20 per cent in Poland, and from 1 per cent to 37 per cent in Estonia,

Table 15.2. *Unemployment rates, selected transition countries, 1998 (%)*

Country	Unemployment rate, 1998 (estimated)
CEE and the Baltic countries	
Bulgaria	12
Czech Republic	7.5
Estonia	9.6
Hungary	7.8
Latvia	9.2
Lithuania	6.4
Poland	10.4
Romania	10.3
Slovakia	11.9
Slovenia	14.5
CIS	
Belarus	2.3
Moldova	1.6[a]
Russia	12.4
Ukraine	3.7

[a] 1997.

Source: European Bank for Reconstruction and Development (1999).

though strong growth should reduce these figures. For less successful reformers, the increase in poverty was even greater, in Romania from 6 per cent to 59 per cent, in Russia from 2 per cent to 50 per cent, and in Ukraine from 2 per cent to 63 per cent, with no likelihood of any short-run improvement.

INEFFECTIVE TARGETING. A third, strategic outcome of transition—ineffective targeting—follows from (*a*). Because of the decline in tax revenues, the problem is critical. A system designed for a flat earnings distribution, continuous employment, and labour shortage predictably misallocates benefits in the face of a diversified distribution. There are two sets of problems. Well-targeted benefits aim to avoid gaps in coverage—in other words, to hit *all* the poor (horizontal efficiency). Immediate failures under this head are inadequate systems of unemployment benefit and poverty relief. A second aspect of good targeting (vertical efficiency) is to avoid leakages—that is, the idea is to hit *only* (or mainly) the poor. Benefits designed for a flat income distribution will inevitably fail this test in the face of a widening distribution, the most glaring example in the transition countries being pensions. High public pension spending was a particular concern in many countries and, for this and other reasons, pension reform became a central—and politically highly salient—issue for policy-makers.

Table 15.3. *Poverty rates selected transition countries, 1987–8 and 1993–5 (% of population)*

Country	Poverty headcount	
	1987–8	1993–5
CEE and the Baltic countries		
Bulgaria	2	15
Czech Republic	0	<1
Estonia	1	37
Hungary	1	4
Latvia	1	22
Lithuania	1	30
Poland	6	20
Romania	6	59
Slovakia	0	<1
Slovenia	0	<1
CIS		
Belarus	1	22
Moldova	4	66
Russia	2	50
Ukraine	2	63
Average CEE and CIS without Central Asia	3	43

Note: The poverty line is 120 international dollars per capita per month.
Source: Milanovic (1998: table 5.1).

1.3. *Resulting reform directions*

Transition thus led to a fundamental reshaping of the economic landscape. As a direct result, the inherited institutions, designed for the old shape, were dysfunctional relative to the needs of a market economy. Strategic reform directions follow directly:

- improved targeting to plug gaps in coverage, notably by strengthening unemployment insurance (Section 2) and also by improving poverty relief.[4]
- improved targeting to reduce leakages, notably by reforming pensions (Section 3).

The parallel arguments for education are discussed in Section 4.

A recurring theme is the need for policy that respects exceptional fiscal constraints, that can be implemented with very limited administrative resources, and

[4] Poverty relief is discussed in Section 2, but only briefly, since poverty relief is outside the remit of this book. For fuller discussion, see Milanovic (1998), and for analysis of social policy more broadly, Eatwell *et al.* (2000).

that does not crowd out institutional capacity from the wide array of other equally urgent and equally important tasks.

2. INSURANCE: ASSISTING LABOUR-MARKET ADJUSTMENT

2.1. *The problem*

Policy-makers face a series of problems directly related to transition.

RISING OPEN UNEMPLOYMENT was both cyclical and structural. The extent of the output decline, and hence falling demand for labour, has already been discussed. Structural change, equally, transcends that experienced in the West. The industrial structure emerging from central planning represented a massive disequilibrium. One response to the complexities of central planning was to have as few entities as possible to plan, with a resulting tendency to giganticism, irrespective of efficiency arguments for decentralization. What emerged from this structural disequilibrium—to oversimplify— were workers with the wrong skills making the wrong products in the wrong place. The burden of unemployment fell particularly on some groups. Women were laid off in larger numbers than men in the early transition; long-term unemployment increased rapidly; and geographical mismatches between jobs and workers produced large regional variations.

AN ACUTE SHORTAGE OF RESOURCES for dealing with these problems was a second strategic problem. Its major source was the collapse in output (which reduced the tax base) coupled with tax systems ill adapted to collecting from the private sector (thus reducing the compliance rate for a given tax base).

AN ACUTE SHORTAGE OF ADMINISTRATIVE CAPACITY in the face of intractable administrative problems was a further constraint. The need for unemployment insurance was completely new, so that there was no pre-existing system on which to build. It is true that there had been employment exchanges in the old system, but their purpose was entirely different—not to find *jobs* for unemployed people, but to find *workers* in an era of labour shortage. The size of the informal economy creates a second problem. In the advanced industrialized countries, as discussed at the start of Chapter 3, unemployment benefits are based on the assumption (unrealistic, but tenable) that the employment/unemployment divide is binary. In transition countries, particularly the slower reformers, the problem is complicated by the extent of informal activity and the existence of small-scale agriculture. Thus the distinction between employment and unemployment becomes blurred, making it difficult to define unemployment and even more difficult to find measurable indicators that can be implemented cost-effectively to determine whether a particular applicant is, or is not, eligible for benefit.

INCENTIVE PROBLEMS. Because of the flat income distribution, the poverty line, unemployment benefit, and minimum wage in the early transition were very close to each other, and the distance between the minimum wage and the average wage was also small in comparison with industrialized countries. Over the first decade of transition the wage distribution decompressed significantly in the advanced reformers, but acute incentive problems remain in countries where wages are low and wage differentials small.

IMPEDIMENTS TO OCCUPATIONAL AND GEOGRAPHICAL LABOUR MOBILITY included inadequate housing markets and the fact that many social benefits were organized by enterprises.

A SKILLS MIX NOT WELL SUITED TO A MODERN MARKET ECONOMY has major implications, discussed in Section 4, for education and training.

2.2. *Policy directions*

DOES HIGHER UNEMPLOYMENT HELP REFORM? The inherited distortions and sharp output decline made it both necessary and desirable for the large state sector to shed labour.[5] However, there is an uncomfortable question about whether higher unemployment speeds reform. At first glance, a rapid shake-out creates a pool of unemployed workers on which the growing private sector can draw. The resulting policy strategy is to subsidize unemployment—for example, through unemployment benefits. The alternative view is that, though some unemployment is necessary, private firms prefer to recruit workers currently employed in the state sector. Unemployment does not signal someone as available for work so much as brand them as a bad worker (which is why their former employer got rid of them first). On this view, high open unemployment is not a prerequisite for reform. The resulting policy strategy is to subsidize employment.

Two patterns of labour-market adjustment to some extent parallel these two different constructs (see World Bank 1996: ch. 4). In most of Central and Eastern Europe, the greater part of adjustment fell on employment. In countries like Russia, in contrast, the initial brunt of adjustment fell on wages. Workers often retained their attachment to their enterprises, even with little or no pay, and thus continued to enjoy some enterprise benefits. Thus disequilibrium manifested itself through underemployment.

It is by no means clear, at least in the early days of reform and in the slower reformers, that the strategy of encouraging unemployment is the right one. Jackman's assessment (1998: 152) of labour market policy concludes:

---

[5] For fuller discussion of reform directions, see Jackman and Rutkowski (1994), Jackman (1998), and Boeri *et al.* (1998).

There would be some point to such a policy if unemployment played a productive role in economic restructuring, but we have seen that the opposite is the case. Unemployment is not the route by which workers move from the declining state sector to the private sector. Unemployed workers are less attractive recruits for private firms than workers in state firms, and a policy leading to higher unemployment may thus have restrained rather than encouraged the growth of the private sector.

Whether unemployment is lower or higher, however, a working system of benefits is essential.

INCOME SUPPORT DURING EARLY TRANSITION: POVERTY RELIEF. During early transition, the design of unemployment benefit needs to address the problems discussed earlier—rising unemployment and an acute scarcity of fiscal and administrative resources. In that context, flat-rate benefits have particular advantages. They are cheap, since nobody receives benefit above the minimum. They are administratively easier than earnings-related benefits: it is still necessary to establish whether a person is eligible but, having done so, there is no need to calculate benefits. A third, more arguable, advantage is that flat-rate benefits, by offering most workers a lower replacement rate[6] than earnings-related benefits, create improved incentives to find work. The first two arguments apply equally to flat-rate pensions.

During early transition, policy thus needs to concentrate resources on protecting the minimum level of benefits—in other words, to concern itself almost entirely with poverty relief. The question is therefore how to address rising poverty in the face of an acute shortage of resources and of administrative capacity. The administrative problems are particularly intractable. Targeting via an income test is administratively demanding at the best of times. Perhaps to an even greater extent than with unemployment, assessment is complicated by the amount of informal activity. It is therefore difficult to measure income accurately or cost-effectively, reducing the usefulness of income testing as a mechanism for targeting.

One way forward is indicator targeting, which awards benefits on the basis of unemployment, ill health, old age, large numbers of children in the family, and similar correlates of poverty.[7] A different approach—as a complement to or substitute for indicator targeting—is through local discretion plus block grants. Localities may be better informed than central government about who is genuinely poor, and thus better able to target on a discretionary basis. However, if central government underwrites the costs of local poverty relief, localities have no incentive to contain costs (another example of the third-party-payment problem discussed in Chapter 2, Section 3). Thus local discretion should be combined with

---

[6] The replacement rate is the ratio of income on benefit to net income when in work—that is, with a 40% replacement rate, an unemployed person receives benefit equal to 40% of his or her previous wage.

[7] On the analytics of targeting, see Barr (1998a: 237–40); on policy, see Grosh (1994); the classic article is by Akerlof (1978).

block grants from the centre to localities. Neither indicator targeting nor local discretion, however, is a complete solution. In the medium term, more ambitious policies become possible, including a partial move towards income testing and a move from discretion towards a rules-based system.

INCOME SUPPORT AS TRANSITION PROGRESSES: INSURANCE AND CONSUMPTION SMOOTHING. As fiscal and administrative capacity grows, the other purposes of cash benefits come back onto the policy agenda—insurance in the case of unemployment and consumption smoothing in the case of pensions—and it becomes possible to collect social-insurance contributions and to link them more tightly to benefits. In this strategy, insurance and consumption smoothing are financed wholly or largely through contributions, with poverty relief increasingly based on tax-funded benefits such as social assistance and family allowance.

The introduction of this type of Western social insurance arrangement, however, requires major changes. Though the old system had something called social insurance, it was—like so many other communist institutions with the same name as Western institutions—very different. First, the connection between contributions and benefits was effectively non-existent. There were generally no worker contributions (another victory of socialism). Benefits were not wholly financed by contributions; and not all of the benefits financed by contributions were remotely connected with potentially insurable risks (for example, such rudimentary social assistance as existed was often financed from contributions). Secondly, contributions were not individualized: enterprises paid contributions *en bloc* on behalf of their workers. As a result, the social insurance/pension authorities knew neither about individual contributors (unnecessary with full employment, when everyone had a full contributions record) nor about individual recipients (unnecessary for universal benefits).

Reform therefore requires (*a*) keeping records of contributions on an individual basis, (*b*) ensuring that such record keeping is by a social-insurance authority not the enterprise, (*c*) introducing a worker contribution alongside the employer contribution, (*d*) using contributions to finance only contributory benefits such as unemployment benefits and pensions, financing benefits such as social assistance from general taxation, and (*e*) ensuring an explicit and well-understood relation between contributions and benefits.[8]

The introduction of an explicit worker contribution merits further discussion. In terms of economic theory, the incidence of contributions is independent of whether they are imposed on the worker or the employer.[9] In political economy

---

[8] For fuller discussion of the reform of social insurance in transition countries, see Barr (1994).

[9] The incidence depends on the relative factor and product demand and supply elasticities and is independent of where the contribution is legally imposed. In theory, therefore, it does not matter how the contribution is shared between worker and employer. This result does not, however, necessarily hold in the short run, nor in situations where markets are not competitive. For further discussion, see Stiglitz (2000: ch. 18).

terms, however, worker contributions give important signals. Before transition, contributions were paid wholly by employers, and enterprises faced a soft budget constraint: as a result, neither workers nor employers faced any incentive to moderate their claims (yet another example of the third-party payment problem). With worker contributions, in contrast, workers immediately see a larger deduction on their pay slip if benefits increase—helping to reduce pressure for higher benefits.

Alongside the reform of benefits, labour-market adjustment also requires action to assist labour mobility.

ADDRESSING CONSTRAINTS ON LABOUR MOBILITY has at least three aspects: job information, policies to promote occupational mobility, and policies to promote geographical mobility. All are relevant to some extent in all labour markets, but have particular salience for transition economies.

Job information is central. In a market economy—in sharp contrast with the old system—the primary responsibility for seeking out job opportunities lies with the individual worker. Thus job information is crucial, and all the more crucial in a situation where the type of jobs, the types of skills required, and their location are changing so quickly and so substantially, making imperfect information an even greater problem than in Western economies. Job information is one aspect of active labour-market policies, the other two being training measures and job creation. In the short run, the most that can be done is to introduce simple, cost-effective job-information and job-matching schemes.

Occupational mobility has a more medium-term horizon. As fiscal and administrative constraints relax, more sophisticated active labour-market policies become an option. However, though there is general agreement about the utility of mechanisms that help to match people with jobs, there is controversy about the cost-effectiveness of publicly organized job training, which appears to have had limited success even in the advanced reformers. Expenditure on such programmes in the transition countries was generally low, usually because rapidly growing expenditure on unemployment benefit crowded out training; and, on limited evidence, programmes were not particularly effective.[10] Alongside active labour-market policies are more general issues of education and training, taken up in Section 4.

Geographical mobility has to overcome at least two sets of impediments. If workers and jobs are in different places, one solution is for workers to move to the jobs. The lack of effective housing markets, however, is a major hindrance. Though the issue cannot be solved in the short term, starting reform *is* an early task. A second impediment is the link between social benefits and the enterprise.

---

[10] For assessment of active labour-market policies, see Godfrey and Richards (1997), OECD (1997c), and Boeri *et al.* (1998).

This, it can be argued, was rational in an era of full employment, jobs for life, and soft budget constraints, but is dysfunctional in a world where not everyone has a job, where labour mobility is high, and where competitive pressures, especially international competitive pressures, make enterprises sensitive to the compliance costs of administering benefits. Thus a major reform direction is to move most benefits out of the enterprise—for example, transferring most administration of contributions and benefits to the social-insurance / pension authorities.

3. PENSIONS

3.1. *The problem*

With unemployment benefit and poverty relief the central targeting problem is to avoid gaps in coverage. With pensions the targeting issue is different—to avoid fiscally unaffordable leakage of benefit. The inherited system of pensions fits badly in several ways with the needs of a market economy.

EASE OF ACCESS TO BENEFIT arose in at least three ways. First, retirement age was low (a further victory of socialism). Secondly, there were pension concessions whereby particular groups of workers (miners, for example) received a pension at an even lower age. Thirdly, the number of pensioners was increased further by generous early retirement provisions in the early transition. 'As a result [of low pensionable age], the typical woman in the Czech Republic enjoys five more years of retirement than her American counterpart, and seven years more than her German counterpart. For men the difference is closer to one year. The comparison for Hungary, Poland and Russia is broadly similar' (World Bank 1996: 78).[11]

UNSUSTAINABLE COST. Pension spending was high in almost all the transition countries, most egregiously Poland, where public pension spending in 1997 was a massive 15 per cent of GDP. Croatia, Latvia, and Macedonia spent about 9 per cent of GDP and the Czech Republic and Hungary around 9 per cent. The cause of such high spending was not generous pensions, but the large number of pensioners arising out of the low retirement age.

Table 15.4 illustrates the scale of the problem. Column (1) shows the age dependency ratio—that is, the fraction of the population of pensionable age; column (2) the system dependency ratio—that is, the fraction of the population receiving pension. If nobody below pensionable age received a pension, the ratio of (2):(1) would be 100 per cent. In practice, there are always some recipients below pensionable age—for example, disability pensioners—so that there will always be some 'leakage'. In Croatia, Latvia, and Lithuania the leakage in 1996 was

---

[11] For further detail, see Barr (1999b: table 11.1).

Table 15.4. *Age dependency ratio and system dependency ratio, selected countries, 1996*

Country	Age dependency ratio (1)	System dependency ratio (2)	(2):(1) (%) (3)
Croatia	32.3[a]	39	121
Estonia	35	46	131
Hungary	36	41	114
Latvia	35	42	120
Lithuania	32	39	122
Poland	28[a]	49[a]	175
Russia	30.5	46[a]	151
Slovenia	29[a]	54[a]	186

[a] 1995 data.
Source: EBRD data.

around 20 per cent, in Poland 75 per cent, and in Slovenia 86 per cent. Thus in the latter two countries, not far short of half of all pensioners were below the official pensionable age.

The large number of pensioners is one part of the sustainability problem; the other is the effect of falling output on the contributions base. There is a potential vicious circle: a combination of high pension spending and an eroded contributions base leads to high payroll contribution rates; these hinder new employment, create incentives for workers and employers to collude in fraud, and encourage informal activity; all these lead to yet higher contribution rates.

PENSIONS WERE GENERALLY LOW. Despite high pension spending and high contributions, pensions in most countries were low, the result of a head-on collision between fiscal constraints and the large number of pensioners. The result is like trying to spread a small piece of butter over an enormous slice of bread.

3.2. *Policy directions*

The inherited system was organized on a Pay-As-You-Go (PAYG) basis. In a balanced such scheme, to return to earlier notation:

$$sWL = PN \tag{15.1}$$

where $s =$ the PAYG social security contribution rate
$W =$ the average real wage
$L =$ the number of workers
$P =$ the average real pension
$N =$ the number of pensioners.

The most pressing actions address the sustainability of pension finance. A second set of reforms concern microeconomic aspects of pension design. Third are options for private pensions. In terms of sustainability, reform can pursue a small number of strategies.

INCREASING OUTPUT. The centrality of output to pension finance was stressed in Chapter 6. Other things being equal, an increase in output is associated with a parallel increase in real wages; thus total contributions, sWL, increase, making it possible to increase pension spending without any increase in the contribution rate, s. As Table 15.1 makes clear, however, in 1999 output in all but a handful of countries remained below its level before transition. Increased output is therefore more of a medium-term solution.

REDUCING THE NUMBER OF PENSIONERS. A reduction in the number of pensioners, N, makes it possible to increase the average pension, P, without an increase in the contribution rate. There has been discussion in many countries about raising the retirement age, and in some, including Poland, Hungary, Croatia, and the Czech Republic, legislation. In practice, however, the average age of retirement barely increased over the 1990s, and in some countries continued to decline. It is open to discussion whether in the short run this is good or bad. Policy has to balance two competing objectives. The argument for raising pensionable age is to reduce public spending. However, a precipitate move has political risks; in addition, the debilitating effects of long-term unemployment, particularly for young workers, is well known. It may be, therefore, that increasing the age of retirement, though essential, is a medium-term policy. Any change will, in any case, need to be phased in gradually.

A second approach to reducing the number of pensioners is through incentives—by withdrawing the right to combine work and pension. Here, too, there are conflicting objectives. The high cost of easy access suggests that there should be a retirement test, whereby pension is partly or wholly withdrawn from anyone who earns more than a small amount. On the other hand, early retirement is a humane and politically appealing way to make older workers redundant, and thus assists the massive restructuring discussed in the context of labour mobility. It may be, therefore, that during the early transition it might be better to consider a *change-of-job* test rather than a *retirement* test, whereby someone of pensionable age who retires but then finds another job can keep at least part of his or her pension.

REDUCING THE AVERAGE PENSION. A third way to reduce expenditure is to reduce the average pension. As a practical matter, pensioners were generally protected relative to other groups. Milanovic (1998: 102–3) finds that 'poverty rates for people of retirement age . . . are only about one half of the country average in

Hungary and Poland, and even less in the Czech Republic and Slovakia'. However, the fact that pensioners were *relatively* protected does not mean that they did not suffer a decline in living standards. In many countries pensions were not indexed, or inadequately indexed. As a result, over time people were pulled down to the minimum pension (which was typically indexed), thus approximating a system of flat-rate pensions. Additional evidence shows that single-person pensioner households—disproportionately very old women—were prominent among the poor.

Perhaps viable short-run options to contain public pension spending are very limited. It may be that this is the right outcome. Both on political grounds and in terms of inter-generational equity, a case can be made for special treatment of the older generation, all or most of whose working lives were during the communist era. 'In much of [Central and Eastern Europe and the former Soviet Union] inflation destroyed the financial savings of the elderly. Unlike the young, they will not have the opportunity to recoup their losses in the market economy. A case can therefore be made on equity grounds for special treatment' (World Bank 1996: 80).

STRENGTHENING THE RELATION BETWEEN CONTRIBUTIONS AND PENSIONS. This type of policy, which is mainly medium term, has less to do with containing total pension spending than with microeonomic efficiency. All the successful reformers have made serious attempts to strengthen the relationship between contributions and benefits, while simultaneously attempting to make pension finance more sustainable. The two most radical reformers, Poland and Latvia, have moved to an almost complete actuarial relationship.

Poland's new pension law, enacted in 1998, is very similar to the Swedish scheme discussed in Chapter 8, Section 3.2. It introduced a universal, mandatory, publicly managed PAYG defined-contribution system.[12] The social-insurance authorities maintain an account for each contributor, who accumulates notional capital.[13] The resulting pension depends only on the notional capital accumulation, the person's age at retirement, and average life expectancy of the relevant cohort. The minimum retirement age is 62 for men and women; other than that, the retirement decision is a matter for individual choice. During a contributor's working life her notional fund is indexed in line with the growth of the real wage bill (and hence in line with trends in productivity and employment); in retirement, pensions are indexed to a pensioner price index.

Latvia, too, introduced notional defined-contribution pensions. Each contributor's social-security account is credited with contributions (up to a ceiling) as

---

[12] For fuller discussion of Poland, see Góra and Rutkowski (1998), and, for a broader assessment, Lindeman *et al.* (2000).

[13] The system also has a small Demographic Reserve Fund.

though it were an explicit savings account, thus creating notional capital. On retirement, a person receives a pension based on his accumulation of notional capital, based on life expectancy at retirement. Retirement age is flexible, with pensions adjusted actuarially.

Hungary adopted less far-reaching reforms to its state pension arrangements.[14] Under reforms in 1998, the first-tier pension was amended by increasing the retirement age to 62 for men and women, strengthening the link between contributions and benefits, increasing the qualifying period for full pension, subjecting benefits to taxation, and shifting indexation from a net-wage basis to half of real earnings growth. As with all the other countries, there is a minimum pension guarantee in the form of a social-assistance pension.

Pension reform in other Central and Eastern European countries—for example, Croatia and the Czech Republic—has been more modest, mostly aimed at improving the sustainability of the PAYG scheme.

In assessing these reforms, the analysis of the effects of pensions on labour supply in Chapter 7, Section 2.1, is highly relevant. There are important gains from strengthening the relationship between contributions and benefits, first, to minimize distortions to individual retirement decisions and, secondly, to encourage compliance with a contributory system, given the strong incentives to evade contributions if workers do not see a clear relationship between contributions and benefits. The latter point is of particular relevance in transition countries, given the output collapse and the resulting pressures on the tax and contributions base, leading to the vicious circle discussed earlier.

Though there is a strong case for strengthening the relationship between contributions and benefits, the extent to which the relationship is *strictly* actuarial is a policy option. It is possible, as in Sweden, Poland, and Latvia, to have state pensions which are almost entirely proportional to contributions. Equally, as discussed in Chapter 7, it is possible to have benefits related at the margin to individual contributions—for example, a person who retires early does so with an actuarially reduced pension.

PHASING IN PRIVATE PENSIONS. Virtually all the transition countries have discussed introducing private pensions, and a significant number have started on legislation. By 2000, the initial phase of reform had already been enacted in Poland, Hungary, Croatia, and Latvia.

The Polish reforms take an integrated approach. Alongside the notional defined-contribution first tier discussed earlier is a mandatory, funded, privately managed, defined-contribution second tier.[15] The two tiers are closely linked: they use the same contributions base and retirement age, both are defined con-

---

[14] See Gerencsér (1997), and International Social Security Association (1998: 16–17).
[15] The economics of pensions were set out in Chapter 6.

tribution, and both are mandatory for people born after 1969. The second-tier pensions are managed by competing funds. Regulation includes constraints on the composition of investments and requirements about disclosure of information. The freedom of individuals to change funds is heavily circumscribed. These arrangements are supplemented by a third tier of voluntary contributions, with incentives to encourage employees and employers to set up voluntary group pension schemes.

Hungary, too, introduced a second-tier pension through individual funded accounts. Such funds may be established by employers, professional associations, the Pensions Insurance Administration, voluntary pension funds, or local governments. Each pension fund must be approved by the newly established Pension Fund Supervision Office. In contrast with Poland, individuals are free to move between funds provided they pay the costs of such a move (see Gerencsér 1997). In further contrast, political support for the reforms is on less firm foundations than in Poland (see Nelson (1998) for discussion of the politics of reform in Hungary, and Nelson (1999: pt. 2) for broader discussion).

Croatia also legislated to bring in second-tier pensions, which are mandatory for people who were under 40 at the time the new scheme started in 2000. The scheme is financed by diverting a fraction of pension contributions to individual accounts. In the late 1990s a number of other countries, notably Estonia and Latvia, were actively considering a mandatory, private, funded second-tier pension.

Kazakhstan is an outlier: in moving to a Chilean-type system, in which mandatory, privately managed, competitive funded pensions replace the state scheme, it is adopting reform that would be radical for any country, and *a fortiori* for a Central Asian country.

In assessing these developments the discussion of earlier chapters is directly relevant. First, the potential gain in terms of output growth of a move towards funding should not be exaggerated (Chapter 7, Sections 1.1–1.3). Secondly, as discussed in Chapter 8, Section 2 and summarized in Table 8.1, there are major prerequisites for successful introduction of private pensions. So far as government is concerned, these include the capacity to maintain macroeconomic stability, the ability to regulate effectively (which in turn depends on the rule of law), and the administrative capacity to collect contributions. They also include important private-sector prerequisites, including a sufficiently well-informed population, financial assets and financial markets, and adequate private-sector capacity for the major tasks of administering pensions and of managing pension funds. A further requirement is the capacity to engender sufficient, and sufficiently long-lasting, political support. The durability of support is particularly important for a policy with such a long-time horizon.

A country like Poland can fulfil these prerequisites, and the political will for reform was there. Thus their reforms make sense. Other advanced reformers such as Hungary, Slovenia, and the Czech Republic also have the necessary capacity. A second group of countries might, at a stretch, be able to implement such reforms, but the question for policy-makers in those countries is whether private pensions are necessarily the most urgent priority, given other demands on scarce public and private capacity. A third group of countries come nowhere close to meeting the prerequisites and should therefore regard the introduction of private pensions as a longer-term option, not as a matter for urgent consideration. As indicated in Chapter 8, Section 2.2, Kazakhstan is certainly not in the first group of countries, and almost certainly not in the second.

4. EDUCATION

The previous two sections argued that the system of income transfers inherited from communism were systematically and predicably ill suited to the needs of a market economy. The same is true of education.

4.1. *The challenge of transition*

Educational achievement under communism was impressive. There was almost universal primary and lower secondary enrolment, high levels of basic literacy and numeracy, and relatively equitable access. Given these successes, the prevailing view in the early transition was that many aspects of education reform could wait. To explain why that view was wrong, it is necessary, first, to return to the objectives of education.

To summarize the discussion of Chapter 10, Section 1, the primary purpose of education policy is to improve educational outcomes by transmitting knowledge and skills *and*, as important, attitudes and values. The latter two, though frequently overlooked, are critical. Achieving this primary objective involves a number of subsidiary ones. Allocative efficiency (also referred to as external efficiency) is concerned with producing the types of educational activities that equip individuals for the societies in which they live, and addresses the issue of the optimal quantity, quality, and mix of educational activities. Productive (or internal) efficiency is concerned with running schools and other institutions as efficiently as possible. Equitable access, a third objective, can be justified both on equity grounds and because it is inefficient to waste talent.

INTERNAL INEFFICIENCY. Reform is necessary, first, because of gross internal inefficiencies in the old education system (see Laporte and Schweitzer 1994). Resources were allocated without regard to student or employer demand. There was poor coordination, with resources often wasted by duplication of facilities, as each enterprise and ministry developed its own. There were no incentives to use resources efficiently and in consequence, gross overstaffing. Analogous problems arose with health care. In both sectors, the problems had the same source as, and similar outcomes to, those of state-owned enterprises generally. The clear solution for most state-owned enterprises was to privatize. That solution, for all the reasons discussed in earlier chapters, does not apply to anything like the same extent to education and health care.

EXTERNAL EFFICIENCY.[16] Addressing internal efficiency is important, but in many ways external efficiency is more important, both intellectually and in policy terms. To start with the old order, two of the stylized facts in Section 1.1—central planning and totalitarian government—are particularly relevant. The resulting education system had two strategic characteristics:

- narrow, specific skills embodied in a mastery of a fixed body of knowledge, to enable workers to fit their allotted place in the central plan;
- lack of questioning attitudes: communist education discouraged independent thinking, which was unnecessary for the central plan and undesirable in a totalitarian environment.

Thus, 'education . . . emphasized conformity for all and specialist expertise for each' (World Bank 1996: 124).

With transition came market forces. In a market economy workers have to respond in a flexible way to the constantly changing demands of a fluid, dynamic system, and therefore need broad, flexible skills. They also need a capacity for independent thought, both in their role as workers and because democracy—a second effect of transition—needs independent thought for a flourishing civil society and an engaged citizenry. What is needed, in other words, are problem-solving skills, imagination, and the initiative to use them.

These are precisely the skills that communist education did *not* give. Though well adapted to the old order, communist education was dysfunctional in at least three ways relative to the needs of a pluralist market economy. First, there were gaps in knowledge. Curricula in subjects such as economics, management science, law, sociology, and psychology were missing, irrelevant, or underemphasized. The problem is greater than it appears: missing subjects lead to missing concepts and, in consequence, to missing words. 'Efficiency', for example, means something very different to a manager seeking to fill his quota under a central plan than to one seeking to increase profit and market share in a competitive system. During the early transition, the term 'income transfers' proved a persistent

---

[16] This section draws on Heyneman (1994), which underpins much of the analysis in World Bank (1996: ch. 8).

problem for interpreters and translators, because there was little understanding of the distinction between wages (mainly related to individual productivity for reasons of economic efficiency) and transfers (mostly paid out of the state budget for distributional reasons). Missing concepts and missing words can create communication problems that impede speedy and effective transfer of knowledge and skills.

A second problem was a lack of broad, flexible skills. Though basic education was in many ways superior to that in many Western countries, subsequent training was too specialized (the old system in Poland taught about 300 occupational skills in secondary technical schools, compared with sixteen broad occupational programmes in Germany). Furthermore, there was little adult education (essential for mobility in a market economy), because the assumption implicit in central planning was of a static world; hence workers were expected to remain in the same occupation throughout their working lives.

A third problem, though harder to document, was a lack of questioning attitudes. It is possible to assess independent thinking, in ascending order of difficulty, by measuring the ability to solve a known type of problem, by the ability to apply a given technique to a new problem, and by the ability to choose which technique to use to solve a new problem. Under communism, the upper end of this taxonomy was regarded with suspicion, and in some countries as seditious.

Figure 15.1 offers some indicative evidence. It shows the results of an international test of skills in mathematics and science designed to give results as comparable as possible across countries.[17] Children in the former Soviet Union, Hungary, and Slovenia have test scores considerably above the international average. These, clearly, are successful systems. However, children in those countries do better in tests of how much they know than of their ability to apply that knowledge in new and unforeseen circumstances. For children in Canada, France, and the UK, the ranking is precisely the reverse.

One interpretation of these results is that the two education systems were successful in achieving their very different objectives. Communist education gave narrow, specific skills to the mass of its population, encouraging the highest international excellence and creativity only in a small elite of politically trustworthy people. Western education seeks to encourage initiative much more democratically.

4.2. *Policy directions: Adapting education to the needs of a market economy*

These results also point to directions for change, both to underpin democracy and to assist the conversion of human capital in support of a market system.

---

[17] For fuller detail, see Education and Testing Service (1992*a*, *b*) and Kovalyova (1994).

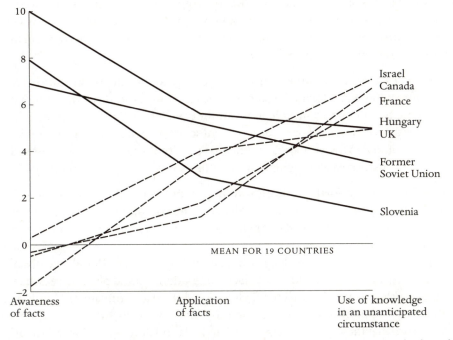

Figure 15.1. *Science and mathematics test performance of children in selected transition and industrial economies*

Note: Data are average scores of 9 and 13 year olds on the second International Assessment of Educational Progress, conducted in 1991. The countries shown are those whose performance was above the mean of a sample of nineteen countries.

Source: World Bank (1966: Fig. 8.1). See also Kovalyova (1994); for technical details, see Education and Testing Service (1992*a*, *b*).

What is needed are changes in all the components of the education package, of which the following are examples.

- Knowledge. The old system brought about levels of knowledge that frequently surpassed those in the West. Those achievements should be preserved, at the same time placing greater emphasis on social-science subjects such as economics and law.
- Skills. The old system achieved high skills, but they tended to be narrow and mechanistic. Reform requires a move towards broader, more flexible skills, together with stronger problem-solving abilities—notably the capacity to apply knowledge in new and unforeseen circumstances.
- Attitudes. Under the old system, workers who showed initiative were frequently regarded as troublemakers; the relationship between employer and worker was regarded as exploitative; and profits were immoral. Reform needs to strengthen the idea that initiative and innovation are praiseworthy.

It should also assist understanding that offering someone a job (subject to suitable regulation) is not exploiting him but giving him an opportunity to earn a living, and that profits are not inherently immoral but (in a properly regulated economy) an engine of growth.

- Values. Under the old system, it was regarded as the duty of the state to look after people. A reformed system should encourage the idea that, though the state has an important role in promoting welfare, citizens—both individually and through various aspects of civil society—need to take responsibility. It should also foster understanding that freedom of expression is an essential and constructive component of a pluralist society governed by consent.

The objective of reform, in short, is to impart problem-solving skills, curiosity, and a capacity for and enjoyment of debate. The communist system gave these skills to a tiny, trusted elite. The challenge of transition is to impart them to the citizenry as a whole.

There are at least four challenges in meeting this objective. Pluralist textbooks are needed, covering revised curricula. Examinations should place increased emphasis on the capacity to use knowledge, as well as to accumulate it. Thirdly, it is necessary to put in place training and more effective assessment of teachers to make sure that they work with the new curricula and develop new ways of teaching. This last element—the need to rejig the human capital of teachers—is perhaps the greatest challenge, in the sense that it requires teachers to teach in a different way. If all one's professional training has been to regard inquisitive, argumentative students as troublemakers, it is hard suddenly to regard them as one of the main joys of teaching.

A fourth challenge is to find additional resources, both for the tasks themselves and to increase teachers' pay. There is a strong and continuing case for public funding and, for the most part, public organization of schools. For tertiary education, in contrast, as discussed in Chapter 13, the strategic way forward involves a mixture of public and private funding and the use of market forces. This area of debate is rising rapidly up the policy agenda in the advanced reforming countries.

Chapter 16

The Welfare State in a Changing World

The world is changing: real incomes are rising, income disparity is tending to increase, family structures are becoming more fluid, the population is ageing, and information and capital flows across national boundaries are instantaneous.

In considering the effects of these changes, writers do not always look at the broader picture. The changes apply equally to private institutions; thus it is insufficient to look at the problems of the welfare state without considering the problems that private institutions would face. Equally, it is mistaken to criticize the welfare state in static terms, ignoring the extensive changes in its institutions over the years across a wide range of countries.

This chapter looks at that broader picture in the context of the forces that influence the shape of the welfare state, including fiscal and political pressures (the 'retreat to the core') and increasing international competition ('globalization').

1. IS THE 'CRISIS' A CRISIS?

The interlinked propositions set out below together argue that the impact of global and other pressures should not be overstated.

PROPOSITION 1: THE WELFARE STATE HAS BENEFITS AS WELL AS COSTS. Almost throughout its history there have been recurring discussions about the costs of the welfare state, and whether those costs are sustainable. In many OECD countries public social spending absorbs 25 per cent of GDP, and in some countries more. Such spending, however, has major benefits. In equity terms, at its narrowest the welfare state provides poverty relief. For many voters and policy-makers it also has broader distributive tasks: to reduce relative poverty, to reduce income inequality and other dimensions of inequality (for example, by gender or ethnicity) and—at its broadest—to tackle social exclusion.

Alongside these equity purposes, as argued throughout the book, the welfare state has an important efficiency role. In the face of market failures it makes possible insurance against major risks and uncertainties, including unemployment, inflation, and important medical risks that private insurance would cover inadequately or not at all. It also facilitates efficient consumption smoothing in respect of old age security and the finance of investment in human capital. The argument, in short, is that a welfare state of some sort would still be necessary even if all distributional problems had been solved—for example, even if the world consisted only of middle-class people.

The efficiency and equity arguments can converge. A distributive approach to relieving poverty operates primarily through income transfers. A structural approach seeks to increase pre-transfer earning capacity by 'equipping the poor of this generation and the potential poor of the next with the means to earn above poverty income through normal employment' (Tobin 1968: 90). This approach seeks to enhance individual skills through education, job training, and health care. Giddens's 'social investment state' (1998) takes a similar approach.

If the welfare state only had costs (this might—perhaps unfairly—be called the Ministry of Finance view), the objective would be to keep public social spending as low as possible. Since it has benefits, the objective is to optimize spending, rather than minimize it. That optimization obviously involves a trade-off between the welfare state and other welfare-increasing activities. What citizens want is growth (that is, rising living standards) and security (that is, reduction of risk and uncertainty). The challenge for the welfare state is simultaneously:

- to promote security by providing mechanisms that make possible consumption smoothing, insurance, and poverty relief; and
- to assist growth, not just passively through fiscally prudent expenditure levels that do not impede growth deriving from other sources, but positively—for example, an effective system of unemployment compensation assists labour mobility and encourages risk taking; a well-designed system of student loans facilitates investment in human capital.

The issue for policy-makers—as always—is to balance competing costs and benefits. Suppose that, in state-of-the-world A ('pure capitalism'), there is little security but rapid growth. If many people, including the better off, are prepared to trade slightly lower growth for greater security, mechanisms to increase security are welfare enhancing. At its broadest, this is a stylized representation of the development of the welfare state in the advanced industrial countries in response to rising real incomes and electoral pressures over the twentieth century. In state-of-the-world B ('communism'), in contrast, there is considerable material security, but growth rates are very low. People are therefore willing (as in the former communist countries) to adopt institutions such as market forces that offer the potential for higher living standards but at a cost of reduced security. In short, too little security reduces well-being; so does too much.

In assessing such trade-offs, economists of all people should need no reminder of the flaws in an argument that looks at costs but ignores benefits. Atkinson

(1999) addresses the argument that the welfare state is unsustainable and should therefore be rolled back, and criticizes it as being too simple.

> The emphasis by economists on the negative economic effects of the welfare state can be attributed to the theoretical framework adopted . . . which remains rooted in a model of perfectly competitive and perfectly clearing markets. *[This] theoretical framework incorporates none of the contingencies for which the welfare state exists . . .* The whole purpose of welfare state provision is missing from the theoretical model.   (1999: 8, emphasis added)

Atkinson's point is that a model (for example, the simple Fisher model in Chapter 2) based on perfect information and market clearing systematically rules out the market failures that it is one of the fundamental tasks of the welfare state to address. The choice of such a model means that analysis inescapably focuses only on the cost side, and implicitly rules out some of the welfare state's main benefits. A richer theoretical treatment—the purpose of this book—that incorporates market failure and government failure leads to a more complex range of outcomes than the simple unsustainability / rollback argument allows. None of this is an argument that fiscal constraints should be ignored, merely that fiscal constraints, market failure, and government failure are each important. This argument leads naturally to:

PROPOSITION 2: STRUCTURE SHOULD NOT BE CONFUSED WITH SCALE. As foreshadowed in Chapter 1, two separate questions arise in considering different pressures on social spending.

- What is the best *structure* of an activity? Which activities should be publicly funded, publicly produced, or both, and which should be largely or wholly private? From an economic perspective, the issue is mainly technical: market allocation is welfare enhancing where the necessary conditions hold; in the presence of major market failures, public activity may improve matters.
- What should be the *scale* of an activity? What is the optimal level of public spending on the welfare state? This is largely a matter of budgetary balance.

As the arguments in earlier chapters make clear, the two questions are logically distinct. Structure is a microeconomic issue: the central question is whether or not market failures are so serious and government sufficiently effective for intervention to be welfare improving. In contrast, scale is largely a macroeconomic issue: unsustainable pension spending, for example, requires tax or contribution rates so high that the resulting disincentives interfere with growth. Scale also has a significant political economy dimension: a country with an individualistic ideology and where risk aversion is not strong will tend to vote for more parsimonious welfare states (what Wilensky and Lebeaux (1965) call a *residual* welfare state); a country where people are more risk averse (hence prepared at the margin to trade growth for security) and/or where social solidarity has a larger role, will vote for wider and deeper welfare states.

This line of argument suggests that, if welfare-state spending is thought to be unsustainable, it does *not* follow that the solution is privatization; rather, it is an argument for reduced spending on the activity. As an illustration, the solution to unsustainable state pensions in the post-communist countries is to reduce the generosity of the system—that is, the issue is one of scale. The extent to which pensions should be private—that is, the structural issue—is entirely separate. In contrast, the argument for substantial reliance on market forces and private finance in tertiary education derives from microeconomic efficiency (that is, structural) arguments, at least as much as from issues of affordability. The distinction between the two very different sets of issues should not be blurred.

PROPOSITION 3: DOMESTIC PRESSURES DO NOT MEAN THE DEMISE OF THE WELFARE STATE. Writers like Glennerster (1998c) ask whether fiscal and political forces exert downward pressure on social spending—the 'retreat to the core'.

Starting with economic arguments, one pressure operates on the demand side. As incomes rise, people move out of public assistance into the private sector. They move from social housing into owner occupation, and from sole reliance on a state pension towards occupational and personal pensions. As a result, the need for large-scale state activity declines, with potential knock-on effects for political support.

There are also pressures on the supply side, not least because the relative price of services rises over time. This is the joint result of the fact, first, that the price of labour tends to rise faster than prices generally (that is, real earnings rise) and, secondly, that services such as health care and education have a high labour content (see Baumol 1996). Such services, therefore, cannot benefit from cost-reducing technological progress as much as (say) car manufacture. Thus real spending on health care and education has to rise year by year just to continue to deliver a constant quantity and quality of service; with technological progress leading to more advanced forms of treatment and with larger numbers of patients or students, pressures towards rising expenditure are even stronger.

Such forces, it is argued, suggest that the welfare state needs to focus on its core activities, to whit those related to poverty relief and those dictated by major market failures. Defined in that way, the broad structure of the welfare state defined by the 'core' hypothesis is exactly compatible with the arguments in this book. Expenditure on such areas (the scale issue) is then determined by a range of factors: by fiscal capacity; and by the level of demand—for example, the number of elderly people requiring medical and long-term care or the number of young people in the education system.

Public choice exerts a third influence on expenditure through the level of political support for public social spending. One determinant is ideology, but path dependency also has an important influence. The USA, for example, has a relatively generous state pension; thus the median voter is signed up, leading to strong and continuing political support for social security. Similar arguments can be made about New Zealand, with its generous, tax-funded citizen's pension, which elicited strong support in a 1997 referendum (see Chapter 8, Section 3.2). In contrast, the UK state pension, having eroded in real terms over the years, is under continuing pressure.

The economic arguments that are the main focus of this book define a circle within which reside the range of efficient and equitable policy options. This line of argument explains why public spending on income transfers, health care, and education in all the advanced industrial countries absorbs a significant fraction of GDP. Political economy arguments define which options within that circle (or, in the case of health care in the USA, outside the circle) are chosen, explaining, at least in part, why spending is higher in some countries than in others and why it is more redistributive in some than in others.

In short, on a plausible interpretation, the retreat to the core, far from illustrating a crisis, shows that the overall shape of the welfare state is adapting in a rational way to economic and technological change.

PROPOSITION 4: GLOBAL PRESSURES SHOULD NOT BE EXAGGERATED. A related but separate question is whether international pressures exert a downward influence on what the welfare state can deliver. The core of the argument is twofold. First, there is international capital mobility. Secondly, because of technological change, economic activity increasingly consists of information that can be transmitted instantly worldwide. Both sets of forces reduce the freedom of a country to conduct an independent economic policy. The argument is important. Many activities are genuinely becoming more global, as exemplified by growing e-commerce. But for at least four reasons the implications for the welfare state are not necessarily apocalyptic.

First, the world is not wholly global. Global competition is powerful but not all powerful. Not all goods are tradeable; and not all factors of production are mobile. Labour mobility is often reduced by individual choice: people generally maximize utility not profit, and therefore often prefer to stay with their family, culture, and language. Mobility is also reduced by constraints, particularly over migration. For these and other reasons, Burtless (1996) concluded that global pressures explain less than one-fifth of the large increase in inequality in the USA since 1970.

Secondly, attempts to cut back public spending can be counterproductive. Parsimonious public funding of health care or pensions may create pressures for employers to offer such benefits. Reduced public spending can therefore backfire: replacing higher taxes by higher employer costs does little, if anything, to improve international competitiveness. At its worst, a budget cap on public spending could be replaced by a Hydra's head of multiple private schemes with open-ended tax concessions, health finance in the USA being very much a case in point.

Thirdly, Western countries can and will adapt. The distinction between structure and scale is acutely relevant in this context. Free movement of capital might mean that low-spending, low-tax countries can exert competitive pressures on social spending in the OECD countries. But even if that is true, it is not an argument for dismantling the welfare state, still less for radical structural change such as privatizing pensions. If policy-makers believe that public spending is incompatible with fiscal constraints, the answer is to make it less generous. For precisely that reason, governments throughout the OECD are taking measures to restrain public spending in general and welfare-state spending in particular.

A final reason why global competitive pressures do not ring the death knell for the welfare state is that the newly industrialized countries will also adapt. Competitive pressures operate in both directions—downwards on higher spenders and upwards on lower spenders. Social spending in industrialized countries has been a superior good: as incomes have risen, electorates have voted for governments that increased the share of social spending in GDP. The fact that that process may have overshot in some countries does not invalidate the premiss. Though family support in East Asia has traditionally been strong, correspondingly reducing the need for publicly funded activities, industrialization and urbanization have led to changes in family structure that, in turn, are leading to demands for rising social expenditures. As discussed in Proposition 5, the outcome of global competition is less likely to be pressures to the lowest common denominator than pressures towards some convergence between the OECD and East Asian countries.

PROPOSITION 5: COUNTRY DIFFERENCES MATTER. Different outcomes in different countries arise either because their objectives differ or because countries face different constraints.

Starting with objectives, consider the balance between individualism and social solidarity. As a very broad illustration, it can be argued that the Americas (North and South) tend to put more weight on individualism (including voluntary charity). This is explicit in much US political discourse; and it is implicit in the pension reforms adopted by Chile in the 1980s. Many European countries, in contrast, give more weight to social solidarity (a term hardly used in US debate). As a result, welfare-state-type institutions in Europe tend to be more fully articulated and welfare-state spending proportionately higher than in America.

Constraints differ across at least four dimensions. Economic constraints are obvious. Countries where income is lower can afford only parsimonious benefits. Countries that face major institutional constraints—less-educated populations, a lack of long-established market institutions, no banking system or capital markets, limited capacity to enforce regulations—can implement only simple structures. Social attitudes vary widely and have a critical bearing on welfare-state institutions. Social spending, for example, is lower in countries where the Confucian tradition allows continued reliance on the extended family. Political constraints are pervasive: in some countries people mount the barricades to defend a system of publicly funded and publicly organized health care; in others they mount the barricades to prevent its introduction.

In comparison with the countries of Central and Eastern Europe, it can be argued that the East Asian economies have a more-or-less single, overriding objective, economic growth, and a political consensus that, by implication, gives a fairly low weight to equity objectives and to social solidarity. They tend to have fairly authoritarian regimes. They face fewer constraints than all but the most advanced reforming countries of Central and Eastern Europe: China apart, they have well-developed market systems, a sophisticated banking system, and well-developed capital markets; and they need no *overall* restructuring. The last, together with their high level of spending on education, means that they have a more appropriate skills mix than the legacy of communist education. Finally, the extended family was part of their historical social structure. The message is *not* that post-communist countries have nothing to learn from those of East Asia, but that East Asian institutions cannot simply be transferred to countries with less clear-cut objectives and very different constraints. Similarly, US institutions will not necessarily take root in countries with different objectives and different constraints.

The same set of arguments explains how institutions may converge. Rising real incomes in East Asia have already led to demands for higher public social spending—for example, systems of unemployment benefit in South Korea, Thailand, Singapore, and Taiwan enacted during the later 1990s. Operating in the same direction, increased urbanization and the declining force of Confucianism create pressures to increased social spending. As an example of weakening family ties, legislation in Singapore in the late 1990s empowered parents to sue children who failed to support them adequately in old age, legislation that would be entirely unnecessary if family ties operated as well as formerly. In Europe, conversely, international competitive pressures (together with population ageing) are likely to exert downward pressure on the generosity of benefits.

These pressures are real, but not overriding. Differences will remain both in objectives and in constraints and, as earlier argument (Proposition 4) suggests, these differences will not be entirely eliminated by international pressures.

Choices remain, as earlier discussion about the range of choice over pension reform makes clear. Country differences matter, and will continue to matter. One size does not fit all.

2. A CONTINUING WELFARE STATE

Esping-Andersen (1996) argues that political and other institutions are enormously important for managing potential conflict between efficiency and distributional objectives. He goes on to argue that during the 1950s and 1960s, and in some countries longer, it was possible to pursue distributional objectives with little efficiency cost because there was an implicit agreement accepting wage restraint as the price of high levels of employment (see also Atkinson and Mogensen 1993 and Blank 1994). That consensus, it can be argued, was what underpinned the early success of Keynesian policies, providing a positive-sum solution to the trade-off between growth and equity. According to this view, institutions have become more fragmented. Because of changes in social norms (Lindbeck *et al.* 1999) and a weakening of some institutions, the trade-off between growth and equity is now less favourable than formerly.[1] Separately, the distribution of pre-tax income has widened in many countries, making the welfare state's Robin Hood function more expensive.

These issues are important. But they do not counsel despair. The welfare state is durable for a rather simple reason: the theoretical argument that underpins its existence will continue to apply. Twenty-first-century changes, though they will cause the welfare state to adapt, do not undermine the overall thrust of that theoretical argument.

THEORY. Though there is no blueprint for the welfare state, all successful institutions go with the grain of economic theory. The theoretical conclusion is that—alongside its role in relieving poverty and reducing inequality—there will be a continuing efficiency role for the state as long as the model in Chapter 2 continues, broadly, to apply. Information problems will, if anything, increase as pension instruments and health care become more complex; such problems will persist until everyone has either an omniscient robot as personal 'minder' or (analytically equivalent), computer-assisted brain power.

Equally, I am not aware of any claim that risk or uncertainty is on the way out. Indeed, it is argued that uncertainties—about variant CJD, global warming, nuclear safety—are increasing. Uncertainty about the likelihood of needing long-term care will persist; the impact of genetic screening on private insurance will increase; and information problems will continue to plague private medical insurers. Private pensions will continue to face uncertainty about future real rates

---

[1] For theoretical discussion of how social customs can influence economic outcomes, see Akerlof (1980).

of return in general, and future rates of inflation in particular; nor is there any reason to suppose that uncertainty facing private lenders of finance to support student loans will diminish. In the face of these continuing problems, the trends discussed below all point to continuing state action to provide, regulate, or facilitate mechanisms that offer insurance and consumption smoothing on better terms than is possible with wholly private mechanisms. This conclusion is robust, even where government takes a minimalist view.

ADAPTATION. None of these arguments, however, suggests an unchanging welfare state. The flexible menu of options emerges throughout the book, notably in Chapters 4, 8, and 13. The menu of country responses also emerges repeatedly. Many current and future adaptations will be direct responses to the twenty-first-century issues discussed in Chapters 5, 9, and 14.

The structure of the welfare state will continue to change.

- Not least because of labour market trends, inequality will be a continuing problem. There will be pressures for social insurance to become more actuarial. Such moves, if well designed, could facilitate labour-market flexibility and enable women, in the face of more fluid family structures, to have their own pension entitlement. None of these adaptations eliminates the state's role, particularly through public or quasi-public provision of unemployment compensation.
- There will be mounting pressure for new insurance instruments (public, private, or mixed) to cover contingencies such as long-term care in old age.
- Continued advances in medical care are likely to increase rather than diminish reliance on public or quasi-public funding.
- The spread of private pensions will put pressure on governments to ensure effective regulation, and possibly also to assist private pensions in the face of unanticipated inflation.
- Technological advance will create pressures for more, and more repeated, investment in human capital. There will be a continuing need for public funding of primary and secondary education and for subsidies for some types of tertiary education.
- There will also be pressures for new lending instruments. Income-contingent loans will increasingly contribute to the finance of tertiary education; and student loans might become a financial asset that financial institutions such as pension funds could hold alongside their portfolios of investment in physical capital. Such adaptations create a continuing role for the state as facilitator in the face of persistent capital-market imperfections.

Other pressures affect the scale of the welfare state.

- In some countries, given demographic pressures, past promises have turned out to be too generous to be compatible with fiscal constraints. Countries have adapted by making promises less generous. Pensions and health care will continue to face resource constraints, creating upward pressure on the age of retirement. As discussed in Chapter 7, these pressures apply equally to public and private pensions.
- Global economic competition is likely to exert downward pressure on social spending in industrialized countries, though, as discussed earlier, there are countervailing upward pressures in countries with less well-developed welfare states.
- In contrast, there might well be upward pressures on education spending.

In the face of all these changes, the word 'adapting' is key. To criticize the welfare state as though it were set in tablets of stone is to make the same mistake as Marx's critique of capitalism—it ignores the fact that both the market system and state institutions adapt. The welfare state faces *problems*; as a result, its institutions *adapt*; this does not mean that there is a *crisis*. The reasons why a welfare state is necessary will not go away; its institutions are robust and responsive; in forms that will continue to evolve, it remains a continuing twenty-first-century challenge.

References

Aaron, Henry J. (1966), 'The Social Insurance Paradox', *Canadian Journal of Economics and Political Science*, 32 (Aug.), 371–4.

——(1982), *Economic Effects of Social Security*, Washington: Brookings Institution.

——(1991), *Serious and Unstable Condition: Financing America's Health Care*, Washington: Brookings Institution.

——(2000), 'The Plight of Academic Medical Centers', *Policy Brief*, 59 (May), Washington: Brookings Institution.

Abel Smith, Brian (1984), *Cost Containment in Health Care*, Occasional Papers in Social Administration No. 73, London: Bedford Square Press.

——(1985), 'Who is the Odd Man Out?: The Experience of Western Europe in Containing the Costs of Health Care', *Health and Society*, 63 / 1: 1–17.

——(1988), 'The Rise and Decline of the Early HMOs: Some International Experiences', *Millbank Quarterly*, 66 / 4: 694–719.

Ackerman, Bruce, and Alstott, Anne (1999), *The Stakeholding Society*, New Haven: Yale University Press.

Agulnik, Phil (2000a), 'Maintaining Incomes after Work: Do Compulsory Earnings-Related Pensions make Sense?', *Oxford Review of Economic Policy*, 16 / 1: 45–56.

——(2000b), 'Individual Accounts and Post-Compulsory Education', in Tony Millns and Wendy Piatt (eds.), *Paying for Learning: The Future of Individual Learning Accounts*, London: Institute for Public Policy Research, 61–72.

——and Barr, Nicholas (2000), 'The Public / Private Mix in UK Pension Policy', *World Economics*, 1 / 1 (Jan.–Mar.), 69–80.

——and Le Grand, Julian (1998), 'Tax Relief and Partnership Pensions', *Fiscal Studies*, 19 / 4: 403–28.

Akerlof, George A. (1970), 'The Market for "Lemons": Qualitative Uncertainty and the Market Mechanism', *Quarterly Journal of Economics*, 84 (Aug.), 488–500, reprinted in George A. Akerlof, *An Economic Theorist's Book of Tales*, Cambridge: Cambridge University Press, 1984, 7–22.

——(1978), 'The Economics of "Tagging" as Applied to the Optimal Income Tax, Welfare Programs and Manpower Planning', *American Economic Review*, 68: 8–19.

——(1980), 'A Theory of Social Custom of which Unemployment may be One Consequence', *Quarterly Journal of Economics*, 94 (June), 749–75.

Arenas de Mesa, Alberto, and Marcel, Mario (1999), 'Fiscal Effects of Social Security Reform in Chile: The Case of the Minimum Pension', paper presented at the APEC Second Regional Forum on Pension Funds Reforms, Viña del Mar, Chile, 26–27 Apr.

Arrow, Kenneth J. (1963), 'Uncertainty and the Welfare Economics of Medical Care', *American Economic Review*, 53: 941–73.

——(1994), 'Medical Information and Medical Insurance: An Ethical Dilemma?', mimeo, Stanford University.

Arulampalam, Wiji, and Stewart, Mark B. (1995), 'The Determinants of Individual Unemployment Durations in an Era of High Unemployment', *Economic Journal*, 105 / 429: 321–32.

Ashenfelter, Orley, and Krueger, Alan (1994), 'Estimating the Returns to Schooling Using a New Sample of Twins', *American Economic Review*, 84: 1157–73.

——and Rouse, Cecilia (1998), 'Income, Schooling and Ability: Evidence from a New Sample of Identical Twins', *Quarterly Journal of Economics*, 113 / 1 (Feb.), 253–84.

Asher, Mukul (1999), 'The Pension System in Singapore', mimeo, National University of Singapore.

Atkinson, Anthony B. (1989), *Poverty and Social Security*, Brighton: Harvester Press.

——(1995), *Incomes and the Welfare State: Essays on Britain and Europe*, Cambridge: Cambridge University Press.

——(1999), *The Economic Consequences of Rolling Back the Welfare State*, London: MIT Press.

——and Hills, John (1998) (eds.), *Exclusion, Employment and Opportunity*, Centre for the Analysis of Social Exclusion, CASEpaper 4, London: London School of Economics, also available from http://sticerd.lse.ac.uk/case.

——and Micklewright, John (1991), 'Unemployment Compensation and Labour Market Transitions: A Critical Review', *Journal of Economic Literature*, 29/4 (Dec.), 1679–727.

——and Mogensen, Gunnar V. (1993), *Welfare and Work Incentives: A North European Perspective*, Oxford: Clarendon Press.

Auerbach, Alan J., and Kotlikoff, Laurence J. (1990), 'Demographics, Fiscal Policy and US Saving in the 1980s and Beyond', in Lawrence H. Summers (ed.), *Tax Policy and the Economy*, iv Cambridge, Mass: MIT Press.

————(1998), *Macroeconomics: An Integrated Approach*, London: MIT Press.

——*et al.* (1989), 'The Economic Dynamics of Ageing Populations: The Case of Four OECD Economies', *OECD Economic Studies* (Spring), 97–130.

——, Kotlikoff, Lawrence, J., and Leibfritz, Willi (1999) (eds.), *Generational Accounting around the World*, Chicago: Chicago University Press.

Australia, Commonwealth Department of Family and Community Services (2000), *The Australian System of Social Protection—An Overview*, Canberra: Department of Family and Community Services.

Barr, Nicholas (1979), 'Myths my Grandpa Taught Me', *Three Banks Review*, 124 (Dec.), 27–55.

——(1987), *The Economics of the Welfare State*, 1st edn., London: Weidenfeld & Nicolson, and Stanford, Calif.: Stanford University Press.

——(1989), *Student Loans: The Next Steps*, Aberdeen University Press for the David Hume Institute, Edinburgh, and the Suntory-Toyota International Centre for Economics and Related Disciplines, London School of Economics.

——(1991), 'Income-Contingent Student Loans: An Idea whose Time has Come', in G. K. Shaw (ed.), *Economics, Culture and Education: Essays in Honour of Mark Blaug*, Cheltenham: Edward Elgar, 155–70.

——(1992), 'Economic Theory and the Welfare State: A Survey and Interpretation', *Journal of Economic Literature*, 30/2: 741–803.

——(1994), 'Income Transfers: Social Insurance', in Nicholas Barr (ed.), *Labor Markets and Social Policy in Central and Eastern Europe: The Transition and Beyond*, New York: Oxford University Press for the World Bank (also available in Hungarian, Romanian, and Russian), 192–225.

——(1997), 'Student Loans: Towards a New Public/Private Mix', *Public Money and Management*, 17/3 (July–Sept.), 31–40.

——(1998a), *The Economics of the Welfare State*, 3rd edn., Oxford: Oxford University Press, and Stanford, Calif.: Stanford University Press.

——(1998b), 'Higher Education in Australia and Britain: What Lessons?', *Australian Economic Review*, 31/2 (June), 179–88.

——(1999a), 'Comments on "Economic Policy and Equity: An Overview" by Amartya Sen', in Vito Tanzi, Ke-young Chu, and Sanjeev Gupta (eds.), *Economic Policy and Equity*, Washington: International Monetary Fund, 44–8.

——(1999b), 'Pension Reform in Central and Eastern Europe: The Good, the Bad and the Unsustainable', in Sami Daniel, Philip Arestis, and John Grahl (eds.), *Essays in Honour of Bernard Corry and Maurice Peston*, iii. *Regulation Strategies and Economic Policies*, Cheltenham: Edward Elgar, 174–91.

——(2000), 'A Strategy for Financing Tertiary Education', Submission to the Education and Science Select Committee, Inquiry into the Resourcing of Tertiary Education, Wellington.

——(forthcoming), *Economic Theory and the Welfare State*, i. *Theory*, ii. *Income Transfers*, and iii. *Benefits in Kind*, International Library of Critical Writings in Economics, Cheltenham: Edward Elgar.

——and Crawford, Iain (1997), 'The Dearing Report, the Government's Response and a View Ahead', in *Third Report: The Dearing Report: Some Funding Issues, Volume II, Minutes of Evidence and Appendices, House of Commons Education and Employment Committee, Session 1997–98*, HC241-II (TSO), 88–103.

——————(1998a), 'Funding Higher Education in an Age of Expansion, *Education Economics*, 6/1: 45–70.

——————(1998b), 'The Dearing Report and the Government's Response: A Critique', *Political Quarterly*, 69/1 (Jan.–Mar.), 72–84.

——————(1998c), 'Private Funds for Higher Education: Third Memorandum to the House of Commons Select Committee on Education and Employment', in *The Funding of Student Loans, Minutes of Evidence and Appendices, House of Commons Education and Employment Committee, Session 1997–98*, HC497-i (TSO), 1–10.

——and Jane Falkingham (1993), *Paying for Learning*, Welfare State Programme, Discussion Paper WSP/94, London: London School of Economics.

——————(1996), *Repayment Rates for Student Loans: Some Sensitivity Tests*, Welfare State Programme, Discussion Paper WSP/127, London: London School of Economics.

——and Low, William (1988), *Student Grants and Student Poverty*, Welfare State Programme, Discussion Paper WSP/28, London: London School of Economics.

——and Whynes, David (1993) (eds.), *Issues in the Economics of the Welfare State*, London: Macmillan.

Barro, Robert (1979), 'On the Determination of the Public Debt', *Journal of Political Economy*, 87/5: 940–71.

Bator, Francis M. (1958), 'The Anatomy of Market Failure,' *Quarterly Journal of Economics*, 72/3 (Aug.), 351–79.

Baumol, William (1996), 'Children of the Performing Arts, The Economics Dilemma: The Climbing Costs of Health Care and Education', *Journal of Cultural Economics*, 20/3: 183–206.

Beatty, R., and McGillivray, W. (1995), 'A Risky Strategy: Reflections on the World Bank Report *Averting the Old Age Crisis*', *International Social Security Review*, 48/3–4: 5–22.

Beenstock, Michael, and Brasse, Valerie (1986), *Insurance for Unemployment*, London: Allen & Unwin.

Belan, Pascal, and Pestieau, Pierre (1999), 'Privatising Social Security: A Critical Assessment', *Geneva Papers on Risk and Insurance*, 24/1: 114–30.

Benzeval, Michaela, Judge, Ken, and Whitehead, Margaret (1995), *Tackling Inequalities in Health*, London: King's Fund.

Beveridge Report (1942), *Social Insurance and Allied Services*, Cmd 6404, London: HMSO.

Blanchflower, David, and Oswald, Andrew (2000), 'Wellbeing over Time in Britain and the USA', working paper, presented at the National Bureau of Economic Research Summer Workshop in Cambridge, Mass, July, also available at www.oswald.co.uk.

Blank, Rebecca (1994) (ed.), *Social Protection versus Economic Flexibility*, Chicago: University of Chicago Press.

Blaug, Mark (1976), 'The Empirical Status of Human Capital Theory: A Slightly Jaundiced Survey', *Journal of Economic Literature* (Sept.), 827–56, reprinted in Mark Blaug, *The Economics of Education and the Education of an Economist*, Cheltenham: Edward Elgar, 1987, 100–28.

——(1984), 'Education Vouchers—It All Depends on What You Mean', in Julian Le Grand and Ray Robinson (eds.), *Privatisation and the Welfare State*, London: Weidenfeld & Nicolson, 160–76.

——(1985), 'Where Are We Now in the Economics of Education?', *Economics of Education Review*, 4/1: 17–28, reprinted in Mark Blaug, *The Economics of Education and the Education of an Economist*, Cheltenham: Edward Elgar, 1987, 129–40.

Blomqvist, A. (1991), 'The Doctor as Double-Agent: Information Asymmetry, Health Insurance and Medical Care', *Journal of Health Economics*, 10/4 (Nov.), 411–32.

Bodie, Zvi, Marcus, Alan J., and Merton, Robert C. (1988), 'Defined Benefit versus Defined Contribution Plans: What Are the Real Tradeoffs?', in Zvi Bodie, John B. Shoven, and David Wise (eds.), *Pensions in the US Economy*, Chicago: Chicago University Press, 139–62.

Boeri, Tito, Burda, Michael, and Köllő, János (1998), *Mediating the Transition: Labour Markets in Central and Eastern Europe*, London: Centre for Economic Policy Research, and New York: Institute for EastWest Studies.

Bonjour, Dorothe, Cherkas, Lyn, Haskel, Jonathan, Hawkes, Denise, and Spector, Tim (2000), 'Estimating Returns to Education Using a New Sample of Twins', mimeo, Queen Mary Westfield College, London.

Breyer, F. (1989), 'On the Intergenerational Pareto Efficiency of Pay-As-You-Go Financed Pension Systems', *Journal of Institutional and Theoretical Economics*, 145: 643–58.

Brooks, Robin (2000), 'What Will Happen to Financial Markets when the Baby Boomers Retire?', mimeo, Fiscal Affairs Department, International Monetary Fund, Washington.

Buchanan, James M., and Tullock, Gordon (1962), *The Calculus of Consent*, Ann Arbor: University of Michigan Press.

Burchardt, Tania (1997), *What Price Security? Assessing Private Insurance for Long-Term Care, Income Replacement during Incapacity, and Unemployment for Mortgators*, Welfare State Programme Discussion Paper WSP/129, London: London School of Economics,.

——(2000), *Enduring Economic Exclusion: Disabled People, Income and Work*, York: Joseph Rowntree Foundation.

——and Hills, John (1997), *Private Welfare Insurance and Social Security: Pushing the Boundaries*, York: Joseph Rowntree Foundation.

Burtless, Gary (1996), 'Rising US Income Inequality and the Growth in World Trade', *Tokyo Club Papers*, 9: 129–59.

——(2000), 'Social Security Privatization and Financial Market Risk', Working Paper No. 10, Center on Social and Economic Dynamics, Feb.

——and Quinn, Joseph F. (2000), 'Retirement Trends and Policies to Encourage Work among Older Americans', paper presented at the annual conference of the National Academy of Social Insurance, Washington, 26–27 Jan.

Bynner, John, and Egerton, Muriel (2000), 'The Wider Benefits of Higher Education', Wider Benefits of Learning Research Centre, Institute of Education, for the Higher Education Funding Council for England in association with the Smith Institute, London.

Callender, Claire, and Kemp, Martin (2000), *Changing Student Finances: Income, Expenditure and the Take-up of Student Loans among Full-Time and Part-Time Higher Education Students in 1998–99*, London: Department for Education and Employment.

Callund, David (1999), 'Chile: Controversy, Difficulty and Solutions', *Geneva Papers on Risk and Insurance*, 24/4 (Oct.), 528–33.

Campbell, J. C., and Ikegami, N. (1998), *The Art of Balance in Health Policy: Maintaining Japan's Low Cost Egalitarian System*, Cambridge: Cambridge University Press.

Campbell, Nigel (1999), *The Decline of Employment among Older People in Britain*, Centre for the Analysis of Social Exclusion, CASEpaper 19, London: London School of Economics, also available at http://sticerd.lse.ac.uk/case.

Card, David (1999), 'The Causal Effect of Education on Earnings', in Orley Ashenfelter and David Card (eds.), *Handbook of Labor Economics*, Amsterdam: North-Holland.

Cardarelli, R., Sefton, J., and Kotlikoff, L. (2000), 'Generational accounting in the UK', *Economic Journal*, 110/467: F547–F574..

Cave, Martin, Dodsworth, Ruth, and Thompson, David (1992), 'Regulatory Reform in Higher Education in the UK: Incentives for Efficiency and Product Quality', *Oxford Review of Economic Policy*, 8/2: 79–102.

Chand, Sheetal K., and Jaeger, Albert (1996), *Aging Populations and Public Pension Schemes*, Occasional Paper 147, Washington: International Monetary Fund.

Chapman, Bruce (1997), 'Conceptual Issues and the Australian Experience with Income Contingent Charges for Higher Education', *Economic Journal*, 107/442 (May), 738–51.

Coase, Ronald H. (1960), 'The Problem of Social Cost', *Journal of Law and Economics* (Oct.), 1–44.

Commission on Social Justice (1994), *Social Justice: Strategies for National Renewal*, London: Vintage.

Commonwealth of Australia (1997), *Learning for Life: Review of Higher Education Financing and Policy: A Policy Discussion Paper*, Canberra: AGPS.

——(1998), *Learning for Life: Review of Higher Education Financing and Policy: Final Report*, Canberra: AGPS.

Cooley, Thomas F., and Soares, Jorge (1999), 'A Positive Theory of Social Security Based on Reputation', *Journal of Political Economy*, 107/1: 135–60.

Culyer, Anthony J. (1993), 'Health Care Insurance and Provision', in Nicholas Barr and David Whynes (eds.), *Issues in the Economics of the Welfare State*, London: Macmillan, 1993, 153–75.

——and Wagstaff, Adam (1993), 'Equity and Equality in Health and Health Care', *Journal of Health Economics*, 12: 431–57.

Dasgupta, Partha, and Maskin, Eric (1986), 'The Existence of Equilibrium in Discontinuous Economics Games I and II', *Review of Economic Studies*, 53: 1–41.

Diamond, Peter (1995), 'Government Provision and Regulation of Economic Support in Old Age', in Michael Bruno and Boris Pleskovic (eds.), *Annual Bank Conference on Development Economics 1995*, Washington: World Bank.

——(1996), 'Social Security Reform in Chile: An Economist's Perspective', in Peter Diamond, David Lindeman, and H. Young (eds.), *Social Security: What Role for the Future?*, Washington: National Academic of Social Insurance, 213–24.

——(1998a), 'The Economics of Social Security Reform', in Douglas Arnold, Michael Graetz, and Alicia Munnell (eds.), *Framing the Social Security Debate: Values, Politics, and Economics*, Washington: Brookings Institution, 38–64.

——(1998b), Testimony before the Committee on Ways and Means, Subcommittee on Social Security, US House of Representatives, 18 June, also available at www.house.gov/ways_means.

——(2001), 'Comments on Rethinking Pension Reform: 10 Myths about Social Security Systems', in Robert Holzmann and Joseph E. Stiglitz with Louise Fox, Estelle James, and Peter R. Orszag (eds.), *New Ideas about Social Security: Toward Sustainable Pension Systems in the 21st Century*, Washington: World Bank, 76–9.

Disney, Richard (2000), 'The Looming Crisis in Public Pension Provision for Many OECD Countries', *Economic Journal*, 100 (Feb.), F1–F23.

Dixon, Jennifer (1997), 'The British NHS—a Funding Crisis?', *Eurohealth*, 3/1 (Spring), 36–7.

Dunleavy, Patrick (1985), 'Bureaucrats, Budgets and the Growth of the State: Reconstructing an Instrumental Model', *British Journal of Political Science*, 15: 299–328.

——(1991), *Democracy, Bureaucracy and Public Choice*, London: Harvester Wheatsheaf.

Dutta, Jayasri, Sefton, James, and Weale, Martin (1999), 'Education and Public Policy', *Fiscal Studies*, 20/4: 351–86.

Eatwell, John, Elmann, Michael, Karlsson, Mats, Nuti, Mario, and Shapiro, Judith (2000), *Hard Budgets, Soft States*, London: Institute for Public Policy Research.

Eddy, David M. (1992), 'Cost-Effectiveness Analysis: A Conversation with my Father', *Journal of the American Medical Association*, 267/12 (Mar.), 1669–75.

Education and Testing Service (1992*a*), *Learning Mathematics*, Princeton: Education and Testing Service.

——(1992*b*), *Learning Science*, Princeton: Education and Testing Service.

Emmerson, Carl, Frayne, Christine, and Goodman, Alissa (2000), *Pressures in UK Healthcare: Challenges for the National Health Service*, London: Institute for Fiscal Studies and King's Fund.

Enthoven, Alain C. (1989), 'What Can Europeans Learn from Americans?', in US HCFA, *Health Care Financing Review*, Annual Supplement, Office of Research and Demonstrations, Health Care Financing Administration, Washington: Government Printing Office, Dec., also published as OECD, *Health Care Systems in Transition: The Search for Efficiency*, Paris: OECD, 1990.

——(1993), 'The History and Principles of Managed Competition', *Health Affairs*, 12, suppl., 24–48.

——(1999), 'Managed Care: What went Wrong? Can it be Fixed?', The Donald C. Ozmun and Donald B. Ozmun and Family Lecture in Management, Mayo Clinic, Rochester, Minn.

Esping-Andersen, Gøspa (1996), 'After the Golden Age? Welfare State Dilemmas in a Global Economy', in Gøspa Esping-Andersen, *Welfare States in Transition: National Adaptations in Global Economies*, London: Sage, 1–31.

Estrin, Saul (1994), 'The Inheritance', in Nicholas Barr (ed.), *Labor Markets and Social Policy in Central and Eastern Europe: The Transition and Beyond*, New York: Oxford University Press for the World Bank (also available in Hungarian, Romanian, and Russian), 53–76.

European Bank for Reconstruction and Development (1999), *Transition Report Update*, London: EBRD.

Eurostat (2000), *ESA95 Manual on Government Deficit and Debt*, Luxembourg: Eurostat.

Evans, Robert, G. (1974), 'Supplier-Induced Demand: Some Empirical Evidence and Implications', in M. Perlman (ed.), *The Economics of Health and Medical Care*, London: Macmillan, 162–73.

——Lomas, Jonathan, Barer, Morris L., *et al.* (1989), 'Controlling Health Expenditures: The Canadian Reality', *New England Journal of Medicine*, 320/9: 571–7.

Falkingham, Jane, and Hills, John (1995), 'Lifetime Incomes and the Welfare State', in Jane Falkingham and John Hills (eds.), *The Dynamic of Welfare: The Welfare State and the Life Cycle*, Hemel Hempstead: Prentice Hall/Harvester Wheatsheaf, 108–136.

——and Johnson, Paul (1995), 'Funding Pensions over the Life Cycle', in Jane Falkingham and John Hills (eds.), *The Dynamic of Welfare: The Welfare State and the Life Cycle*, Hemel Hempstead: Prentice Hall/Harvester Wheatsheaf, 204–17.

Feldstein, Martin S. (1974), 'Social Security, Induced Retirement and Aggregate Capital Accumulation', *Journal of Political Economy*, 82: 905–26.

——(1996), 'The Missing Piece in Policy Analysis: Social Security Reform', *American Economic Review*, 86/2 (May), 1–14.

Flemming, John S. (1978), 'Aspects of Optimal Unemployment Insurance', *Journal of Public Economics*, 10: 403–5.

Friedman, Milton (1962), *Capitalism and Freedom*, Chicago: University of Chicago Press.

Fuchs, Victor R. (1988), 'The "Competition Revolution" in Health Care', *Health Affairs*, 7/3: 5–24.

Gale, William (1998), 'The Effects of Pensions on Wealth: A Re-Evaluation of Theory and Evidence', *Journal of Political Economy* (Aug.), 706–23.

Geanakoplos, John, Mitchell, Olivia S., and Zeldes, Stephen P. (1998), 'Would a Privatized Social Security System Really Pay a Higher Rate of Return?', in Douglas R. Arnold, Michael J. Graetz, and Alicia H. Munnell (eds.), *Framing the Social Security Debate: Values, Politics, and Economics*, Washington: Brookings Institution, 137–57.

————(1999), 'Social Security Money's Worth', in Olivia S. Mitchell, Robert J. Myers, and Howard Young, *Prospects for Social Security Reform*, Philadelphia: University of Pennsylvania Press, 79–151.

Gerencsér, L. (1997), *Information on the Pension Reform in Hungary*, Budapest: Central Administration of the National Pension Insurance Fund.

Giddens, Anthony (1998), *The Third Way: The Renewal of Social Democracy*, Cambridge: Polity Press.

Glennerster, Howard (1993), 'The Economics of Education: Changing Fortunes', in Nicholas Barr and David Whynes (1993), *Issues in the Economics of the Welfare State*, London: Macmillan, 176–99.

——(1997a), *Paying for Welfare: Towards 2000*, 3rd edn., Hemel Hempstead: Prentice Hall/Harvester Wheatsheaf.

——(1997b), 'Education', in Howard Glennerster and John Hills (eds.), *The State of Welfare: The Economics of Social Spending*, Oxford: Oxford University Press, 27–74.

——(1998a), 'Solutions for Long-Term Care', *New Economy*, 5/1: 24–9.

——(1998b), 'Competition and Quality in Health Care: The UK Experience', *International Journal for Quality in Health Care*, 10/5: 403–10.

——(1998c), 'Priorities for Welfare', *Times Higher Education Supplement*, 1344, 7 Aug. 1998, 16–17.

——Merrett, Stephen, and Wilson, Gail (1968), 'A Graduate Tax', *Higher Education Review*, 1/1: 26–38.

Godfrey, M., and Richards, P. (1997) (eds.), *Employment Policies and Programmes in Central and Eastern Europe*, Geneva: ILO.

Góra, Marek, and Rutkowski, Michal (1998), 'The Quest for Pension Reform: Poland's Security through Diversity', Social Protection Discussion Paper 9815, World Bank, Washington.

Greenaway, David, and Haynes, Michelle (2000), *Funding Universities to Meet National and International Challenges*, Nottingham: University of Nottingham, also available at www.nottingham. ac.uk/economics/funding.

Grosh, Margaret (1994), *Administering Targeted Social Programs in Latin America: From Platitudes to Practice*, Washington: World Bank.

Grout, Paul (1983), 'Education Finance and Imperfections in Information', *Economic and Social Review*, 15/1 (Oct.), 25–33.

Gruber, Jonathan, and Wise, David (1999), *Social Security and Retirement around the World*, Chicago: University of Chicago Press.

Hannah, Leslie (1986), *Inventing Retirement*, Cambridge: Cambridge University Press.

Hansen, W. Lee, and Weisbrod, Burton A. (1969), 'The Distribution of Costs and Direct Benefits of Public Higher Education: The Case of California', *Journal of Human Resources*, 4/2 (Spring), 176–91.

————(1978), 'The Distribution of Subsidies to Students in California Public Higher Education: Reply', *Journal of Human Resources*, 13/1 (Winter), 137–9.

Hanushek, Eric A. (1986), 'The Economics of Schooling: Production and Efficiency in Public Schools', *Journal of Economic Literature*, 23/3: 1141–77.

——(1996), 'Measuring Investment in Education', *Journal of Economic Perspectives*, 10/4: 9–30.

Harper, Peter S. (1992), 'Genetic Testing and Insurance', *Journal of the Royal College of Physicians*, 26/2 (Apr.), 184–7.

Harrison, A. H., Dixon, J., New, B., and Judge, K (1997a), 'Is the NHS Sustainable?', *British Medical Journal*, 314: 296–8.

———— ———— ———— ————(1997b), 'Can the NHS Cope in the Future?', *British Medical Journal*, 314: 139–42.

Hayek, Friedrich A. (1945), 'The Use of Knowledge in Society', *American Economic Review*, 35: 519–30.

Heller, Peter (1998), *Rethinking Public Pension Reform Initiatives*, IMF Working Paper, WP/98/61, Washington: International Monetary Fund.

Hellwig, Martin (1987), 'Some Recent Developments in the Theory of Competition in Markets with Adverse Selection', *European Economic Review*, 31: 319–25.

Heyneman, Stephen P. (1994), *Education in the Europe and Central Asia Region: Policies of Adjustment and Excellence*, Europe and Central Asia Region, Report No. IDP-145, Washington DC: World Bank (also in Russian).

Himmelstein, David U., and Woolhandler, Steffie (1991), 'The Deteriorating Administrative Efficiency of the US Health Care System', *New England Journal of Medicine*, 324/18: 1253–7.

Hochman, Harold, and Rodgers, James (1969), 'Pareto Optimal Distribution', *American Economic Review*, 41/4: 542–57.

Holzmann, Robert (1997), 'Pension Reform, Financial Market Development, and Economic Growth: Preliminary Evidence from Chile', *IMF Staff Papers*, 44/2: 149–78.

——(1999), 'On the Economic Benefits and Fiscal Requirements of Moving from Unfunded to Funded Pensions', in M. Buti, D. Franco, and L. Pench (eds.), *The Welfare State in Europe*, Cheltenham: Edward Elgar, 139–96.

——(2000a), 'The World Bank Approach to Pension Reform', *International Social Security Review*, 53/1: 11–31.

——(2000b), 'Can Investments in Emerging Markets Help to Solve the Aging Problem', mimeo, World Bank, Washington.

Homburg, S. (1990), 'The Efficiency of Unfunded Pension Schemes', *Journal of Institutional and Theoretical Economics*, 146: 640–7.

International Federation of Accountants (1998), 'Guideline for Governmental Financial Reporting', Exposure Draft, issued for comment by 31 July.

International Social Security Association (1998), *Trends in Social Security*, 1998(2).

Jackman, Richard (1998), 'Unemployment and Restructuring', in Peter Boone, Stanislaw Gomulka, and Richard Layard, *Emerging from Communism: Lessons from Russia, China, and Eastern Europe*, London: MIT Press, 123–52.

——and Rutkowski, Michal (1994), 'Labour Markets: Wages and Employment', in Nicholas Barr (ed.), *Labor Markets and Social Policy in Central and Eastern Europe: The Transition and Beyond*, New York: Oxford University Press for the World Bank (also available in Hungarian, Romanian, and Russian), 121–59.

James, Estelle (1998), 'New Models for Old-Age Security: Experiments, Evidence, and Unanswered Questions', *World Bank Research Observer*, 13/2 (Aug.), 271–301.

——(2001), 'Comments on Rethinking Pension Reform: 10 Myths about Social Security Systems', in Robert Holzmann and Joseph E. Stiglitz, with Louise Fox, Estelle James, and Peter R. Orszag (eds.), *New Ideas about Social Security: Toward Sustainable Pension Systems in the 21st Century*, Washington: The World Bank, 63–70.

Jongbloed, Ben (1999), 'Funding Higher Education in the Netherlands', personal communication.

Kawachi, I, Kennedy, B. P., and Wilkinson, R. G. (2000), *Society and Population Health: Reader*, i. *Income Inequality and Health*, New York: New Press.

King, Jacqueline (1999) (ed.), *Financing a College Education: How it Works, How it's Changing*, Phoenix, Ariz.: American Council on Education and Oryx Press.

Kotlikoff, Laurence J. (1992), *Generational Accounting: Knowing Who Pays, and When, for What we Spend*, New York: Maxwell Macmillan International.

——and Raffelhueschen, B. (1999), 'Generational Accounting Round the Globe', *American Economic Review*, 89/2: 161–6.

——and Seeger, Charles (2000), 'Look Abroad to Solve the Pensions Crisis', *Financial Times*, US edn., 25 Apr., p. 17.

Kovalyova, Galina (1994), 'Comparative Assessments of Students in Science and Math', in Stephen P. Heynemann, (ed.), *Education in the Europe and Central Asia Region: Policies of Adjustment and Excellence*, Europe and Central Asia Region, Report No. IDP-145, Washington: World Bank.

Laporte, Bruno, and Schweitzer, Julian (1994), 'Education and Training', in Nicholas Barr (ed.), *Labor Markets and Social Policy in Central and Eastern Europe: The Transition and Beyond*, New York: Oxford University Press for the World Bank (also available in Hungarian, Romanian, and Russian), 260–87.

Le Grand, Julian (1982), *The Strategy of Equality*, London: George Allen & Unwin.

——(1989), 'Markets, Welfare and Equality', in Julian Le Grand and Saul Estrin (eds.), *Market Socialism*, Oxford: Clarendon Press.

——(1991a), 'The Theory of Government Failure', *British Journal of Political Science*, 21: 423–42.

——(1991b), 'Equity in the Distribution of UK National Health Service Resources', *Journal of Health Economics*, 10/1 (May), 1–9.

——(1992), 'The Distribution of Health Care Revisited', *Journal of Health Economics*, 10: 239–45.

——(1995), 'The Strategy of Equality Revisited: Reply', *Journal of Social Policy*, 24/2: 187–91.

——and Nissan, David (2000), *A Capital Idea: Start-Up Grants for Young People*, London: Fabian Society.

——and Vizard, Polly (1998), 'The National Health Service: Crisis, Change or Continuity?', in Howard Glennerster and John Hills (1998) (eds.), *The State of Welfare*, 2nd edn., Oxford: Oxford University Press, 75–121.

——Mays, Nicholas, and Mulligan, Jo-Ann (1998), *Learning from the NHS Internal Market*, London: King's Fund.

Lindbeck, Assar, Nyberg, Sten, and Weibull, Jorgen (1999), 'Social Norms and Economic Incentives in the Welfare State', *Quarterly Journal of Economics*, 114/1: 1–35.

Lindeman, David, Rutkowski, Michal, and Sluchynskiyy, Oleksiy (2000), *The Evolution of Pension Systems in Eastern Europe and Central Asia: Opportunities, Constraints, Dilemmas and Emerging Practices*, Washington: World Bank.

Loewenstein, George (1999), 'Is More Choice Always Better?, *Social Security Brief*, 7, Washington: National Academy of Social Insurance, also available at http://www.nasi.org/ SocSec/Briefs.

Lucas, Robert E. (1987), *Models of Business Cycles*, Oxford: Basil Blackwell.

McGuire, Alistair (1996), 'Is There Adequate Funding of Health Care?', in Anthony J. Culyer and Adam Wagstaff (eds.), *Reforming Health Care Systems: Experiments with the NHS*, Proceedings of Section F (Economics) of the British Association for the Advancement of Science, Loughborough 1994, Cheltenham: Edward Elgar, 134–49.

Mackenzie, G. A., Gerson, Philip, and Cuevas, Alfredo (1997), *Pension Regimes and Saving*, Occasional Paper 153, Washington: International Monetary Fund.

McPherson, Michael S., and Shapiro, Morton Owen (1998), *The Student Aid Game: Meeting Need and Rewarding Talent in American Higher Education*, Princeton: Princeton University Press.

Manning, Willard G., Newhouse, Joseph P., Duan, Naihua, Keeler, Emmett B., Liebowitz, Arleen, and Marquis, Susan M. (1987), 'Health Insurance and the Demand for Medical Care: Evidence from a Randomized Experiment', *American Economic Review*, 77/3 (June), 251–77.

Marmot, M. G., Davey Smith, G., Stanseld, S., Patel, C., North, F., Head, J., White, I., Brunner, E., and Feeney, A. (1991), 'Health Inequalities among British Civil Servants: The Whitehall II Study', *Lancet*, 337, 8 June, pp. 1387–93.

Marshall, Alfred (1961), *Principles of Economics*, 9th edn., London: Macmillan.

Meade, James E. (1952), 'External Economies and Diseconomies in a Competitive Situation', *Economic Journal*, 62: 54–67.

Merton, Robert (1983), 'On the Role of Social Security as a Means for Efficient Risk Sharing in an Economy where Human Capital is not Tradeable,' in Zvi Bodie and John Shoven (eds.), *Issues in Pension Economics*, Chicago: University of Chicago Press.

——Bodie, Zvi, and Marcus, Alan (1987), 'Pension Plan Integration as Insurance Against Social Security Risk,' in Zvi Bodie, John Shoven, and David Wise (eds.), *Issues in Pension Economics*, Chicago: University of Chicago Press.

Milanovic, Branko (1998), *Income, Inequality and Poverty during the Transition from Planned to Market Economy*, Washington: World Bank.

Miles, David (2000), 'Moving to Funded Pension Schemes', CEPR/RES public meeting, 3 Feb.

Millns, Tony (2000), 'Individual Learning Accounts and Tertiary Education', in Tony Millns and Wendy Piatt (eds.), *Paying for Learning: The Future of Individual Learning Accounts*, London: Institute for Public Policy Research, 1–10.

Modigliani, Franco, Ceprini, Maria Luisa, and Muralidhar, Arun (2000), 'An MIT Solution to the Social Security Crisis', Sloan Working Paper No. 4051, Massachusetts Institute of Technology, Aug.

Morris, J., Cook, D., and Shaper, G. (1994), 'Loss of Employment and Mortality', *British Medical Journal*, 308: 1135–9.

Mossialos, Elias, and Le Grand, Julian (1999) (eds.), *Health Care and Cost Containment in the European Union*, Aldershot: Ashgate.

Mueller, Dennis C. (1997) (ed.), *Perspectives on Public Choice: A Handbook*, Cambridge: Cambridge University Press.

Muralidhar, Arun, and van der Wouden, Ronald J. P. (1998a), *Reforming Pension Reform—the Case for Contributory Defined Benefit Second Pillars*, Working Paper Series 98–003, Washington: World Bank, May.

——————(1998b), *Welfare Costs of Defined Contribution Plans—the Case for an Alternative*, Working Paper Series 98–006, Washington: World Bank, June.

Murthi, Mamta, Orszag, Michael, and Orszag, Peter (1999), 'The Charge Ratio on Individual Accounts: Lessons from the UK Experience', Working Paper 2/99, Birkbeck College, London, Mar.

Narendranathan, Wiji, Nickell, Stephen, and Stern, Jon (1985), 'Unemployment Benefits Revisited', *Economic Journal*, 95: 307–29.

National Westminster Bank (1997), *A Changing Nation: Retirement Provision for the 21st Century*, London: National Westminster Bank.

Nellis, John (1999), *Time to Rethink Privatization in Transition Economies?*, Discussion Paper No. 38, Washington: International Finance Corporation.

Nelson, Joan (1998), 'The Politics of Pensions and Health Care Delivery Reforms in Hungary and Poland', paper to Focus Group on Fiscal Reforms, Collegium Budapest, 27–28 Mar., Budapest.

——(1999), *Reforming Health and Education: The World Bank, the IDB, and Complex Institutional Change*, Washington: Overseas Development Council.

New, Bill (1999), 'Paternalism and Public Policy', *Economics and Philosophy*, 15: 62–83.

——(2000), 'Justifying State Interventions: The Case of Paternalism', Ph.D. thesis, London School of Economics.

Newhouse, Joseph P. (1993), *Free for All: Lessons from the RAND Health Insurance Experiment*, Cambridge, Mass: Harvard University Press.

New Zealand Ministry of Education (1998), *Tertiary Education in New Zealand: Policy Directions for the 21st Century*, White Paper (Nov.), Wellington: Ministry of Education.

Niskanen, William A. (1971), *Bureaucracy and Representative Government*, Chicago: Aldine Atherton.

North, F., Syme, S. L., Feeney, A., *et al.* (1993), 'Explaining Sociological Differences in Sickness Absence: The Whitehall II Study', *British Medical Journal*, 306, 6 Feb., 363.

Nuttall, S., Blackwood, R., Bussell, B., Cliff, J., Conrall, M., Cowley, A., Gatenby, P., and Webber, J. (1995), 'Financing Long-Term Care in Great Britain', *Journal of the Institute of Actuaries*, 121 / 1: 1–68.

OECD (1992), *The Reform of Health Care: A Comparative Analysis of Seven OECD Countries*, Paris: OECD.

——(1994), *The Reform of Health Care Systems: A Comparative Analysis of Seventeen OECD Countries*, Paris: OECD.

——(1996), *Caring for Frail Elderly People: Policies in Evolution*, Paris: OECD.

——(1997a), *Thematic Review of Higher Education*, Paris: OECD.

——(1997b), *Thematic Review of the First Years of Tertiary Education: Country Note: Denmark*, Paris: OECD.

——(1997c), *Lessons from Labour Market Policies in the Transition Economies*, Paris: OECD.

——(1998), *Education at a Glance: OECD Indicators*, Paris: OECD.

Orszag, Peter R. (1999), *Individual Accounts and Social Security: Does Social Security Really Provide a Lower Rate of Return?*, Washington: Center on Budget and Policy Priorities, also available at http:/ /www.cbpp.org.

——and Stiglitz, Joseph E. (2001), 'Rethinking Pension Reform: 10 Myths about Social Security Systems', in Robert Holzmann and Joseph E. Stiglitz, with Louise Fox, Estelle James, and Peter R. Orszag (eds.), *New Ideas about Social Security: Toward Sustainable Pension Systems in the 21st Century*, Washington: World Bank, 17–62.

Panel on Privatization of Social Security (1998), *Evaluating Issues in Privatizing Social Security*, Report of the Panel on Privatization of Social Security, Washington: National Academy of Social Insurance.

Pauly, Mark V. (1974), 'Overinsurance and Public Provision of Insurance: The Roles of Moral Hazard and Adverse Selection', *Quarterly Journal of Economics*, 88: 44–62.

——(1986), 'Taxation, Health Insurance and Market Failure in the Medical Economy', *Journal of Economic Literature*, 24 (June), 629–75.

——(1990), 'The Rational Non-Purchase of Long-Term Care Insurance', *Journal of Political Economy*, 98 / 1: 153–68.

Pestieau, Pierre, and Possen, Uri M. (2000), 'Investing Social Security in the Equity Market. Does it Make a Difference?', *National Tax Journal*, 53 / 1: 41–57.

Powell, M (1995), 'The Strategy of Equality Revisited', *Journal of Social Policy*, 24(2): 163–91.

Preker, Alexander, and Feachem, Richard (1994), 'Health and Health Care' in Nicholas Barr (ed.), *Labor Markets and Social Policy in Central and Eastern Europe: The Transition and Beyond*, New York: Oxford University Press for the World Bank (also available in Hungarian, Romanian, and Russian), 288–321.

Quah, Danny (1996), *The Invisible Hand and the Weightless Economy*, Centre for Economic Performance, Occasional Paper No. 12, London: London School of Economics.

Ravallion, Martin (1996), 'Issues in Measuring and Modelling Poverty', *Economic Journal*, 106 (Sept.), 1328–44.

Ravallion, Martin and Datt, Gaurav (1995), 'Is Targeting through a Work Requirement Effective?', in Dominique van de Walle and Kimberly Nead (1995) (eds.), *Public Spending and the Poor: Theory and Evidence*, Washington: Johns Hopkins University Press, 413–44.

Rees, Ray (1989), 'Uncertainty, Information and Insurance' in John Hey 1989) (ed.), *Current Issues in Microeconomics*, London: Macmillan, 47–78.

Robertson, David (1997), 'The Learning Bank: Rethinking the Funding of Relationships in British Higher Education', *Higher Education Review*, 29/2: 17–33.

——and Mason, Geoff (2000), 'Individual Learning Accounts and Tertiary Education', in Tony Millns and Wendy Piatt (eds.), *Paying for Learning: The Future of Individual Learning Accounts*, London: Institute for Public Policy Research, 50–60.

Robinson, Ray, and Steiner, Andrea (1998), *Managed Health Care*, Buckingham: Open University Press.

Romer, Paul (1993), 'Ideal Gaps and Object Gaps in Economic Development', *Journal of Monetary Economics*, 32: 338–69.

Ross, Stanford (2000), 'Doctrine and Practice in Social Security Pension Reforms', *International Social Security Review*, 53/2: 3–29.

Rothschild, Michael, and Stiglitz, Joseph E. (1976), 'Equilibrium in Competitive Insurance Markets: An Essay on the Economics of Imperfect Information', *Quarterly Journal of Economics*, 90: 629–49.

Royal Economic Society (2000), 'The Pensions Problem', *Royal Economic Society Newsletter*, 109 (Apr.), 11–13.

Saltman, Richard B., Busse, Reinhard, and Mossialos, Elias (forthcoming) (eds.), *Regulating Entrepreneurial Behavior in European Health Care*, European Observatory Series, Milton Keynes: Open University Press.

Samuelson, Paul A. (1954), 'The Pure Theory of Public Expenditures', *Review of Economics and Statistics*, 36/4 (Nov.), 387–9.

——(1958), 'An Exact Consumption-Loan Model of Interest with or without the Social Contrivance of Money', *Journal of Political Economy*, 56/6 (Dec.), 467–82.

Sen, Amartya K. (1999), 'Economic Policy and Equity: An Overview', in Vito Tanzi, Ke-young Chu, and Sanjeev Gupta (eds.), *Economic Policy and Equity*, Washington: International Monetary Fund, 28–43.

Shapiro, Judith (1995), 'The Russian Mortality Crisis and its Causes', in Anders Aslund (ed.), *Russian Economic Reform at Risk*, London: Pinter, 149–78.

Sloan, Frank A., and Norton, Edward C. (1997), 'Adverse Selection Bequests, Crowding out, and Private Demand for Insurance: Evidence from the Long-Term Care Insurance Market', *Journal of Risk and Uncertainty*, 15/3: 201–19.

Sparkes, Jo (1999), *Schools, Education and Social Exclusion*, Centre for the Analysis of Social Exclusion, CASEpaper 29, London: London School of Economics, also available at http://sticerd.lse.ac.uk/case.

Stern, Jon (1982), 'Unemployment Inflow Rates for Autumn 1978', Centre for Labour Economics, Discussion Paper No. 129, London School of Economics.

Stiglitz, Joseph E. (1983), 'Risk, Incentives and Insurance: The Pure Theory of Moral Hazard', *Geneva Papers on Risk and Insurance*, 8(26): 4–33.

——(1999), 'Whither Reform? Ten Years of the Transition', Keynote Address, Annual Bank Conference on Development Economics, World Bank, Washington.

——(2000), *Economics of the Public Sector*, 3rd edn., New York and London: Norton.

Sweden, Federation of Social Insurance Offices (1998), 'Sweden', *The Future of Social Security*, Stockholm: Federation of Social Insurance Offices, 192–203; updates available at http://www.pension.gov.se.

Thompson, Lawrence (1998), *Older and Wiser: The Economics of Public Pensions*, Washington: Urban Institute.

Thurow, Lester (1996), *The Future of Capitalism: How Today's Economic Forces Shape Tomorrow's World*, London: Nicholas Brealey.

Tiebout, Charles (1956), 'A Pure Theory of Local Expenditures', *Journal of Political Economy* (Oct.), 416–24.

Tobin, James (1968), 'Raising the Incomes of the Poor', in Kermit Gordon (ed.), *Agenda for the Nation*, Washington: Brookings Institution.

Tullock, Gordon (1970), *Private Wants, Public Means*, New York: Basic Books.

——(1971), 'The Charity of the Uncharitable', *Western Economic Journal*, 9: 379–92.

UK Committee of Vice-Chancellors and Principals (1996), *Our Universities, Our Future, Special Report 4: The Case for a New Higher Education Funding System*, London: Committee of Vice-Chancellors and Principals.

UK Department for Education and Employment (1998a), 'Letter and Memorandum by the Department for Education and Employment', in *The Funding of Student Loans, Minutes of Evidence and Appendices, House of Commons Education and Employment Committee, Session 1997–98*, HC497-i, London: 150, 10–12.

——(1998b), *Individual Learning Accounts* (ILA1), London: Department of Education and Employment.

——(1999), *Individual Learning Accounts: A Summary of Progress*, London: Department of Education and Employment.

UK Department of Health (2000), *The NHS Plan: The Government's Response to the Royal Commission on Long Term Care*, CM 4818-II, London: TSO.

UK Department of Social Security (1993), *Containing the Costs of Social Security—the International Context*, London: HMSO.

——(1997), 'Guaranteed, Secure Pensions for All Says Peter Lilley', Press Release 97/044, Department of Social Security, London.

——(1998), *A New Contract for Welfare: Partnership in Pensions*, Cm 4179, London: TSO, December.

UK Further Education Funding Council (1997), *Learning Works: Widening Participation in Further Education* (the Kennedy Report), Coventry: Further Education Funding Council.

UK Government Actuary's Department (1978), *The Financing of Occupational Pension Schemes, Evidence of the Government Actuary's Department to the Committee to Review the Functioning of Financial Institutions*, London: HMSO.

UK National Committee of Inquiry into Higher Education (the Dearing Committee) (1997a), *Higher Education in the Learning Society: Summary Report*, London: HMSO, also available at http://www.leeds.ac.uk/educol/ncihe.

——(1997b), *Higher Education in the Learning Society: Main Report*, London: HMSO, also available at http://www.leeds.ac.uk/educol/ncihe.

——(1997c), *Higher Education in the Learning Society: Appendix 5: Higher Education in other Countries*, London: HMSO, also available at http://www.leeds.ac.uk/educol/ncihe.

——(1997d), *Higher Education in the Learning Society: Report 7, Rates of Return to Higher Education*, London: HMSO, also available at http://www.leeds.ac.uk/educol/ncihe.

——(1997e), *Higher Education in the Learning Society: Report 13, Individual Learning Accounts and a Learning Bank*, London: HMSO, also available at http://www.leeds.ac.uk/educol/ncihe.

UK Pension Law Review Committee (1993), *Pension Law Reform, Report of the Pension Law Review Committee, Volume I, Report; Volume II, Research*, London: HMSO.

UK Royal Commission (1999a), *With Respect to Old Age: Long-Term Care—Rights and Responsibilities, A Report by the Royal Commission on Long Term Care*, Cm 4192-I, London: TSO.

UK Royal Commission (1999*b*), *With Respect to Old Age: Long-Term Care—Rights and Responsibilities, Research Volume 1*, Cm 4192-II/I, London: TSO.

UK Treasury Select Committee (1998), *The Mis-Selling of Personal Pensions, Ninth Report, Volume 1, Report and Proceedings of the Committee*, HC712-1, London: TSO.

Varian, Hal R. (1999), *Intermediate Microeconomics*, 5th edn., New York and London: Norton.

Westwood, Andy (2000), 'What do Employers Want? Do they Know? And should we Listen?', in Caroline Mager and Peter Robinson (eds.), *The New Learning Market*, London: FEDA and Institute for Public Policy Research, 93–112.

Wilensky, Harold L., and Lebeaux, Charles N. (1965), *Industrial Society and Social Welfare*, New York: Free Press; London: Collier-Macmillan.

Wilkinson, Richard (1996), *Unhealthy Societies: The Afflictions of Inequality*, London: Routledge.

Winston, Gordon (1999), 'Subsidies, Hierarchies and Peers: The Awkward Economics of Higher Education', *Journal of Economic Perspectives*, 13/1 (Winter), 13–26.

Woodhall, Maureen (1990), *Student Loans in Higher Education: 1 Western Europe and the USA*, Educational Forum Series No. 1, Paris: International Institute for Educational Planning.

World Bank (1993), *Poland: Income Support and the Social Safety Net during the Transition*, Washington: World Bank.

——(1994*a*), *Averting the Old Age Crisis*, New York: Oxford University Press.

——(1994*b*), *Higher Education: The Lessons of Experience*, Washington: World Bank.

——(1996), *World Development Report 1996: From Plan to Market*, New York: Oxford University Press.

——(1999), *World Development Indicators*, Washington: World Bank.

Index

Aaron, H. 63, 64, 91, 102, 118
Abel Smith, B. 60, 61
Ackerman, B. and Alstott, A. 238
Actuarial *see* insurance
administrative costs:
  higher education 183–4, 215
  pensions 117, 122
adverse selection:
  and genetic screening 74–5
  and long-term care 82
  and medical insurance 20–1, 55, 56–7
  pooling equilibrium 21, 74–5
  separating equilibrium 21, 75
  and student loans 176–8, 182
  theory 20–1
  and unemployment insurance 37
  see also insurance; social insurance
Agulnik, P. 134, 238 n.
Agulnik, P. and Barr, N. 115
Agulnik, P. and Le Grand, J. 150
Akerlof, G. 16 n., 20, 57 n., 270 n.
allocative efficiency 28–9, 51, 161–2, 258, 259–60
annuities:
  market risk 115–16, 135
  transactions costs 116
Arenas de Mesa, A. and Marcel, M. 138
Arrow, K. 16 n., 23, 74, 77
Arulampalam, W. and Stewart, M. 46
Ashenfelter, O. and Krueger, A. 168 n.
Ashenfelter, O. and Rouse, C. 168 n.
Asher, M. 138
Atkinson, A. 20 n., 24, 33, 57 n., 107, 264–5
Atkinson, A. and Hills, J. 31, 170
Atkinson, A. and Micklewright, J. 40 n.
Atkinson, A. and Mogenson, G. 40 n., 270
Auerbach, A. *et al.* 102, 109 n.
Auerbach, A. and Kotlikoff, L. 11 n., 102
Australia:
  health finance 58–9
  higher education 208–11, 212–15
  pension system 13, 99–100, 133, 134, 135, 140,
    142–3
  student loans 233
  West Report 210–11

Barr, N. 4, 13 n., 18 n., 96, 97, 164, 185, 202, 203,
  210 n., 212, 224 n., 225, 243, 250 n., 252 n.
Barr, N. and Crawford, I. 186 n., 195 n., 201 n., 203,
  227 n.
Barr, N. and Falkingham, J. 186 n., 204, 225, 229, 235
Barr, N. and Low, W. 205
Barr, N. and Whynes, D. 20 n.

Barro, R. 109
Bator, F. 16 n.
Baumol, W. 82 n., 266
Beatty, R. and McGillivray, W. 137
Beenstock, M. and Brasse, V. 33, 38, 41–2, 44, 45
Belan, P. and Pestieau, P. 118, 120
Benzeval, M., Judge, K., and Whitehead, M. 51
Blanchflower, D. and Oswald, A. 164
Blank, R. 270
Blaug, M. 166 n., 196 n.
Blomqvist, A. 57
Bodie, Z., Marcus, A., and Merton, R. 93 n.
Boeri, T., Burda, M., and Kollo, J. 248 n., 251 n.
Bonjour, D. *et al.* 168 n.
Breyer, F. 118, 120
British Medical Association (BMA) 37
Brooks, R. 13 n., 98 n.
Buchanan, J. and Tullock, G. 27
Bulgaria 243
Burchardt, T. 79 n., 81
Burchardt, T. and Hills, J. 18 n., 40, 45, 81, 83
Burtless, G. 114, 267
Burtless, G. and Quinn, J. 111
Bynner, J. and Egerton, M. 165

Callender, C. and Kemp, M. 205
Callund, D. 116, 137
Campbell, J. and Ikegami, N. 68
Campbell, N. 111
Canada:
  education 260
  health finance 58–9, 61, 62, 67–9, 70, 147
  pension funding 101, 123, 126, 134, 135, 147
capital markets, information problems 7, 175–8
capital mobility 103
Card, D. 167 n.
Cardarelli, R., Sefton, J., and Kotlikoff, L. 109 n.
Cave, M., Dodsworth, R., and Thompson, D. 196
Chand, S. and Jaeger, A. 105
Chapman, B. 208 n., 209, 220
Chile, pension reform 104, 115–16, 117, 123, 128,
    133, 135, 136–8, 142
choice:
  educational 173–4
  see also risk; uncertainty
classification problem 200
  higher education 183–4, 190, 200, 218–19, 223–5
Coase, R. 15
coinsurance 58
competition:
  advantages 53, 59
  and cost containment 59

Index

competition (*cont.*):
  in higher education 196–7
  perfect 14
compliance rates 137
compulsion 24, 37, 42–3, 134
consumer sovereignty, higher education 159, 192, 216
consumption:
  rivalry 15
  smoothing 5, 87, 89, 101, 134, 138, 142, 152, 156–7, 250
Cooley, T. and Soares, J. 141 n.
cost sharing 58–9
countries *see* Australia; Bulgaria; Canada; Chile; Croatia; Czech Republic; Denmark; Estonia; France; Germany; Hungary; Japan; Kazakhstan; Latvia; Lithuania; Netherlands; New Zealand; Norway; Poland; Romania; Russia; Singapore; Slovakia; Slovenia; Sweden; UK; Ukraine; USA
Croatia, pension reform 252–7
Culyer, A. 18 n., 20 n., 21 n.
Culyer, A. and Wagstaff, A. 67 n.
Czech Republic 243–4, 252, 254–5

Dasgupta, P. and Maskin, E. 57 n.
Dearing Report, UK 195 n., 203, 210, 236
debt:
  pension 105–10
  public 101
  see also student loans
demographic change 13
  pension funding 96–110
Denmark 208 n.
  higher education 208 n.
diagnosis-related groups *see* medical insurance
Diamond, P. 104, 111, 114, 117, 121, 123, 137
disability insurance 31, 79
Disney, R. 96
divorce 150, 154, 155
Dixon, J. 67 n.
Dunleavy, P. 27
Dutta, J., Sefton, J., and Weale, M. 167 n.

early retirement 111, 139
Eatwell, J. *et al.* 106, 136, 246 n.
Eddy, D. 52 n.
education:
  benefits of 159, 162, 164–5, 217, 258
  and capital markets 7, 159, 175–8
  efficient levels of spending on 59, 167–70
  and equity 171–2, 180
  establishing causality 166–70
  'good education' defined 161–4, 172
  higher *see* higher education
  Hungary 260
  information problems 7, 26, 159, 171–8
  market forces 159
  measuring inputs and outputs 164–6

school level 26, 159, 171–3
screening hypothesis 166–7
student loans *see* student loans
sub-degree studies 234–6
tertiary 159, 173–4, 234–6
  see also higher education
test scores 166
and values 162–4
vocational 200, 234
vouchers 162–3
efficiency:
  allocative 4, 28–9, 51, 161–2, 258, 259–60
  definition 161
  dynamic 4, 162
  and equity 29, 161, 258
  productive 4, 162, 258–9
  static 4, 162
elitism 216
Emmerson, C., Frayne, C., and Goodman, A. 66 n.
employment:
  and health 51
  see also unemployment insurance
endogenous growth theory 165
Enthoven, A. 60 n., 63, 64, 65 n.
equality of opportunity 5, 161, 215–16
equity 5, 29, 52, 58, 67, 189, 197–8, 201, 216
  and education 171–2, 180
  and efficiency 2, 29, 161, 258
  generational 109
Esping-Andersen, G. 270
Estonia 245, 257
Estrin, S. 103
Evans, R. 61, 663
Evans, R. et al. 61
excludability 15–16
expectations:
  educational 221–2
  and retirement behaviour 102
external effects 15, 16

Falkingham, J. and Hills, J. 1
Falkingham, J. and Johnson, P. 151
family:
  breakdown 24
  formation 148, 149, 150
Feldstein, M. 101, 118
finance:
  intervention by 13–14
  and production 14
  health *see* health care, medical insurance
  higher education *see* higher education
  long-term care *see* long-term care
Fisher model 5–6, 11–13, 19, 87, 159, 175, 182, 238, 265
Flemming, J. 38
France 260
Friedman, Milton, *Capitalism and Freedom* 27, 185
Fuchs, V. 59
funded pensions *see* retirement pensions

Gale, W. 102
Geanakoplos, J., Mitchell, O., and Zeldes, S.
    106 n., 118, 119, 120, 121
generational accounting 109
genetic screening 72–9
    adverse selection 74–5
    information problems and 55
    policies towards 75–8
    preferred options 78–9
    problems for insurance 31, 55, 72–4
    uninsurable risks 73, 74
Gerencser, L. 256 n., 257
Germany:
    health finance 65, 68, 69, 70
    long-term care 85–6
    welfare beneficiaries 28
Giddens, A. 264
Glennerster, H. 4, 59, 83, 166 n., 167 n., 186, 266
global pressures 267–8
Godfrey, M. and Richards, P. 251 n.
Gora, M. and Rutkowski, M. 255 n.
government failure 26–8, 106, 215
graduate tax 179, 186, 218–19
Greenaway, D. and Haynes, M. 193, 201, 202
Gresham's law 74, 77
Grout, P. 184 n.
Gruber, J. and Wise, D. 111

Hannah, L. 33
Hansen, W. and Weisbrod, B. 180 n.
Hanushek, E. 166
Harper, P. 72
Harrison, A.H., Dixon, J., New, B., and Judge K.
    67 n.
Hayek, F. 23
health, and employment 51
health care:
    access to 64, 67, 69
    Canada 58–9, 61, 62, 67–9
    competition and 64, 67, 69
    cost containment 63–4, 66–7, 68–9
    Germany 65, 68, 69, 70
    information problems 52–3
    Netherlands 65, 68, 78
    policy objectives 50–2
    as proportion of GDP 63–4
    UK 61–2, 63, 66–7, 70–1
    USA 56, 59–61, 62–6, 70–1, 74
    waiting lists 64, 67, 69
    see also medical insurance
health finance see health care; medical insurance
health maintenance organizations see medical
    insurance
Heller, P. 98 n., 124 n.
Hellwig, M. 57 n.
Heyneman, S. 259 n.
higher education:
    access to 192, 198, 200, 201, 202, 205–6, 214,
        215–16, 219, 220–2, 237

administrative costs 183–4, 215
Australia 208–11, 212–15
classification problem 183–4, 190, 200, 218–19,
    223–5
competition 196–7
consumer sovereignty 159, 192, 216
Dearing Report (UK, 1997) 170, 176 n., 195 n.,
    203, 210
debate about nature of 191
default rates 200
Denmark 208 n.
expansion 193–4
finance see strategy for financing
income-contingent loans for see student loans
Latin America 214
lessons from international experience 198–215
market forces 173–4
myths about policy 215–19
Netherlands 206–7, 212–15
New Zealand 211–15
private and external benefits 195
private funding, and 223–33
producer sovereignty 192–3
scholarships 220, 221
size of university system 193–4
strategy for financing 180–1, 194–8, 220–2
student loans see student loans
Sweden 207–8, 212–215
UK 173, 201–6, 212–15
USA 173, 180, 181, 198–201, 212–15
vouchers 196–7
West Report, Australia 210–11
see also student loans
Himmelstein, D. and Woolhandler, S. 64 n.
Hochman, H. and Rodgers, J. 27
Holzmann, R. 102, 104, 112, 116, 121 n., 130,
    132
Homburg, S. 118
house insurance 33, 34
Hungary:
    education 260
    output growth 243
    pension reform 252–8
hygiene laws 25

imperfect information see information
incentives 5, 180
income transfers 14
income-contingent repayments 179, 185, 209, 215,
    220–1
    and ability-to-pay principle 185–6, 187
    addressing capital market imperfections 184–5,
        187
    and benefit principle 185, 187
    criticisms 203–6
    efficiency advantages 184–5, 187, 203
    equity advantages 185–6, 187
    intuition of 186–7
    philosophical advantages 185–6, 187

income-contingent repayments (*cont.*):
  and social insurance 179, 186
increasing returns to scale 15–16
index funds 115
indexed funds 113–114, 115
individual learning accounts 160
  and student loans 226 n., 236–8
individualization 149, 150, 155, 268
inflation 112–14
  medical care 82 n.
  and pensions 92
informal economy 247
information:
  about financial markets 129
  about the future 17
  about price 17
  about quality 16–17
  asymmetry 20, 57–8
  and capital markets 175–8
  consumer ignorance 94
  dilemma 74
  and education market 171–4
  and higher education access 221–2
  imperfect 5–6, 11, 13–17, 19–23, 52–62, 80–3,
    93–5, 171–8
  in insurance markets *see* insurance
  perfect 16–17, 18–24
  problems 14, 52–62
information problems, capital markets 175–8
insurance:
  actuarial 6, 18–19, 34, 113
  adverse selection *see* adverse selection
  asymmetric information and 20, 57–8
  and certainty 18
  common shock 112–14
  genetic screening *see* genetic screening
  health care *see* medical insurance
  individual risk 18–19
  long-term care *see* long-term care insurance
  moral hazard *see* moral hazard
  pooling equilibrium 21, 74–5
  rationing of cover 76
  separating equilibrium 21, 75
  social *see* social insurance
  third-party payment problem 22, 57–8, 60,
    82–3
  and uncertainty 24
  see also medical insurance; social insurance;
    unemployment insurance
interest rates 103
  student loans 189, 204–5, 212–14
international comparisons *see* countries
International Learning Bank 234
International Monetary Fund (IMF) 125
internationalization 149, 151, 154, 155–6
invalidity pensions 89
investment:
  foreign 99–100
  index funds 115

pension funds *see* retirement pensions
tracker funds 115
see also savings
investment-swap approach 131

Jackman, R. 242 n., 248–9
Jackman, R. and Rutkowski, M. 248 n.
James, E. 96, 101, 110, 116, 135–6
Japan, health care 68

Kawachi, I., Kennedy, B. P., and Wilkinson, R.G.
  50
Kazakhstan, pension reform 129 n., 132, 257, 258
King, J. 198 n.
Kotlikoff, L. J. 109
Kotlikoff, L. J. and Raffelhueschen, B. 109 n.
Kotlikoff, L. J. and Seeger, C. 130
Kovalyova, G. 260 n.

Labour markets:
  distortions 110
  mobility 74, 93, 111, 149, 153–4, 248, 251–2
  post-communist 247–52
Laporte, B. and Schweitzer, J. 258
Latin America, higher education 214
Latvia 252–3, 255–6
Le Grand, J. 28, 66 n., 67 n., 180 n., 197
Le Grand, J., Mays, N., and Mulligan, J. 67
Le Grand, J. and Nissan, D. 238
Le Grand, J. and Vizard, P. 66 n.
life expectancy 50–1, 81, 146
lifelong learning 193
Lindbeck, A., Nyberg, S., and Weibull, J. 270
Lindeman, D., Rutkowski, M., and Sluchynskiyy, O.
  132 n., 255 n.
Lithuania 252–3
loans *see* student loans
Loewenstein, G. 117
long-term care insurance:
  adverse selection 82
  finance *see* insurance problems; self-insurance;
    social insurance
  Germany 85–6
  information problems 80–1
  insurance problems 31, 81–3
  moral hazard 82–3
  preferred options 83–6
  self-insurance 80, 84
  social insurance approach 83–6
  UK 80, 82, 83, 85
  uncertainty 55, 81–2
low life-time earnings, and student loans 229
Lucas, R.E. 23

Macedonia 252
McGuire, A. 67 n.
Mackenzie, G., Gerson, P., and Cuevas, A. 101 n.,
  102, 104
McPherson, M. and Shapiro, M. 198 n.

Manning, W., Newhouse, J., Duan, N., Keeler, E., Liebowitz, A., and Marquis, S. 60
marginal social benefits 162, 217
marginal social costs 162, 217
markets:
  capital 175–8
  and education 7, 159, 171–4
  efficiency assumptions 161–2
  failure 26–8, 106, 215
  government and, borderline between state intervention, and 2, 215
Marmot, M.G., Davey Smith, G., Stanseld, S., Patel, C., North, F., Head, J., White, I., Brunner, E., and Feeney, A. 51
Marshall, A. 168–9, 193
Meade, J. 15, 60 n.
medical developments 24
medical insurance:
  and access 64, 67, 69
  and adverse selection 20–1, 55, 56–7
  Canada 58–9, 61, 62, 67–9, 70, 147
  consumer choice 65, 67, 69
  cost containment:
    incentive-based mechanisms 58–61, 63–4, 66–7, 68–9
    regulation 58, 61–2
  diagnosis-related groups 61, 63
  elective treatment 57
  gaps 64
  Germany 65, 68, 69, 70
  health maintenance organizations 59–60, 63, 64–5
  information problems 19, 21–2, 26, 54–62
  labour mobility 74
  managed care 63
  moral hazard 21–3, 57–8
  Netherlands 65, 68, 78
  objectives of 50–2
  pooling equilibrium 21, 56
  preferred providers 59
  prospective payment 59, 63
  regulation of medical spending 58, 59, 61–2
  risk-rated premiums 54–6
  separating equilibrium 21, 56–7
  Stanford scheme 64–6, 68, 79
  strategies for 66
  UK *see* health care
  USA 56, 59–61, 74
  waiting lists 64, 67, 69
  see also health care
Merton, R. 116 n.
Merton, R., Bodie, Z., and Marcus, A. 116 n.
Milanovic, B. 246 n., 254
Miles, D. 115
Millns, T. 237
Modigliani, F., Ceprini, M., and Muralidhar, A. 152 n.
monopolies 14, 27
  supply side 67
moral hazard:
  long-term care insurance 82–3

medical insurance 21–3, 57–8
pensions 134
theory 21–3
third-party payment problem 22, 57–8, 60, 82–3
unemployment insurance 37–40
see also insurance; social insurance
Morris, J., Cook, D., and Shaper, G. 51
mortgage repayment student loans 179
  administrative problems 183–4
  efficiency problems 182, 200
  equity problems 182, 200
Mossialos, E. and Le Grand, J. 61, 62 n., 69
motor insurance 26, 33
  compulsion 43
Mueller, D. 27
Muralidhar, A. and van der Wouden, R. 152 n.
Murthi, M., Orszag, M., and Orszag, P. 117
myths:
  about higher education funding 215–19
  government role 122–4
  macroeconomic 96–110
  pension design 87, 96–124

Narendranathan, W., Nickell, S., and Stern, J. 46
National Health Service, UK 61–2, 63, 66–7, 70–1
National Westminster Bank 94
Nellis, J. 122
Nelson, J. 257
Netherlands:
  health care 65, 68, 78
  higher education 206–7, 212–15
  student loans 206–7
New, B. 16, 17, 172 n.
New Zealand:
  higher education finance 211–15
  pension system 133, 140, 146, 155, 267
  student loans 233
Newhouse, J. 60
Niskanen, W. 27
North, F., Syme, S. L., Feeney, A. et al. 51
Norway, pension funding 101, 147
Nuti 106
Nuttall, S., Blackwood, R., Bussell, B., Cliff, J., Conrall, M., Cowley, A., Gatenby, P., and Webber, J. 82

OECD 59, 61, 85, 170, 191, 251 n.
Orszag, P. 117, 118, 119, 121
Orszag, P. and Stiglitz, J. 94, 96, 102, 111, 117

parental contributions, student loans 205–6
Pareto optimality 23, 121
Pauly, M. 21, 22, 57, 82
pay-as-you-go schemes 84 n., 87, 90–1, 93, 96, 98–124, 126
  see also retirement pensions
pension funds:
  acquisition of student debt 233
  and economic growth 89, 101–4

pension funds (*cont.*):
  performance 151–2
  see also retirement pensions
performance-based funding 206, 207
Pestieau, P. and Possen, U. 120
Poland:
  education 260
  output growth 243
  retirement pensions 130–2, 252–8
  unemployment 243
political sustainability 3, 127–8
pollution 27
pooling equilibrium, adverse selection 21, 74–5
population ageing 87, 96–110, 126, 144–8
  and education 170
  retirement pensions 87, 96–110, 126, 144–8
post-communist reform:
  education:
    inherited problems 164, 170, 258–60
    policy directions 260–2
  labour market adjustment:
    inherited problems 36, 47, 247–8
    policy directions 248–52
  pensions:
    inherited problems 103, 122, 245, 252–3
    policy directions 123, 129 n., 132, 146, 253–8
  poverty relief 242, 249–50
  transition:
    initial effects 241–6
    reform directions 246–7
    simple analytics of 241–7
poverty:
  block grants 249–50
  indicator targeting 249
  post-communist 243–6
  relief 5, 12–13, 128, 242, 249–50
  transient 12–13
Powell, M. 67 n.
preferred providers *see* medical insurance
Preker, A. and Feachem, R. 51 n.
premiums:
  medical insurance 54–6
  rises in 45
  risk-related distributional effects 44–5
  unemployment insurance 47–8
pressure groups 27
price regulation 14
private goods 15
privatization, unemployment benefits 48
productive efficiency 162, 258–9
productivity, and pensions 99
protection of individuals 43–5
public accounts, pensions 107–8
public goods 15–16, 217
public production 14, 15–16

Quah, D. 148
quality regulation 14, 43–4
quantity regulation 14

Ravallion, M. 128 n., 164
Ravallion, M. and Datt, G. 21 n.
redistribution 24, 47–8, 49, 133–4, 137, 142, 152
  higher education 197
Rees, R. 18 n., 20 n., 21 n.
regulation 13–14, 128–9
rejectability 15–16
residential care *see* long-term care insurance
retirement pensions:
  accumulated rights 149–50, 153
  administrative costs 117, 122
  age dependency ratio 96–7, 144
  age of retirement 109–10, 126, 140, 146, 254
  annuities market risk 92, 112–13, 115–16, 122, 135
  Australia 99–100, 133, 134, 135, 140, 142–3
  Canada 101, 123, 126, 134, 135, 147
  centrality of output 89–91, 98–9, 103–4, 108–9, 144–5
  Chile 104, 115–16, 117, 123, 128, 133, 135, 136–8, 142–3
  Croatia 252–8
  defined benefit schemes 90–1, 92–3, 110–11, 113, 149, 152–4
  defined contribution schemes 90, 92, 94, 110, 112–13, 149–52
  demographic shocks 92, 96–100, 114, 121
  dependency ratio 96–7, 144
  design questions 110–22, 125–43, 151–2
  divorce and 150, 154, 155
  early retirement 111, 139
  economics of 6, 89–95
  equivalence proposition 118–21
  expectations 102
  family structure and 148, 149, 150, 269
  flexibility 147–8
  funded schemes 87, 90–1, 96, 98–124
  and government role 113–14, 122–4, 128
  growth effects of 101–4
  Hungary 130, 132, 252–8
  incentive effects:
    growth 101–4
    labour supply 110–12, 126
  indexation 113–14, 135, 136, 145, 255
  information problems and 93–94, 116–18, 129
  investment risk 92, 114–15, 122
  Kazakhstan 129 n., 132, 257, 258
  labour supply effects of 110–12
  macroeconomic shocks 92, 112–14, 121
  management risk 92, 114, 121–2
  myths about 6, 96–124
  New Zealand 133, 140, 146, 155, 267
  Norway 101, 147
  objectives 89, 133–5
  pay-as-you-go schemes 84 n., 87, 90–1, 93, 96, 98–124, 126
  perceptions of 126
  Poland 252–8, 130–2
  policy choices 125, 132–43
  political risk 92, 114, 121, 122–4

population ageing 87, 96–110, 126, 144–8
portable 148–57, 234
post-communist reform 252–8
prerequisites 104–5, 126–32, 257–8
private v. public 126, 256–8
public 107–8
public accounts 107–8
public spending and 100–1, 109–10, 126
real wage growth and 118–22
reduction 97, 109–10, 145–6, 254–5
regulation 128–9
risks:
    diversification 112–16
    for individual pensioners 92–3, 137, 147, 152
    for pension schemes 91–2, 147, 153
    Russia 132
Singapore 101, 135, 138, 142–3, 269
social insurance *see* social insurance
stakeholder 115
state pensions 14, 105, 110–11, 155–6
surplus building 147
Sweden 111, 123, 138–9, 142, 207–8
system dependency ratio 96–7, 144
and taxation 89, 106, 111
tiers of 133–5
transition costs 118–22
UK 94, 103, 104, 115, 117, 128, 133, 134, 140,
    142–3, 146, 156, 267
and uncertainty 91–2
USA 94, 101, 117, 126, 134, 135, 140–1, 142–3, 146,
    147, 156, 267
returns, rates of 137, 152
risk:
    annuities market risk, pensions and 18–20
    common shock 19, 54
    facing individual pensioners 92–3, 137, 147, 152
    facing pension schemes 91–2, 147, 153
    facing providers of student loans 12, 176–8, 182,
        225, 229–30
    facing student borrowers 18, 175–6
    genetic screening and 72–4
    individual 19, 54
    investment risk, pensions and 92, 114–15, 122
    management risk, pensions and 112–16
    medical insurance premiums and 54–6
    premium rates 54–6
    protection against 18
    and uncertainty 5–6, 20
    unemployment insurance and 44–5
    uninsurable 19, 73, 74
    see also adverse selection; insurance; moral hazard;
        social insurance; uncertainty
Robertson, D. 237 n.
Robertson, D. and Mason, G. 237 n.
Robinson, R. and Steiner, A. 60, 63
Romania 243, 245
Romer, P. 165
Ross, S. 141
Rothschild, M. and Stiglitz, J. 20 n., 57 n.

Royal Economic Society 115
Russia 132, 245
    retirement pensions 132

Saltman, R., Busse, R., and Mossialos, E. 59
Samuelson, P. 16, 91, 118
savings 12
    and pension funding 101–4
    voluntary 102
school leavers, unemployment 47
self-employment 46–7, 149
self-insurance 80, 84
Sen, A. 164
separating equilibrium, adverse selection 21, 75
Shapiro, J. 51 n.
sick pay 31
Singapore, pension system 101, 135, 138, 142–3, 269
Sloan, F. and Norton, E. 82
Slovakia 243–4
Slovenia 243–4, 253, 260
social insurance:
    compulsion 24
    differences from private insurance 24
    flexibility 139
    home responsibility protection 150 n., 155
    and pension provision 151–2
    post-communist countries 250–1
    as response to information failure 23–4
    shared between husband and wife 150, 155
    see also adverse selection; insurance; medical
        insurance; moral hazard
Sparkes, J. 170
stakeholder pensions 115
Stanford scheme (medical insurance) 64–6, 68, 79
state intervention *see* government failure; market;
    social insurance
state pensions *see* retirement pensions
Stern, J. 45
Stiglitz, J. 4 n., 14 n., 18 n., 21 n., 43 n., 122,
    165 n., 217 n., 250 n.
student loans:
    adverse selection 176–8, 182
    Australia 233
    basic design elements 179–80, 188
    capital market imperfections 182, 184–5
    debt sales 225–6
    default risk 229–30
    employers' contributions 236–7
    front-end funding 225–6
    graduate tax 179, 186, 218–19
    hermetically-sealed fund 226–7
    income-contingent repayments *see* income-
        contingent repayments
    and individual learning accounts 236–8
    information problems 182
    interest rates 189, 204–5
    and labour mobility 229, 233–4
    and low life-time income 229
    market interest rates and 189

student loans (*cont.*):
mortgage repayment *see* mortgage repayment student loans
Netherlands 206–7
New Zealand 233
parental contributions 205–6
private finance and 183, 184, 189–90, 223–33
risk and uncertainty:
facing borrowers 182, 188
facing lenders 182, 225, 229–30
strategy for 220–2
Sweden 233
UK 201–6, 233
USA 198–201, 231, 233
see also higher education; income-contingent repayments; mortgage repayments
Student Loans Company 231–2
subsidies:
interest rates 189, 212–14, 217
lump-sum 15
per-unit 14
Pigovian 43
sustainability, political and fiscal 128–9
Sweden:
health care 61–2
higher education 207–8, 212–15
retirement pensions 111, 123, 138–39, 142, 207–8
student loans 233
unemployment insurance 48
welfare beneficiaries 28

taxation:
as disincentive 5
graduate 179, 186, 218–19
health care through 66–7, 68
investment subsidies 217
and pensions 89, 106, 111
see also social insurance
tertiary education 234–6
see also higher education; student loans
test scores, education 166
third-party payment problem 22, 57–8, 60, 82–3
see also insurance
Thompson, L. 89 n., 101 n., 102, 123, 139 n.
Thurow, L. 169
Tiebout, C. 28
Tobin, J. 264
tracker funds 115
trade unions, insurance provision 41–2
transactions costs 58
annuities 116
transition *see* post-communist reform
transition costs, pensions 118–22, 137–8
transition generation 121
trust, public 129
tuition fees 202, 206, 208–9, 211, 212, 214
and access 219
flexible 220
Tullock, G. 27, 28

twenty-first century issues:
genetic screening 72–9
individual learning accounts 236–8
long-term care 79–86
population ageing 87, 96–110, 126, 144–8
portable pensions 148–57
private funding for tertiary education 223–33
rationalizing tertiary education funding 234–6
student loans with international labour mobility 229, 233–4
unemployment 49

UK:
health care 61–2, 63, 66–7, 70–1
higher education 173, 201–6, 212–15
long-term care 80, 82, 83, 85
national health service 61–2, 63, 66–7, 70–1
pension system 94, 103, 104, 115, 117, 128, 133, 134, 135, 140, 142–3, 146, 156, 267
Royal Commission on long-term care 80, 82, 83, 85
school education 260
student loans 201–6, 233
Ukraine 245
uncertainty:
facing individual pensioners 92–3, 137, 147, 152
facing pension schemes 91–2, 147, 153
facing providers of student loans 12, 182, 225, 229–30
facing student borrowers 182, 188
and insurance 24
and long-term care insurance 81–2
and medical insurance 54–5, 72–4
in post-communist countries 241, 250–1
and retirement pensions 91–2
and risk 5–6, 20
see also information; risk; social insurance
unemployment:
benefits 249–51
post-communist 243–5, 248–9
school leavers 47
see also unemployment insurance
unemployment insurance:
adverse selection 37
compulsion 37, 42–3
credit loan insurance 41
distributional effects of risk-rated premiums 36–7, 44–5
moral hazard and 31, 37–40
mortgage protection policies 31, 40–1
objectives 34–5
operational problems with private schemes 31, 33–4, 42–6
post-communist 247
private, conclusions about 46–9
probabilities, calculation of 45–6, 72–5
Sweden 48
technical problems 35–42
trade union schemes 41–2

universities:
  academic freedom 192
  economic freedom 192
  entrepreneurial activities 181
  and reform 248–9
  see also higher education; student loans
USA:
  health care 56, 59–61, 62–6, 70–1, 74
  higher education 173, 180, 181, 198–201, 212–15
  medical insurance 56, 59–61, 74
  pension system 94, 101, 117, 126, 134, 135, 140–1,
    142–3, 146, 147, 156, 267
  student loans 198–201, 231, 233
  welfare beneficiaries 28, 231, 233

Varian, H. 11 n.
voluntarism argument 42
vouchers, educational 162–3

waiting lists, health care 64, 67, 69
welfare state:

beneficiaries 27–8
and certainty 12–13
crisis 263–70
definition 4
global pressures 2–3, 267–8
objectives 1–2, 4–5, 186, 270–2
'Piggy bank' function 1–2
residual 265–6
'Robin Hood' function 1, 270
  see also redistribution
West Report, Australia 210–11
Westwood, A. 237
Wilensky, H. and Lebeaux, C. 265
Wilkinson, R. 50 n.
Winston, G. 196
Woodhall, M. 198 n.
World Bank 51 n., 116, 125, 130–1, 132, 243, 248,
    252, 255, 259
  higher education study 198–9
  pensions study (1994) 132, 136, 137
World Development Report (1996) 127